THE WORLD ALMANAC® FOR KIDS 2013

WORLD ALMANAC® BOOKS
An Imprint of Infobase Learning

THE WORLD ALMANAC® FOR KIDS 2013

Project Management: Robert Famighetti
New Content: RJF PUBLISHING

Contributors: Emily Dolbear, Jacqueline Laks Gorman, Lisa M. Herrington, Geoffrey M. Horn, Amanda Hudson, William A. McGeveran
Photo Research: Edward A. Thomas
Index Editor: Nan Badgett

Design: Q2A/BILL SMITH
Chief Creative Officer: Brian Kobberger
Project Manager: Rosanne Guararra
Design: Brock Waldron, Shanin Glenn, Geron Hoy, Deirdre Jennings, Brian Lora, Orville Ottey
Production: Robergeau Duverger, Julia Edwards, Matthew Gaddis, Nancy Mace, Ronald Ottaviano, Doug Teece, Mie Tsuchida, Richard Welch, Luke Zeigler

INFOBASE LEARNING
Editorial Director: Laurie E. Likoff
Senior Editor: Sarah Janssen
Project Editor: Edward A. Thomas

World Almanac® Books
An imprint of Infobase Learning
132 West 31st Street
New York NY 10001

Hardcover	Paperback
ISBN-13: 978-1-60057-166-4	ISBN-13: 978-1-60057-167-1
ISBN-10: 1-60057-166-2	ISBN-10: 1-60057-167-0

For Library of Congress cataloging information, please contact the publisher.

The World Almanac® for Kids is distributed in paperback to the trade by Simon & Schuster, and to schools and libraries at special discounts by Infobase Learning. For more information, contact (800) 322-8755 or visit www.InfobaseLearning.com.

You can find *The World Almanac® for Kids* online at www.worldalmanac.com

Book printed and bound by RR Donnelley, Crawfordsville, IN
Date printed: July 2012
Printed in the United States of America

RRD BSG 10 9 8 7 6 5 4 3 2 1

The addresses and content of Web sites referred to in this book are subject to change. Although *The World Almanac® for Kids* carefully reviews these sites, we cannot take responsibility for their content.

CONTENTS

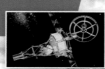

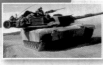

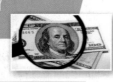

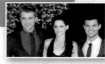

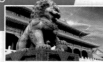

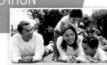

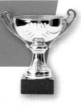

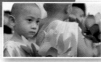

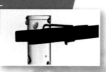

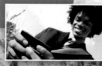

FACES & PLACES

IN THE NEWS

DEEP DIVE

Explorer and filmmaker James Cameron made a 7-mile solo dive in a submersible into the deepest part of the Pacific Ocean on March 26, 2012.

VIOLENCE IN SYRIA

Children carried signs opposing the government in an April 2012 protest march. Since 2011, thousands of Syrians calling for democracy have been killed.

ON THE ROCKS

The cruise ship *Costa Concordia* ran aground off the coast of an Italian island on January 13, 2012. More than 30 people lost their lives.

NEW LEADER

Kim Jong Un took over as all-powerful ruler of North Korea after his father died in December 2011.

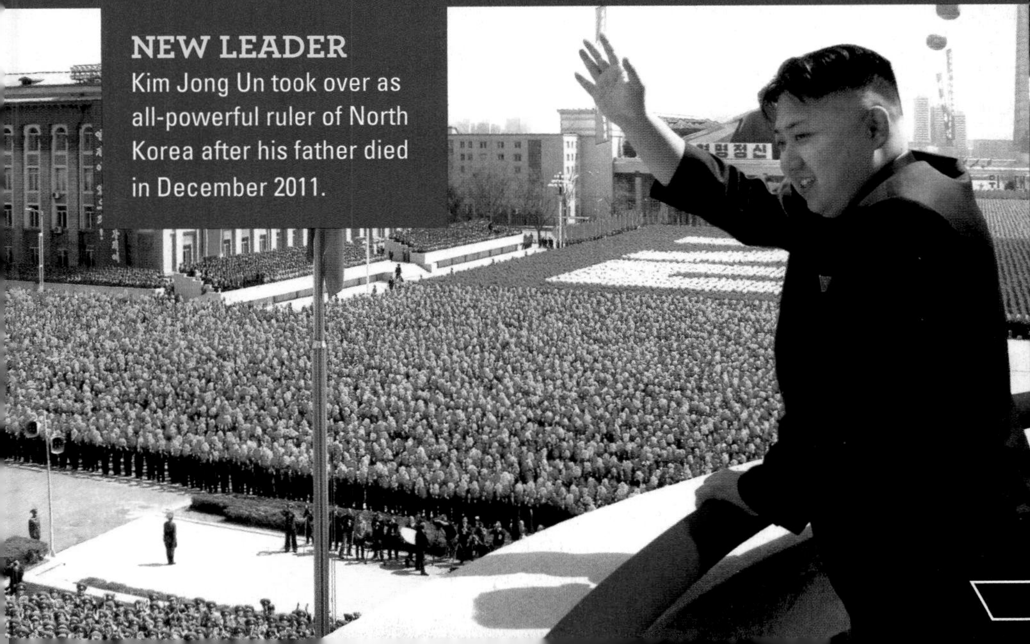

IN THE NEWS

TORN APART

A couple looked over the remains of their home after a tornado swept through Harrisburg, Illinois, in February 2012. Many tornadoes struck the Midwest and South in winter and spring.

A SAD CASE

Trayvon Martin, an unarmed African-American teenager, was shot to death on February 26, 2012, by a man patrolling in a gated community in Florida. Here, protesters rally on behalf of the teen.

BATTLE FOR THE WHITE HOUSE

President Barack Obama and former Massachusetts Governor Mitt Romney both had their sights set on winning the November 2012 election for president.

FINAL FLIGHT

The space shuttle *Discovery*, carried on top of a jet, was flown over Washington, D.C., in April 2012, on its way to retirement at the National Air and Space Museum.

TELEVISION

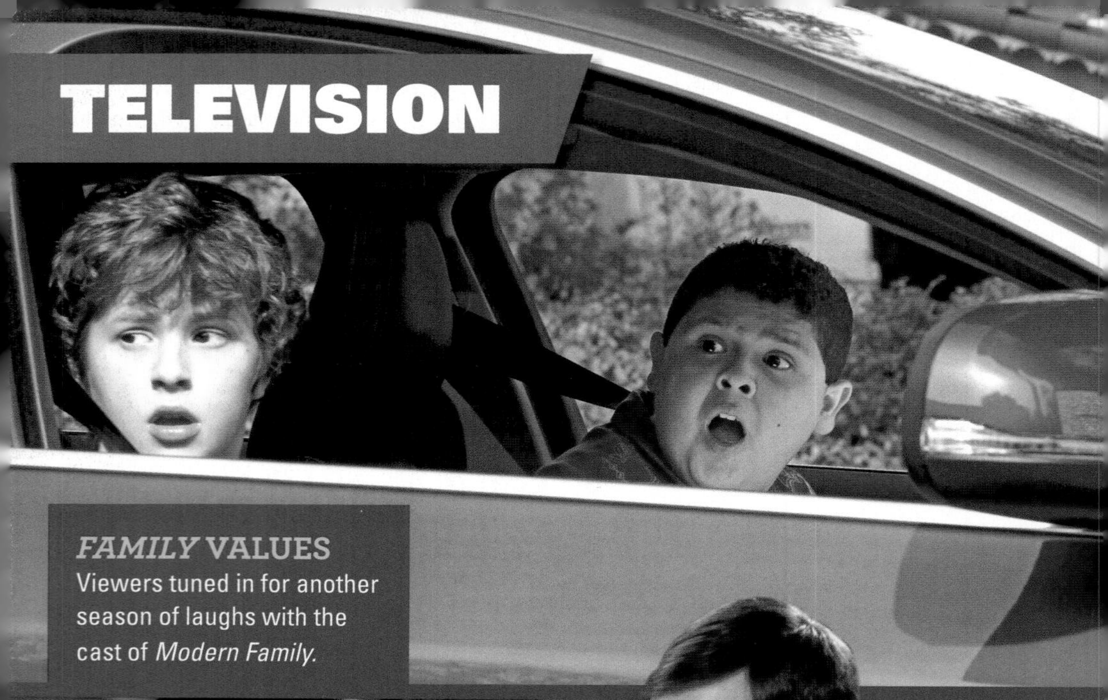

***FAMILY* VALUES**
Viewers tuned in for another season of laughs with the cast of *Modern Family.*

COSMIC COMEDY
Leonard and Sheldon experimented with science—and humor—on *The Big Bang Theory*.

VOICE VICTOR

R&B singer Jermaine Paul, coached by team leader Blake Shelton, was the Season 2 winner of *The Voice*.

PRETTY AND POPULAR

In June 2012, fans welcomed the third season of *Pretty Little Liars*, based on the books by Sara Shepard.

MOVIES

***GAMES* GOLD**
Millions of moviegoers lined up to cheer on Jennifer Lawrence as Katniss Everdeen in *The Hunger Games.*

BACK IN *BLACK*
Actors Will Smith and Tommy Lee Jones returned as Agents J and K in *Men in Black III.*

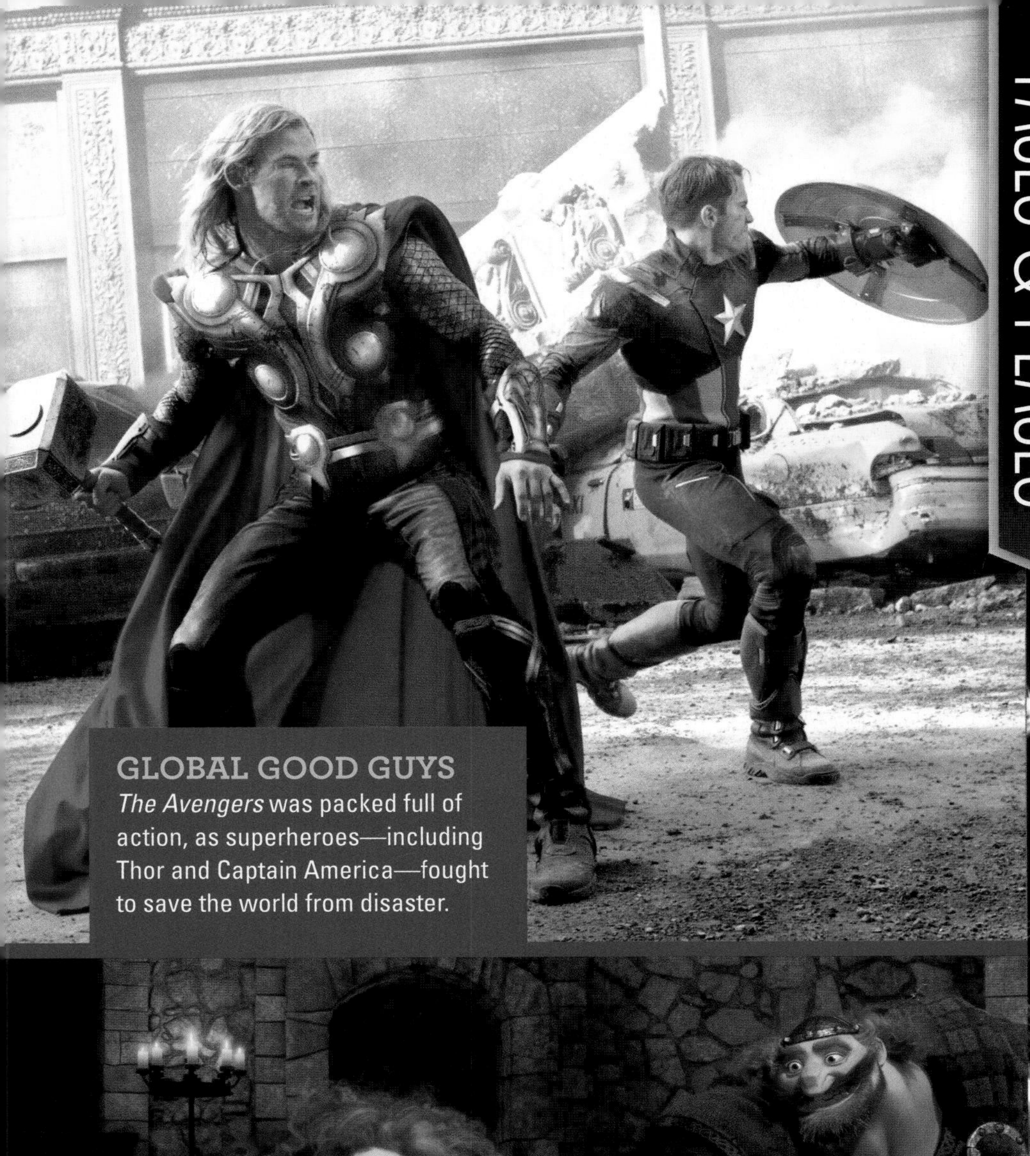

GLOBAL GOOD GUYS

The Avengers was packed full of action, as superheroes—including Thor and Captain America—fought to save the world from disaster.

BOLD AND *BRAVE*

Kelly Macdonald provided the voice for the daring Princess Merida in the animated film *Brave.*

MOVIES

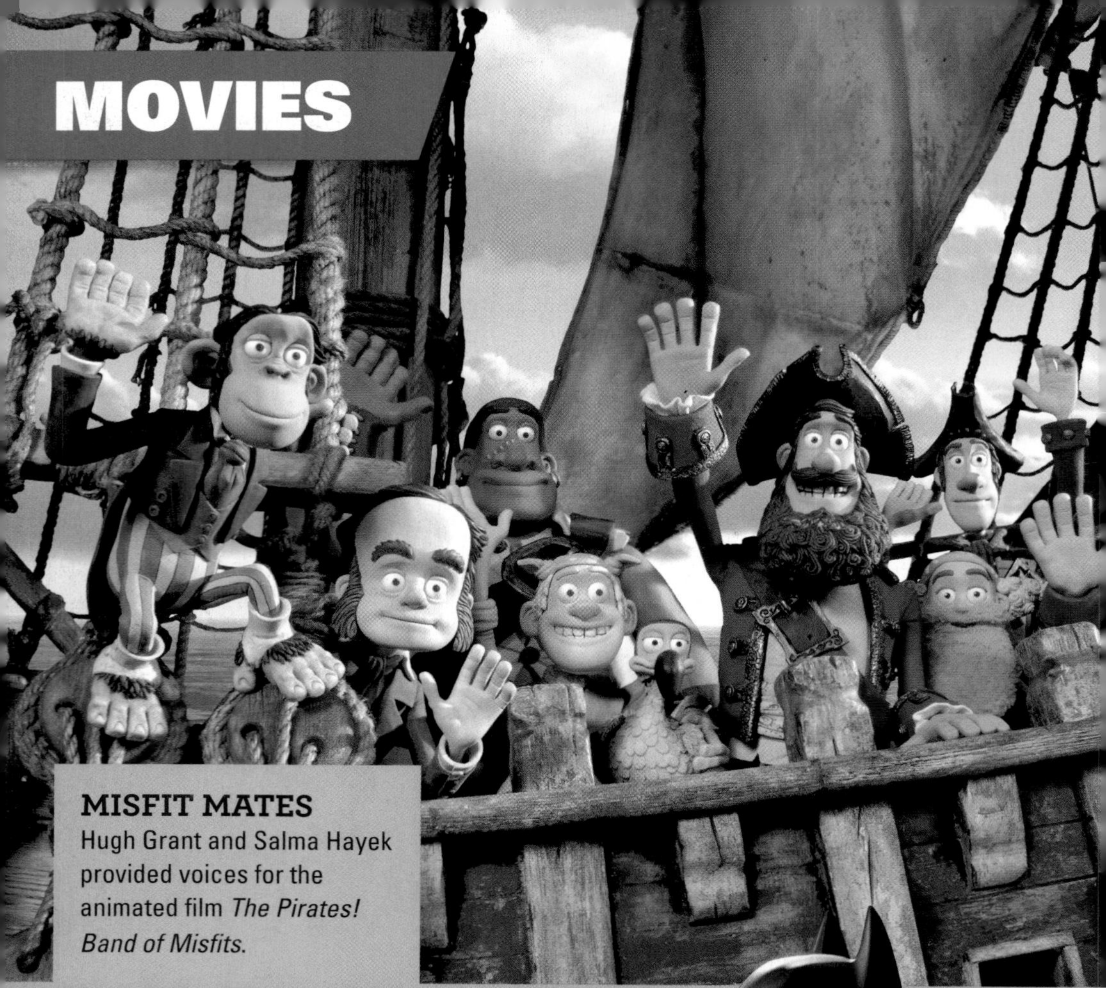

MISFIT MATES
Hugh Grant and Salma Hayek provided voices for the animated film *The Pirates! Band of Misfits.*

BATMAN BALE
Christian Bale put on his Batman suit for the third time in *The Dark Knight Rises.*

SPIDEY SENSE
Actor Andrew Garfield stepped into the role previously played by Tobey Maguire in *The Amazing Spider-Man*.

TRUE LOVE
Moviegoers fell for Channing Tatum and Rachel McAdams in the emotional love story *The Vow*.

MUSIC

AMAZING ADELE

Powerhouse vocalist Adele took home six Grammy Awards in 2012—including record, song, and album of the year.

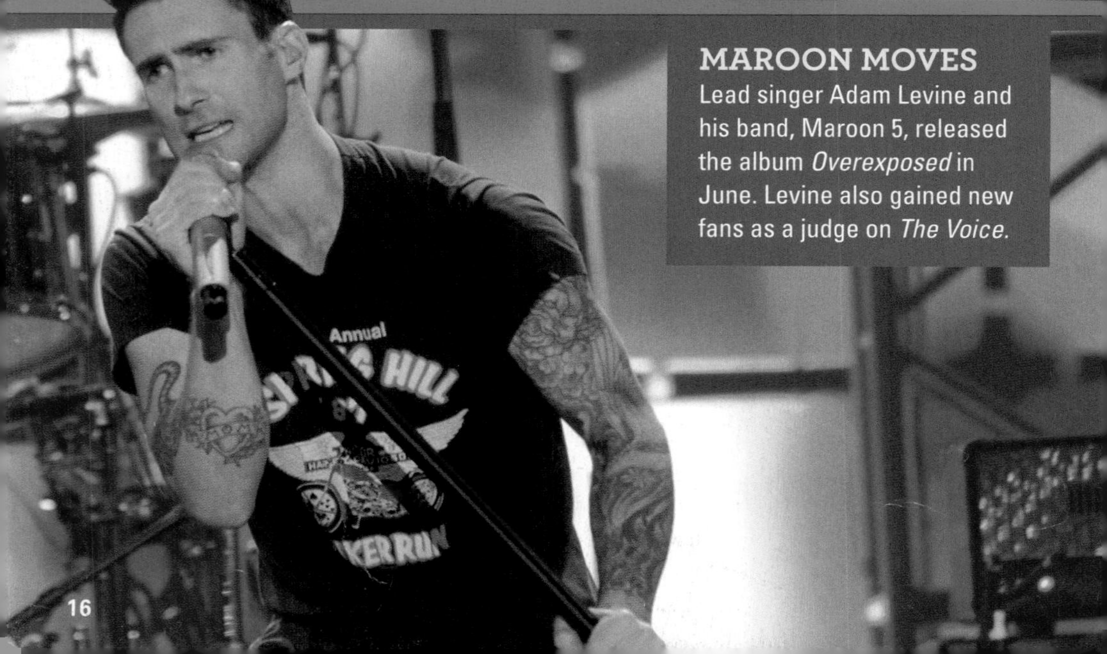

MAROON MOVES

Lead singer Adam Levine and his band, Maroon 5, released the album *Overexposed* in June. Levine also gained new fans as a judge on *The Voice.*

BOY BAND

Zayn Malik, Niall Horan, Harry Styles, Liam Payne, and Louis Tomlinson became household names as their band, One Direction, caught the attention of fans all over the world.

TAYLOR'S YEAR

As she prepared to release a new album in 2012, Taylor Swift was named Entertainer of the Year for the second time by the Academy of Country Music.

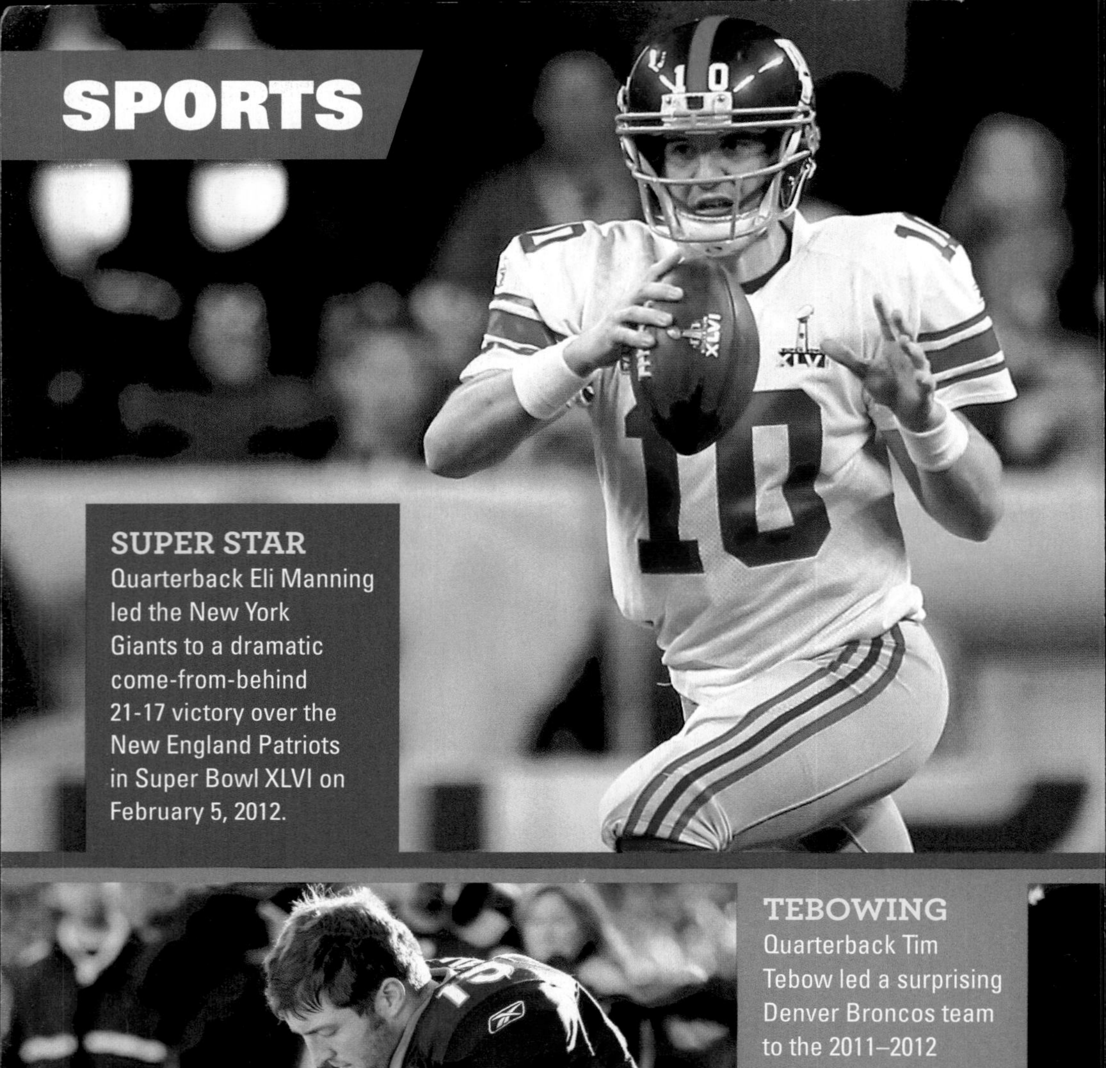

SUPER STAR

Quarterback Eli Manning led the New York Giants to a dramatic come-from-behind 21-17 victory over the New England Patriots in Super Bowl XLVI on February 5, 2012.

TEBOWING

Quarterback Tim Tebow led a surprising Denver Broncos team to the 2011–2012 NFL playoffs. Known for kneeling to pray ("Tebowing") on the field, he joined the New York Jets in March 2012.

PERFECT!

San Francisco's Matt Cain pitched a perfect game June 13, 2012—the first in the Giants' team history. It was also the fifth no-hitter in the early months of the 2012 baseball season.

DOMINATING PRESENCE

Overpowering on both offense and defense, center Brittney Griner (42) starred as Baylor won the NCAA women's championship in 2012.

SPORTS

SPEED ON SKIS

In 2012, Lindsey Vonn captured the overall World Cup women's championship for the fourth time in five years.

REPEAT WINNER

Averaging 140.256 mph, Matt Kenseth (17) sped to his second victory in the Daytona 500 in February 2012.

HOT HAND

Led by LeBron James, the Miami Heat won the NBA championship in June 2012. James averaged 28.6 points in the Finals and was named MVP.

DRAMATIC DECEMBER

Baylor quarterback Robert Griffin III won the Heisman Trophy for best college player of 2011, then led his team to a 67-56 win in the Valero Alamo Bowl.

ANIMALS

→How many types of venomous snakes can be found in the world? PAGE 26

Weird Animal Facts

Furry or scaly, creepy or crawly, schoolbus-sized or microscopic—animals can often surprise us. Here are some facts about the Animal Kingdom.

Vogelkop Bowerbird

The Vogelkop bowerbird, which lives in the mountains of New Guinea, has some of the most unusual courtship behaviors scientists have ever seen. When it is time to find a mate, males will build a bower (or shelter) that resembles a tiny apartment. They then decorate their bowers with flowers, stones, leaves, and any other objects they can find in the area. As the birds get older and more experienced, their bowers become fancier. Females visit the bowers of competing males, choosing the mate whose display appeals to them the most.

Colossal Squid

The colossal squid is the largest squid in the ocean, in terms of weight, and also the largest invertebrate. Invertebrates are animals that do not have backbones. The colossal squid lives in very deep water in the Southern Ocean. It can reach 46 feet in length, can weigh well over 200 pounds, and has the largest eyes of any animal. When one of these giant meat-eating creatures swallows a meal, the food must take an unusual path. Food must pass from the mouth down the squid's narrow esophagus, which travels right through its doughnut-shaped brain!

LIFE ON EARTH

This time line shows how life developed on Earth. The earliest life forms are at the top of the chart. The most recent are at the bottom. All numbers are years before the present.

Precambrian	4.6 billion	Formation of Earth
	3.8 billion–542 million	First evidence of life on Earth. All life is in water. Early single-celled bacteria and achaea appear, followed by multi-celled organisms, including early animals.
Paleozoic	542–443 million	Animals with shells (called trilobites) and some mollusks form. Primitive fish and corals develop. Evidence of the first primitive land plants.
	443–417 million	Coral reefs form. Other animals, such as the first known freshwater fish, develop. Relatives of spiders and centipedes develop.
	417–354 million	The first trees and forests appear. The first land-living vertebrates, amphibians, and wingless insects appear. Many new sea creatures also appear.
	354–290 million	Reptiles develop. Much of the land is covered by swamps.
	290–248 million	A mass extinction wipes out 95% of all marine life.
Mesozoic	248–206 million	In the Triassic period, marine life develops again. Reptiles also move into the water. Reptiles begin to dominate the land areas. Dinosaurs and mammals develop.
	206–144 million	The Jurassic is dominated by giant dinosaurs. In the late Jurassic, birds evolve.
	144–65 million	In the Cretaceous period, new dinosaurs appear. Many insect groups, modern mammal and bird groups also develop. A global extinction of most dinosaurs occurs at the end of this period.
Cenozoic	65–1.8 million	Ancestors of modern-day horses, zebras, rhinos, sheep, goats, camels, pigs, cows, deer, giraffes, elephants, cats, dogs, and primates begin to develop.
	1.8 million–10,000	Large mammals such as mammoths, saber-toothed cats, and giant ground sloths develop. Modern human beings evolve.
	10,000–present	Human civilization develops.

ANIMAL KINGDOM

The world has so many animals that scientists looked for a way to organize them into groups. A Swedish scientist named Carolus Linnaeus (1707–1778) worked out a system for classifying both animals and plants. We still use it today.

The Animal Kingdom is separated into two large groups—animals with backbones, called **vertebrates**, and animals without backbones, called **invertebrates**.

These large groups are divided into smaller groups called **phyla**. And phyla are divided into even smaller groups called **classes**. The animals in each group are classified together when their bodies are similar in certain ways.

VERTEBRATES
Animals with Backbones

FISH	Swordfish, tuna, salmon, trout, halibut, goldfish
AMPHIBIANS	Frogs, toads, mud puppies
REPTILES	Turtles, alligators, crocodiles, lizards
BIRDS	Sparrows, owls, turkeys, hawks
MAMMALS	Kangaroos, opossums, dogs, cats, bears, seals, rats, squirrels, rabbits, chipmunks, porcupines, horses, pigs, cows, deer, bats, whales, dolphins, monkeys, apes, humans

INVERTEBRATES
Animals without Backbones

PROTOZOA	The simplest form of animals
COELENTERATES	Jellyfish, hydra, sea anemones, coral
MOLLUSKS	Clams, snails, squid, oysters
ANNELIDS	Earthworms
ARTHOPODS	
Crustaceans	Lobsters, crayfish
Centipedes and Millipedes	
Arachnids	Spiders, scorpions
Insects	Butterflies, grasshoppers, bees, termites, cockroaches
ECHINODERMS	Starfish, sea urchins, sea cucumbers

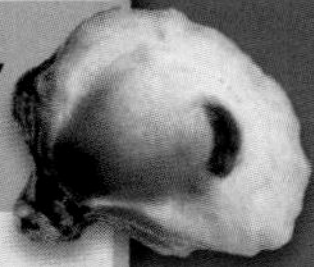

HOMEWORK TIP

How can you remember the animal classifications from most general to most specific? Try this sentence:

King **P**hilip **C**ame **O**ver **F**rom **G**reat **S**pain.

K = Kingdom; **P** = Phylum; **C** = Class; **O** = Order; **F** = Family; **G** = Genus; **S** = Species

ZOOS: PAST AND PRESENT

Throughout history, humans have been curious about wild animals. Zoos have given people a way to safely observe these animals up close. Fossils found in Egypt suggest the first zoo dates back to 3500 B.C.

For many years, zoos were very different from the ones we know today. Animals were often kept in small cages and given only the most basic care. As time went by and people became more knowledgeable about animals, zoos began to change. In today's zoos, animals live in open areas designed to be like their native habitats.

Modern zoos also do much more than just house animals. Through breeding programs, zoos work to increase the populations of endangered species that are at risk of becoming extinct. Animals raised in zoos may later be released into the wild. And zoos are sometimes the only homes for types of animals that have already become extinct in nature.

Here's a look at just a few of today's major zoos.

San Diego Zoo

More than 3,700 animals can be found in the San Diego Zoo, which opened in 1916. It is home to five giant pandas—the largest population of giant pandas in North America. The zoo has been at the forefront of conservation efforts and captive breeding programs for these critically endangered animals. The San Diego Zoo was a pioneer in "cage free" exhibits—its first, for lions, was opened in 1922.

Philadelphia Zoo

The first zoo in the United States opened in Philadelphia in 1874. In that first year, the Philadelphia Zoo was home to 813 animals. Today, there are more than 1,300. The Philadelphia Zoo is known for successfully breeding animals that do not breed well in captivity—the zoo welcomed the first captive chimpanzee born in the U.S. in 1928.

Chester Zoo

The most popular zoo in the United Kingdom, Chester Zoo has been in operation since 1931. It now holds more than 8,000 animals and an extensive collection of endangered plants. Visitors to the zoo can participate in a "zookeeper for a day" program that focuses on a chosen animal. Proceeds from the program are put toward the zoo's conservation efforts, which include breeding endangered animals.

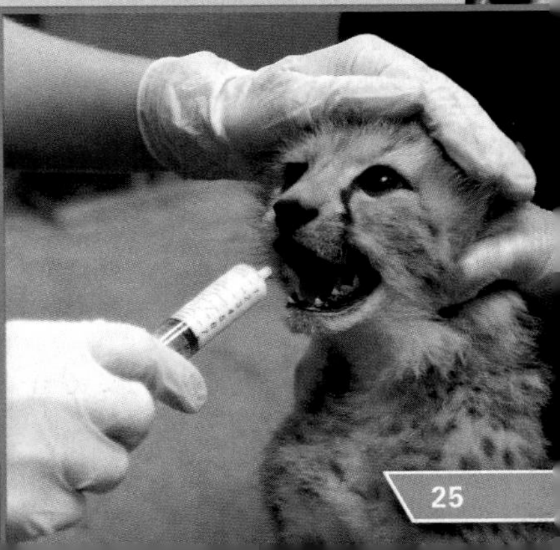

BIGGEST, SMALLEST, *FASTEST* in the World

World's BIGGEST Animals

Marine mammal: Blue whale (100 feet long, 200 tons)

Heaviest land mammal: African bush elephant (12 feet high, 4-7 tons)
Tallest land mammal: Giraffe (18 feet tall)

Reptile: Saltwater crocodile (20-23 feet long, 1,150 pounds)

Heaviest snake: Green anaconda (16-30 feet, 550 pounds)
Longest snake: Reticulated python (26-32 feet long)

Fish: Whale shark (40-60 feet long, 10-20 tons)

Bird: Ostrich (9 feet tall, 345 pounds)

Insect: Stick insect (15 inches long)

World's *FASTEST* Animals

Marine mammal: Killer whale and Dall's porpoise (35 miles per hour)

Land mammal: Cheetah (70 miles per hour)

Fish: Sailfish (68 miles per hour, leaping)

Bird: Peregrine falcon (200 miles per hour)

Insect: Dragonfly (35 miles per hour)

Snake: Black mamba (14 miles per hour)

World's SMALLEST Animals

Mammal: Bumblebee bat (1.1-1.3 inches)

Fish: *Paedocypris progenetica* or stout infantfish (0.31-0.33 inches)

Bird: Bee hummingbird (1-2 inches)

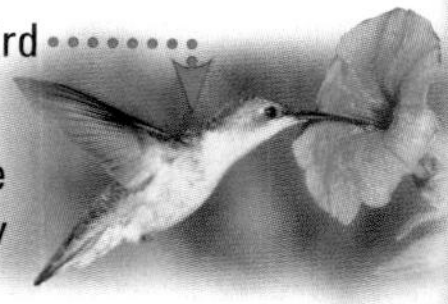

Snake: Thread snake and brahminy blind snake (4.25 inches)

Lizard: Jaragua sphaero and Virgin Islands dwarf sphaero (0.63 inch)

Insect: Fairyfly (0.01 inch)

HOW FAST DO ANIMALS RUN?

This table shows how fast some animals can move on land. A snail can take more than 30 hours just to go 1 mile. But humans at their fastest are still slower than many animals. The human record for fastest speed for a recognized race distance is held by Usain Bolt, who set a world record in 2009 in the 100-meter dash of 9.58 seconds, for an average speed of about 23 miles per hour.

ANIMAL	SPEED (miles per hour)
Cheetah	70
Pronghorn	60
Elk	45
Ostrich	40
Rabbit	35
Giraffe	32
Grizzly bear	30
Elephant	25
Wild turkey	15
Crocodile	10
Tiger beetle	5.5
Snail	0.03

How Long Do Animals LIVE?

Most animals do not live as long as humans do. A monkey that's 14 years old is thought to be old, while a person at that age is still considered young. The average life spans of some animals in the wild are shown here. An average 10-year-old boy in the U.S. can expect to live to be about 74.

ANIMAL	AVERAGE LIFE SPAN
Galapagos tortoise	100+ years
Blue whale	80 years
Alligator	50 years
Chimpanzee	50 years
African elephant	35 years
Bottlenose dolphin	30 years
Horse	20 years
Tiger	16 years
Lobster	15 years
Cat (domestic)	15 years
Tarantula	15 years

ANIMAL	AVERAGE LIFE SPAN
Dog (domestic)	13 years
Camel (bactrian)	12 years
Pig	10 years
Deer (white-tailed)	8 years
Kangaroo	7 years
Chipmunk	6 years
Guinea pig	4 years
Mouse	3 years
Opossum	1 year
Worker bee	6 weeks
Adult housefly	1-3 weeks

SNAKES: *Fact or Fiction?*

Many people are afraid of snakes. These reptiles can move quickly and often surprise people. Some types of snakes are also venomous. Venomous snakes have a special type of saliva that is harmful to humans and other animals. But snakes are useful to humans in many ways. Many small snakes eat insects, and larger snakes eat rodents. Learn the facts about these often misunderstood creatures.

Fact or fiction? Snakes are slimy.
FICTION. Snakes are covered in scales made of keratin, the same substance that makes up human fingernails. They feel cool and dry.

Fact or fiction? Most snakes are venomous.
FICTION. Of the roughly 3,000 species of snakes worldwide, only 400 are venomous. The vast majority of snakes are harmless to humans. Because some snakes are venomous, however, they should always be avoided in the wild.

Fact or fiction? Snakes do not have eyelids.
FACT. The eyes of a snake are protected by a clear scale, but snakes cannot blink or close their eyes, even when sleeping. Contrary to popular myth, snakes cannot "hypnotize" their prey by staring at it.

Fact or fiction? Rattlesnakes always shake their tails before striking.
FICTION. Rattlesnakes do not always rattle before striking. A threatened rattlesnake may strike with no warning at all, so people must be extremely careful if they come in contact with one. Rattlesnakes are generally not aggressive toward humans, however, and usually will retreat if given the opportunity.

WHAT ARE GROUPS OF ANIMALS CALLED?

Here are some (often odd) names for animal groups.

BEARS: ***sleuth*** of bears
CATS: ***clowder*** of cats
CATTLE: ***drove*** of cattle
CROCODILES: ***bask*** of crocodiles
CROWS: ***murder*** of crows
FISH: ***school*** or ***shoal*** of fish
FLIES: ***swarm*** or ***cloud*** of flies
FOXES: ***skulk*** of foxes
GIRAFFES: ***tower*** of giraffes
HARES: ***down*** of hares
HAWKS: ***cast*** of hawks
HYENAS: ***cackle*** of hyenas
JELLYFISH: ***smack*** of jellyfish
KITTENS: ***kindle*** or ***kendle*** of kittens
LEOPARDS: ***leap*** of leopards
MONKEYS: ***troop*** of monkeys
MULES: ***span*** of mules
NIGHTINGALES: ***watch*** of nightingales
OWLS: ***parliament*** of owls
OYSTERS: ***bed*** of oysters
PEACOCKS: ***muster*** of peacocks
RAVENS: ***unkindness*** of ravens
SHARKS: ***shiver*** of sharks
SQUIRRELS: ***dray*** or ***scurry*** of squirrels
TURTLES: ***bale*** of turtles
WHALES: ***pod*** of whales

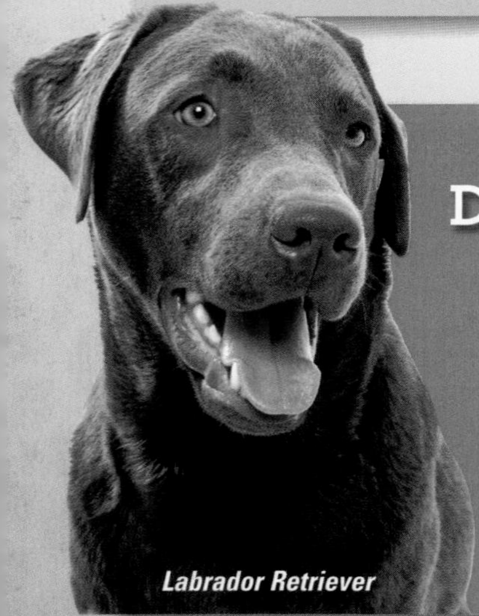

Labrador Retriever

DOGS AT THE TOP

Here are the most popular dog breeds in the United States.

1. Labrador Retriever
2. German Shepherd Dog
3. Beagle
4. Golden Retriever
5. Yorkshire Terrier
6. Bulldog
7. Boxer
8. Poodle
9. Dachshund
10. Rottweiler

Source: American Kennel Club, 2011

PETS Q&A

Which breed of dog is the largest? The tallest dog breed is the Irish Wolfhound, which can reach 35 inches at the shoulder and weigh 150 pounds. The heaviest breed is the English Mastiff, which can reach 32 inches at the shoulder and weigh 250 pounds.

True or false? Chow Chows are the only breed of dog with blue-black tongues. False. Other breeds share this trait, including the Shar-Pei.

True or false? Adult cats do not meow at other cats. True. Kittens meow to their mothers, but adult cats use the "meow" sound only to communicate with humans.

Chow Chow

WHICH PET IS RIGHT FOR YOU?

Freshwater fish (like goldfish), cats, and dogs—in that order—are the three most popular pets in the United States. If your family has decided to get a pet, how can you decide which type will be the best fit for you?

Freshwater Fish are an excellent option if you live in a small space or if any family members suffer from allergies. Some people think that fish require very little work and care, but this is not necessarily the case. Fish do not need to be walked or taken on regular trips to a veterinarian, but responsible fish owners keep the bowl or tank very clean and research which types of fish can share a living space. Even a simple goldfish in a bowl can be a big commitment—a goldfish may live for 10 years!

Cats are very popular pets, and with good reason. They can be playful and affectionate, but they are independent in many ways. Most cats use a litter box indoors, and they keep clean by licking themselves. But cats must be taken to a veterinarian at least once a year, and cats with claws often tear furniture or clothing. Many people are allergic to cats, so it is important for all family members to spend time with a cat before bringing one home.

Dogs are well-known for being loyal and loving to their owners. But of all the popular pets, dogs require the most work. Puppies often take many months to be housebroken, or trained to relieve themselves only outside. Adult dogs need daily exercise, and many breeds require regular grooming. Dogs are often given to animal shelters by owners who are overwhelmed by the need to care for them. Once your family has decided to get a dog, animal shelters are a great place to start your search!

ENDANGERED SPECIES

When a species becomes extinct, the variety of life on Earth is reduced. In the world today, many thousands of known species of animals and plants are in danger of becoming extinct. Humans have been able to save some endangered animals and are working to save more.

Some Endangered Animals

GIANT PANDA One of the world's most beloved animals is also one of the most threatened. Giant pandas are found in the wild only in China, and they must eat large amounts of bamboo—their primary food source—every day. It is estimated that fewer than 1,600 giant pandas can be found in the wild.

Reasons for population decline:
- Low rate of reproduction
- Loss of habitat due to increased development

KAKAPO This large parrot is one of the most unusual and rare birds in the world. It is the only parrot that is nocturnal (active at night), and it does not fly. The Kakapo will walk for miles at night in its native New Zealand. It is estimated that only about 100 of these birds can be found in the wild.

Reasons for population decline:
- Habitat loss due to deforestation
- Introduction of non-native species by humans
- Hunting by humans for its skin and feathers, which were made into capes

BACTRIAN CAMEL Bactrian camels, found in the Gobi Desert of Mongolia and China, are the only species of camel left in the wild. The Bactrian is related to the more common Arabian camel, but unlike the Arabian, it has two humps on its back. Experts estimate that fewer than 1,000 remain in the wild.

Reasons for population decline:
- Hunting by humans
- Habitat loss due to mining and other factors
- Low rate of reproduction

Success Stories

FLORIDA PANTHER The Florida panther, a type of cougar, is Florida's state animal. In 1989, studies showed that fewer than 50 of these big cats could be found in the wild. Although the Florida panther is still endangered, captive breeding programs and habitat protection efforts have kept this animal from becoming extinct.

GRAY WOLF Gray wolves could once be found all across the continent of North America. By the middle of the 20th century, their numbers had been drastically reduced, as farmers often killed wolves to protect their livestock. Thanks to efforts to save their natural habitats and reintroduce wolves into some areas, the gray wolf population is now thriving.

On the Brink

South China Tiger

True to its name, the South China tiger was once found in several provinces of southern China. The tiger is officially listed as critically endangered and can still be found in zoos, but scientists have not seen one in its native habitat since the 1970s. Most experts believe that the South China tiger is extinct in the wild.

Animals Word Scramble

Unscramble these words to find the names of some of the animals you've read about in this chapter.

lrioFad atnerph
ahhecet
soolacsl duqsi
aarngkoo
aintg anpad
atrciBan alemc

ANSWERS ON PAGES 334-336.

Working Animals

People and animals have worked together for thousands of years. The first animals to become domesticated, or comfortable with humans, were wolves. Wolves are the ancestors of the dogs that people live with—and sometimes work with—today. Many types of animals have been trained by people to do important jobs. Here are just a few examples.

Cats

When people think about working animals, cats are not usually first on the list! But cats provide many valuable services for people. Cats eat mice and other rodents, and they are often used for pest control on farms or in cities. They are also brought to places where people might need cheering up, such as hospitals. Studies have shown that petting an animal can improve a person's mood and even lower blood pressure. "Therapy cats" can provide this valuable service to patients.

Horses

Horses have played an important part in human history. Before the invention of cars, people traveled on horseback or in horse-drawn vehicles. Horses were also used to pull plows on farms, to herd cattle on ranches, to move goods in horse-drawn wagons, and to carry soldiers into battle. Today, police officers work on horseback to see above crowds and get into areas where cars can't travel. Horses are also used in search-and-rescue missions, because they can travel faster than people over rugged terrain. Some farmers still use horses to herd livestock and plow fields.

Dogs

Dogs work at more jobs than any other domesticated animal. They work with law enforcement officers to help find people who are lost or to sniff out bombs and other chemicals. Dogs who work with military personnel have been trained to spot snipers or find buried explosives. Service dogs may guide people who cannot see, alert hearing-impaired people to things they cannot hear, or give warnings when a person is about to have a seizure. Dogs protect and herd livestock on farms, and they have been trained to find bedbugs, termites, or other pests.

On the JOB Veterinarian

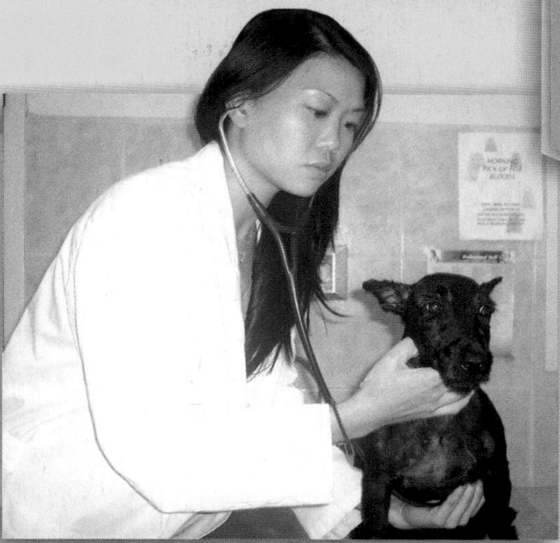

Veterinarians are doctors who take care of animals. Some work mostly with small animals, such as dogs and cats, in vet clinics. Some specialize in one type of illness or work with large animals on farms or in zoos. **Vivian Ng**, a veterinarian who works in a clinic, agreed to talk to *The World Almanac for Kids* about her work.

What do you do in a typical day?

I see patients, perform surgeries, and interact with people. I am a small animal vet, which means I primarily work with cats and dogs. It's important for me to communicate with owners about how to give the best care for their pet. When a pet is sick, my biggest challenge is figuring out what is wrong. Animals can't tell us why they're sick or how they are feeling. Another important part of my job is performing spay and neuter surgeries. These surgeries help prevent overpopulation of dogs and cats.

What interests and strengths of yours make this job right for you?

I have always been interested in animals—my pets are like family to me. This connection makes me more compassionate in my work. I think compassion and clear-headedness are extremely important in this career. There are many emergency situations that require vets to stay calm and think clearly.

What kind of education or training did you need to get in order to do your job?

I have a doctor of veterinary medicine degree from the Atlantic Veterinary College of the University of Prince Edward Island.

What do you like best about your job? What is most challenging?

I love the diversity. You can choose to interact with large animals, small animals, exotics (like hedgehogs and snakes), marine animals, or zoo animals. You might try different career paths—such as private practice, research, public health, or teaching. Not all veterinarians take care of pets. What I find most rewarding is to be able to help animals feel better and to help to comfort their worried owners. There are many days that are long and stressful, and that is challenging—but knowing that I made a difference in an animal's life makes it worthwhile.

ART

→How have carved masks been used in many African cultures? PAGE 36

What is art?

The answer is up for debate. People who study this question are studying aesthetics (ess-THET-ics), which is a kind of philosophy. Usually art is something about life or about the world that an artist interprets for an audience.

Why do we need art?

Sometimes art simply gives us pleasure, as when we look at a painting of a beautiful scene. Art can also make us think. Works of art sometimes get us to rethink ideas we take for granted. Sometimes they give us insights into the character of people.

Artists express their ideas in their art, and their work can help the rest of us understand our world and ourselves better.

Art Q&A

When I see a work of art in a museum, what should I look for?

Look at the artwork without thinking too hard about it. How does it make you feel? Happy, sad, confused, silly? Study the work, and try to discover the colors, shapes, or textures that create those feelings in you.

Look at the information card next to the work of art. Usually, it will tell you who created it, when it was made, and what media (materials) were used. You can compare it to other works of art by the same artist, from the same time, or in the same medium.

Different Kinds of Art

Through history, artists have painted pictures of nature (landscapes), pictures of people (portraits), and pictures of flowers in vases, food, and other objects (still lifes). Today many artists create pictures that do not look like anything in the real world. These are examples of abstract art.

Photography, too, is a form of art. Photos record both the commonplace and the exotic and help us look at events in new ways.

Sculpture is a three-dimensional form made from clay, stone, metal, or other material. Sculptures can be large, like the Statue of Liberty. Some are realistic. Others have no form you can recognize.

Artists work with many materials. Some artists today use computers and video screens to create their art.

Little Fourteen-Year-Old Dancer by Edgar Degas

ART ALL-STARS

These works of art helped change the way we see the world around us.

LEONARDO DA VINCI (1452–1519)
The Lady with the Ermine (1496)

Leonardo lived in Italy at a time of great creativity known as the Renaissance. Most famous as a painter, he was also a scientist, inventor, musician, and map-maker. His best-known painting is the *Mona Lisa*, but he did a number of other portraits of women that feature fascinating facial expressions and delicate lighting.

JOHANNES VERMEER (1632–1675)
Young Woman with a Water Pitcher (1660s)

Vermeer lived and worked in the Dutch city of Delft. He painted small canvases, usually of beautifully lit interiors. His work seems to capture a moment in time, and peace and calm fill his pictures of people doing everyday things. He is considered one of the greatest painters of all time.

BERENICE ABBOTT (1898–1991)
Blossom Restaurant (1935)

Born in Ohio, Berenice Abbott became one of America's foremost photographers. She is particularly known for her series of photos called *Changing New York*, which captured the city as it rapidly modernized in the 1930s.

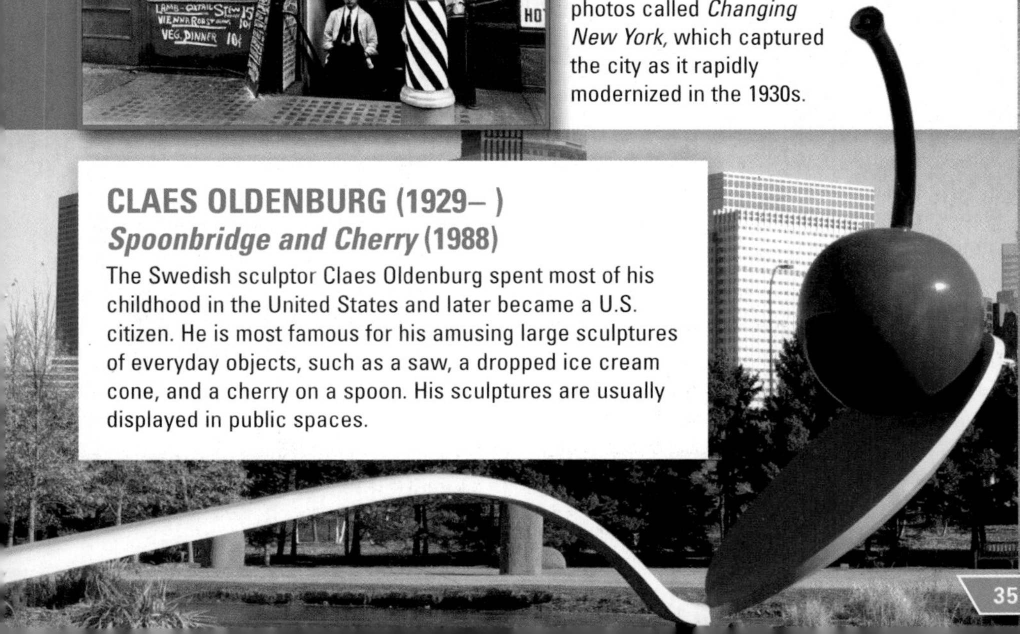

CLAES OLDENBURG (1929–)
Spoonbridge and Cherry (1988)

The Swedish sculptor Claes Oldenburg spent most of his childhood in the United States and later became a U.S. citizen. He is most famous for his amusing large sculptures of everyday objects, such as a saw, a dropped ice cream cone, and a cherry on a spoon. His sculptures are usually displayed in public spaces.

Art Around the World

Throughout history, all cultures have created their own art forms. This art reflects each culture's traditions and beliefs. Here are a few of the different artistic traditions that are found around the globe.

African Masks

Many African peoples have created masks for use in religious ceremonies. The wooden masks are beautifully carved and sometimes elaborately decorated. They can represent people from earlier generations or such things as good and evil spirits. Sometimes they have a mix of human and animal features, which is meant to represent the close relationship between people and nature. African masks have influenced the work of many Western artists, including the painter Pablo Picasso.

Australian Aboriginal Art

For Australian Aborigines, traditional art is connected to what they call the "Dreamtime." This is a sacred time that began in the past, during which people developed ways of living and creating art. "Dreaming" is the total of everything that is known and understood. This idea is expressed in Aboriginal art through symbols that represent important aspects of life, including animals, human activities, and natural phenomena such as rain.

Japanese Landscape Painting

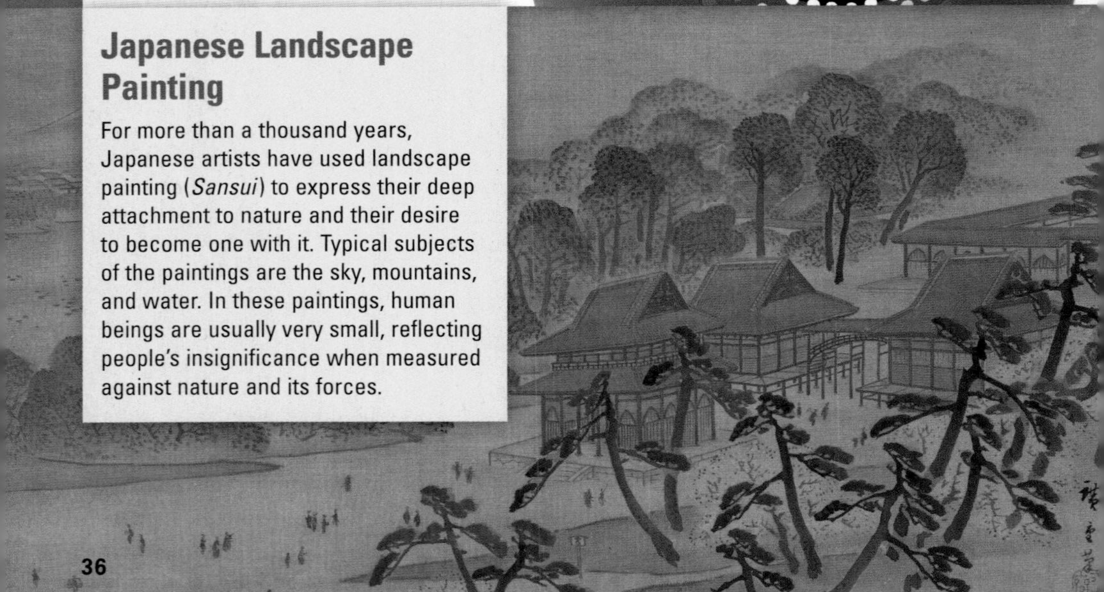

For more than a thousand years, Japanese artists have used landscape painting (*Sansui*) to express their deep attachment to nature and their desire to become one with it. Typical subjects of the paintings are the sky, mountains, and water. In these paintings, human beings are usually very small, reflecting people's insignificance when measured against nature and its forces.

Color Wheel

This color wheel shows how colors are related to each other.

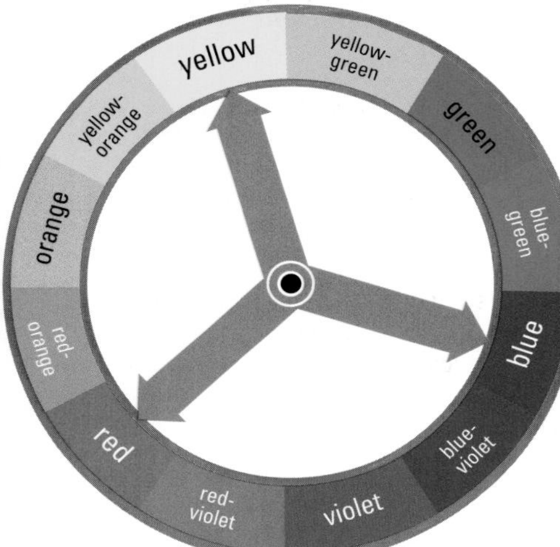

Primary colors The most basic colors are RED, YELLOW, and **BLUE**. They're called primary because you can't get them by mixing any other colors. In fact, the other colors are made by mixing red, blue, or yellow. Arrows on this wheel show the primary colors.

Secondary colors **ORANGE**, **GREEN**, and **VIOLET** are the secondary colors. They are made by mixing two primary colors. You make orange by mixing yellow and red, or green by mixing yellow and blue. On the color wheel, **GREEN** appears between **BLUE** and **YELLOW**.

Tertiary colors When you mix a primary and a secondary color, you get a tertiary, or intermediate, color. **BLUE-GREEN** and **YELLOW-GREEN** are intermediate colors.

More Color Terms

VALUES

The lightness or darkness of a color is its value. Tints are light values made by mixing a color with white. **PINK** is a tint of **RED**. Shades are dark values made by mixing a color with black. **MAROON** is a shade of **RED**.

COMPLEMENTARY COLORS

Contrasting colors that please the eye when used together are called complementary colors. These colors appear opposite each other on the wheel and don't have any colors in common. **RED** is a complement to **GREEN**, which is made by mixing **YELLOW** and **BLUE**.

COOL COLORS

Cool colors are mostly **GREEN**, **BLUE**, and **PURPLE**. They make you think of cool things like water and can even make you feel cooler.

WARM COLORS

Warm colors are mostly **RED**, **ORANGE**, and **YELLOW**. They suggest heat and can actually make you feel warmer.

ANALOGOUS COLORS

The colors next to each other on the wheel are from the same "family." **BLUE**, **BLUE-GREEN**, and **GREEN** all have **BLUE** in them and are analogous colors.

BIRTHDAYS

→What symbol represents a Gemini? PAGE 42

Taye Diggs

JANUARY
BIRTHSTONE: GARNET

1 J. D. Salinger, author, 1919
2 Taye Diggs, actor, 1971
3 Eli Manning, football player, 1981
4 Isaac Newton, scientist, 1643
5 January Jones, actress, 1978
6 Carl Sandburg, poet, 1878
7 Katie Couric, journalist, 1957
8 Stephen Hawking, physicist, 1942
9 Catherine (Kate Middleton), Duchess of Cambridge, 1982
10 George Foreman, boxer, 1948
11 Mary J. Blige, singer, 1971
12 Christiane Amanpour, journalist, 1958
13 Liam Hemsworth, actor, 1990
14 LL Cool J, rapper/actor, 1968
15 Rev. Martin Luther King Jr., civil rights leader, 1929
16 Albert Pujols, baseball player, 1980
17 Michelle Obama, first lady, 1964
18 Mark Messier, hockey player, 1961
19 Paul Cézanne, artist, 1839
20 Buzz Aldrin, astronaut, 1930
21 Hakeem Olajuwon, basketball player, 1963
22 Diane Lane, actress, 1965
23 John Hancock, patriot, 1737
24 Edith Wharton, author, 1862
25 Etta James, singer, 1938
26 Paul Newman, actor, 1925
27 Hannah Teter, snowboarder, 1987
28 Ariel Winter, actress, 1998
29 Oprah Winfrey, TV personality, 1954
30 Christian Bale, actor, 1974
31 Justin Timberlake, singer, 1981

FEBRUARY
BIRTHSTONE: AMETHYST

1 Langston Hughes, poet, 1902
2 Shakira, singer, 1977
3 Elizabeth Blackwell, first woman physician in U.S., 1821
4 Rosa Parks, civil rights leader, 1913
5 Hank Aaron, baseball player, 1934
6 Ronald Reagan, 40th president, 1911
7 Laura Ingalls Wilder, author, 1867
8 John Grisham, author, 1955
9 Carole King, musician, 1942
10 Elizabeth Banks, actress, 1974
11 Taylor Lautner, actor, 1992
12 Abraham Lincoln, 16th president, 1809
13 Grant Wood, artist, 1891
14 Drew Bledsoe, football player, 1972
15 Matt Groening, cartoonist, 1954
16 John McEnroe, tennis player, 1959
17 Billie Joe Armstrong, musician, 1972
18 Jillian Michaels, TV personality, 1974
19 Amy Tan, author, 1952
20 Justin Verlander, baseball player, 1983
21 Ashley Greene, actress, 1987
22 Edna St. Vincent Millay, poet, 1892
23 Dakota Fanning, actress, 1994
24 Steve Jobs, computer innovator, 1955
25 George Harrison, musician, 1943
26 Fats Domino, musician, 1928
27 John Steinbeck, author, 1902
28 Linus Pauling, scientist, 1901
29 Herman Hollerith, statistician, 1860

Abraham Lincoln

Danica Patrick

MARCH
BIRTHSTONE: AQUAMARINE

1 Justin Bieber, singer, 1994
2 Bryce Dallas Howard, actress, 1981
3 Alexander Graham Bell, inventor, 1847
4 Knute Rockne, football coach, 1888
5 Eva Mendes, actress, 1974
6 Elizabeth Barrett Browning, poet, 1806
7 Jenna Fischer, actress, 1974
8 Kenneth Grahame, author, 1859
9 Bow Wow, actor/rapper, 1987
10 Carrie Underwood, singer, 1983
11 Benji and Joel Madden, musicians, 1979
12 Mitt Romney, politician, 1947
13 Will Clark, baseball player, 1964
14 Albert Einstein, physicist/ Nobel laureate, 1879
15 Eva Longoria, actress, 1975
16 Lauren Graham, actress, 1967
17 Nat King Cole, musician, 1919
18 Adam Levine, musician, 1979
19 Bruce Willis, actor, 1955
20 Fred Rogers, TV personality, 1928
21 Johann Sebastian Bach, composer, 1685
22 Reese Witherspoon, actress, 1976
23 Jason Kidd, basketball player, 1973
24 Peyton Manning, football player, 1976
25 Danica Patrick, racecar driver, 1982
26 Robert Frost, poet, 1874
27 Mariah Carey, singer, 1970
28 Lady Gaga, singer, 1986
29 Cy Young, baseball player, 1867
30 Eric Clapton, musician, 1945
31 Cesar Chavez, labor leader, 1927

APRIL
BIRTHSTONE: DIAMOND

1 Rachel Maddow, TV host, 1973
2 Marvin Gaye, singer, 1939
3 Jane Goodall, scientist, 1934
4 Maya Angelou, poet, 1928
5 Booker T. Washington, educator, 1856
6 Paul Rudd, actor, 1969
7 Francis Ford Coppola, director, 1939
8 Taylor Kitsch, actor, 1981
9 Kristen Stewart, actress, 1990
10 John Madden, sportscaster, 1936
11 Joss Stone, singer, 1987
12 Claire Danes, actress, 1979
13 Thomas Jefferson, 3rd president, 1743
14 Pete Rose, baseball player, 1941
15 Emma Watson, actress, 1990
16 Kareem Abdul-Jabbar, basketball player, 1947
17 Jennifer Garner, actress, 1972
18 America Ferrera, actress, 1984
19 James Franco, actor, 1978
20 Don Mattingly, baseball player, 1961
21 Queen Elizabeth II, British monarch, 1926
22 Robert J. Oppenheimer, physicist, 1904
23 Dev Patel, actor, 1990
24 Kelly Clarkson, singer, 1982
25 Ella Fitzgerald, singer, 1917
26 Channing Tatum, actor, 1980
27 Samuel Morse, inventor, 1791
28 Harper Lee, author, 1926
29 Dale Earnhardt Sr., race car driver, 1951
30 Dianna Agron, actress, 1986

Maya Angelou

Adele

MAY
BIRTHSTONE: EMERALD

1 Tim McGraw, musician, 1967
2 David Beckham, soccer player, 1975
3 Sugar Ray Robinson, boxer, 1921
4 Audrey Hepburn, actress, 1929
5 Adele, singer, 1988
6 George Clooney, actor, 1961
7 Johannes Brahms, composer, 1833
8 Enrique Iglesias, singer, 1975
9 Billy Joel, musician, 1949
10 Bono, musician/activist, 1960
11 Cory Monteith, actor, 1982
12 Tony Hawk, skateboarder, 1968
13 Robert Pattinson, actor, 1986
14 Miranda Cosgrove, actress, 1993
15 Emmitt Smith, football player, 1969
16 Megan Fox, actress, 1986
17 Sugar Ray Leonard, boxer, 1956
18 Tina Fey, actress/comedian, 1970
19 Malcolm X, militant civil rights activist, 1925
20 Busta Rhymes, rapper, 1972
21 John Muir, naturalist, 1838
22 Novak Djokovik, tennis player, 1987
23 Margaret Wise Brown, author, 1910
24 Bob Dylan, musician, 1941
25 Mike Myers, actor, 1963
26 Lenny Kravitz, actor/ musician, 1964
27 Chris Colfer, actor, 1990
28 Jim Thorpe, athlete, 1888
29 John F. Kennedy, 35th president, 1917
30 Cee Lo Green, singer, 1974
31 Walt Whitman, poet, 1819

JUNE
BIRTHSTONE: PEARL

1 Marilyn Monroe, actress, 1926
2 Zachary Quinto, actor, 1977
3 Anderson Cooper, journalist, 1967
4 Angelina Jolie, actress, 1975
5 Mark Wahlberg, actor, 1971
6 Cynthia Rylant, author, 1954
7 Michael Cera, actor, 1988
8 Kanye West, musician, 1977
9 Natalie Portman, actress, 1981
10 Maurice Sendak, author/ illustrator, 1928
11 Peter Dinklage, actor, 1969
12 Anne Frank, diary writer, 1929
13 William Butler Yeats, poet, 1865
14 Kevin McHale, actor, 1988
15 Neil Patrick Harris, actor, 1973
16 Tupac Shakur, rapper/actor, 1971
17 Venus Williams, tennis player, 1980
18 Sir Paul McCartney, musician, 1942
19 Zoe Saldana, actress, 1978
20 Nicole Kidman, actress, 1967
21 Prince William of Great Britain, Duke of Cambridge, 1982
22 Meryl Streep, actress, 1949
23 Bob Fosse, choreographer, 1927
24 Solange Knowles, singer, 1986
25 Sonia Sotomayor, U.S. Supreme Court justice, 1954
26 Derek Jeter, baseball player, 1974
27 Ed Westwick, actor, 1987
28 John Cusack, actor, 1966
29 Nicole Scherzinger, singer, 1978
30 Michael Phelps, Olympic champion, 1985

Maurice Sendak

Sofía Vergara

JULY
BIRTHSTONE: RUBY

1 Carl Lewis, Olympic champion, 1961
2 Ashley Tisdale, actress, 1986
3 Tom Cruise, actor, 1962
4 Neil Simon, playwright, 1927
5 P. T. Barnum, showman/circus founder, 1810
6 George W. Bush, 43rd president, 1946
7 Michelle Kwan, figure skater, 1980
8 Jaden Smith, actor/rapper, 1998
9 Tom Hanks, actor, 1956
10 Sofía Vergara, actress, 1972
11 E. B. White, author, 1899
12 Andrew Wyeth, painter, 1917
13 Harrison Ford, actor, 1942
14 Jane Lynch, actress, 1960
15 Rembrandt van Rijn, artist, 1606
16 Will Ferrell, actor, 1967
17 Donald Sutherland, actor, 1935
18 Kristen Bell, actress, 1980
19 Edgar Degas, artist, 1834
20 Gisele Bündchen, model, 1980
21 Ernest Hemingway, author, 1899
22 Selena Gomez, actress/singer 1992
23 Daniel Radcliffe, actor, 1989
24 Jennifer Lopez, actress/singer, 1969
25 Walter Payton, football player, 1954
26 Taylor Momsen, actress, 1993
27 Alex Rodriguez, baseball player, 1975
28 Beatrix Potter, author, 1866
29 Danger Mouse, musician, 1977
30 Laurence Fishburne, actor, 1961
31 J. K. Rowling, author, 1965

AUGUST
BIRTHSTONE: PERIDOT

1 Yves Saint Laurent, designer, 1936
2 Sam Worthington, actor, 1976
3 Tom Brady, football player, 1977
4 Barack Obama, 44th president, 1961
5 Neil Armstrong, astronaut, 1930
6 Andy Warhol, artist, 1928
7 Charlize Theron, actress, 1975
8 Matthew Henson, explorer, 1866
9 Eric Bana, actor, 1968
10 Antonio Banderas, actor, 1960
11 Alyson Stoner, actress, 1983
12 Pete Sampras, tennis player, 1971
13 Alfred Hitchcock, filmmaker, 1899
14 Tim Tebow, football player, 1987
15 Jennifer Lawrence, actress, 1990
16 Steve Carell, actor, 1963
17 Robert De Niro, actor, 1943
18 Meriwether Lewis, explorer, 1774
19 Bill Clinton, 42nd president, 1946
20 Demi Lovato, actress/singer, 1992
21 Usain Bolt, Olympic champion, 1986
22 Giada De Laurentiis, chef, 1970
23 Jeremy Lin, basketball player, 1988
24 Rupert Grint, actor, 1988
25 Blake Lively, actress, 1987
26 Keke Palmer, actress, 1993
27 Alexa Vega, actress, 1988
28 Jack Black, actor, 1969
29 Lea Michele, actress, 1986
30 Cameron Diaz, actress, 1972
31 Van Morrison, musician, 1945

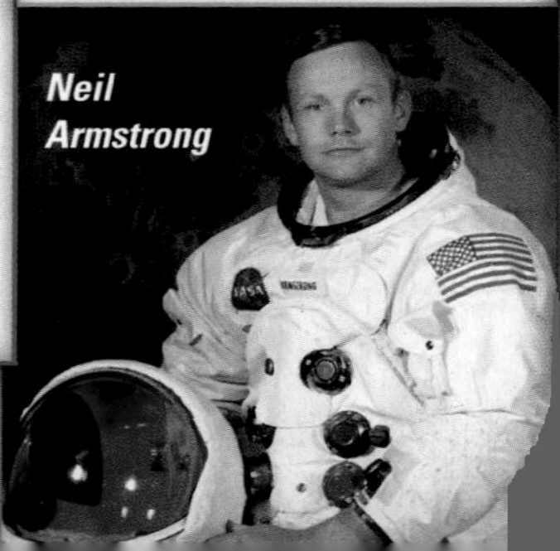

Neil Armstrong

Ray Charles

SEPTEMBER
BIRTHSTONE: SAPPHIRE

1 Rachel Zoe, stylist, 1971
2 Christa McAuliffe, teacher/astronaut, 1948
3 Shaun White, snowboarder, 1986
4 Beyoncé Knowles, singer/actress, 1981
5 Werner Herzog, director, 1942
6 Roger Waters, musician, 1943
7 Buddy Holly, musician, 1936
8 Pink, singer, 1979
9 Michelle Williams, actress, 1980
10 Roger Maris, baseball player, 1934
11 Ludacris, rapper, 1977
12 Jennifer Hudson, singer/actress, 1981
13 Roald Dahl, author, 1916
14 Tyler Perry, director, 1969
15 Prince Harry of Great Britain, 1984
16 Amy Poehler, actress/comedian, 1971
17 Rasheed Wallace, basketball player, 1974
18 Lance Armstrong, cyclist, 1971
19 Jim Abbott, baseball player, 1967
20 Red Auerbach, basketball coach, 1917
21 Stephen King, author, 1947
22 Andrea Bocelli, singer, 1958
23 Ray Charles, musician, 1930
24 Jim Henson, Muppet creator, 1936
25 Will Smith, actor/rapper, 1968
26 T. S. Eliot, poet, 1888
27 Gwyneth Paltrow, actress, 1972
28 Al Capp, cartoonist, 1909
29 Kevin Durant, basketball player, 1988
30 Elie Wiesel, author, 1928

OCTOBER
BIRTHSTONE: OPAL

1 Rod Carew, baseball player, 1945
2 Mohandas Gandhi, activist, 1869
3 Stevie Ray Vaughan, musician, 1954
4 Anne Rice, author, 1941
5 Jesse Eisenberg, actor, 1983
6 Olivia Thirlby, actress, 1986
7 Simon Cowell, TV personality, 1959
8 Matt Damon, actor, 1970
9 John Lennon, musician, 1940
10 Maya Lin, sculptor and architect, 1960
11 Steve Young, football player, 1961
12 Josh Hutcherson, actor, 1992
13 Jerry Rice, football player, 1962
14 Usher, singer, 1978
15 Penny Marshall, actress/director, 1943
16 John Mayer, musician, 1977
17 Eminem, rapper/actor, 1972
18 Lindsey Vonn, skier, 1984
19 Ty Pennington, TV personality, 1965
20 Danny Boyle, director, 1956
21 Dizzy Gillespie, trumpet player, 1917
22 Ichiro Suzuki, baseball player, 1973
23 Amandla Stenberg, actress, 1998
24 Brian Vickers, racecar driver, 1983
25 Katy Perry, singer, 1984
26 Keith Urban, musician, 1967
27 Theodore Roosevelt, 26th president, 1858
28 Nolan Gould, actor, 1998
29 Winona Ryder, actress, 1971
30 Matthew Morrison, actor, 1978
31 Willow Smith, singer/actress, 2000

Josh Hutcherson

Louisa May Alcott

NOVEMBER
BIRTHSTONE: TOPAZ

1 Penn Badgley, actor, 1986
2 James K. Polk, 11th president, 1795
3 John Barry, composer, 1933
4 Matthew McConaughey, actor, 1969
5 Johnny Damon, baseball player, 1973
6 Emma Stone, actress, 1988
7 Marie Curie, scientist/Nobel laureate, 1867
8 Margaret Mitchell, author, 1900
9 Carl Sagan, scientist, 1934
10 Miranda Lambert, musician, 1983
11 Leonardo DiCaprio, actor, 1974
12 Ryan Gosling, actor, 1980
13 Robert Louis Stevenson, author, 1850
14 Condoleezza Rice, diplomat, 1954
15 Georgia O'Keefe, artist, 1887
16 Maggie Gyllenhaal, actress, 1977
17 Rachel McAdams, actress, 1978
18 Owen Wilson, actor, 1968
19 Calvin Klein, fashion designer, 1942
20 Joe Biden, 47th vice president, 1942
21 Troy Aikman, football player, 1966
22 Scarlett Johansson, actress, 1984
23 Miley Cyrus, singer/actress, 1992
24 Sarah Hyland, actress, 1990
25 Donovan McNabb, football player, 1976
26 Charles Schulz, cartoonist, 1912
27 Kathryn Bigelow, director, 1951
28 Jon Stewart, TV host, 1962
29 Louisa May Alcott, author, 1832
30 Elisha Cuthbert, actress, 1982

DECEMBER
BIRTHSTONE: TURQUOISE

1 Sarah Silverman, actress/comedienne, 1970
2 Lucy Liu, actress, 1968
3 Amanda Seyfried, actress, 1985
4 Jay-Z, rapper, 1969
5 Walt Disney, cartoonist/filmmaker, 1901
6 Otto Graham, football player/coach, 1921
7 Larry Bird, basketball player/coach, 1956
8 Nicki Minaj, rapper, 1982
9 Felicity Huffman, actress, 1962
10 Bobby Flay, chef, 1964
11 Hailee Steinfeld, actress, 1996
12 Frank Sinatra, singer/actor, 1915
13 Taylor Swift, singer, 1989
14 Vanessa Hudgens, actress/singer, 1988
15 Adam Brody, actor, 1979
16 Jane Austen, author, 1775
17 Chase Utley, baseball player, 1978
18 Christina Aguilera, singer, 1980
19 Jake Gyllenhaal, actor, 1980
20 Jonah Hill, actor, 1983
21 Samuel L. Jackson, actor, 1948
22 Diane Sawyer, journalist, 1945
23 Eddie Vedder, musician, 1964
24 Stephenie Meyer, author, 1973
25 Clara Barton, American Red Cross founder, 1821
26 Carlton Fisk, baseball player, 1947
27 Louis Pasteur, scientist, 1822
28 Denzel Washington, actor, 1954
29 Charles Goodyear, inventor, 1800
30 LeBron James, basketball player, 1984
31 Diane von Fürstenberg, designer, 1946

Jane Austen

WHAT'S YOUR SIGN?

Astrology is a study of the positions of celestial bodies—such as the sun, moon, planets, and stars—that looks to find connections between these bodies and things that happen on Earth. Most scientists do not believe that there are connections. Still, many people enjoy learning about astrology and using it for entertainment.

The Zodiac is very important to people who follow astrology. The zodiac is a belt-shaped section of the sky that has been divided into twelve constellations. A constellation is a cluster of stars that can be seen from Earth. Astrologers believe that every person is influenced by one of these twelve constellations—or twelve signs—depending on his or her birthday. For example, a person born between July 23 and August 22 is a Leo. Leos are said to be confident and generous, but stubborn.

A Horoscope is a prediction about a person's future based on his or her astrological sign. Daily or monthly horoscopes can be found in many newspapers and magazines, in print or online, and on other websites.

Signs of the Zodiac

Here are the signs of the zodiac, with the approximate date span and symbol for each.

Aries
March 21 - April 19
RAM

Taurus
April 20 - May 20
BULL

Gemini
May 21 - June 20
TWINS

Cancer
June 21 - July 22
CRAB

Leo
July 23 - August 22
LION

Virgo
August 23 - September 22
MAIDEN

Libra
September 23 - October 22
SCALES

Scorpio
October 23 - November 21
SCORPION

Sagittarius
November 22 - December 21
ARCHER

Capricorn
December 22 - January 19
GOAT

Aquarius
January 20 - February 18
WATER CARRIER

Pisces
February 19 - March 20
FISHES

DID YOU KNOW? The *Shēngxiào*, or Chinese zodiac, is a system that relates every birth year to a different animal. For example, people who were born in 2002 (a year of the horse) are said to be cheerful and charming.

Celebrity Crossword Puzzle

Think you know a lot about celebrities? It's time to put that knowledge to the test! Fill in the words that go with each clue. If you're stumped, the answers can all be found in *The World Almanac for Kids*. Look in these chapters: Birthdays, Books, Faces & Places, Movies & TV, and Music & Dance. Good luck!

Hint: When the clue is about a person, the answer could be the person's full name or just the person's last name.

ANSWERS ON PAGES 334-336.

ACROSS

6. *The Pirates! Band of Misfits* voice

7. Author of *The Lorax*

9. Super Bowl halftime star

12. Racecar driver born in March

13. Maroon 5 singer

14. Actor who plays Percy Jackson

DOWN

1. All-time top grossing movie

2. Academy Award-winning actress for *The Help*

3. Second book of The Hunger Games series

4. Star of *The Amazing Spider-Man*

5. Kids' Choice Awards host

8. Director of *The Hobbit: An Unexpected Journey*

10. Singer with the best-selling album of 2011

11. Love story starring Channing Tatum and Rachel McAdams

15. Twilight series author

BOOKS

→What was E. B. White's first children's book? PAGE 45

2012 BOOK AWARDS

Caldecott Medal
For the artist of the best children's picture book
2012 winner: ***A Ball for Daisy***, by Chris Raschka

"A BRILLIANT BOOK." —Dave Barry
A New York Times bestselling novel by the National Book Award Finalist
Jack Gantos
DEAD END IN NORVELT

Newbery Medal
For the author of the best children's book
2012 winner:
Dead End in Norvelt, by Jack Gantos

Michael L. Printz Award
For excellence in literature written for young adults
2012 winner:
Where Things Come Back, by John Corey Whaley

Coretta Scott King Award
For artists and authors whose works encourage expression of the African American experience
2012 winners:
Author Award:
Heart and Soul*: *The Story of America and African Americans, by Kadir Nelson

Illustrator Award:
Underground*: *Finding the Light to Freedom, illustrated by Shane W. Evans

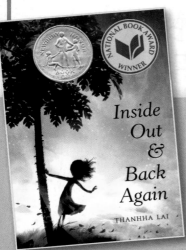

NEW BOOK SPOTLIGHT

***Inside Out & Back Again*, by Thanhha Lai, tells the story of 10-year-old Hà. The young girl and her family are forced to flee their home in Saigon during the Vietnam War. They move to Alabama. In the book, Hà writes in verse about her struggle as she leaves her old life behind and starts fresh in a whole new world. The book is based on the author's personal experience.**

FAMOUS CHILDREN'S AUTHORS

Author	TRY the Books
 **Suzanne Collins** (1962–) is the author of The Hunger Games trilogy. She began her career writing for children's television. The Hunger Games series is rooted in her interest in Greek mythology. She got the idea for the books while watching TV. She observed people competing on a reality show on one channel and fighting a war on another channel.	• ***The Hunger Games*** • ***Catching Fire*** • ***Mockingjay***
Kate DiCamillo (1964–) won the Newbery Medal for *The Tale of Despereaux*. She was inspired to write it after a friend's son asked her to create an unlikely hero with exceptionally large ears. The book follows the adventures of Despereaux the mouse on his quest to rescue a princess.	• ***Because of Winn-Dixie*** • ***The Tiger Rising***
 **Stephenie Meyer** (1973–) is the author of the world-famous Twilight vampire-romance series. Her four novels have sold more than 100 million copies and been translated into 37 languages. In June 2003, a dream sparked the idea for the series. Three months later, she finished writing *Twilight*, her first novel in the saga. It was published in 2005.	• ***Twilight*** • ***New Moon*** • ***Eclipse*** • ***Breaking Dawn***
 **Walter Dean Myers** (1937–) was born Walter Milton Myers in West Virginia. After his mother died when he was only two, his foster parents, Florence and Herbert Dean, raised him in New York City. He changed his middle name to honor them. Growing up, Myers loved basketball and writing.	• ***Monster*** • ***Lockdown*** • ***Scorpions*** • ***Somewhere in the Darkness***
Gary Paulsen (1939–) worked a variety of jobs—including as an engineer, construction worker, and truck driver—before realizing he wanted to be a writer. He has written more than 175 books. In addition to writing, Paulsen trains dogs for the Iditarod sled race in Alaska.	**The Brian Saga:** ***Hatchet, The River, Brian's Winter, Brian's Return,*** **and** ***Brian's Hunt***
E. B. White (1899–1985), born Elwyn Brooks White, is the author of the beloved children's classics *Stuart Little, The Trumpet of the Swan,* and *Charlotte's Web*. White worked as a reporter, essayist, and magazine writer. *Stuart Little*, his first children's book, was published in 1945.	• ***Charlotte's Web*** • ***The Trumpet of the Swan***

Cool Reads

Calling all bookworms! There are two main types of literature: **fiction** and **nonfiction**. Fiction is a made-up story. Nonfiction, on the other hand, is a true story. Within these two groups are different types of stories called **genres** (ZHAHN-ruhz). Check out these recommended reads from various genres.

FICTION

ADVENTURE, FANTASY, AND SCIENCE FICTION

These stories transport you to imaginary worlds filled with unusual characters and magical creatures.

TRY THESE ***The Hunger Games***, by Suzanne Collins; **Percy Jackson & the Olympians** series, by Rick Riordan; ***A Wrinkle in Time***, by Madeleine L'Engle

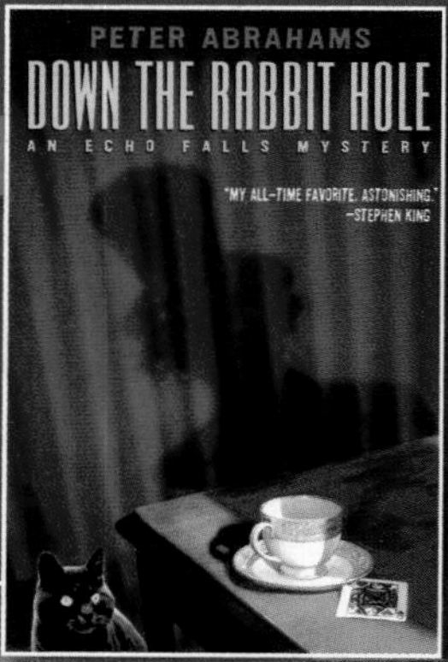

MYSTERIES AND THRILLERS

These suspense-filled tales follow a secret that needs to be uncovered or a crime that needs to be solved.

TRY THESE ***Down the Rabbit Hole: An Echo Falls Mystery***, by Peter Abrahams; ***The Egypt Game,*** by Zilpha Keatley Snyder; ***The House With a Clock in Its Walls***, by John Bellairs

REALISTIC FICTION

Do you enjoy reading stories that you can relate to? This genre is about real-life situations that kids and teens deal with every day.

TRY THESE ***13 Gifts***, by Wendy Mass; ***Tales of a Fourth Grade Nothing***, by Judy Blume

HISTORICAL FICTION

Authors of this genre put a new twist on history. They take exciting historical events or periods and place intriguing fictional characters smack in the middle of them.

TRY THESE ***Al Capone Does My Shirts***, by Gennifer Choldenko; ***Bud, Not Buddy,*** by Christopher Paul Curtis

MYTHS AND LEGENDS

These made-up stories go way back. Many tell of how things in nature came to be.

TRY THESE ***Amazing Greek Myths of Wonder and Blunders,*** by Mike Townsend; ***The Girl Who Helped Thunder and Other Native American Folktales***, by James Bruchac and Joseph Bruchac

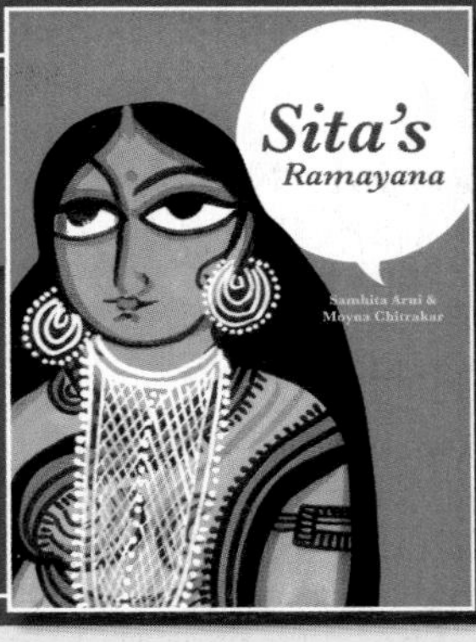

GRAPHIC NOVELS, COMICS, AND MANGA

These types of books convey their stories with drawings and text.

TRY THESE ***Diary of a Wimpy Kid,*** by Jeff Kinney; ***Sita's Ramayana,*** written by Samhita Arni and illustrated by Moyna Chitrakar

NONFICTION

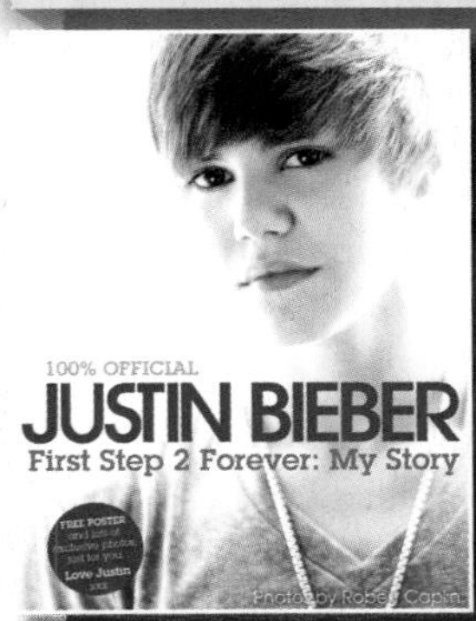

MEMOIRS, BIOGRAPHIES, AND AUTOBIOGRAPHIES

Do you like reading about the details of a real person's life? Then get up-close and personal with this genre!

TRY THESE ***Justin Bieber: First Step 2 Forever: My Story***, by Justin Bieber; ***Music Was It: Young Leonard Bernstein,*** by Susan Goldman Rubin; ***Rosa Parks: My Story***, by Rosa Parks with Jim Haskins

HISTORY

Books in this genre can be about an event, an era, a country, or even a war.

TRY THESE ***All Stations! Distress!: April 15, 1912, The Day the Titanic Sank,*** by Don Brown; ***Blizzard of Glass: The Halifax Explosion of 1917***, by Sally M. Walker

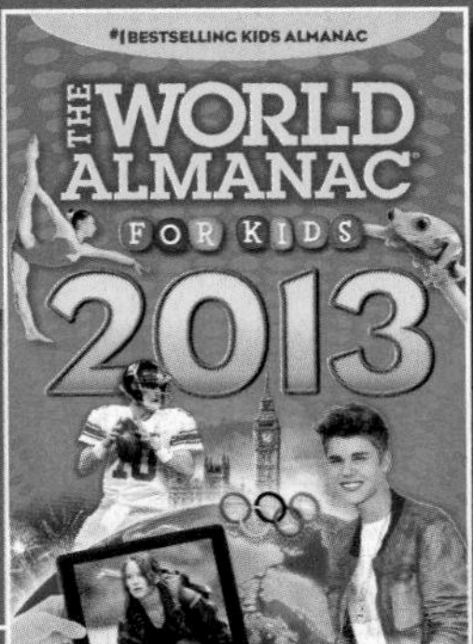

REFERENCE

Reference books provide reliable facts and sources of information. Almanacs, atlases, dictionaries, and encyclopedias are examples of reference books.

TRY THIS ***The World Almanac for Kids***

BOOKS THROUGH TIME

If a Roman emperor wanted to read a book, he had to unroll it from a scroll. Around A.D. 100, the codex was invented. It was made up of a stack of pages stitched together at the side and protected by a cover. Books on paper that we read today look something like a codex.

In the Middle Ages, books were made by monks who copied them by hand onto prepared animal skins called parchment (see right). The monks often decorated the pages with beautiful color illustrations called illuminations. Books were scarce and very expensive, and few people who were not priests or monks could read.

A big change came with the inventions of paper and printing in China. Paper came into Europe through the Muslim world and was common by the 14th century. Johann Gutenberg of Germany perfected printing in the 1450s. Once books could be printed they became more common.

At first, books were still not easy to make. A typesetter had to put each letter into place individually. Once all the letters for the page were in place, they were covered with ink and printed, one page at a time, by hand on a press. By the 19th century, however, steam-powered presses could print out hundreds of pages at a time. Another invention was the linotype machine, which stamped out individual letters and set them up much faster than a typesetter could. Today, many people read books using electronic devices.

Who Am I?

I was born in Hawaii in 1937, the middle child of three children. My father was a dentist in the U.S. Army, so our family moved around a lot. I had four children, whom I raised in Maine. My first book, *A Summer to Die*, was published in 1977. The fictional work was inspired by the loss of my sister. My books have explored many issues, from terminal illness to the Holocaust. Two of my books have won Newbery Medals—*Number the Stars* (1990) and *The Giver* (1994). *The Giver* is the first book in a trilogy, followed by *Gathering Blue* (2000) and *Messenger* (2004). A fourth book called *Son*—based on the death of my son—makes the trilogy a quartet in fall 2012.

Answer: Lois Lowry

DIGITAL READS

→ E-Books and E-Readers

The age of the electronic book is here! The number of people reading e-books is skyrocketing. More than 100 million e-books are now sold each year. Some well-known e-book readers include the Kindle, the Nook, and the Sony Reader.

E-readers allow users to download books, magazines, newspapers, and other material wirelessly from the Internet. They have a number of interactive features. You can control screen brightness, type size, and other aspects of how each page looks. On some devices, you turn a page using a page button. On others, you run your finger across the screen.

Some e-readers have a keyboard, which allows you to add comments to the page as you read. Others have a touch screen keyboard. Some allow website access and some let you download books as audio files.

→ Time for Tablets!

Tablets are a line of computers that allow you to read books and also access the Internet, play music, e-mail, watch videos, and download apps with the touch of your finger. Thin and light, a tablet is like a laptop computer, e-reader, and smartphone combined. One of the most popular is Apple's iPad. In March 2012, the third version of the iPad was released. This new iPad featured a sharper display among its improvements. Apple said that, after the new version was released, the company sold more than 3 million iPads in less than four days.

BUILDINGS

→What is the most photographed building in Poland? PAGE 52

TALLEST BUILDINGS IN THE WORLD

Here are the world's tallest buildings as of 2012, with the year each was completed. Heights listed don't include antennas or other outside structures.

Burj Khalifa (Khalifa Tower)
Dubai, United Arab Emirates (2010)
Height: 162 stories, 2,717 feet

Makkah Royal Clock Tower Hotel
Mecca, Saudi Arabia (2012)
Height: 120 stories, 1,971 feet

Taipei 101
Taipei, Taiwan (2004)
Height: 101 stories, 1,667 feet

World Financial Center
Shanghai, China (2008)
Height: 101 stories, 1,614 feet

International Commerce Center
Hong Kong, China (2010)
Height: 108 stories, 1,588 feet

Petronas Towers 1 & 2
Kuala Lumpur, Malaysia (1998)
Height: each building is 88 stories, 1,483 feet

A New Landmark

In 2012, work was almost complete on a major new skyscraper—One World Trade Center, being built in New York City near the site of the World Trade Center towers destroyed in the September 11, 2001, terrorist attacks. One World Trade Center will have 105 stories and, if completed as planned, will be the tallest building in the U.S. (In 2012, that honor was held by the Willis Tower in Chicago, at 1,450 feet.) One World Trade Center is designed to rise 1,776 feet into the air (a reference to the year the American colonies declared independence). The environmentally friendly building will house offices, restaurants, shops, an observation deck, and two broadcast studios.

WORLD'S TALLEST WHEN BUILT

Great Pyramid of Giza, Egypt
Built c. 2250 B.C. Height: 480 feet

Washington Monument, Washington, D.C. Built 1848–1884. Height: 555 feet

Eiffel Tower, Paris, France
Built 1887–89. Height: 984 feet

Chrysler Building, New York, NY
Built 1930. Height: 1,046 feet

Empire State Building, New York, NY
Built 1931. Height: 1,250 feet

DID YOU KNOW?

The 19th-century French engineer Alexandre-Gustave Eiffel is best known for designing the Eiffel Tower in Paris. But that is not the only world-famous landmark he helped create. Eiffel also designed the strong but flexible frame that is inside the Statue of Liberty. The metal frame supports the outside of the statue and also allows it to bend with the wind and expand and contract as the temperature changes.

A Short History of Tall Buildings

Throughout history, tall buildings have been symbols of power, wealth, and personal importance. Think about how impressed we are by the ancient Pyramids in Egypt, and then imagine how much more impressive they must have seemed to ancient people, who weren't used to seeing such enormous structures. But, in addition to trying to impress other people, the makers of tall buildings had to figure out how to support them and keep them from collapsing from their own weight. One answer was to have a huge, thick base that could support the weight above. The base of the Washington Monument, for example, has walls that are 15 feet thick!

By the 1880s, three **key factors in the evolution of tall buildings** were in place:

1. A NEED FOR SPACE Crowded cities had less space for building, and land got expensive. To create more space, buildings had to go up instead of out.

2. BETTER STEEL PRODUCTION Mass-producing steel meant more of it was available for construction. Long vertical **columns** and horizontal girders could be joined to form a strong cube-like grid that was lighter than a similar one made of stone or brick. Weight was also directed down the columns to a solid **foundation**, usually underground, instead of to walls.

3. THE ELEVATOR Tall buildings need elevators! The first elevator, powered by steam, was installed in a New York store in 1857. Electric elevators came along in 1880.

As buildings got taller, a new problem sprang up—**wind**. Too much movement could damage buildings or make the people inside uncomfortable. Some tall buildings, like New York's Citicorp Center, actually have a counter-weight near the top. A computer controls a 400-ton weight, moving it back and forth to lessen the building's sway.

In places such as California and Japan, **earthquakes** are a big problem, and special techniques are needed to make tall buildings safer from quakes.

IT'S ***NOT*** ALL ABOUT . . . TALL!

When it comes to buildings, the tall ones grab people's attention. But many other buildings are interesting and fun to look at. Here are a few really cool buildings.

THE CROOKED HOUSE, Sopot, Poland

The Crooked House was built in 2004 and is part of a shopping center. Its designers said they were influenced by children's fairytale illustrations by two Polish writers. The style of the building is similar to other buildings around it, but the Crooked House looks as if it has collapsed from exhaustion or perhaps melted in the sun. It is said to be the most-photographed building in the entire country.

COMMUNITY BOOKSHELF, Kansas City, Missouri

A "wall of books" decorates the exterior of the parking garage for the Kansas City Central Library. Completed in 2006, the garage was designed by a local architecture firm. Each "book" measures about 9 feet wide and 25 feet high. The titles were chosen by the city's residents and include books of local interest, as well as classics such as Mark Twain's *The Adventures of Huckleberry Finn.*

ELEPHANT BUILDING (CHANG BUILDING), Bangkok, Thailand

This unusual building, completed in 1997, is located in a business district of Bangkok. It has 32 stories and is 335 feet tall. Inside, there are apartments, shops, and office space. The elephant is Thailand's national animal, so the design honors an important part of the country's heritage. Far from being beautiful, the structure has actually won a competition for the world's ugliest building!

30 ST. MARY AXE, London, England

The unusual office tower in the financial center of London opened in 2004. It was carefully designed to be energy efficient and uses sunlight to heat the interior during the winter. The building's unique shape has earned it the nickname "the Gherkin" (a gherkin is a kind of pickle). It has appeared in a number of films, including *Harry Potter and the Half-Blood Prince.*

HISTORICAL WONDERS

DOME OF THE ROCK

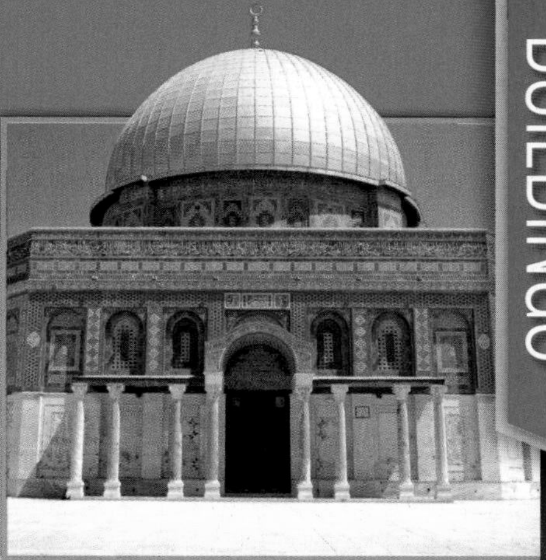

Jerusalem, Israel; built late 600s

The Dome of the Rock is the oldest Islamic monument still standing. A shrine, it was built over a rock sacred to both Muslims and Jews. Its 25-meter dome is covered with gold. Because the structure is considered the center of the Earth for the Arabs who built it, there are exits leading north, east, south, and west.

BOROBUDUR TEMPLE

Java, Indonesia; built 700s–800s

The stone temple at Borobudur was built as a shrine to Buddha and as a destination for Buddhist pilgrims. The base is in the form of a pyramid. Above it are five square terraces, topped by five circular platforms, all lavishly carved. As pilgrims climbed the different levels, they symbolically went through different levels of the Buddhist religion. Rediscovered and restored in the 19th century, the site is now Indonesia's biggest tourist attraction.

EL CASTILLO PYRAMID

Chichén-Itzá, Mexico; built 800–1200

El Castillo is the greatest pyramid at Chichén-Itzá, a center of Mayan civilization. Historians believe that the pyramid served as a calendar. It has 91 steps on each of its four sides. If you count the step onto the platform at the top, the total number of steps is 365, the number of days in a year. The base of the northern side of the pyramid is decorated with huge plumed serpents.

ALHAMBRA PALACE

Granada, Spain; built 1300s

The sprawling Alhambra palace was a royal residence. It was built by Muslim leaders from North Africa who ruled much of Spain at that time. Created on the site of a 9th-century fort, the palace complex also contains a bath and a mosque. Its architecture is in the Moorish style. All the rooms open onto interior courtyards surrounded by graceful arcades (covered walkways). The carvings that surround the arches and the lavish fountains and reflecting pools in the courtyards add to the beauty of the complex.

BRIDGES

There are four main bridge designs: beam, arch, truss, and suspension or cable-stayed.

BEAM

The beam bridge is the most basic kind. A log across a stream is a simple style of beam bridge. Highway bridges are often beam bridges. The span of a beam bridge, or the length of the bridge without any support under it, needs to be fairly short. Long beam bridges need many supporting poles, called piers.

ARCH

You can easily recognize an arch bridge, because it has arches holding it up from the bottom. The columns that support the arches are called abutments. Arch bridges were invented by the ancient Greeks.

TRUSS

The truss bridge uses mainly steel beams, connected in triangles to increase strength and span greater distances.

SUSPENSION

On suspension bridges, the roadway hangs from smaller cables attached to a pair of huge cables running over two massive towers. The ends of the giant cables are anchored firmly into solid rock or huge concrete blocks at each end of the bridge. The weight of the roadway is transferred through the cables to the anchors. On a cable-stayed bridge, the cables are attached directly from the towers (pylons) to the deck.

BUILDING QUIZ

Can you match each building in the left column with a description in the right column?

Alhambra	Tallest building in the world
The Crooked House	Biggest tourist attraction in Indonesia
Borobudur Temple	Palace in Spain
Burj Khalifa	Most photographed building in Poland

ANSWERS ON PAGES 334-336.

PARTS OF A SUSPENSION BRIDGE

Anchorage Main cables are attached here, adding strength and stability

Deck Surface of the bridge

Main cable Primary load-bearing cables, secured by anchorages

Pier Supports for pylons

Pylon Tower supports that hold up cables and decks

Suspender cable Vertical cables that hold up the deck

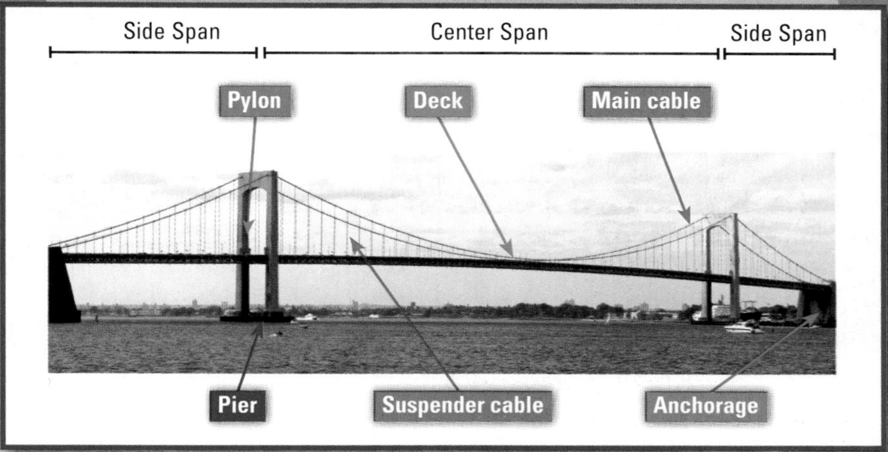

DAM FACTS

Dams are built to control the flow of rivers. They can provide water for drinking or farming, prevent flooding, and create electricity. The first dams were embankment dams built thousands of years ago out of walls of rocks and dirt to prevent flooding or to make lakes called reservoirs for irrigation. Today, most dams are made of concrete. "Hydroelectric" dams are used to generate electricity by channeling the force of rivers and waterfalls into tunnels in the dam to move enormous machines called turbines.

Bonneville Dam on the Columbia River

CALENDAR

→When is Veterans Day? PAGE 62

CALENDAR BASICS

Holidays and calendars go hand in hand. Using a calendar, you can see what day of the week it is and look for the next special day. Calendars divide time into days, weeks, months, and years. According to our calendar, also known as the Gregorian calendar, a year is the time it takes for one revolution of Earth around the Sun: 365¼ days. To make things easier, most years have just 365 days. Then, every four years we add an extra day, February 29, in "leap years," such as 2012.

→ THE NAMES OF THE MONTHS

→ **JANUARY** named for the Roman god Janus, guardian of gates (often shown with two faces, looking backward and forward)

→ **FEBRUARY** named for Februalia, a Roman time of sacrifice

→ **MARCH** named for Mars, the Roman god of war (the end of winter meant fighting could begin again)

→ **APRIL** "aperire," Latin for "to open," as in flower buds

→ **MAY** named for Maia, the goddess of plant growth

→ **JUNE** "Junius," the Latin word for the goddess Juno

→ **JULY** named after the Roman ruler Julius Caesar

→ **AUGUST** named for Augustus, the first Roman emperor

→ **SEPTEMBER** "septem," Latin for seven (the Roman year began in March)

→ **OCTOBER** "octo," the Latin word for eight

→ **NOVEMBER** "novem," the Latin word for nine

→ **DECEMBER** "decem," the Latin word for ten

→ OTHER CALENDARS

The Gregorian calender is used by the United States and much of the rest of the world. But some nations and religions use other calendars.

→ **ISLAMIC CALENDAR** The Islamic calendar is used by Muslim people around the world. Twelve lunar months, each beginning with the new Moon, make up the year. The year is 354 days long (355 days in leap years). Al-Hijra/ Muharram (Islamic New Year) in Islamic year 1435 starts at Moon crescent on November 3, 2013.

→ **JEWISH CALENDAR** The Jewish calendar has months of 29 and 30 days, and its years are either 12 or 13 months long. It is a lunar-solar calendar, which means its months are lunar, but its years adjust to the movement of Earth around the Sun. It is the official calendar in Israel and is used as a religious calendar by Jewish people worldwide. Rosh Hashanah (New Year) in the year 5774 begins at sundown on September 4, 2013, on the Gregorian calendar.

→ **CHINESE CALENDAR** The Chinese calendar is a lunar-solar calendar that runs on a 60-year cycle. Within the cycle, years are given one of twelve animal designations: Rat, Ox, Tiger, Rabbit, Dragon, Snake, Horse, Sheep, Monkey, Rooster, Dog, and Pig. On February 10, 2013, the Year of the Snake starts.

HOLIDAY HIGHLIGHTS

Each month brings new chances to celebrate famous people, historic events, and special occasions. On federal holidays, U.S. government offices are closed as are many schools and businesses. There are also other holidays that might not mean a day off from school, but they are still enthusiastically celebrated. Holidays marked with an asterisk (*) are federal holidays.

JANUARY 2013

January is National Oatmeal Month and National Skating Month. Learn how to ice skate—for free—at events at participating ice rinks nationwide. Grab a bowl of oatmeal beforehand for a nutritious way to stay warm from the inside out.

* January 1: New Year's Day

Until the year 1753, New Year's Day was celebrated on March 25 every year. When the Gregorian calendar was adopted in 1582, the date was switched to January 1.

* JANUARY 21: MARTIN LUTHER KING JR. DAY

Martin Luther King Jr. Day takes place on the third Monday in January. The holiday honors the famous civil rights leader who was born on January 15, 1929.

FEBRUARY 2013

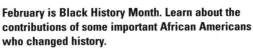

February is Black History Month. Learn about the contributions of some important African Americans who changed history.

February 2: Groundhog Day

On February 2, thousands of people gather in the small town of Punxsutawney, Pennsylvania, to see if Punxsutawney Phil will see his shadow. According to legend, if the famous groundhog sees his shadow, winter will last six more weeks. If he doesn't, spring will come early.

FEBRUARY 10: CHINESE NEW YEAR

The year 4711 begins on February 10 according to China's traditional lunar-solar calendar. The celebration lasts for 15 days, ending with the Lantern Festival.

February 14: Valentine's Day

Valentine's Day is mostly a way to celebrate those you care about. People have been exchanging Valentine cards with loved ones since the 1500s.

* February 18: Presidents' Day

Observed on the third Monday in February, Presidents' Day honors George Washington and Abraham Lincoln. Both presidents were born in February. George Washington was born on February 22, 1732, and Abraham Lincoln was born on February 12, 1809.

MARCH 2013

March is Women's History Month. From science to sports, discover some of history's leading ladies. March is also National Nutrition Month. It is a good time to learn how to eat well and stay fit all year long.

MARCH 17: ST. PATRICK'S DAY

This day honors the patron saint of Ireland. Festivities include wearing green, attending parades, and eating corned beef and cabbage, a traditional Irish food.

March 20: First Day of Spring

Today marks the first day of spring in the Northern Hemisphere. Also known as the Vernal Equinox, the first day of spring is observed when the center of the Sun appears directly above Earth's equator.

At sundown, March 25: Passover

This Jewish holiday celebrates the freeing of Israelites from slavery in ancient Egypt. The eight-day celebration (seven in Israel) includes a seder meal and other religious rituals.

March 31: Easter

This Christian holiday celebrates the resurrection of Jesus Christ. Traditions include coloring eggs and filling Easter baskets with candy and gifts.

APRIL 2013

April is National Poetry Month. Visit the library for books of poetry (try *Where the Sidewalk Ends*, by Shel Silverstein). Then try writing some of your own.

April 1: April Fools' Day

People have been celebrating April Fools' Day with pranks and gags for more than 400 years.

APRIL 22: EARTH DAY

First celebrated in the United States in 1970, Earth Day is an occasion for people to take action and care for our environment. Today, more than one billion people around the globe commemorate Earth Day.

MAY 2013

May is National Bike Month. Riding your bike is a great way to stay fit and have fun. Be sure to wear a helmet every time you ride, even if you're going just a short distance.

May 5: Cinco de Mayo

This holiday commemorates Mexico's defeat of the French army in the Battle of the Puebla on this day in 1862.

May 12: Mother's Day

Since 1914, Mother's Day has been celebrated on the second Sunday of May. Each year, more than 155 million cards are bought and given to moms across the United States. And that doesn't even include the special homemade cards that moms receive!

* MAY 27: MEMORIAL DAY

Originally celebrated in honor of members of the military who died during the Civil War, Memorial Day now honors all men and women who have died while serving in the U.S. military. It falls on the last Monday in May.

JUNE 2013

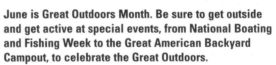

June is Great Outdoors Month. Be sure to get outside and get active at special events, from National Boating and Fishing Week to the Great American Backyard Campout, to celebrate the Great Outdoors.

June 14: Flag Day

Celebrated on June 14, this day remembers the adoption of the first version of the Stars and Stripes by the Continental Congress in 1777. Flag Day is not an official federal holiday, but many communities hold celebrations to honor the American flag.

JUNE 16: FATHER'S DAY

This day that celebrates fathers falls on the third Sunday in June.

June 19: Juneteenth

Juneteenth, also known as Emancipation Day, celebrates a military order on June 19, 1865, that formally completed the freeing of the slaves.

June 21: First Day of Summer

The first day of summer in the Northern Hemisphere is observed on the Summer Solstice, when the Sun rises and sets the farthest north on the horizon and daylight hours are longest.

JULY 2013

July is Cell Phone Courtesy Month. This month reminds the more than 233 million cell phone users in the United States to be more aware of how cell phone use in public places affects other people.

July 1: Canada Day

Canada Day (called Dominion Day until 1982) celebrates the creation of the Dominion of Canada on July 1, 1867. Like the Fourth of July in the United States, Canada Day is celebrated with parades and fireworks.

* JULY 4: INDEPENDENCE DAY

Commonly known as the Fourth of July, this federal holiday marks the anniversary of the adoption of the Declaration of Independence on July 4, 1776. Americans celebrate with picnics, parades, barbecues, and fireworks.

July 14: Bastille Day

This holiday commemorates the beginning of the French Revolution by the storming of the Bastille, an event that eventually led to the formation of modern France.

AUGUST 2013

August is American Adventures Month. Celebrate vacations in North, South, and Central America by going on one of your own or remembering a fun vacation you've taken in the past.

AT MOON CRESCENT, AUGUST 7: EID AL-FITR

This Muslim holiday marks the end of Ramadan, the Islamic month of fasting. During Ramadan, observers refrain from eating from dawn to sunset. A special meal is part of Eid al-Fitr festivities to celebrate the end of fasting.

SEPTEMBER 2013

September is Library Card Sign-Up Month and Hispanic Heritage Month (September 15–October 15). Take advantage of the library to learn about the 500-year-old roots of Hispanic culture in the Americas.

* September 2: Labor Day

A federal holiday that takes place on the first Monday in September, Labor Day celebrates workers with a day off in their honor. Labor Day has its roots in the late 19th-century labor movement, when workers began to organize to demand shorter hours and fairer pay. It was made a federal holiday in 1894.

At sundown, September 4-6: Rosh Hashanah

Rosh Hashanah is a two-day holiday that celebrates the beginning of the Jewish new year. The day is marked with prayer and symbolic foods, such as apples dipped in honey.

At sundown, September 13-14: Yom Kippur

Also known as the Day of Atonement, Yom Kippur is the holiest and most solemn day of the year for Jewish people. The holiday is observed with fasting and prayer to atone, or make up, for one's sins.

September 17: Constitution or Citizenship Day

Constitution Day is celebrated on September 17, the date the U.S. Constitution was signed in 1787.

SEPTEMBER 22: FIRST DAY OF AUTUMN

Today is the first day of autumn, or fall, in the Northern Hemisphere. Also known as the Autumnal Equinox, the first day of fall occurs when the center of the Sun appears directly above Earth's equator.

OCTOBER 2013

Smile! October is National Dental Hygiene Month—a time to brush up on keeping your teeth healthy.

* October 14: Columbus Day

Celebrated on the second Monday in October, Columbus Day marks Christopher Columbus's landing on an island in the Bahamas, then thought of as the New World, in 1492.

At Moon crescent, October 14-15: Eid al-Adha

This Muslim holiday celebrates Abraham's willingness to sacrifice his son Ishmael to Allah prove his faith. The celebration includes a special meal, prayer, and other rituals.

OCTOBER 31: HALLOWEEN

Halloween always falls on the last day of October. Popular ways to celebrate include trick-or-treating and going to costume parties.

NOVEMBER 2013

November is National American Indian Heritage Month. Learn about Native Americans and their roles in American history.

November 3: Diwali

This Hindu holiday is also known as the Festival of Lights. People decorate their homes with lights, candles, and oil lamps to celebrate.

November 5: Election Day

The first Tuesday after the first Monday in November, Election Day is a mandatory holiday in some states.

* November 11: Veterans Day

On this special day, Americans honor U.S. veterans—men and women who have served in the armed forces.

* NOVEMBER 28: THANKSGIVING

Every year on the fourth Thursday in November, Americans take the day to honor the people, events, and things in their lives for which they are thankful.

At sundown, November 27-December 5: Hanukkah

Also known as the Festival of Lights, this Jewish holiday lasts eight days and commemorates the rededication of the Holy Temple in Jerusalem. Each night, families light a candle in a special holder called a menorah.

DECEMBER 2013

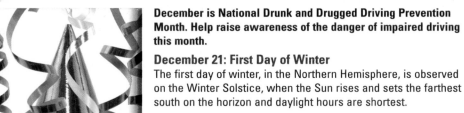

December is National Drunk and Drugged Driving Prevention Month. Help raise awareness of the danger of impaired driving this month.

December 21: First Day of Winter

The first day of winter, in the Northern Hemisphere, is observed on the Winter Solstice, when the Sun rises and sets the farthest south on the horizon and daylight hours are shortest.

* December 25: Christmas

This Christian holiday celebrates the birth of Jesus Christ. People celebrate by decorating trees, exchanging presents, and gathering with family and friends.

December 26-January 1, 2014: Kwanzaa

This week-long holiday honors African culture. People light candles in holders called kinaras and exchange gifts to celebrate.

DECEMBER 31: NEW YEAR'S EVE

This day isn't technically a holiday, but you'll find a lot of people celebrating the end of one year and the start of the next.

MORE WAYS TO CELEBRATE

Mark your calendar! Here are some other special days you don't want to miss.

January 17: Kid Inventors' Day — Celebrate young minds on the birthday of Ben Franklin, who invented the first swim fins at age 12.

February 3: Super Bowl XLVII — The year's biggest game is the grand finale of the NFL season. The Super Bowl returns to New Orleans for the first time since before Hurricane Katrina in 2005.

March 3: National Anthem Day — *O say, can you see...* "The Star-Spangled Banner," written by Francis Scott Key during the War of 1812, officially became the U.S. national anthem on March 3, 1931.

April 26: National Arbor Day — Give a tree a hug today. Arbor Day, observed each year on the last Friday in April, encourages people to plant and care for trees.

May 4: Kentucky Derby — Known as "The Most Exciting Two Minutes in Sports," the Kentucky Derby is held each year on the first Saturday in May at Churchill Downs in Louisville, Kentucky.

June 8: World Oceans Day — Catch the wave! Help protect the world's oceans, which cover about 70 percent of Earth's surface.

July 21: National Ice Cream Day — Let's all scream for ice cream! Also known as "Sundae Sunday," National Ice Cream Day celebrates America's popular dessert on the third Sunday in July.

August 26: Women's Equality Day — On this day in 1920, the 19th Amendment to the U.S. Constitution was ratified, giving women the right to vote.

September 8: National Grandparents Day — This special day honors grandparents and their wisdom.

October 16: Dictionary Day — Learn a new word in honor of the birthday of Noah Webster, the father of the American dictionary.

November 7: International Tongue Twister Day — "Peter Piper picked a peck of pickled peppers." Can you say that three times fast? Celebrate this day by practicing some of your favorite tongue twisters.

December 4: National Cookie Day — Bake up a batch of your favorite cookies to celebrate this sweet day!

DID YOU KNOW? Daylight Saving Time is when we turn our clocks ahead by an hour in the spring. That gives us more light at the end of the day during warmer weather. We turn the clocks back in the fall. In 2013, Daylight Saving Time begins on March 10 and ends on November 3.

→What hidden secret does luminol reveal? PAGE 64

FORENSICS:

Using Science to Solve Crimes

The use of scientific evidence to solve crimes is known as **forensics**. Many different methods can be used to help find out the facts in a case and identify suspects.

FINGERPRINTS: In 1880, a court in Japan made the first-ever use of fingerprints to charge a person with a crime. Later advances in technology have made it easier to use fingerprint evidence in solving crimes. Certain chemicals can show up a hidden fingerprint, and modern computer networks allow investigators to quickly compare the fingerprints from a crime scene to the prints of many known individuals on file.

GUNS: A bullet that has gone through a gun barrel may pick up markings that can help identify the gun that was used to fire it.

DNA: DNA, or genetic, evidence can be very helpful in identifying individuals. Except in identical twins, every person's DNA is unique. Investigators often gather it from sources such as blood, saliva, and skin.

CHEMISTRY: Chemistry is a valuable tool for solving crimes. For example, an investigator may apply a chemical such as luminol at a crime scene to make hidden bloodstains visible. Well-equipped crime labs use the latest techniques to learn the makeup of unknown substances found at a crime scene.

DID YOU KNOW?

Before many modern forensic techniques were developed, the world's most famous fictional detective was solving crimes by observing things carefully and analyzing evidence such as fingerprints, footprints, tobacco ash, and bloodstains. Sherlock Holmes was created by a Scottish eye doctor named Sir Arthur Conan Doyle. Holmes appears in 60 short stories and novels by Doyle published between 1887 and 1927. Since then, many movies and TV shows have featured the Sherlock Holmes character.

On the JOB Deputy Sheriff

Many jobs in law enforcement involve tracking down and arresting people who may be guilty of a crime or keeping those people in custody while their cases go through the courts. **Morgan McCann** is a deputy sheriff in Hennepin County, Minnesota, one of the largest counties in the United States, and he works at the county jail. He agreed to talk to *The World Almanac for Kids* about his work.

What do you do in a typical day?

When a police department from any city or town in our county charges someone with a crime, that person is brought to our jail to stay until he or she goes court or is released for some other reason. Most days, I work either in the housing area, where the inmates stay, or in the intake area, where people are processed as they come into the jail.

What interests and strengths of yours make this job right for you?

I am a very creative person, and I enjoy my work because it's different every day. There is a lot of variety interacting with the different law enforcement agencies and the courts. I like to use my problem-solving skills to deal with whatever comes along. We focus on helping the inmates access the necessary resources and understand the legal process, so that they can get out of jail when the law allows. Last year, we booked 34,503 people! Each one has his or her own story, and the problems to go with it.

What kind of education or training did you need to get in order to do your job?

In Minnesota, as in many other states, a college degree is required to work as a licensed peace officer. Once you have a college degree, you can apply to be accepted into an additional year of training that prepares you with the specific skills used in law enforcement.

What do you like best about your job? What is most challenging?

I enjoy the feeling that I'm doing the most I can to make sure the rules are followed so everyone can have the best possible outcome. A lot of what I do is focused on safety. Some people are put in the jail because they are dangerous to other people in the community. Keeping the dangerous people in jail keeps the community safe. I also have to make sure the people in our jail remain safe. Sometimes, I have to work at night or on holidays, and I miss events with my family. But my family is very supportive, and we make up those times. I get the satisfaction that what I'm doing makes a difference to others.

DISASTERS

→What caused the tsunami off Indonesia in 1883 that killed 36,000 people? PAGE 67

EARTHQUAKES

There are thousands of earthquakes each year. Most are small, but about 1 in 500 causes damage. Some quakes are incredibly powerful and destructive, such as the huge quake in Japan in March 2011 and the somewhat smaller quake that hit the Philippines in February 2012. ▶

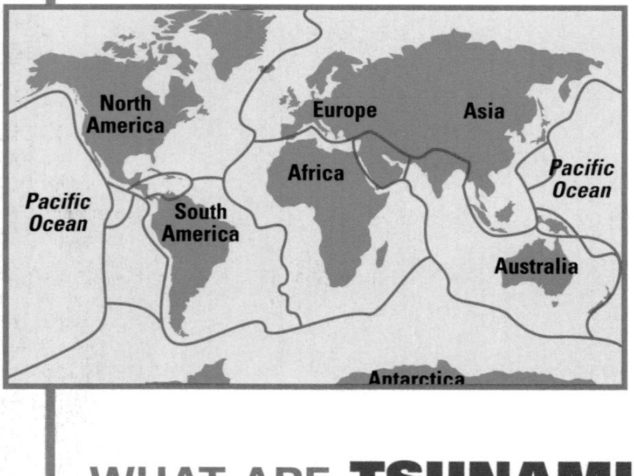

WHAT CAUSES **EARTHQUAKES?**

To understand earthquakes, imagine Earth as an egg with a cracked shell. The cracked outer layer (the eggshell) is called the lithosphere, and it is divided into huge pieces called plates (see map). The plates are constantly moving away from, toward, or past one another. Earthquakes result when plates collide or scrape against each other. The cracks in the lithosphere are called faults. Many quakes occur along these fault lines.

WHAT ARE **TSUNAMIS?**

Tsunami (pronounced ***tsoo-NAH-mee***) comes from two Japanese words: "tsu" (harbor) and "nami" (wave). Tsunamis are huge waves. They are sometimes called tidal waves, but they have nothing to do with the tides.

The strongest tsunamis happen when a big part of the sea floor lifts along a fault (see map above), pushing up a huge volume of water. Many times this happens after an undersea earthquake. The waves move at speeds of up to 500 miles per hour. As they near shore, they slow down, and the great energy forces the water upward into big waves.

MAJOR EARTHQUAKES

These earthquakes are among the largest and most destructive since 1960.

Year	Location	Magnitude	Deaths (estimated)
1960	near Chile	9.5	5,000
1970	Northern Peru	7.8	66,000
1976	Tangshan, China	8.0	255,000
1988	Soviet Armenia	7.0	55,000
1989	United States (San Francisco area)	7.1	62
1990	Western Iran	7.7	40,000
1999	Western Turkey	7.4	17,200
2001	Western India	7.9	30,000
2004	Sumatra, Indonesia	9.0	225,000
2005	Pakistan and India	7.6	80,000
2008	Sichuan, China	7.9	87,857
2010	Haiti	7.0	222,570
2011	Northeastern Japan	9.0	15,800+
2012	Central Philippines	6.9	100+

MAJOR TSUNAMIS

These are some of the most destructive tsunamis in recent centuries.

Year	Location	What Happened?	Deaths (estimated)
1755	Lisbon, Portugal	Three earthquakes struck Portugal's capital within 10 minutes, creating a tsunami with waves up to 100 feet high.	100,000–200,000
1782	South China Sea near Taiwan	After a major underwater earthquake, a tsunami sent waves inland more than 60 miles.	40,000
1883	Indonesia	The Krakatau, or Krakatoa, volcano erupted four times, causing a massive tsunami more than 100 feet tall. On the island nearest the volcano, there were no survivors.	36,000
1908	Southern Italy	A major earthquake triggered a devastating tsunami.	123,000
2004	Indian Ocean	After a 9.0-magnitude earthquake hit Indonesia, a tsunami with waves up to 100 feet high struck 14 countries.	225,000
2011	Northeastern Japan	A 9.0-magnitude earthquake touched off a huge tsunami.	15,800+

VOLCANOES

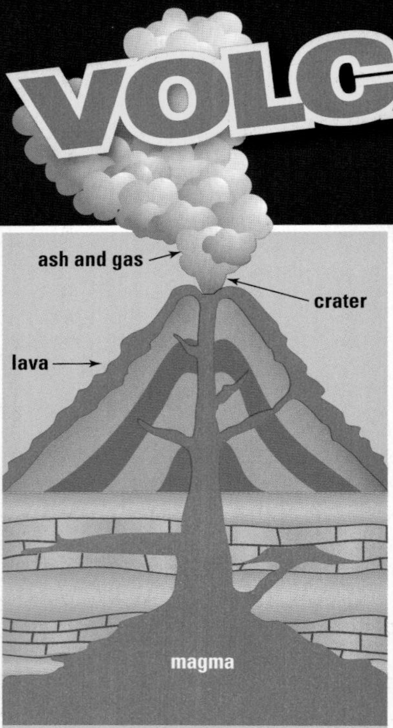

A volcano is a mountain or hill (cone) with an opening on top known as a crater. Hot melted rock (magma), gases, and other material from inside Earth mix together and rise up through cracks and weak spots. When enough pressure builds up, the magma can escape, erupting through the crater. Magma that comes out of the crater is called lava. Lava may be hotter than 2,000°F. The cone of a volcano is often made of layers of lava and ash that have erupted, then cooled.

Some Famous **Volcanic Eruptions**

Year	Volcano (place)	Deaths (estimated)
79	Mount Vesuvius (Italy)	16,000
1586	Kelut (Indonesia)	10,000
1792	Mount Unzen (Japan)	14,500
1815	Tambora (Indonesia)	10,000
1883	Krakatau, or Krakatoa (Indonesia)	36,000
1902	Mount Pelée (Martinique)	28,000
1980	Mount St. Helens (U.S.)	57
1982	El Chichón (Mexico)	1,880
1985	Nevado del Ruiz (Colombia)	23,000
1986	Lake Nyos (Cameroon)	1,700
1991	Mount Pinatubo (Philippines)	800

Where is the **RING of FIRE?**

The hundreds of active volcanoes near the edges of the Pacific Ocean make up what is called the **Ring of Fire.** They mark the boundary between the plates under the Pacific Ocean and the plates under the surrounding continents. (Earth's plates are explained on page 66, with the help of a map.) The Ring of Fire runs from Alaska, along the west coast of North and South America, to the southern tip of Chile. The ring also runs down the east coast of Asia. Starting in the far north, it passes through Japan, the Philippines, and New Guinea. It continues down past Australia. Some of the most destructive volcanic eruptions ever recorded have occurred along the Ring of Fire.

HOW WAS **Hawaii** FORMED?

Hawaii is a 1,500-mile-long chain of islands in the middle of the Pacific Ocean. These islands are the tops of volcanoes, and they were formed by a **hot spot**. This is an area deep inside Earth that spews lava up through the ocean floor. Over time, as more and more lava emerges, cools, and hardens, the volcanic cone rises above the surface. Over thousands of years, the islands drift to the northwest as Earth's plates move (see page 66), and new islands are formed over the hot spot. This process is still going on today.

HURRICANES

Categories 1 74-95 mph **2** 96-110 mph **3** 111-130 mph **4** 131-155 mph **5** over 155 mph

Hurricanes—called typhoons or cyclones in the Pacific—are Earth's biggest storms. When conditions are right, they form over the ocean from collections of storms and clouds known as tropical disturbances. Strong winds create a wall of clouds and rain that swirl in a circle around a calm center called the eye.

The eye develops as **warm, moist air** is forced upward in the storm by **denser, cooler air**. From the outer edge of the storm to the inner eye, the pressure drops and wind speeds rise sharply, creating swirling **convection currents** around the eye. If wind speeds reach 39 mph, the storm is named. If wind speeds top 74 mph, the storm is called a **hurricane**. Hurricanes are classified into five categories (see above) depending on their wind speeds.

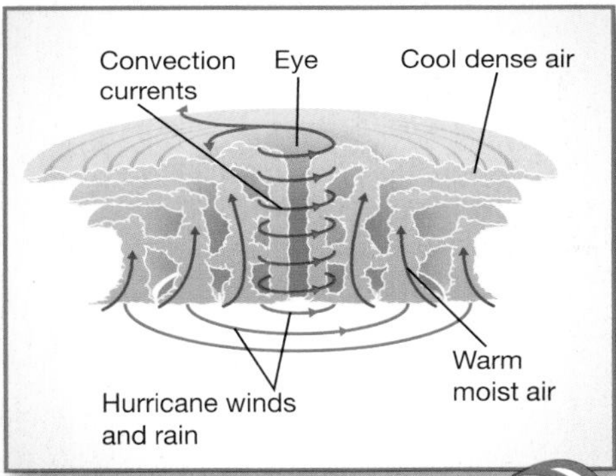

Hurricanes can be up to 300 miles wide. On land, the storm can snap trees and tear buildings apart. Strong winds blowing toward shore can create a rise in the ocean water called a **storm surge**. It can combine with heavy rains to cause flooding and massive damage.

For the Atlantic Ocean, Caribbean Sea, and Gulf of Mexico, hurricane season runs from June 1 to November 30.

NOTABLE U.S. HURRICANES

Date	Location	What Happened?	Deaths (estimated)
Sept. 8, 1900	Galveston, TX	Category 4 storm flooded the island with 15-foot waves.	8,000+
Sept. 16-17, 1928	Central/ southern FL	Category 5 storm, the fourth-largest to hit the U.S. mainland, caused 9-foot waves.	1,836
Sept. 19, 1938	NY, CT, RI, MA	"The Long Island Express," with storm surges rising 10-25 feet, caused $306 million in damages.	600+
Aug. 25-29, 2005	LA, MS, AL, GA, FL	Hurricane Katrina, with 175 mph winds and a 25-foot high storm surge, caused about $125 billion in damage.	1,833

Hurricane Names

The U.S. began using women's names for hurricanes in 1953 and added men's names in 1979. When all letters (except Q, U, X, Y, and Z) are used in one season, any additional storms are named with Greek letters.

2013 Atlantic Hurricane Names:

Angel, Barry, Chantal, Dorian, Erin, Fernand, Gabrielle, Humberto, Ingrid, Jerry, Karen, Lorenzo, Melissa, Nestor, Olga, Pablo, Rebekah, Sebastien, Tanya, Van, Wendy

Long Island Express hurricane of 1928

TORNADOES

Categories

WEAK

EF0: 65-85 mph

EF1: 86-110 mph

STRONG

EF2: 111-135 mph

EF3: 136-165 mph

VIOLENT

EF4: 166-200 mph

EF5: over 200 mph

Tornadoes, or twisters, are rapidly spinning columns of air. They usually form when winds change direction, speed up, and spin around in or near a thunderstorm.

Tornadoes can happen any time that the weather is right, but they are more common between March and July. They can happen in any state, but strong tornadoes often touch down in the U.S. Midwest and Southeast. A group of states including Texas, Oklahoma, Kansas, Nebraska, Iowa, and South Dakota is sometimes called Tornado Alley because of the large number of twisters that occur in the region.

According to the National Oceanic and Atmospheric Administration (NOAA), about 1,000 tornadoes occur in the U.S. each year.

Tornadoes are measured by how much damage they cause. In February 2007, the U.S. began using the Enhanced Fujita (EF) Scale (top left) to measure tornadoes. The EF-Scale provides an estimate of a tornado's wind speed based on the amount of damage. If a tornado doesn't hit anything, it may be hard to classify it.

Wind speeds are difficult to measure directly, because measuring instruments can be destroyed in more violent winds. The highest speed ever recorded—302 mph—was taken in May 1999 in an Oklahoma tornado.

U.S. Tornado Records

(since record keeping began in 1950)

YEAR: The 1,817 tornadoes reported in **2004** topped the previous record of 1,424 in 1998.

MONTH: In **April 2011**, there were a total of 758 tornadoes, easily passing the old record of 542 set in May 2003.

SINGLE EVENT: On **April 25-28, 2011**, an estimated 305 tornadoes touched down in Alabama and a number of other states, mostly in the Southeast, causing more than 300 deaths.

DID YOU KNOW? A string of tornadoes hit the U.S. Midwest on February 29, 2012. The storms flattened hotels in the tourist town of Branson, Missouri, and killed six residents of Harrisburg, Illinois. A total of at least 12 fatalities was recorded across the region.

The Lusitania

OTHER MAJOR DISASTERS

SHIP DISASTERS

Date	Location	What Happened?	Deaths
April 14, 1912	near Newfoundland	Luxury liner *Titanic* collided with iceberg.	1,503
May 7, 1915	Atlantic Ocean, near Ireland	British steamer *Lusitania* torpedoed and sunk by German submarine.	1,198
Jan. 30, 1945	Baltic Sea	Liner *Wilhelm Gustloff* carrying German refugees and soldiers sunk by Soviet sub. Highest death toll for a single ship.	9,000
Jan. 13, 2012	Off coast of Italy	Cruise ship *Costa Concordia* capsized after hitting rocks close to shore.	30+

AIRCRAFT DISASTERS

Date	Location	What Happened?	Deaths
May 6, 1937	Lakehurst, NJ	German zeppelin (blimp) *Hindenburg* caught fire as it prepared to land.	36
March 27, 1977	Tenerife, Canary Islands	Two Boeing 747s collide on the runway of Los Rodeos airport.	582
Sept. 11, 2001	New York, NY; Arlington, VA; Shanksville, PA	Two hijacked planes crashed into the World Trade Center, one plane hit the Pentagon, and a fourth went down in a PA field.	Nearly 3,000

EXPLOSIONS AND FIRES

Date	Location	What Happened?	Deaths
March 25, 1911	New York, NY	Triangle Shirtwaist Factory caught fire, trapping garment workers, mostly women.	146
Nov. 28, 1942	Boston, MA	Fire swept through the Coconut Grove nightclub; patrons panicked. Deadliest nightclub fire in U.S. history.	146
Dec. 3, 1984	Bhopal, India	A pesticide factory explosion spread toxic gas. Worst industrial accident in history.	15,000

FLOODS

Date	Location	What Happened?	Deaths
1927	Mississippi River	From Illinois to Louisiana, the Mississippi River overflowed its banks, flooding 16 million acres of land and leaving 600,000 people homeless. Most destructive river flood in U.S. history.	500
Aug. 1931	China	Vast flooding on the Huang He River. Highest known death toll from a flood.	3,700,000

ENERGY

→What is Fracking? PAGE 74

Energy can take many forms. Electricity is a form of energy. The Sun's warmth is energy in the form of heat. The energy we use every day—to heat and light buildings, travel around, run machinery, and power our electronic devices—comes from many sources. Some of these are **renewable** and will not get used up over time. Others are **nonrenewable** and will run out.

Which Countries Produce and Use the MOST ENERGY?

The United States produces about 15% of the world's energy—more than any other country except China—but it also uses 20% of the world's supply. The table on the left lists the world's top ten energy producers and the percentage of the world's production that each nation was responsible for in 2008. One of these countries—Saudi Arabia—is the world's largest oil producer. The table on the right lists the world's top energy users and the percentage of the world's energy that each nation consumed that same year.

TOP ENERGY PRODUCERS

Country	Percent
China	16%
United States	15%
Russia	11%
Saudi Arabia	5%
Canada	4%
India	3%
Iran	3%
Indonesia	3%
Australia	3%
Norway	2%

TOP ENERGY USERS

Country	Percent
United States	20%
China	17%
Russia	6%
Japan	5%
India	4%
Germany	3%
Canada	3%
France	2%
Brazil	2%
South Korea	2%

WHERE DOES U.S. ENERGY COME FROM?*

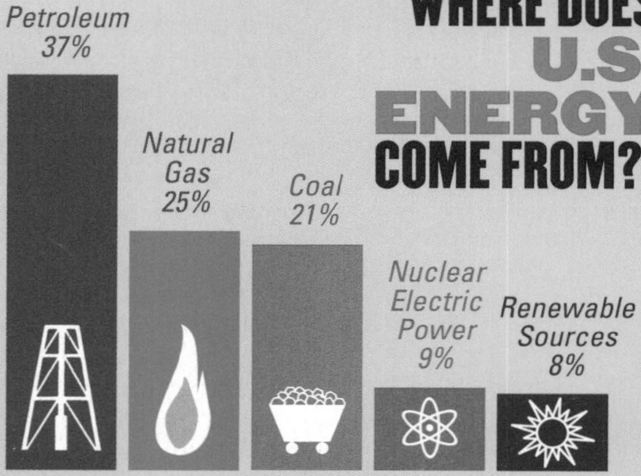

*2010

Sources of ENERGY

NONRENEWABLE sources are limited.

The fossil fuels—mainly **coal, oil,** and **natural gas**—are the most common sources of energy in the U.S. They are the decayed remains of ancient animals and plants. These fossil fuels took millions of years to form. If we run out, it will take millions of years for new supplies to be made. **Uranium**, the element that is split to power U.S. nuclear reactors, is fairly abundant. However, U-235, the type of uranium used for fuel in nuclear power plants, is relatively rare.

RENEWABLE sources of energy will never run out.

The force of moving water, such as a river or waterfall, can create **hydropower**. It is one of the oldest sources of energy. **Ocean energy** uses the motion of the tides or the power of breaking waves to produce energy. The Sun's light can be converted into **solar power**. Steady winds can be used to spin giant propellers, generating **wind power**. **Biomass** is renewable material made from plants or animals. This material, including wood or garbage, can be burned to make energy. Heat from within Earth, called **geothermal energy**, can be collected at natural hot springs where hot magma boils surface water.

How Do We POWER Homes?

The most common uses of energy in the home are to control heating and cooling and to provide electricity for lighting and appliances.

Most electricity is generated at power stations by wheel-shaped engines called **turbines**. Water, wind, or steam can be used to push turbines. Water is heated into steam by burning biomass or fossil fuels, by splitting uranium atoms during nuclear fission, or by using the heat of sunlight. More than two-fifths of America's electricity is generated from burning coal. Some homes have solar "collectors" that capture the Sun's energy for use in heating water or solar panels that convert sunlight directly into electricity. Many people in the U.S. use natural gas, delivered to their home through pipes, for heat and hot water.

RENEWABLE Energy in Action

Wind farms are made up of large numbers of towers called wind turbines. Their blades spin in the wind, and a turbine in each one changes the energy of motion into electricity. Most wind farms are on land, but some, such as Great Britain's Walney wind farm, are offshore. Walney is the world's largest offshore wind farm.

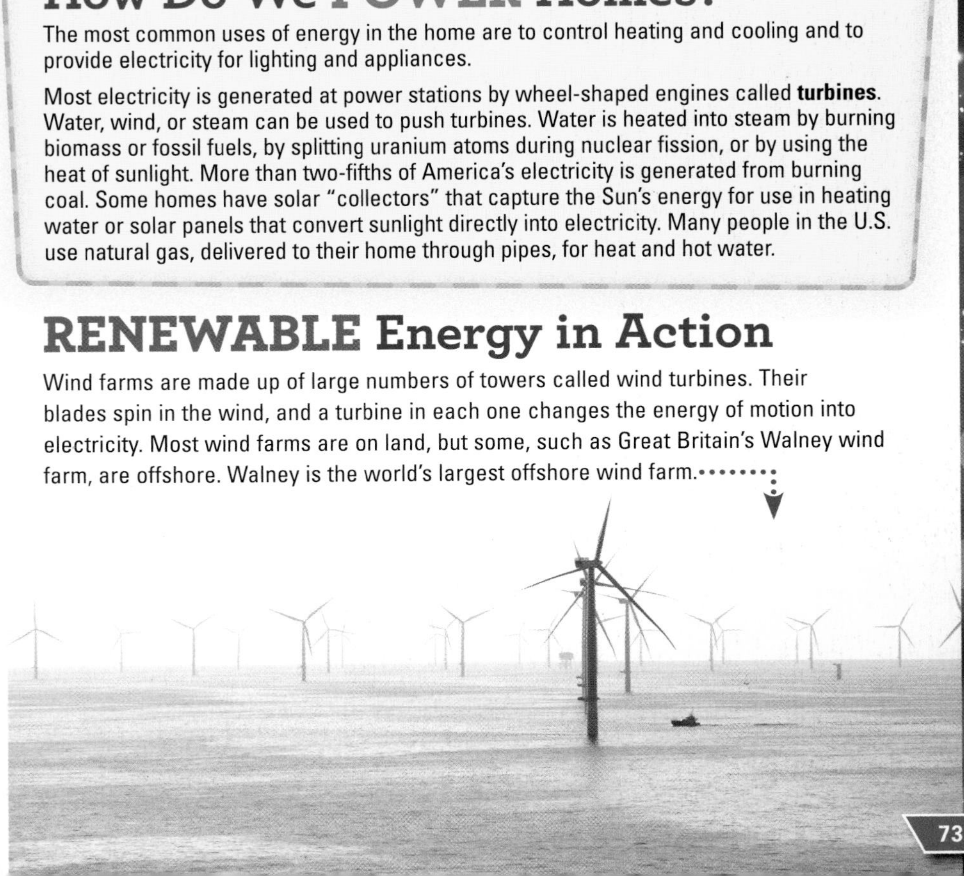

ENERGY TOPICS

What Is "FRACKING"?

"Fracking," short for "hydraulic fracturing," is a technique for drilling as much as 4 miles deep into rock formations to get oil or natural gas. Once a very deep hole is drilled, water or chemicals under great pressure are used to create openings called "fractures" in the rock. Oil or gas trapped in the rock seeps into and fills the fractures. This oil or gas can then be extracted.

Fracking has been around since the 1940s, but it has grown in popularity as energy companies look for new sources of supplies. The technique is controversial. People who support it say that it can help the U.S. import less oil from foreign countries. People who oppose it say that the chemicals used in the process can get into water supplies and harm wildlife and people who drink the water. Some scientists also claim that the natural gas produced through fracking gives off more pollutants than natural gas from other sources.

How Does a NUCLEAR POWER PLANT Work?

There are different types of nuclear power plants, but they all rely on one basic fact: when the nucleus of an atom of uranium is split, a tremendous amount of energy is produced.

Atoms are made up of three different kinds of particles: protons, neutrons, and electrons. Protons and neutrons are found in the atom's nucleus, or core. Electrons orbit around the nucleus. When the nucleus is split, in a process called **nuclear fission**, two new nuclei are created. In addition, energy is released.

The energy produced by fission is used to boil water, so that it turns into steam. This steam turns the blades of a machine called a turbine, producing electricity.

The uranium used as fuel is in long rods. Neutrons hit these **fuel rods** to split the uranium atoms. By having the right number of neutrons hit the right amount of fuel at the right speed, scientists can create a **chain reaction** in which atoms keep splitting at a controlled rate, producing a steady supply of energy. Cool water and devices called **control rods** keep the fuel rods from getting too hot and keep the chain reaction from getting out of control. The chain reaction takes place inside thick concrete **containment structures**, so that radioactivity doesn't leak out of the plant.

PRODUCING ELECTRICITY:

Pros & Cons

Nuclear Fission

Pros: No greenhouse gases; produces a large amount of energy from a small amount of fuel; cannot explode like a nuclear bomb.

Cons: Creates dangerous nuclear waste that takes thousands of years to become safe; accidents might contaminate large areas with radiation; expensive.

Hydroelectric

Pros: Does not pollute or heat the water or air; no waste products, runs nonstop; very inexpensive.

Cons: Massive dams are expensive and difficult to build; alters the environment around the dam; can affect fish migratory patterns.

Biomass

Pros: Reduces trash in landfills; cuts down on release of methane; plants, such as corn for ethanol, are a renewable resource.

Cons: Burning some trash releases toxins and some greenhouse gases into the air; leaves ash; plants require large farms and specific climate conditions; could raise food prices.

Wind

Pros: Clean; land for wind farms can be used for other purposes like farming; can be built offshore.

Cons: Wind farms take up a lot of space; can kill birds if placed in migratory paths; require winds of at least 12 to 14 mph; can be noisy.

Solar

Pros: No pollution; little maintenance required.

Cons: Solar panels are expensive and take up a lot of space; energy can't be gathered when the Sun isn't shining; manufacturing the solar cells produces waste products.

Fossil Fuels

(primarily coal)

Pros: Affordable because equipment is in wide use; needs smaller space to generate power than most other sources.

Cons: Limited supply; major contributor to global warming; causes chemical reactions that create acid rain and smog; releases pollutants that cause breathing problems like asthma, can harm land and pollute water.

"Greener" Cars, Cleaner Air

About 750 million motor vehicles, most of them passenger cars, fill the world's roads. Nearly all of these vehicles burn fossil fuels, mainly gasoline or diesel fuel, putting gases and dust particles into the air. The gases and particles that come out of a vehicle's tail pipe are called **emissions**, and some of them are harmful to people's health. Some emissions contribute to **smog** and other types of air pollution. Some, such as carbon dioxide, are known as **greenhouse gases**, which promote global warming. The 21st century has seen a surge of interest in reducing the harmful emissions from cars and trucks in order to reduce harm to the environment. More and more "green" cars, offering reduced or even zero emissions, have come on the market. Additional models are in the works.

ELECTRIFYING!

One way to deal with the emission problem is to replace gasoline or diesel fuel with some other power source for cars—such as electricity. **Electric cars** don't give off any emissions at all. They first appeared at the end of the 19th century but failed to catch on, largely because the batteries they used had a very limited capacity. Batteries are better today, and electric cars are beginning to make a comeback. The Nissan Leaf, for example, can go about 100 miles on a single charge, so it's useful for people who don't need to drive long distances.

Batteries are not the only possible source of electricity. A lot of effort has been devoted, for example, to studying **hydrogen fuel cells** as a means of powering cars. These devices, when provided with a supply of hydrogen, can make the hydrogen combine with oxygen, a process that yields electricity and a very nonpolluting by-product: water. Many auto companies are working on developing hydrogen-fueled cars.

HYBRID CARS

A popular approach to dealing with automobile emissions in recent years has been not to eliminate them but to reduce them. Carmakers brought out vehicles called hybrid cars that feature both a gasoline (or diesel) engine and an electric motor. The two power sources work together to make the vehicle go, and its fossil fuel consumption is much less than in a traditional vehicle.

The first hybrid car to go on sale in the U.S. was the little Honda Insight in December 1999. Ten years later there were more than 20 models of hybrid cars on the U.S. market. In 2011, about 275,000 hybrids were sold in the United States. The Toyota Prius remained one of the most popular models. In 2011, it passed 1 million total sales since its introduction in the U.S. in the year 2000.

CLEANER-BURNING CARS

Carmakers have also brought out nonelectric, fuel-burning cars that are less polluting than those of the past. Some of these vehicles reduce emissions by using alternative fuels, such as biofuels or the relatively clean-burning fossil fuel natural gas. Also, engines in many modern gasoline and diesel cars are simply more efficient and run more cleanly. They offer better fuel economy (and thus a lower rate of emissions per mile).

On the JOB Solar Energy Company Owner

Dan Sabia has his own solar energy company that designs and installs rooftop solar energy systems. These systems convert sunlight into electricity. He agreed to talk to *The World Almanac for Kids* about his work.

What do you do in a typical day?

I'm out a lot during the day. I visit buildings where my crews are installing solar panels, to make sure everything is going OK. I also visit and talk with new customers who want a solar energy system. It's important to make sure the building faces south and has no trees shading the roof, so that the solar panels can absorb enough sunlight to produce energy.

What interests and strengths of yours make this job right for you?

Even as a child, I was interested in how things were built and how they worked. At that time, there was no such thing as a career in solar energy. It wasn't until I was much older that I realized I could take my hands-on carpentry, construction, and architectural abilities and put those toward something that's good for our planet.

What kind of education or training did you need to get in order to do your job?

I spent many years as a facilities manager for a college and then a large school district, making sure everything operated safely and efficiently. Before starting my own solar energy company, I took courses in renewable energy technology.

What do you like best about your job? What is most challenging?

One of the main challenges is getting the word out that solar energy really is a practical way to produce electricity. Another challenge is that the solar energy business is seasonal. Solar panels can't be installed on rooftops if the temperature is below freezing or the weather is wet. The things I like best about my job are helping the environment and educating people about the advantages of renewable energy. It gives me tremendous satisfaction to know that my efforts are making the planet a cleaner and better place to live.

ENVIRONMENT

→What year was the warmest ever recorded? PAGE 80

LIVING GREEN

Protecting the environment is important to humans and every other living thing on Earth. Helping the environment includes keeping air, water, and soil as clean as possible. It also includes preserving Earth's resources for the future, saving the many **biomes** around the world in which different plants and animals live, and reducing the amount of **greenhouse gases** that are being added to the air and are likely changing Earth's climate. Everyone can have an impact, however small, on protecting the environment. Here are some ways people are "living green."

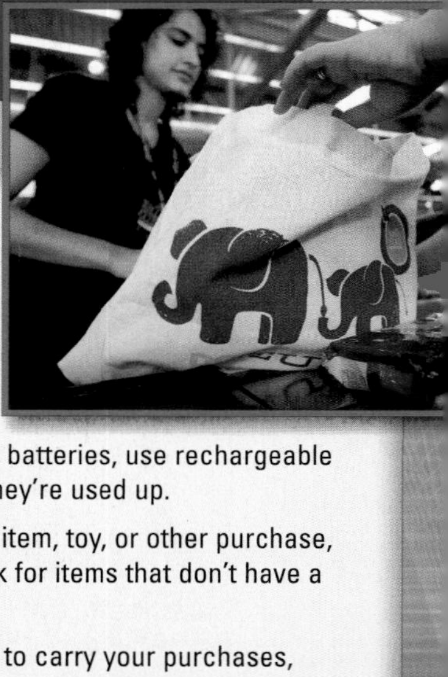

SHOPPING GREEN

- **Rent or reuse:** Every time something new is made, energy and raw materials are used up to make it. If you or your family needs to use something for a short time, find out whether it can be rented, rather than bought new. You also might find used books, toys, party decorations, and even clothing at garage sales or thrift shops.
- **Think about batteries:** When you buy something that requires batteries, use rechargeable batteries rather than batteries that just go into the trash when they're used up.
- **Check out packaging:** The more packaging there is on a food item, toy, or other purchase, the more trash there will be to throw away. When shopping, look for items that don't have a lot of wasteful packaging.
- **Reuse bags:** Bring your own reusable bags to the supermarket to carry your purchases, rather than getting plastic bags at the store.
- **Be aware of ingredients:** Try to buy only products that don't contain harmful chemicals and that are produced in a way that does the least harm to the environment. You can find "green" shampoos, household cleansers, and clothing—all made without harmful chemicals.

TRAVELING GREEN

- **Walk or bike:** Try walking or biking to places that aren't too far away, rather than depending on a car. Most cars burn fuel and put pollution into the air.
- **Use trains and buses:** Encourage your family to think about using a train or a bus the next time you go on vacation, rather than driving.
- **Think about carpooling:** Set up carpools for traveling to places that you and your friends go to all the time, rather than having everyone go in separate cars.

EATING GREEN

- **Think local:** Eat foods that are grown locally so that they don't have to be shipped long distances. Shipping foods by truck or airplane is a major source of air pollution. Is there a greenmarket or a farmer's market near where you live that sells locally produced food?
- **Remember the season:** Eat fresh fruits and other foods that are in season. When you eat a fruit that's not in season, you're eating something that had to be picked and stored and then shipped a long way to your neighborhood store—all of which uses energy and causes pollution.
- **Check out gardening:** Think about planting a small vegetable garden in your yard. If you don't have a yard, maybe there's a community garden in your neighborhood where people are growing their own food. Could you suggest that your school start a small garden?

THINKING GREEN EVERY DAY

- **Avoid things you use once:** Avoid products that you use just once and then throw away, such as plastic forks, knives, and cups. Try taking your lunch in a container that you can wash and reuse many times, rather than putting it in a paper bag that you'll just throw away.
- **Save water:** Make sure you turn off the faucet tightly to avoid drips that waste water. Don't let the water run when you're not using it—for example, while you brush your teeth. Take showers rather than baths, because they use much less water—and keep your showers short.
- **Use tap water:** Drink tap water rather than bottled water. Making the bottles and shipping the water both use energy. You can fill a glass container with tap water and chill it in the refrigerator so that it will be cold.
- **Be smart about using appliances:** Don't run a half-full washing machine or dishwasher. Wait until the machine is full, and you can clean twice as much using the same amount of water and energy.
- **Conserve electricity:** To save electricity, turn off the lights when you leave a room. Turn off TVs, computers, and other devices when they're not being used.
- **Use the sponge:** Instead of using paper towels to wipe up spills, use a sponge. Paper towels become trash.

DID YOU KNOW?

Trains are far more fuel-efficient than trucks for moving freight. A train can move a ton of cargo between 156 and 512 miles on a single gallon of fuel! That's much more than the 68 to 133 miles a truck can move a ton of freight per gallon of fuel used.

What Is GLOBAL WARMING?

What Is the Greenhouse Effect?

Global warming is a gradual increase in the average temperature at Earth's surface. Earth reflects back into space about 30% of the Sun's rays that reach it. Some rays are absorbed by Earth's surface and converted into heat energy. The heat radiates from the surface, and some of it escapes into space. But some is prevented from escaping by **greenhouse gases** in the atmosphere. The most common greenhouse gases are water vapor, carbon dioxide, methane, nitrous oxide, ozone, and fluorinated gases. Most greenhouse gases occur naturally, and they help to make life on Earth possible. Without this natural **greenhouse effect**, Earth would be about 60°F colder than it is today.

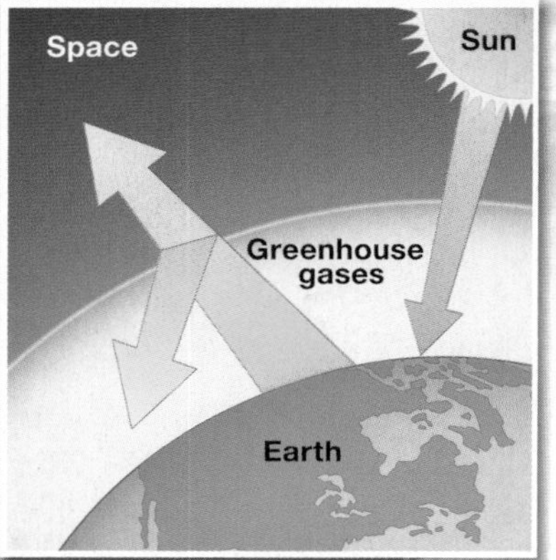

Why Are Greenhouse Gases Increasing?

Since the mid-1700s, humans have been releasing more and more greenhouse gases into the atmosphere. Mostly these additions have come from burning fossil fuels—such as coal, natural gas, and oil—which produce carbon dioxide. Factories, farms, and **landfills** (places where trash is dumped) also give off greenhouse gases. **Deforestation** (cutting down or otherwise destroying forests) adds to the problem, because trees absorb carbon dioxide.

There is more carbon dioxide and methane in the atmosphere today than has been normal for the last 650,000 years, trapping more of the Sun's energy. The decade from 2000 to 2009 was the warmest recorded since good temperature records began in 1880, and 2010 was the warmest single year ever since 1880. Almost all scientists believe humans are the main cause of this global warming.

Sources of Carbon Dioxide Released by Burning Fossil Fuels in the U.S. in 2010*

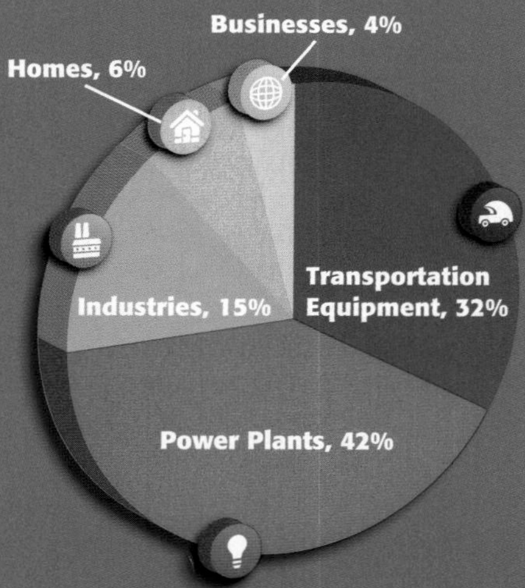

*Percentages do not add to 100% because of rounding.

How Do We Know about Global Warming?

Worldwide records of climate have been kept since around the mid-1800s. They show global increases in air and ocean temperatures, a rise in sea level, and melting glaciers. Today, weather balloons, ocean buoys, and satellites provide even more information.

Scientists drill thousands of feet into ice caps in Antarctica and Greenland to remove ice core samples. The layers of ice and air pockets trapped in them can be read like a timeline of climate change over the past 800,000 years.

What Will Happen?

RISING SEA LEVELS: Scientists have created computer climate models that identify patterns and make predictions. In the short run, average temperatures may go up or down in a given year. But in the long run, current estimates predict that they will rise. In fact, by the year 2100, Earth's average temperature may increase at least 2°F and oceans will rise 7 inches. The worst-case scenarios suggest that Earth could warm by more than 11°F and sea levels could rise 2 feet or more.

As Earth warms, sea levels rise:

- Water expands slightly as it warms.
- The ice sheets covering Greenland and the Arctic Sea are melting. Also, chunks of ice (icebergs) are breaking away from ice sheets in Antarctica and Greenland.
- Glaciers are melting in non-polar regions, producing more water. ▲
- As ice melts, it exposes darker land or sea, which is less reflective and absorbs more heat.

MELTING POLAR ICE: The Arctic region may warm up more than many other places because of the albedo effect, or a surface's power to reflect light. Ice reflects the Sun's rays. With less ice on Earth, more of the Sun's heat will be absorbed by the oceans. Warmer water raises sea levels and melts ice faster.

CHANGING WATER CYCLE: Warmer air affects the water cycle (see page 82). More water evaporates, and the atmosphere can hold more water vapor. Places with plenty of water will have more rain and floods. But in places where water is scarce, evaporation will dry out the land even more. Vapor will take more time to condense, meaning less rain and more droughts.

Rising sea levels already threaten some coastal settlements and small Pacific islands.

Many scientists believe that warmer oceans will lead to more intense tropical cyclones (also called hurricanes and typhoons).

As environments change, animals must find new homes or they may become extinct. Warmer global climates will allow disease-carrying creatures such as mosquitoes to spread to new places.

Water, Water EVERYWHERE

Earth is the water planet. More than two-thirds of its surface is covered with water, and every living thing on it needs water to live. Humans can survive for about a month without eating food, but only for about a week without drinking water. People also use water for cooking and cleaning, to produce power, to irrigate farmland, and for recreation.

About 97% of the world's water is salt water in the oceans and inland seas, which can be drunk only after special treatment. Another 2% of the water is frozen in ice caps and glaciers. Half of the 1% left is too far underground to be reached. That leaves only 0.5% for all the people, plants, and animals on Earth.

THE WATER CYCLE

Water is the only thing on Earth that exists naturally in **all three normal physical states**: solid (ice), liquid, and gas (water vapor). The water cycle describes how water changes as it moves through the environment. The cycle has no starting or ending point but is driven by the Sun.

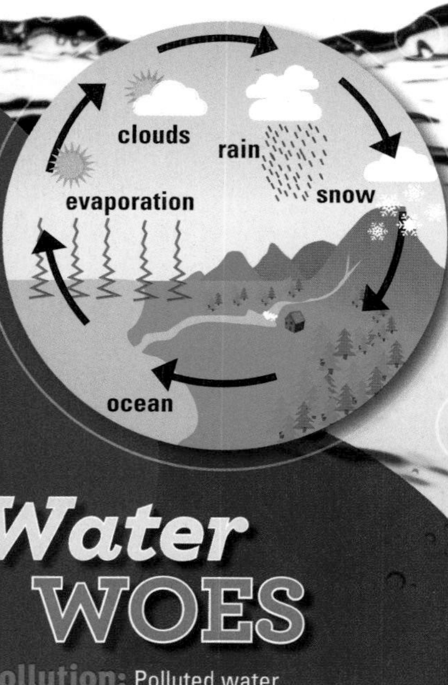

HOW DOES WATER GET INTO THE AIR?

Heat from the Sun causes surface water in oceans, lakes, swamps, and rivers to turn into water vapor. This is called **evaporation**. Plants release water vapor into the air as part of the process called **transpiration**. Animals release a little bit when they breathe and when they perspire.

HOW DOES WATER COME OUT OF THE AIR?

Warm air holds more water vapor than cold air. As the air rises into the atmosphere, it cools and the water vapor **condenses**—changes back into tiny water droplets. These droplets form clouds. As the drops get bigger, gravity pulls them down to Earth as **precipitation** (such as rain, snow, or sleet).

WHERE DOES THE WATER GO?

Depending on where the precipitation lands, it can: **1.** evaporate back into the atmosphere, **2.** run off into streams and rivers, **3.** be absorbed by plants, **4.** soak down into the soil as groundwater, or **5.** fall as snow on a glacier and be trapped as ice for thousands of years.

Water WOES

Pollution: Polluted water can't be used for drinking, swimming, or watering crops, nor can it provide a good habitat for plants and animals. Major sources of water pollutants are sewage, chemicals from factories, fertilizers and pesticides, and landfills that leak.

Overuse: When more water is taken out of lakes and reservoirs (for drinking, washing, watering lawns, and other uses) than is put back in, the water levels begin to drop. This can be devastating. In some cases, lakes become salty or dry up completely.

WHERE GARBAGE GOES

The disposal of garbage is a serious issue. The problem is that we now produce more garbage than our natural environment can absorb.

WHAT HAPPENS TO THINGS WE THROW AWAY?

LANDFILLS

About half of our trash goes to places called landfills. A **landfill** (or dump) is a low area of land that is filled with garbage. Most modern landfills are lined with a layer of plastic or clay to try to keep dangerous liquids from seeping into the soil and underground water supplies (**groundwater**). The number of landfills is one-fourth of what it was in 1988, but they're much larger.

The Problem with LANDFILLS

Because of the unhealthy materials many of them contain, landfills do not make good neighbors. But where can we dispose of waste?

INCINERATORS

One way to get rid of trash is to burn it. Trash can be burned in a furnace-like device called an **incinerator** to make electricity.

The Problem with INCINERATORS

Leftover ash and smoke from burning trash such as rubber tires may contain harmful chemicals, including greenhouse gases. Pollutants can make it hard for some people to breathe. They can harm plants, animals, and people.

Reduce, Reuse, Recycle

Reducing garbage helps protect the environment. Reuse products. Recycle products so that materials can be used again rather than become garbage.

What Is Made from RECYCLED MATERIALS?

- ***From* RECYCLED PAPER we get newspapers, cereal boxes, wrapping paper, cardboard containers, and insulation.**
- ***From* RECYCLED PLASTIC we get soda bottles, benches, bike racks, cameras, backpacks, carpeting, and clothes.**
- ***From* RECYCLED ALUMINUM we get cans, cars, bicycles, computers, and pots and pans.**
- ***From* RECYCLED GLASS we get glass jars and tiles.**
- ***From* RECYCLED RUBBER we get mousepads, shoe soles, floor tiles, and playground equipment.**

HOME SWEET BIOME

A biome is a large natural area that is home to certain types of plants. The animals, climate, soil, and even the amount of water in the region also help distinguish a biome. There are many kinds of biomes in the world. But the following types cover most of Earth's surface.

Forests

Evergreen forest, Europe

Forests cover about one-third of Earth's land surface. Pines, hemlocks, firs, and spruces grow in the cool **evergreen forests** farthest from the equator. These trees are called evergreens because they keep their leaves year-round. They are also known as **conifers** because they produce cones.

Temperate forests tend to have warm, rainy summers and cool, snowy winters. They often are home to **deciduous trees** (trees that lose their leaves in the fall and grow new ones in the spring), such as maple, oak, beech, and poplar. Mixtures of deciduous trees and evergreens also occur, and some temperate forests are primarily coniferous. Areas where temperate forests can be found include the United States, southern Canada, southern Chile, Europe, Asia, eastern Australia, and New Zealand.

Still closer to the equator are the **tropical rain forests**, home to the greatest variety of plants on Earth. Typically, more than 80 inches of rain fall each year. Tropical trees stay green all year. They grow close together, shading the ground. There are several layers of trees. The top, **emergent layer** has trees that can reach 200 feet in height. The **canopy**, which gets lots of sunlight, comes next, followed by the **understory**. The **forest floor**, covered with roots, gets little sunlight. Many plants cannot grow there.

ayers of a tropical rain forest

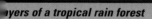

Tropical rain forests are found mainly in Central America, South America, Africa, Southeast Asia, and Australia and nearby islands. They once covered as much as 12% of Earth's land surface or nearly 7 million square miles. Today, because of destruction by humans, fewer than 2.5 million square miles of rain forest remain. Half the plant and animal species in the world live there. The Amazon rain forest in South America is the world's largest tropical rain forest.

Tundra

Tundra, the coldest biome, is a treeless plain. In the Arctic tundra—located in the northernmost regions of North America, Europe, and Asia surrounding the Arctic Ocean—the temperature rarely rises above 50°F. Water in the ground freezes the subsoil solid **(permafrost)** so plant and tree roots can't dig down. Most plants are mosses and lichens without roots. In some areas, the top layer of soil thaws for about two months each year. This may allow wildflowers or small shrubs to grow. Alpine tundra is located on top of the world's highest mountains (such as the Himalayas, Alps, Andes, and Rockies). Plants and low shrubs may be found here, and patches of permafrost may occur.

What Is the Tree Line? On mountains, there is an altitude above which trees will not grow. This is the **tree line** or **timberline**.

Deserts

Desert, Nevada

The driest areas of the world are the **deserts**. They receive less than 10 inches of rain in a year. Some desert areas have very few plants. But others contain an amazing number of plants that store water in thick bodies or roots deep underground. Rain can make fields of wildflowers bloom. Shrubby sagebrush and spiny cacti are native to dry regions of North and South America. Prickly pear, barrel, and saguaro cacti can be found in the southwestern United States. Date palms grow in desert oases of the Middle East and North Africa.

Savanna, Tanzania

Grasslands

Areas that are too dry to have green forests but not dry enough to be deserts are **grasslands**. The most common plants are grasses. Cooler grasslands are found in the Great Plains of the United States and Canada, in the steppes of Europe and Asia, and in the pampas of Argentina. Drier grasslands called steppes have short grasses and are used for grazing cattle and sheep. In **prairies**, characterized by tall grasses, there is a little more rain. The warmer grasslands, called **savannas**, are found in central and southern Africa, Venezuela, southern Brazil, and Australia. Most savannas have moist summers and cool, dry winters.

Marine

Reef, Belize

Covering more than two-thirds of Earth's surface, marine regions are the largest biome. The marine biome includes the **oceans, coastal areas, tidal zones,** and **coral reefs**. Reefs are found most often in relatively shallow warm water, including coastal waters of the Caribbean Sea. Like tropical rain forests, reefs are home to thousands of species of plant and animal life. Australia's Great Barrier Reef is the largest in the world.

FASHION

→Which fashion designer is the daughter of a former member of The Beatles? PAGE 88

Must-Have Fashions

All over the world, fashion trends often start with young people. Sometimes, kids take clothing or accessories from previous decades and tweak them to create fresh styles. Here are some trends seen around the world.

GEEK CHIC

"Geek chic" has become popular with today's young people—guys and girls are wearing plaid shirts and heavy, dark-framed glasses. The outfits may be paired with Mary Jane-style shoes or canvas sneakers.

R&B star Usher ▶

PLATFORMS

Some fashion-forward teens are sporting platform sneakers—the taller, the better. The look is especially popular in Tokyo, Japan, where teens might personalize their look by matching the sneakers with tights or socks.

NEON

Bright neon colors are the rage in many areas, but especially in New York City. Sunglasses, sneakers, and leggings in bright pinks and greens can be seen throughout the city.

◀ *Radio host Rocsi Diaz*

ALL-NATURAL

Teens and adults alike are hooked on environmentally friendly clothing made with organic fabrics, such as hemp and organic cotton. Toms shoes—made with "green" materials—can be seen all over the world.

Toms founder Blake Mycoskie ▶

BLASTS FROM THE PAST

Around the globe and in every period of history, people have chosen their own styles and created new looks. These styles may seem unusual to us today, but they were the height of fashion then. Here are a few examples.

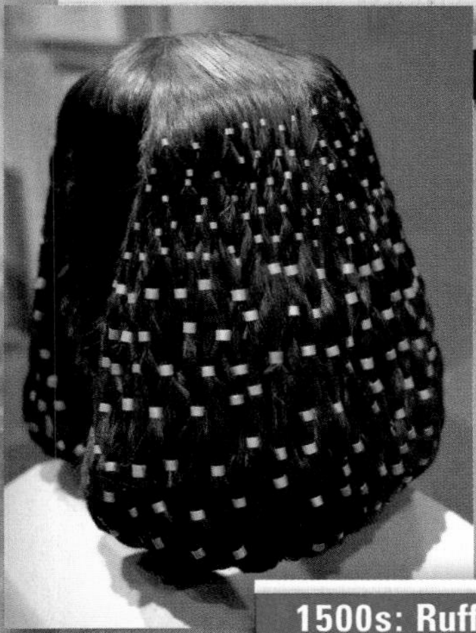

100s B.C.: Wigs

Wigs were very popular for men and women in Egypt in the second century B.C. The wealthiest members of society shaved their heads to prevent lice and to help keep cool in the extreme heat of the climate. They wore wigs for formal occasions and to protect their bare heads from the sun. The elaborately decorated wigs were generally made of human, sheep, or horse hair.

1500s: Ruffs

Fashionable men and women in the 1500s in Spain wore a large fabric ruffle, or ruff, around their necks. Ruffs got larger toward the end of the century—by the 1580s, some ruffs were more than a foot wide and needed wire to hold them up.

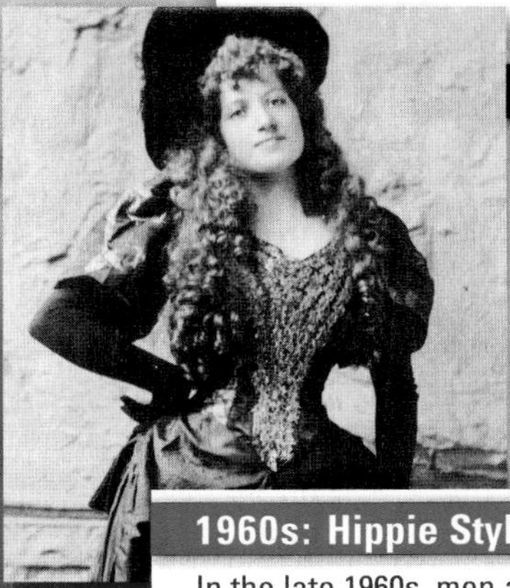

1800s: Corsets

In the 1800s, women in England went to extreme measures to make their waists look smaller. Corsets, often lined with whalebone or steel, were worn under dresses and tied so tightly that many women suffered from health problems as a result.

1960s: Hippie Style

In the late 1960s, men and women embraced the "hippie" style that first became popular in San Francisco, California. Pants with very wide bell-bottoms, brightly colored skirts, beads, and headbands helped create the look. Peace signs were often used to accessorize the outfits, which were usually worn by people who opposed the Vietnam War.

SOME FAMOUS **FASHION DESIGNERS**

RALPH **LAUREN**

Ralph Lauren—originally named Ralph Lifshitz—was born in New York City in 1939. He became interested in fashion while in middle school, after taking a part-time job at a department store. Lauren worked as a designer for a few years before starting his own company and creating his own brand, Polo. He rose to fame with the design of his simple collared shirts with a horse and rider logo. His brands now include Polo Ralph Lauren, Polo Sport, and the Ralph Lauren Collection. One of the world's best-known and most successful designers, he is estimated to be worth about $7.5 billion.

STELLA **McCARTNEY**

Born in 1971, Stella McCartney is the daughter of singer/songwriter and former Beatle Paul McCartney and his wife Linda. Stella began designing her own clothing as a teenager, and at age 15, she was hired as an intern with designer Christian Lacroix. Her design career took off from there. Linda McCartney was an animal-rights activist, and Stella has followed in her footsteps. She is a committed vegetarian who uses no fur or leather in her designs. Today, Stella McCartney designs both high-end clothing for celebrities and also more affordable fashions sold in stores such as Target and the Gap. She also has a line of organically made skin care products that are never tested on animals.

Actress Kristen Stewart, wearing a Stella McCartney design ▶

JAY-**Z**

Originally named Shawn Corey Carter, Jay-Z was born in Brooklyn, New York, in 1969. He rose to rap stardom in the 1990s. In 1999, Jay-Z expanded his career into fashion design. With partner Damon Dash, he created the clothing company Rocawear. The clothing was inspired by hip-hop culture and sold in department stores. Though Jay-Z sold the rights to the brand in 2007, he kept a stake in the company and continues to oversee the company's products and marketing. Today, Rocawear is extremely successful, with annual sales of about $700 million.

On the JOB Fashion Designer

Fashion is always changing, and fashion designers are the people who help decide what those changes will be. **Meredith Evans** (right), a fashion designer who works for a clothing manufacturer, agreed to talk to *The World Almanac for Kids* about her work.

sketches by Meredith Evans ▼

What do you do in a typical day?

My days are hectic! I manage a team of people, so I always need to be sure they are clear about what needs to be done that day. I direct the creative part of our clothing line—inspiration for colors, fabrics, silhouettes, prints, and patterns we'll use. And I manage the business side of things, too. I work with our merchandising and marketing teams to make sure what we are developing fits in with the sales strategy for the season. I also prepare many presentations and have a lot of meetings with clients. These clients are the buyers for the large retail chains that we sell our clothing to.

What interests and strengths of yours make this job right for you?

I am a creative person and love fashion, but I also like business, so this job is a good combination of both.

What kind of education or training did you need to get in order to do your job?

I have a bachelor of fine arts degree from the Parsons School of Design in New York City.

What do you like best about your job? What is most challenging?

I like the fast pace and I like that no two days are ever the same. It's never boring! It is a lot of pressure, however, to always need to be one step ahead of the trends.

GAMES

→ In what year was Microsoft's Xbox introduced? PAGE 91

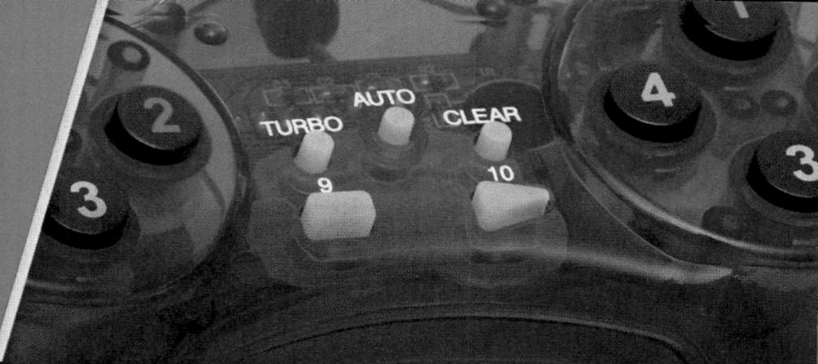

TOP SELLERS

Nintendo rules in sales of games developed for traditional platforms. The Mario franchise is the most successful video game series of all time, with more than 225 million games sold. Here are the five all-time top-selling individual games.

Game	Console	U.S. Release	Units Sold*
Wii Sports	Wii	2006	78.98 million
Super Mario Bros.	NES	1985	40.24 million
Mario Kart Wii	Wii	2008	32.06 million
Pokémon Red / Green / Blue	Game Boy	1998	31.37 million
Tetris	Game Boy	1989	30.26 million

*Through June 11, 2012; sales figures are worldwide. Source: VGChartz

GAME SPOTLIGHT: ANGRY BIRDS

Rovio, a company based in Finland, released *Angry Birds* in 2009 for touchscreen smartphones. In the game, a player uses a slingshot to launch colorful birds at green pigs that stole their eggs. *Angry Birds* quickly became the most popular game on the iPhone. It is now available on other platforms and has been downloaded more than 700 million times.

WHAT'S NEW?

Eagerly awaited sequels to some popular games were released in 2012.

Kid Icarus Uprising: The long-awaited sequel to 1991's *Kid Icarus: Of Myths and Monsters* follows Pit, the trusted servant of the good Palutena. Players on Nintendo 3DS control Pit as he takes to the sky to battle the evil Medusa and her Underworld Army.

Major League Baseball 2K12: The newest version of the popular baseball game featured advanced hitting and pitching controls, lifelike animations, and commentary from real announcers. Game users could play along as the real baseball season took place.

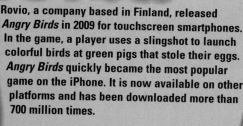

GAMING TIMELINE

1972 The Magnavox Odyssey is the first commercial home video-game console. The system has no sound.

1975 The home version of Atari's *Pong* debuts. It features two lines (or paddles) that players use to hit a dot back and forth.

1977 The Atari VCS (later renamed the 2600) is the first popular system to feature cartridges for different games.

1980 The pie-shaped pellet-eating character Pac-Man chomps its way into arcades. ▶

1985 Known as Famicom in Japan, the Nintendo Entertainment System invades the United States.

1989 Nintendo's first handheld game system, Game Boy, is a huge hit.

1995 Sony releases its popular PlayStation, which uses CD-Roms instead of cartridges.

2001 Home computer giant Microsoft gets into the action with the Xbox.

2004 The Nintendo DS (dual-screen) ushers in a new era of handheld gaming.

2006 Nintendo Wii changes gaming with the introduction of wand-like controllers.

2008 Nintendo *Wii Fit* features a balance board that allows users to exercise as they play.

2010 The motion-sensing Kinect system for the Xbox 360 console allows users to play games without the need of a controller.

2012 Sony's PlayStation Vita gives users a full-motion 3-D gaming experience in portable form, with built-in satellite navigation and access to cellphone networks. ▲

THE ART OF VIDEO GAMES

A 2012 exhibit at the Smithsonian's American Art Museum in Washington, D.C., explored 40 years in the history of video games from an artistic point of view. The exhibit traced the evolution of games, focusing on visual effects and the creative use of new technologies. The public was invited to vote on the 80 games selected to be included in the exhibit. In addition, five games—including perennial favorites *Pac-Man, Super Mario Bros.*, and *Myst*—were available for visitors to play. The exhibit was scheduled to travel to museums in 10 cities through early 2016.

GEOGRAPHY

→What Chinese explorer sailed to Africa in the early 1400s? PAGE 95

SIZING UP PLANET EARTH

The word "geography" comes from the Greek word **geographia**, meaning "writing about Earth." It was first used by the Greek scholar Eratosthenes, who was head of the great library of Alexandria in Egypt. Around 230 B.C., when many people believed the world was flat, he did a remarkable thing. He calculated Earth's circumference. His figure of about 25,000 miles was close to the modern measurement of 24,901 miles!

Actually, Earth is not perfectly round. It's flatter at the poles and bulges out a little at the middle. This bulge around the equator is due to Earth's rotation. Although Earth seems solid to us, it is really slightly plastic, or flexible. As Earth spins, material flows toward its middle, piling up and creating a slight bulge. Earth's diameter is 7,926 miles at the equator, but only 7,900 miles from North Pole to South Pole. The total surface area of Earth is 196,940,000 square miles.

Geography 1 2 3

Longest Rivers	**1. Nile (Egypt and Sudan)—4,160 miles** **2. Amazon (Brazil and Peru)—4,000 miles** **3. Chang (China)—3,964 miles (formerly called the Yangtze)**
Tallest Mountains	**1. Mount Everest (Tibet and Nepal)—29,035 feet** **2. K2 (Kashmir)—28,250 feet** **3. Kanchenjunga (India and Nepal)—28,208 feet**
Biggest Islands	**1. Greenland (Atlantic Ocean)—840,000 square miles** **2. New Guinea (Pacific Ocean)—306,000 square miles** **3. Borneo (Pacific Ocean)—280,100 square miles**
Biggest Desert Regions	**1. Sahara Desert (North Africa)—3.5 million square miles** **2. Australian Deserts—1.3 million square miles** **3. Arabian Peninsula—1 million square miles**
Biggest Lakes	**1. Caspian Sea (Europe and Asia)—143,244 square miles** **2. Superior (U.S. and Canada)—31,700 square miles** **3. Victoria (Kenya, Tanzania, Uganda)—26,828 square miles**
Highest Waterfalls	**1. Angel Falls (Venezuela)—3,212 feet** **2. Tugela Falls (South Africa)—2,800 feet** **3. Monge Falls (Norway)—2,540 feet**

Reading a MAP

DIRECTION Maps usually have a **compass rose** that shows you which way is north. On most maps, like this one, it's straight up. The compass rose on this map is in the upper left corner.

DISTANCE As you can see, the distances on a map are much shorter than the distances in the real world. The **scale** shows you how to estimate the real distance. This map's scale is in the lower left corner.

PICTURES Maps usually have little pictures or symbols to represent real things such as roads, towns, airports, or other points of interest. The map **legend** (or **key**) tells what they mean.

FINDING PLACES Rather than use latitude and longitude to locate features, many maps use a grid with numbers on one side and letters on another. An index, listing place names in alphabetical order, gives a letter and a number for each. The letter and number tell you in which square to look for a place on the map's grid. For example, Landisville can be found at A1.

USING THE MAP People use maps to help them travel from one place to another. What if you lived in East Petersburgh and wanted to go to the Hands-on-House Children's Museum? First, locate the two places on the map. East Petersburgh is C1, and the Hands-on House Children's Museum is E1. Next, look at the roads that connect them and decide on the best route. One way is to travel east on Route 722, then southeast on Valley Road until you see the Children's Museum.

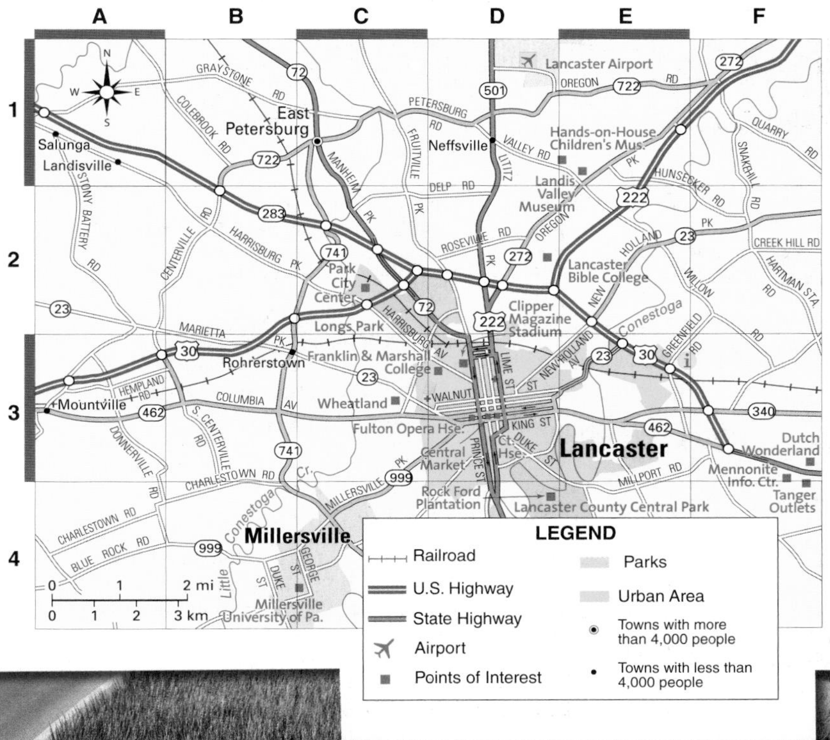

EARLY EXPLORATION

AROUND 1000 — **Leif Ericson**, from Iceland, explored "Vinland," which may have been the coasts of northeast Canada and New England.

1271–1295 — **Marco Polo** (Italian) traveled through Central Asia, India, China, and Indonesia.

1488 — **Bartolomeu Dias** (Portuguese) explored the Cape of Good Hope in southern Africa.

1492–1504 — **Christopher Columbus** (Italian) sailed four times from Spain to America and started colonies there.

1497–1498 — **Vasco da Gama** (Portuguese) sailed farther than Dias, around the Cape of Good Hope to East Africa and India.

1513 — **Juan Ponce de León** (Spanish) explored and named Florida.

1513 — **Vasco Núñez de Balboa** (Spanish) explored Panama and reached the Pacific Ocean.

1519–1521 — **Ferdinand Magellan** (Portuguese) sailed from Spain around the tip of South America and across the Pacific Ocean to the Philippines, where he died. His expedition continued around the world.

1519–1536 — **Hernán Cortés** (Spanish) conquered Mexico, traveling as far west as Baja California.

1527–1542 — **Alvar Núñez Cabeza de Vaca** (Spanish) explored the southwestern United States, Brazil, and Paraguay.

1532–1535 — **Francisco Pizarro** (Spanish) explored the west coast of South America and conquered Peru.

1534–1536 — **Jacques Cartier** (French) sailed up the St. Lawrence River to the site of present-day Montreal.

1539–1542 — **Hernando de Soto** (Spanish) explored the southeastern United States and the lower Mississippi Valley.

1603–1613 — **Samuel de Champlain** (French) traced the course of the St. Lawrence River and explored the northeastern United States.

1609–1610 — **Henry Hudson** (English), sailing from Holland, explored the Hudson River, Hudson Bay, and Hudson Strait.

1682 — **Robert Cavelier, sieur de La Salle** (French), traced the Mississippi River to its mouth in the Gulf of Mexico.

1768–1778 — **James Cook** (English) charted the world's major bodies of water and explored Hawaii and Antarctica.

1804–1806 — **Meriwether Lewis and William Clark** (American) traveled from St. Louis along the Missouri and Columbia rivers to the Pacific Ocean and back.

1849–1859 — **David Livingstone** (Scottish) explored Southern Africa.

SOME FAMOUS

EXPLORERS

These explorers, and many others, risked their lives on trips to explore faraway and often unknown places. Some sought fame. Some sought fortune. Some just sought challenge. All of them increased people's knowledge of the world.

1371–1433 ZHENG HE

Chinese explorer who in the early 1400s built a fleet of enormous wooden ships and explored the Indian Ocean and beyond. He sailed into the Persian Gulf and reached Somalia in East Africa. Zheng He brought back to China ivory, pearls, spices, and many other valuable trade goods.

1451–1506 CHRISTOPHER COLUMBUS

Italian navigator who sailed for Spain. He had hoped to find a fast route to Asia by going west from Europe. Instead he became the first European (other than the Vikings) to reach America, landing in the Bahamas in October 1492.

1480–1521 FERDINAND MAGELLAN

Portuguese explorer who sailed from Spain in 1519, seeking a western route to the Spice Islands of Indonesia. He became the first European to cross the Pacific Ocean but was killed by natives in the Philippines. Because he passed the easternmost point he had reached on an earlier voyage, he is considered the first person to circumnavigate Earth.

1732–1820 DANIEL BOONE

American pioneer and explorer. As a young man, he explored the territory of Kentucky for two years. Using an old Indian trail, he led a group through the Cumberland Gap from Virginia into Kentucky and later went on to blaze hundreds of miles of new trails for settlers to use throughout the territory.

1866–1955 MATTHEW HENSON

The first famous African-American explorer. As an assistant to explorer Robert Peary (1856–1920), he traveled on seven expeditions to Greenland and the Arctic region. In April 1909, Peary and Henson became the first to reach, or nearly reach, the North Pole. (Recent research suggests they may have fallen short by about 30 to 60 miles.)

1942– ROBERT BALLARD

American navy commander and underwater archaeologist. Ballard was the first person to locate the remains of the luxury liner *Titanic*, which sank in 1912. He also located other historic ships, such as the World War II battleship *Bismarck*.

1951– SALLY RIDE

American astronaut who, in 1983, became the first American woman to go into space. She joined NASA in 1978 and served as a mission specialist on two space shuttle missions. Ride was the first person to operate a robot arm in space. After leaving NASA, Ride taught physics at the University of California and then started her own company to encourage girls to pursue careers in science.

LOOKING AT OUR WORLD

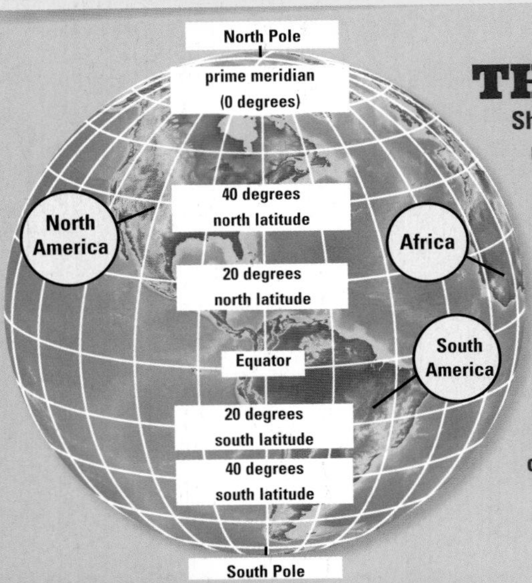

THINKING GLOBAL

Shaped like a ball or sphere, a globe is a model of our planet. Like Earth, it's not perfectly round. It is an oblate spheroid (called a "geoid") that bulges a little in the middle.

In 1569, Gerardus Mercator found a way to project Earth's curved surface onto a flat map. One problem with a Mercator map (like the one on page 97) is that land closer to the poles appears bigger than it is. Australia looks smaller than Greenland on this type of map, but in reality it's not.

LATITUDE AND LONGITUDE

Imaginary lines that run east and west around Earth, parallel to the equator, are called **parallels**. They tell you the **latitude** of a place, or how far it is from the equator. The equator is at 0 degrees latitude. As you go farther north or south, the latitude increases. The North Pole is at 90 degrees **north latitude**. The South Pole is at 90 degrees **south latitude**.

Imaginary lines that run north and south around the globe, from one pole to the other, are called **meridians**. They tell you the degree of **longitude**, or how far east or west a place is from the prime meridian (0 degrees).

Which Hemispheres Do You Live In?

Draw an imaginary line around the middle of Earth. This is the **equator**. It splits Earth into two halves called **hemispheres**. The part north of the equator, including North America, is the **northern hemisphere**. The part south of the equator is the **southern hemisphere**.

An imaginary line called the **Greenwich meridian** or **prime meridian** divides Earth into east and west. It runs north and south around the globe, passing through the city of Greenwich in England. North and South America are in the **western hemisphere**. Africa, Asia, and most of Europe are in the **eastern hemisphere**.

THE TROPICS OF CANCER AND CAPRICORN

If you find the equator on a globe or map, you'll often see two dotted lines running parallel to it, one above and one below (see pages 150–151). The top one marks the Tropic of Cancer, an imaginary line marking the latitude (about 23°27′ North) where the sun is directly overhead on June 21 or 22, the beginning of summer in the northern hemisphere.

Below the equator is the Tropic of Capricorn (about 23°27′ South). This line marks the sun's path directly overhead at noon on December 21 or 22, the beginning of summer in the southern hemisphere. The area between these dotted lines is the tropics, where it is consistently hot because the sun's rays shine more directly than they do farther north or south.

THE SEVEN CONTINENTS AND FIVE OCEANS

ARCTIC OCEAN
5,427,000 square miles
3,953 feet avg. depth

NORTH AMERICA
Area: 9,352,000 square miles
2012 estimated population: 546,875,000
Highest pt.: Mt. McKinley (AK), 20,320 ft
Lowest pt.: Death Valley (CA), –282 ft

EUROPE
Area: 4,033,000 square miles
2012 estimated population: 735,757,000*
Highest pt.: Mt. Elbrus (Russia), 18,510 ft
Lowest pt.: Caspian Sea, –92 ft
*Includes all of Russia.

ASIA
Area: 17,041,000 square miles
2012 estimated population: 4,223,292,000
Highest pt.: Mt. Everest (Nepal/Tibet), 29,035 ft
Lowest pt.: Dead Sea (Israel/Jordan), –1,348 ft

ATLANTIC OCEAN
29,637,900 square miles
12,880 feet avg. depth

PACIFIC OCEAN
60,060,700 square miles
13,215 feet avg. depth

OCEANIA (including Australia)
Area: 3,455,000 square miles
2012 estimated population: 35,834,000
Highest pt.: Jaya, New Guinea, 16,500 ft
Lowest pt.: Lake Eyre, Australia, –52 ft

INDIAN OCEAN
26,469,500 square miles
13,002 feet avg. depth

SOUTH AMERICA
Area: 6,884,000 square miles
2012 estimated population: 404,379,000
Highest pt.: Mt. Aconcagua (Arg.), 22,834 ft
Lowest pt.: Valdes Peninsula (Arg.), –131 ft

AFRICA
Area: 11,675,000 square miles
2012 estimated population: 1,077,187,000
Highest pt.: Mt. Kilimanjaro (Tanzania), 19,340 ft
Lowest pt.: Lake Assal (Djibouti), –512 ft

ANTARCTICA
Area: 5,400,000 square miles
2012 population: no permanent residents
Highest pt.: Vinson Massif, 16,864 ft
Lowest pt.: Bently Subglacial Trench, –8,327 ft

SOUTHERN OCEAN
7,848,300 square miles
14,750 feet avg. depth

WHAT'S INSIDE PLANET EARTH?

Starting at Earth's surface and going down, you find the lithosphere, the mantle, and then the core.

The **lithosphere**, Earth's rocky crust, extends for about 60 miles.

The dense, heavy inner part of Earth is divided into a thick shell, the **mantle**, surrounding an innermost sphere, the **core**. The mantle extends from the base of the crust to a depth of about 1,800 miles and is mostly solid.

Then there is Earth's core. It has two parts: an inner sphere of scorchingly hot, solid iron almost as large as the Moon and an outer region of molten iron. The inner core is much hotter than the outer core. The intense pressure near the center of Earth squeezes the iron in the inner core into a solid ball nearly as hot as the surface of the Sun. Scientists believe the core formed billions of years ago during the planet's fiery birth. Iron and other heavy elements sank into the planet's hot interior while the planet was still molten. As this metallic soup cooled over millions of years, crystals of iron hardened at the center.

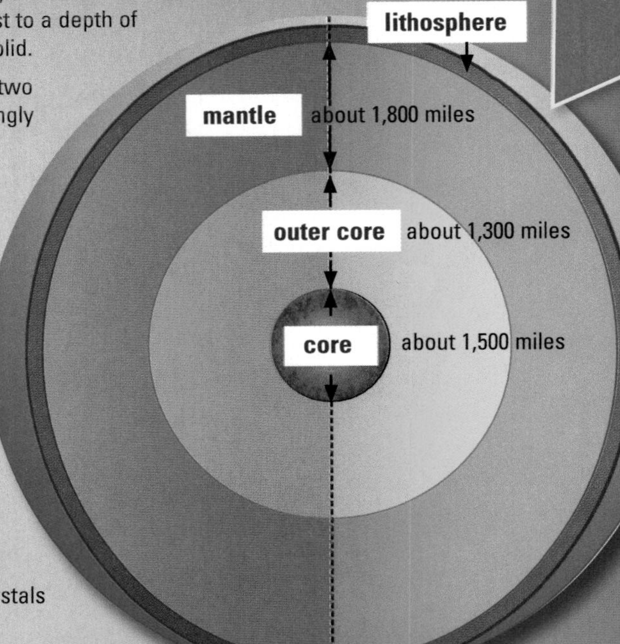

In 1996, after nearly 30 years of research, it was found that, like Earth itself, the inner core spins on an axis from west to east, but at its own rate, outpacing Earth by about one degree per year.

HOMEWORK TIP

There are three types of rock:

1 IGNEOUS rocks form from underground magma (melted rock) that cools and becomes solid. Granite is an igneous rock made from quartz, feldspar, and mica.

2 SEDIMENTARY rocks form on low-lying land or the bottom of seas. Layers of small particles harden into rock such as limestone or shale over millions of years.

3 METAMORPHIC rocks are igneous or sedimentary rocks that have been changed by chemistry, heat, or pressure (or all three). Marble is a metamorphic rock formed from limestone.

CONTINENTAL DRIFT

Earth's landmasses didn't always look the way they do now. The continents are always in motion. It was only in the early 20th century, though, that a geologist named Alfred Lothar Wegener came up with the theory of continental drift. Wegener got the idea by looking at the matching rock formations on the west coast of Africa and the east coast of South America. He named the enormous continent that existed more than 250 million years ago Pangaea. The maps below show how the continents have moved since then. They are still moving, athough most move no faster than your fingernails grow—about 2 inches a year.

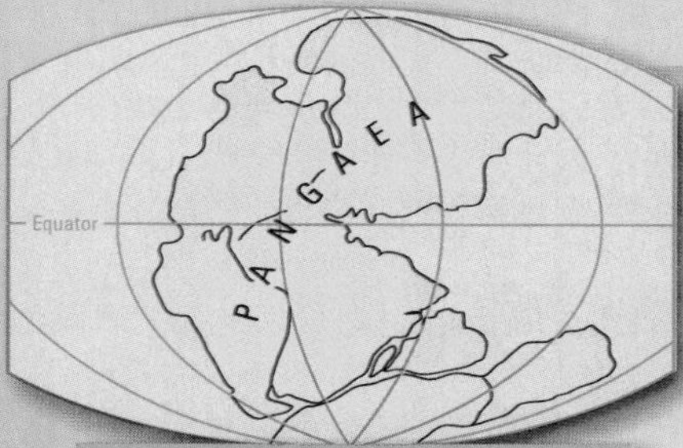

Permian
251 million years ago

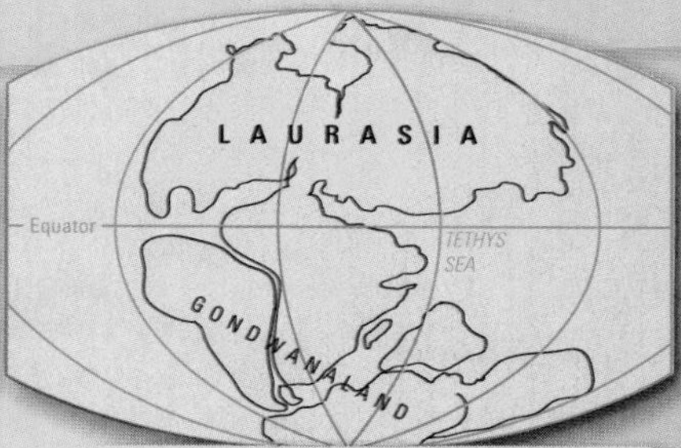

Triassic
200 million years ago

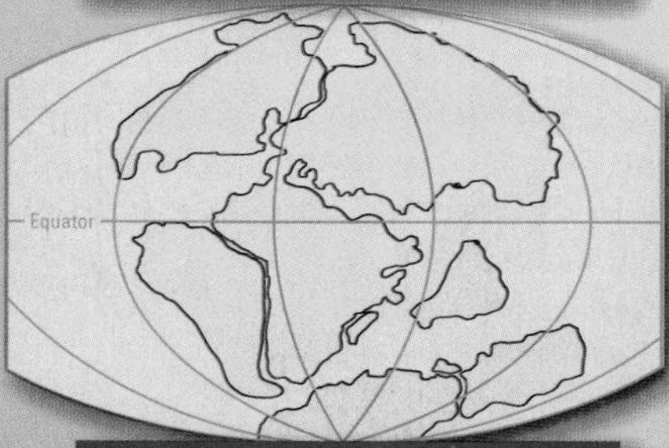

Jurassic
145 million years ago

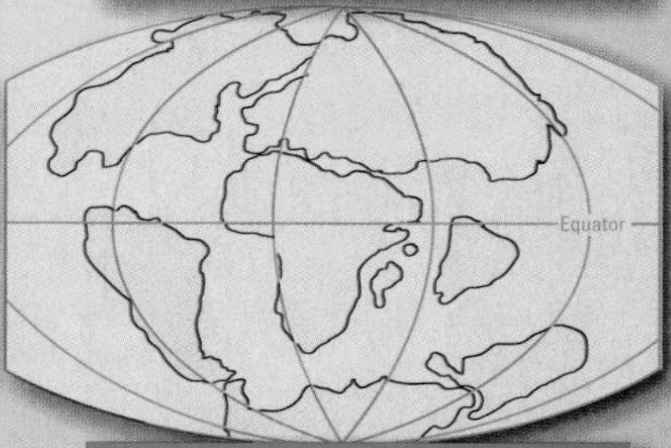

Cretaceous
65 million years ago

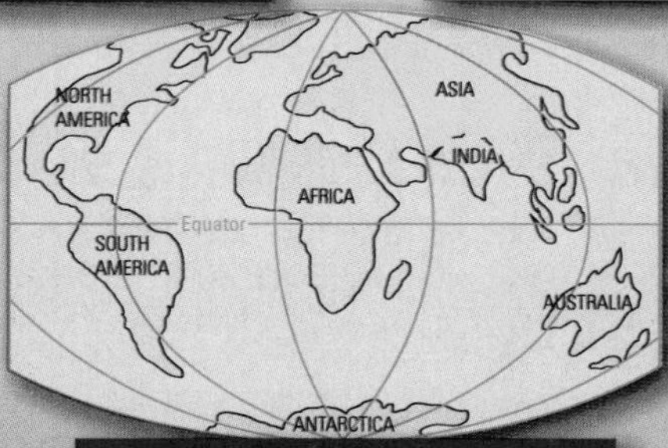

Present Day

HEALTH

→About how much does the human brain weigh? PAGE 105

KIDS' HEALTH ISSUES

ALLERGIES

Our immune systems protect us from harmful substances. Certain people's immune systems, however, try to fight off even harmless substances. Common **allergens**—the things people are allergic to—include dust mites, pollen from trees and grass, peanuts, shellfish, and cats, dogs, or other pets. If a person inhales, eats, or touches an allergen, he or she might have an allergic reaction. The person might look as if he or she has a cold or have trouble breathing. In severe cases, a person can die from an allergic reaction.

ASTHMA

About 9 million kids in the United States have **asthma**. Asthma is a condition that makes breathing difficult. It is caused when the airways narrow and can't carry as much air to the lungs. Allergens, polluted air, and exercise are some of the things that can trigger an asthma attack. Asthma can't be cured, but medication can help prevent or treat attacks.

EATING DISORDERS

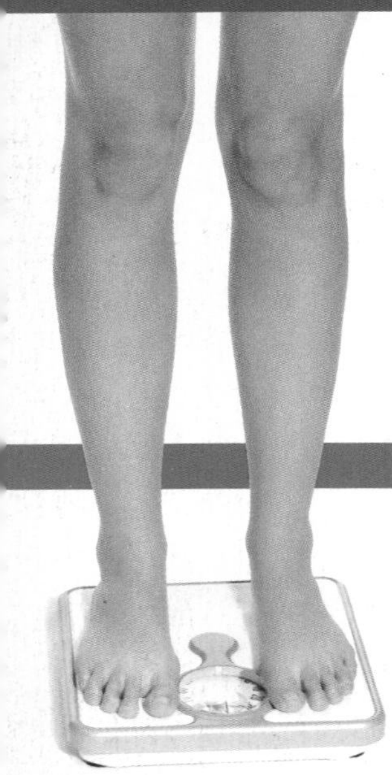

Many of the millions of Americans who have an eating disorder are teenagers. Some have **anorexia nervosa**, a condition in which the person has an overwhelming desire to be thin. **Anorexics** may think they are fat even when they are significantly underweight. They skip meals and drastically reduce the amount of food they eat. They lose so much weight that they endanger their health.

Other teenagers suffer from **bulimia nervosa**, also known as bulimia. **Bulimics** alternate between bingeing, when they eat huge amounts of food, and purging, when they empty their bodies of everything they've eaten. Unlike anorexics, most bulimics are of normal or above-normal weight.

OBESITY

Generally, someone who is significantly overweight is considered obese. Since 1980, obesity rates have tripled among kids in the United States. Nearly one in three kids today is overweight or obese. When people eat more calories than they burn off through physical activity, their bodies store the extra calories as fat. Being obese can lead to health problems, such as heart disease and diabetes.

BALANCE YOUR PLATE!

Do you want to make sure you're eating a well-balanced diet? Then follow MyPlate! The U.S. government created the MyPlate symbol to show kids and adults how to eat right.

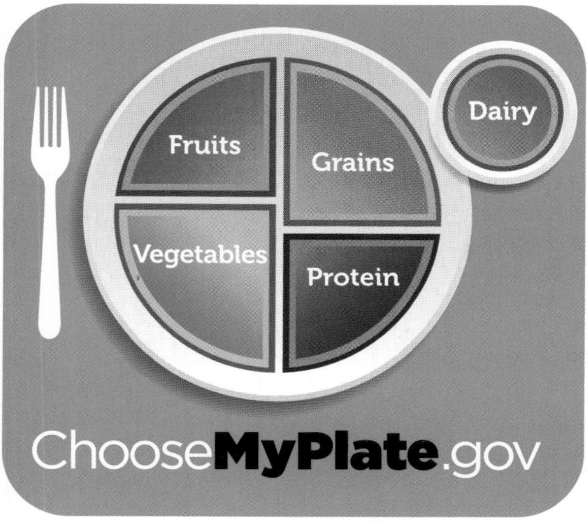

The large plate in the symbol is divided into four sections—fruits, vegetables, grains, and protein. The sections are different sizes to represent how much of each food group should be on your plate for a healthful meal. The small circle next to the plate stands for dairy foods, such as milk, cheese, and yogurt.

FOOD FOR THOUGHT

Check out these tips that go along with the MyPlate symbol to help people make healthful food choices.

BALANCING CALORIES

→Enjoy your food, but eat less.

→Avoid oversized portions.

FOODS TO INCREASE

→Make half your plate fruits and vegetables.

→Drink fat-free or low-fat (1%) milk.

→Make at least half your grains whole grains.

For more information, visit ChooseMyPlate.gov

FOODS TO REDUCE

→Compare sodium (salt) in foods such as soup, bread, and frozen meals—and choose the foods with lower numbers.

→Drink water instead of sugary drinks.

DID YOU KNOW? In 2011, MyPlate replaced the food pyramid, which had been used for nearly 20 years. Many nutrition experts thought the pyramid was confusing and didn't offer enough clear guidance on how much of different types of food to eat.

YOUR BODY

Know What Goes Into It

HOW TO READ A FOOD LABEL

Every food product approved by the Food and Drug Administration (FDA) has a label that describes its nutrients. For instance, the chips label on this page shows the total calories, fat, cholesterol, sodium, carbohydrate, protein, and vitamin content per serving.

A serving size is always defined (here, it is about 12 chips or 28 grams). This label shows that there are 9 servings per container. Don't be fooled by the calorie count of 140—these are calories per serving and not per container. If you ate the entire bag of chips, you would have eaten 1,260 calories!

Nutrition Facts

Serving Size 1 oz. (28g/About 12 chips)
Servings Per Container About 9

Amount Per Serving	
Calories 140	Calories from Fat 60
	% Daily Value*
Total Fat 7g	**11%**
Saturated Fat 1g	**5%**
Trans Fat 0g	
Cholesterol 0mg	**0%**
Sodium 170mg	**7%**
Total Carbohydrate 18g	**6%**
Dietary Fiber 1g	**4%**
Sugars less than 1g	
Protein 2g	

Vitamin A 0%	Vitamin C 0%
Calcium 2%	Iron 2%
Vitamin E 4%	Thiamin 2%
Riboflavin 2%	Vitamin B6 4%
Phosphorus 6%	Magnesium 4%

* Percent Daily Values are based on a 2,000 calorie diet. Your daily values may be higher or lower depending on your calorie needs:

	Calories:	2,000	2,500
Total Fat	Less than	65g	80g
Sat Fat	Less than	20g	25g
Cholesterol	Less than	300mg	300mg
Sodium	Less than	2,400mg	2,400mg
Total Carbohydrate		300g	375g
Dietary Fiber		25g	30g

Calories per gram:
Fat 9 • Carbohydrate 4 • Protein 4

WHY You Need To Eat:

Fats help kids grow and stay healthy. Fats contain nine calories per gram—the highest calorie count of any type of food. So you should limit (but not avoid) fatty foods. Choose unsaturated fats, like the fat in nuts, over saturated fats and trans fats, like the fat in doughnuts.

Carbohydrates are a major source of energy for the body. Simple carbohydrates are found in white sugar, fruit, and milk. Complex carbohydrates, also called starches, are found in bread, pasta, and rice.

Cholesterol is a soft, fat-like substance produced by your body. It's also present in animal products such as meat, cheese, and eggs but not in plant products. Cholesterol helps with cell membrane and hormone production, but there are two main types. Bad cholesterol, or LDL, gets stuck easily in blood vessels, which can lead to a heart attack or stroke. Good cholesterol, or HDL, helps break down bad cholesterol.

Proteins help your body grow and make your immune system stronger. Lean meats and tofu are good options.

Vitamins and Minerals are good for all parts of your body. For example, vitamin A, found in carrots, promotes good vision; calcium, found in milk, helps build bones; and vitamin C, found in fruits, helps heal cuts.

SOME FATTY FOODS

Ice cream
Doughnuts
Cheeseburgers
Chocolate candy
French fries

SOME LOW-FAT FOODS

Strawberries
Oatmeal
Plain popcorn
Carrots
Bell peppers
Apples

HAVE FUN GETTING FIT

WHY WORK OUT?

Exercise is a great way to prevent obesity and improve health. Children should get at least 60 minutes of exercise every day. Be sure to make exercise fun. Do yoga, bike, swim, shoot hoops, or play catch with a friend. The table below shows how many calories you'll burn from different types of activities.

HOW TO WORK OUT

→Begin with a five-minute warm-up! Warm-up exercises heat the body up so muscles are ready for more intense activity. Warm-up exercises include jumping jacks, walking, and stretching.

→After warming up, do an activity that you like, such as running or playing basketball with your friends. This increases your heart rate.

→After working out, cool down for 5 to 10 minutes. Cooling down lets your heart rate slow gradually. Walking is an example of a cool-down activity. Afterward, do some stretching. This helps your muscles remove waste, such as lactic acid, made when you exercise. Be sure to drink water during and after exercise.

→Building up strength through your workouts can be very beneficial. This doesn't mean you should lift the heaviest weights possible! It's better to do more lifts using light weights (1/2 lb or 1 lb) than fewer lifts with very heavy weights. Give your body time to recover between strength workouts.

ACTIVITY	CALORIES PER MINUTE
Racquetball	10
Jogging (6 miles per hour)	8
Martial arts	8
Basketball	7
Soccer	6
Bicycling (10-12 miles per hour)	5
Raking leaves	4
Skating or rollerblading (easy pace)	4
Swimming (25 yards per minute)	3
Walking (3 miles per hour)	3
Yoga	3
Playing catch	2

DID YOU KNOW?

Do you want to perform better in school? Then get up and go! Experts say that exercise not only keeps your body healthy but also boosts brainpower. Find fun ways to incorporate fitness into your day, such as taking the stairs instead of the elevator, walking your dog, or going on a nature hike.

BODY Basics

Your body is made up of many parts. Even though we are all individuals, our bodies share similar structures. These structures make up different systems in the body.

CIRCULATORY SYSTEM

In the circulatory system, the **heart** pumps **blood**. Blood travels through tubes, called **arteries**, to all parts of the body. Blood carries oxygen and food that the body needs to stay alive. **Veins** carry blood back to the heart.

DIGESTIVE SYSTEM

The digestive system moves food through the **esophagus**, **stomach**, and **intestines**. As food passes through, some of it is broken down into tiny particles called **nutrients**. Nutrients enter the bloodstream and are carried to all parts of the body. The digestive system changes whatever food isn't used into waste that is eliminated from the body.

ENDOCRINE SYSTEM

The endocrine system includes glands. There are two kinds of glands. **Exocrine glands** produce liquids such as sweat and saliva. **Endocrine glands** produce chemicals called **hormones**. Hormones control body functions like growth.

NERVOUS SYSTEM

The nervous system enables us to think, feel, move, hear, and see. It includes the **brain**, the **spinal cord**, and **nerves** throughout the body. Nerves in the spinal cord carry signals between the brain and the rest of the body. The brain has three major parts. The **cerebrum** controls thinking, speech, and vision. The **cerebellum** is responsible for physical coordination. The **brain stem** controls the respiratory, circulatory, and digestive systems.

RESPIRATORY SYSTEM

The respiratory system allows us to breathe. Air enters the body through the nose and mouth. It goes through the **windpipe**, or **trachea**, to two tubes called **bronchi**, which carry air to the **lungs**. Oxygen from the air is absorbed by tiny blood vessels in the lungs. The blood then carries oxygen to the heart, from where it is sent to the body's cells.

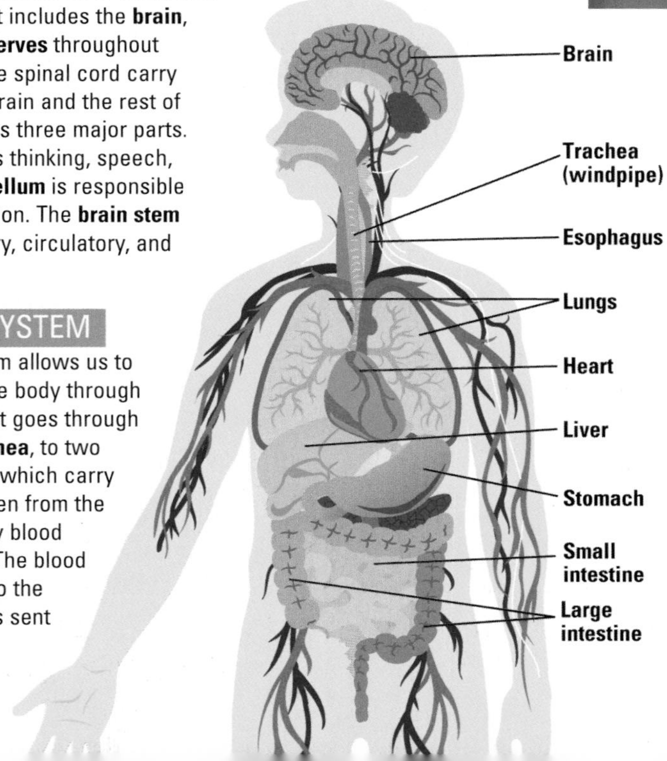

What the Body's Systems Do

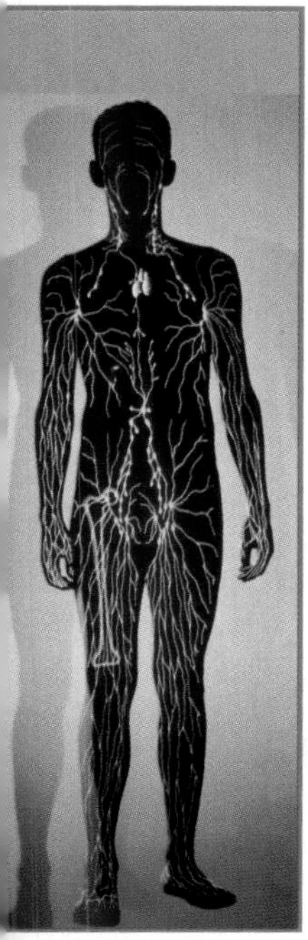

MUSCULAR SYSTEM

Muscles are made up of elastic fibers. There are three types of muscles. **Skeletal muscles** help the body move—they are the large muscles we can see. **Smooth muscles** are found in our digestive system, blood vessels, and air passages. **Cardiac muscle** is found only in the heart. Smooth and cardiac muscles are **involuntary muscles**—they work without us having to think about them.

REPRODUCTIVE SYSTEM

Through the reproductive system, adult human beings are able to create new human beings. Reproduction begins when a man's **sperm** cell fertilizes a woman's **egg** cell.

URINARY SYSTEM

This system, which includes the **kidneys**, cleans waste from the blood and regulates the amount of water in the body.

IMMUNE SYSTEM

The immune system protects your body from diseases by fighting against certain outside substances, or **antigens**. This happens in different ways. For example, white blood cells called **B lymphocytes** learn to fight viruses and bacteria by producing **antibodies** to attack them. Sometimes, as with allergies, the immune system makes a mistake and creates antibodies to fight a substance that's really harmless.

SKELETAL SYSTEM

The skeletal system is made up of **bones** that hold the body upright. It also gives your body its shape, protects your organs, and works with your muscles to help you move. Babies are born with 350 bones. By adulthood, some of the bones have grown together for a total of 206.

Brain Power

The typical human brain only weighs about three pounds. But it's like the control center of the body, responsible for making sure everything functions properly. Different parts of the brain do different things.

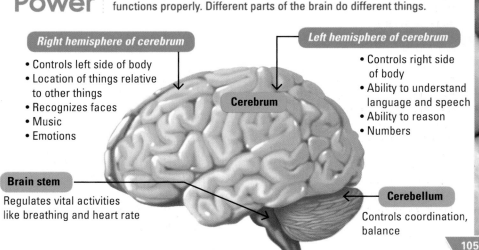

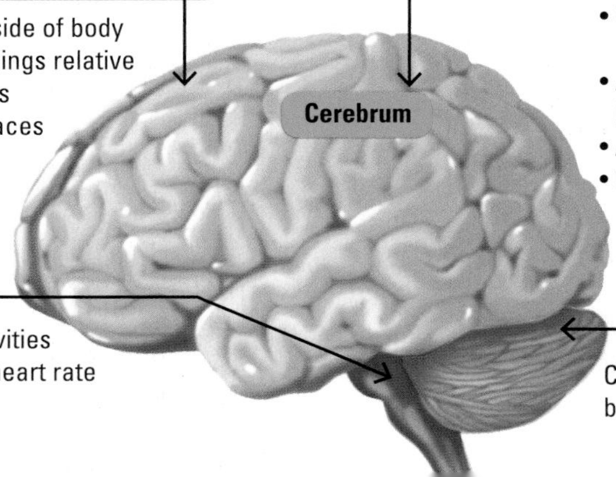

THE Five SENSES

Your senses gather information about the world around you. The five senses are **hearing**, **sight**, **smell**, **taste**, and **touch**. You need senses to find food, resist heat or cold, and avoid situations that might be harmful. Your ears, eyes, nose, tongue, and skin sense changes in the environment. Nerve receptors send signals about these changes to the brain, where the information is processed.

1 HEARING

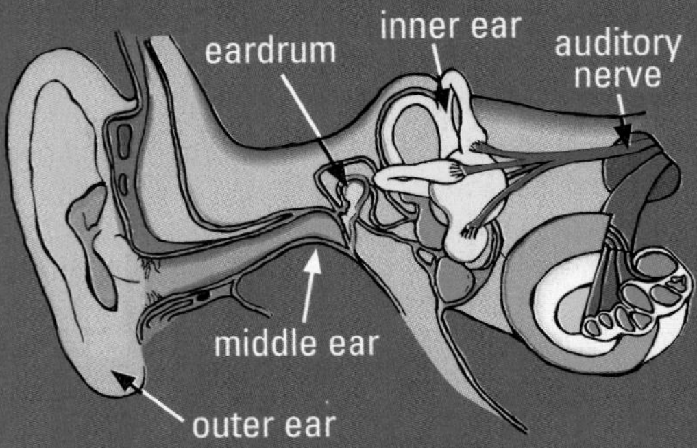

The human ear is divided into three parts—the outer, middle, and inner. The **outer ear** is mainly the flap we can see on the outside. Its shape funnels sound waves into the **middle ear**, where the eardrum is located. The **eardrum** vibrates when sound waves hit it, causing three tiny bones behind it to vibrate as well. These vibrations are picked up in the **inner ear** by tiny filaments of the **auditory nerve**. This nerve changes the vibrations into nerve impulses and carries them to the brain.

2 SIGHT

The **lens** of the eye is the first stop for light waves, which tell you the shapes and colors of things around you. The lens focuses light waves onto the **retina**, located on the back wall of the eye. The retina has light-sensitive nerve cells. These cells translate the light waves into patterns of nerve impulses that travel along the **optic nerve** to your brain, where an image is produced. So in reality, all the eye does is collect light. It is the brain that actually forms the image.

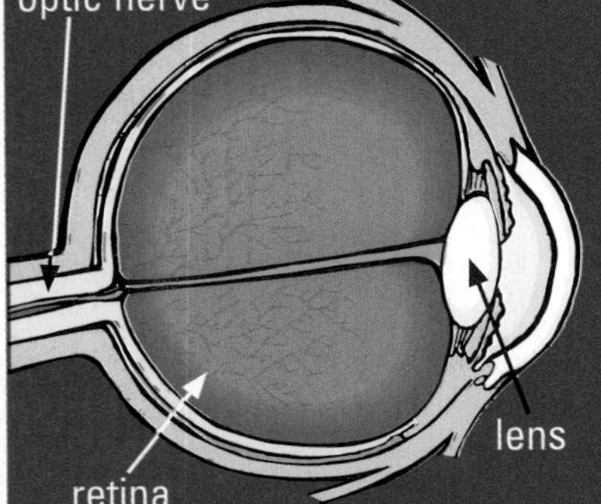

DID YOU KNOW? **Blinking cleans and moistens our eyes. Babies need to blink only about once every minute. By adulthood, people blink about 10 to 15 times a minute.**

3 SMELL

In our noses are nerve cells called **olfactory receptors**. Tiny mucus-covered hairs from these receptors detect chemicals in the air. These chemicals make what we call odor, or scent. This information then travels along the **olfactory nerves** to the brain. Nerves from the olfactory receptors connect with the **limbic system**, the part of the brain that deals with emotions. That's why we tend to like or dislike a smell right away. The smell can leave a strong impression on our memory, and very often a smell triggers a particular memory.

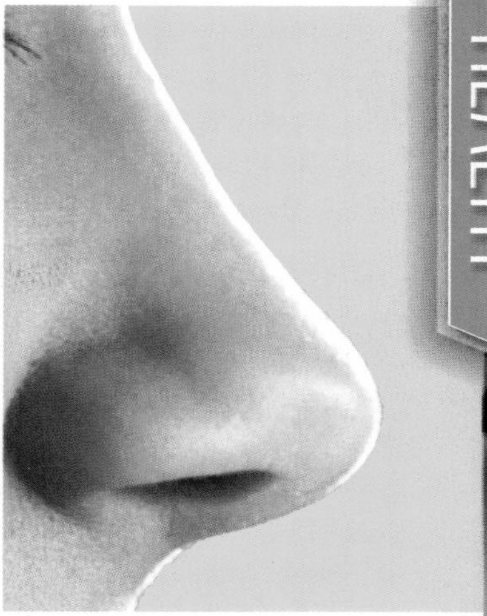

4 TASTE

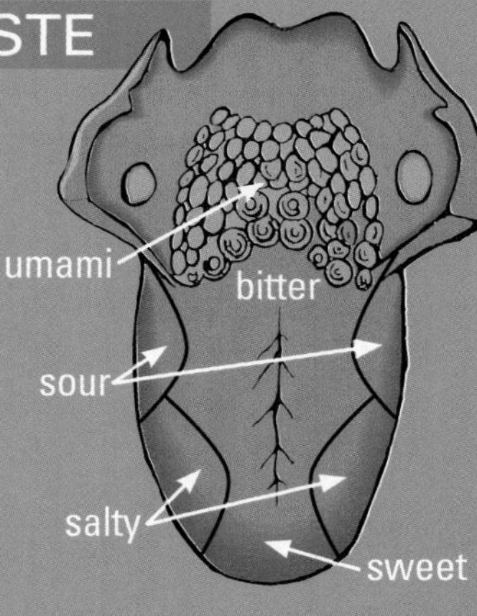

Taste buds are the primary receptors for taste. They are located on the surface and sides of the tongue, on the roof of the mouth, and at the back of the throat. These buds can detect five qualities—**sweet** (like sugar), **sour** (like lemons), **salty** (like chips), **bitter** (like coffee), and **umami** or savory flavors (like meat). Taste signals come together with smell signals in the same part of your brain. That's why you need both senses to get a food's full flavor.

5 TOUCH

Your sense of touch allows you to feel temperature, pain, and pressure. These environmental factors are all sensed by nerve fibers located in the **epidermis**, the outer layer of skin, and the **dermis**, the second layer of skin, throughout the body. As with all the other senses, nerves send information to the brain through the nervous system. The skin on your hands has more nerve endings than almost any other part of your body—about 1,300 in every square inch!

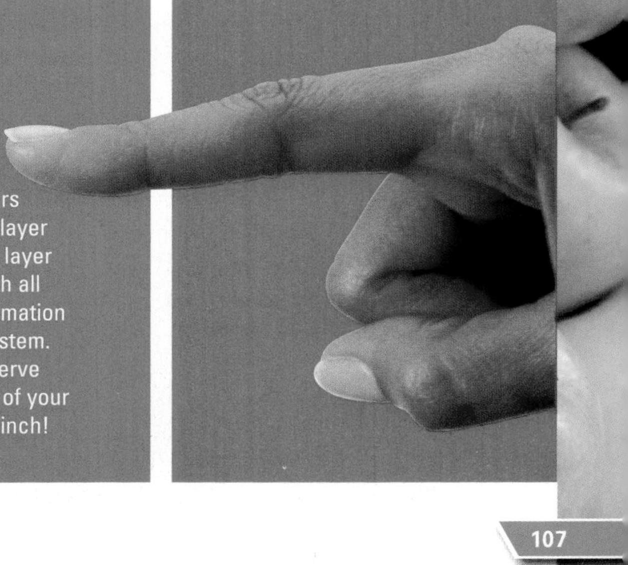

HOMEWORK HELP

→What is the difference between "its" and "it's"? PAGE 109

If you need to study for an exam or write a research paper, there are helpful hints in this chapter.

HOMEWORK TIP

There are many study and learning tips throughout *The World Almanac for Kids*. Look for the **"Homework Tip"** icon!

In other chapters, you can find lots of information on topics you may write about or study in school. **Facts About Nations,** pages 152–177, and **Facts About the States,** pages 292–309, are good places to look. For math tips and formulas, look up the chapter on **Numbers**. For good books to read and write about, see the **Books** chapter.

Those Tricky TESTS

GETTING READY

Being prepared for a test can relieve some of your jitters and can make test taking a lot easier! Here are some tips to help you get ready.

→Take good notes in class and keep up with assignments, so you don't have to learn material at the last minute!

→Make a study schedule and stick to it! Don't watch TV or listen to distracting music while studying.

→Start reviewing early if you can—don't wait until the night before the test.

→Go over the headings, summaries, and questions in each chapter to review key points. Read your notes and highlight the most important topics.

→Get a good night's sleep, and eat a good breakfast before the test.

THE BIG EVENT

Follow these suggestions for smooth sailing during test time:

→If you are allowed, skim through the entire exam so you know what to expect and how long it may take.

→As you start each part of the exam, read directions carefully.

→Read each question carefully before answering. For a multiple-choice question, check every possible answer before you decide on one.

→Don't spend too much time on any one question. Skip hard questions and go back to them at the end.

→Keep track of time so you can pace yourself. Use any time left at the end to go back and review your answers. Make sure you've written the answer you meant to select.

WHICH ONE DO I USE?

When you need to write answers for a school assignment or write a research paper, you'll want to be careful to use words correctly. There are many examples in English of two words (or even three) that sound alike but that mean different things. Words that sound alike but have different meanings are called **homonyms**. Here are a few.

Its/It's

Its is a possessive. That means that it shows ownership. For example:

➔ **Each sport has its own rules.**

It's, on the other hand, is a contraction of *it is*. For example:

➔ **It's time to leave for school.**

Affect/Effect

Affect is a verb that means *to change* or *to influence*. Here's an example:

➔ **Our picnic was affected by the rain.**

Effect is a noun that means *result* or *impact*. For example:

➔ **What effect did the rain have on your picnic?**

Principal/Principle

Principal means *most important*. For example:

➔ **What are the principal products of France?**

The head of a school is also usually called a *principal*.

A *principle*, on the other hand, is a standard or rule that people live by. For example:

➔ **An important principle stated in the Declaration of Independence is that all men are created equal.**

Compliment/Complement

A compliment is a flattering remark:

➔ **He paid me a nice compliment about my new dress.**

To *complement* something means to *complete* it or to *supply a needed portion* of it. Here's an example:

➔ **My partner's work on the research paper complemented my own efforts.**

They're/There/Their

They're is a contraction of *they are:*

➔ **They're coming to visit at noon.**

There refers to a place and means the opposite of *here*.

➔ **Put the dishes over there.**

Finally, the third form, *their*, is a possessive adjective and means *belonging to them*.

➔ **Where are their coats?**

Capital/Capitol

Capital means the city where a state or country has its government.

➔ **The capital of the United States is Washington, D.C.**

Capitol, on the other hand, is the name of the building where members of the government meet.

➔ **The U.S. Capitol is the building where Congress meets in Washington, D.C.**

How to Write a RESEARCH PAPER

Doing Research

To start any paper or project, the first thing to do is research.

- **Encyclopedias are a good place to start.** They give you an overview of the subject.
- **The electronic catalog** of your school or public library can help you find information. A librarian can assist you.

- You can also use **the Internet**.
- As you read each source, **write down the facts and ideas** that you may need. Note the title, author, and other key information about each source.

Writing It Down

The next step is to organize your facts. **Develop a rough outline** of your ideas in the order in which they'll appear. Then, write a draft of your paper. It should contain three main parts:

INTRODUCTION The paper's introduction, or first paragraph, explains your topic and your point of view on it. It should let readers know what to expect from your paper.

BODY The body of the paper develops your ideas. Use specific facts, examples, and details to make your points clear and convincing. Use separate paragraphs for each new idea, and use words and phrases that link one paragraph to the next so your ideas flow smoothly.

CONCLUSION Summarize your main points in the final paragraph.

Showing Your Sources

You may need to do a **bibliography** at the end of your paper. This is a list of all the sources you used to prepare the report. Here are some guidelines for how to cite commonly used types of sources.

FOR A BOOK: **Author. *Title.* City Published: Publisher, Year.**
Jones, Phil. *Science Foundations: Kingdoms of Life.* New York: Chelsea House, 2011.

FOR A MAGAZINE ARTICLE: **Author. "Article Title." *Magazine Title,* Date of Issue, Pages.**
Dybas, Cheryl Lyn. "Messengers from the Arctic." *Natural History,* February 2012, 30–37.

FOR ONLINE (INTERNET): **Author. "Entry Title." *Database Name,* Date of Publication. Database Company. URL (date accessed).**
Allard, Cat. "Salem Witch Trials." *Issues & Controversies in American History,* April 10, 2006. Infobase Publishing. http://icah.infobaselearning.com/issue.aspx?ID=107569 (accessed March 29, 2012).

RESEARCH ON THE INTERNET

USING LIBRARY RESOURCES

Your school or public library is a great place to start. It probably has a list (catalog) of its books and of periodicals (newspapers and magazines) available from computers at the library, or even from home over the Internet through your library's web site. You can search using **keywords** (words that describe your subject) in three basic ways: by **author**, by **title**, or by **subject**.

For example, doing a subject search for "Benjamin Franklin" will give you a list of books and articles about him, along with their locations in the library.

Your library may also subscribe to online reference databases that companies create especially for research. These are accessible over the Internet and could contain almanacs, encyclopedias, reference books, other nonfiction books, or collections of articles. You can access these databases from the library, and maybe even from home from your library's web site.

When you write your report, don't copy directly from books, articles, or the Internet—that's **plagiarism**, a form of cheating. Keep track of all your **sources**—the books, articles, and web sites you use—and list them in a **bibliography**.

Why shouldn't I just search the Internet?

The library's list may look just like other information on the Internet. But these sources usually have been checked by experts. This is not true of all the information on the Internet. It could come from almost anybody, and it may not be trustworthy.

When can I use the Internet?

The Internet is still a great way to look things up. You can find addresses or recipes, listen to music, or find things to do. You can look up information on hobbies or musical instruments, or read a magazine or newspaper online.

If you search the Internet on your own, make sure the web site you find is reliable. A U.S. government site or a site produced by a well-known organization is usually your best bet The addresses of these sites often end in *.gov* or *.org.*

USING A SEARCH ENGINE

The best way to find web sites is to use a search engine. Here are a few:

Yahoo Kids (kids.yahoo.com)
Kidsclick (www.kidsclick.org)
CyberSleuth Kids (cybersleuth-kids.com)

Start by typing one or two search terms—words that describe your topic. The search engine scans the Internet and gives you a list of sites that contain them. The results appear in a certain order, or **rank**. Search engines use different ways of measuring which web sites are likely to be the most helpful. The site that's listed first may not have what you want. Explore as many of the sites as possible.

INVENTIONS

→Who invented Popsicles? PAGE 113

INVENTION TIMELINE

YEAR	INVENTION	INVENTOR (COUNTRY)
105	paper	Cai Lun (China)
1440s	printing press/movable type	Johann Gutenberg (Germany)
1590	2-lens microscope	Zacharias Janssen (Netherlands)
1608	telescope	Hans Lippershey (Netherlands)
1714	mercury thermometer	Gabriel D. Fahrenheit (Germany)
1752	lightning rod	Benjamin Franklin (U.S.)
1783	parachute	Sebastien Lenormand (France)
1800	electric battery	Alessandro Volta (Italy)
1804	steam locomotive	Richard Trevithick (England)
1837	telegraph	Samuel F. B. Morse (U.S.), Charles Wheatstone (England), & William F. Cooke (England)
1842	anesthesia (ether)	Crawford W. Long (U.S.)
1870s	telephone*	Antonio Meucci (Italy), Alexander G. Bell (U.S.)
1879	practical lightbulb	Thomas A. Edison (U.S.)
1886	automobile (gasoline)	Karl Benz (Germany)
1892	moving picture viewer	Thomas A. Edison & William K. Dickson (U.S.)
1894	cereal flakes	Will Keith Kellogg (U.S.)
1897	diesel engine	Rudolf Diesel (Germany)
1923	television**	Vladimir K. Zworykin (U.S.)
1926	liquid-fuel rocket engine	Robert H. Goddard (U.S.)
1928	penicillin	Alexander Fleming (Scotland)
1930	packaged quick-frozen food	Clarence Birdseye (U.S.)
1933	FM radio	Edwin Armstrong (U.S.)
1939	jet airplane	Hans von Ohain (Germany)
1942	electronic computer	John V. Atanasoff & Clifford Berry (U.S.)
1955	TV wireless remote control	Eugene Polley (U.S.)
1957	digital image	Russell Kirsch (U.S.)
1971	CAT scanner	Godfrey N. Hounsfield (England)
1973	personal computer	André Thi Truong (France)
1975	digital camera	Steven Sasson (U.S.)
1989	World Wide Web	Tim Berners-Lee (England)
2007	iPhone	Apple (U.S.)
2012	computer eyeglasses	Google (U.S.)

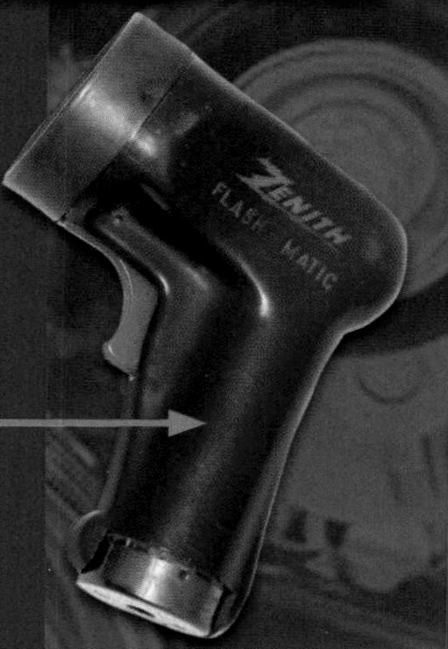

*Meucci developed a type of telephone (early 1870s); Bell received a patent for a telephone in 1876.

**Others who helped invent the television in the 1920s were Philo T. Farnsworth and John Baird.

They've Come a Long Way

Many inventions that changed our lives have also changed a great deal themselves over the years. Here are just a couple of examples.

Automobiles

What was the first automobile like? One of the earliest was a steam-powered tricycle, designed in 1769 by Nicholas-Joseph Cugnot of France. Karl Benz in Germany invented the first gasoline-powered car in 1886. Henry Ford's Model T came along in 1908. This low-priced five-seater had two forward speeds and oil lamps on the sides.

By the 1950s, U.S. manufacturers were producing large luxury cars with automatic features. When gas prices went up in the 1970s, Americans started buying smaller, more fuel-efficient vehicles, such as the Japanese-made Honda Civic. Advances in the next three decades included air bags, anti-skid brakes, and navigation systems.

Honda Civic, 1975

Environmental concerns have led to vehicles with new power sources. Today's engineers have developed electric, hybrid (gasoline and electric powered), and hydrogen-fueled cars. Some even run on vegetable oil! In the future, computer-controlled cars may drive themselves, navigating the way, moving at a safe speed, and avoiding other vehicles on the road.

Thermometers

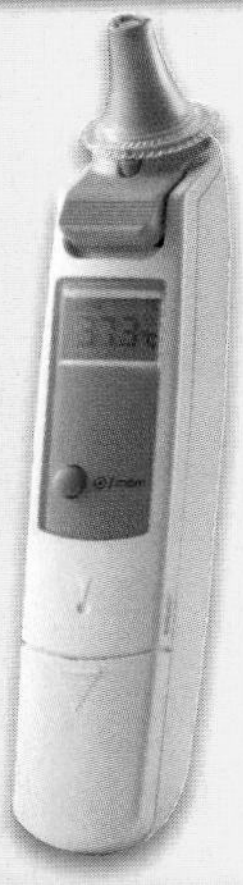

To measure a fever, you need a reliable thermometer. The earliest medical thermometers were large and slow to use. In 1866 in England, Sir Thomas Allbutt invented the first modern thermometer for patients. The device, 6 inches long, took about five minutes to get a reading. Like today's liquid thermometers, it had a glass tube with liquid in it that expanded as the temperature rose.

The latest thermometers are much faster and easier to use. It takes just one minute in the mouth for a dot-matrix thermometer—a single-use, plastic strip with a dotted grid—to check for fever. A digital thermometer records with an electronic sensor and works in a matter of seconds. An infrared one fits in your ear canal to measure eardrum temperature.

One day, perhaps you'll monitor your core temperature around the clock by swallowing a NASA-developed capsule. This thermometer pill of the future could help prevent heatstroke in athletes or improve surgeries.

DID YOU KNOW?

Many popular inventions were discovered by accident. In 1905, a young Frank Epperson left a stirring stick in his drink overnight, creating a frozen treat that he marketed as a Popsicle two decades later. Play-Doh modeling clay began in 1933 as a wallpaper-cleaning product. An accident even led to today's hockey puck. In 1839, Charles Goodyear spilled a rubber-sulfur mixture onto a hot stove, discovering a strong material called vulcanized rubber. The rubber, later used for bicycle and car tires, replaced the wood in hockey pucks in the late 1880s.

LANGUAGE

→What does *Buon compleanno!* mean? PAGE 115

TOP LANGUAGES

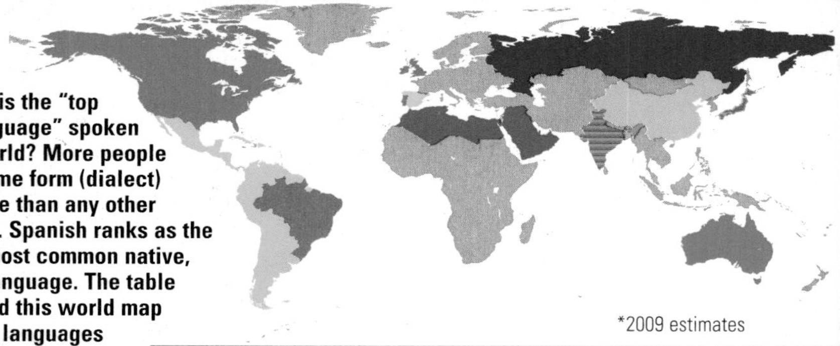

What is the "top language" spoken in the world? More people speak some form (dialect) of Chinese than any other language. Spanish ranks as the second most common native, or first, language. The table below and this world map show the languages with at least 100 million native speakers.*

*2009 estimates

LANGUAGE	KEY PLACES WHERE SPOKEN	NATIVE SPEAKERS
Chinese	China, Taiwan	1,213 million
Spanish	Latin America, Spain	329 million
English	U.S., Canada, Britain, Australia	328 million
Arabic	Middle East, North Africa	221 million
Hindi	India	182 million
Bengali	Bangladesh, India	181 million
Portuguese	Portugal, Brazil	178 million
Russian	Russia	144 million
Japanese	Japan	122 million

Which LANGUAGES Are SPOKEN in the UNITED STATES?

Most Americans speak English at home. But since the beginning of American history, immigrants have come to the U.S. from all over the world. Many have brought other languages with them.

The table below lists the most frequently spoken languages in the U.S. in 2010, according to the Census Bureau.

LANGUAGE USED AT HOME	SPEAKERS 5 YEARS AND OLDER
1 Speak only English	229,673,150
2 Spanish or Spanish Creole	36,995,602
3 Chinese	2,808,692
4 Tagalog	1,573,720
5 Vietnamese	1,381,488
6 French (including Patois, Cajun)	1,322,650
7 Korean	1,137,325
8 German	1,067,651
9 Arabic	864,961
10 African languages	862,441

LANGUAGE USED AT HOME	SPEAKERS 5 YEARS AND OLDER
11 Russian	854,955
12 Other Asian languages	839,294
13 French Creole	746,702
14 Other Indic languages	741,339
15 Italian	725,223
16 Portuguese or Portuguese Creole	688,326
17 Hindi	609,395
18 Polish	608,333
19 Japanese	443,497
20 Other Indo-European languages	435,615

LANGUAGE Express

Ciao!
(Italian)
Hello!
(English)
Salam!
(Arabic)

Surprise your friends and family with words from other languages.

English	Arabic*	Chinese	French	Italian
January	yanāyir	yi-yue	janvier	gennaio
February	fibrāyir	er-yue	février	febbraio
March	māris	san-yue	mars	marzo
April	abrīl *or* ibrīl	si-yue	avril	aprile
May	māyū	wu-yue	mai	maggio
June	yūnyū *or* yūnya	liu-yue	juin	giugno
July	yūlyū *or* yūlia	qi-yue	juillet	luglio
August	aġustus	ba-yue	août	agosto
September	sibtambir	jiu-yue	septembre	settembre
October	uktūbar	shi-yue	octobre	ottobre
November	nūfambir	shi-yi-yue	novembre	novembre
December	dīsambir	shi-er-yue	décembre	dicémbre
blue	asrag	lan	bleu	azzurro
red	ahmar	hong	rouge	rosso
green	akhdar	lu	vert	verde
yellow	asfar	huang	jaune	giallo
black	aswad	hei	noir	nero
white	abyad	bai	blanc	bianco
Happy birthday!	Eid meelad sa'eed!	Sheng-ri kuai le!	Joyeux anniversaire!	Buon compleanno!
Hello!	Salam!	Ni hao!	Bonjour!	Ciao!
Good-bye!	Ma salamah!	Zai-jian!	Au revoir!	Arrivederci!
fish	samakah	yu	poisson	pesci
bird	altair	niao	oiseau	uccello
horse	hisan	ma	cheval	cavallo
one	wahed	yi	un	uno
two	ithnaan	er	deux	due
three	thalatha	san	trois	tre
four	arba'a	si	quatre	quattro
five	khamsa	wu	cinq	cinque

*The line over a vowel indicates a long sound.

WEIRD LANGUAGE FACTS

A word in the English language pronounced the same way when the last four letters are removed is: *Queue*.

The only letter in the alphabet with three syllables is: *W*.

A word that contains ten words without rearranging any letters is: *Therein* (*there*, *in*, *the*, *he*, *her*, *here*, *ere*, *therein*, *herein*, and *rein*).

¡Say It in Español!

After English, Spanish is the most commonly spoken language in the U.S. Almost 37 million people speak Spanish at home. That's 12 percent of all people in the U.S.

Pronouncing Spanish Words

A	w**a**ter
E	b**e**t
I	f**ee**t
O	sl**ow**
U	t**u**be

In Spanish, the vowels only make one type of sound. The sound each vowel makes in Spanish is the same sound it makes in the English words at left.

Also, if you see the letters *j*, *g*, or *x* followed by a vowel, pronounce them like the English *h*. So, *frijoles* (beans) sounds like free-HOLE-lehs. *México* sounds like MAY-hee-co. The *h* in Spanish is always silent. So *hermano* (brother) sounds like er-MAN-o.

Try pronouncing the Spanish on this page.

Basic Spanish Phrases

Hello	Hola
Good-bye	Adiós
How are you?	¿Cómo estás?
Please	Por favor
Thank you	Gracias
What is your name?	¿Cómo te llamas?

Find the False Friends

Some Spanish and English words that look or sound the same have similar meanings. But some of these words can have very different meanings. They are called false friends. Can you spot which of these Spanish words have false friends? Check the answers to see if you're right!

bigote
blanco
carpeta
doctor
éxito
motel
piano

Answers: There are four false friends: *bigote* means "a moustache," not "a bigot"; *blanco* means "white," not "blank"; *carpeta* means "a folder," not "a carpet"; and *éxito* means "success," not "an exit." The other three words mean the same thing in Spanish and English: *doctor, motel*, and *piano*.

FOOD

At dinner, try asking your sister if she'd like more *ensalada*.

Your Bedroom
Es Su Dormitorio

Do you know what an *almohada* is? See if you can say and remember these items from a bedroom (*dormitorio*) in Spanish.

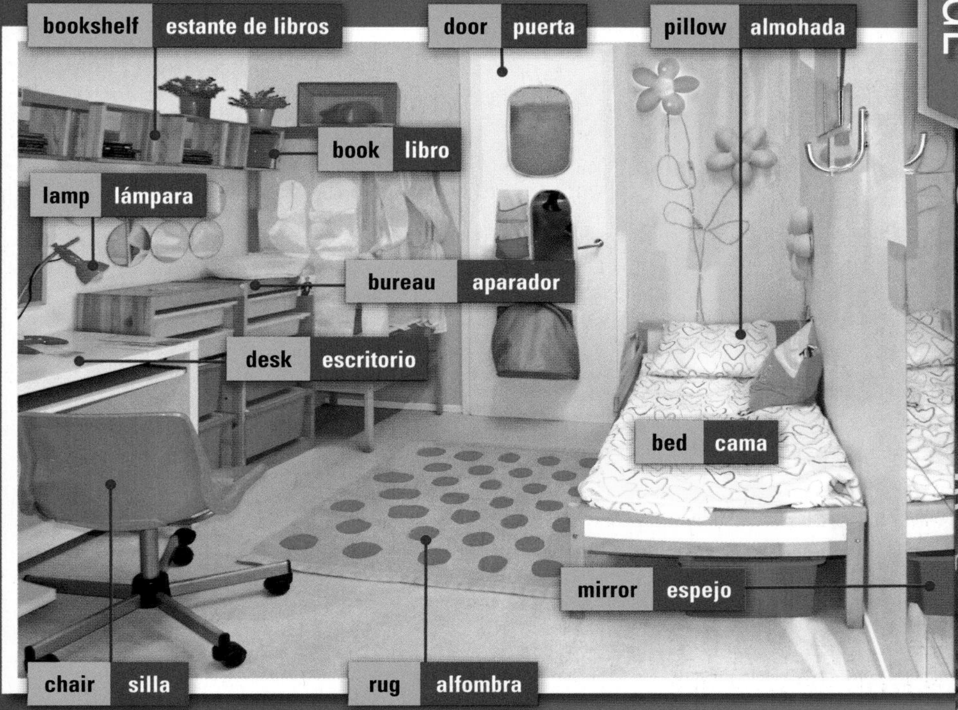

Numbers

1	uno	3	tres	5	cinco	7	siete	9	nueve
2	dos	4	cuatro	6	seis	8	ocho	10	diez

Joke en Español

PATIENT: *Doctor, doctor, no puedo recordar nada.*
(Doctor, doctor, I can't remember anything.)

DOCTOR: *Vaya, y desde cuando tiene usted este problema?*
(Wow, and how long have you had this problem?)

PATIENT: *¿Qué problema?* (What problem?)

The English Language

New Words

English is always changing as new words are born and old ones die out. Many new words come from the latest technology, from sports, or from slang.

bestie: a person's best friend

brain candy: widely appealing, undemanding entertainment

chillax: to calm down and relax

fist bump: a gesture in which two people greet each other or celebrate by bumping their fists together

retweet: to repost or forward a message posted by another user on the social networking service Twitter

walk-off: a hit that ends a baseball game immediately by causing the winning run to score for the home team in the last inning

FACTS ABOUT ENGLISH

- According to the *Oxford English Dictionary*, the English language contains between 250,000 and 750,000 words. (Some people count different meanings of the same word as separate words and include unusual technical terms.)
- The most frequently used letters of the alphabet are *e, t, a*, and *o*, in that order.
- The 30 most common words in the English language are: *the, of, and, a, to, in, is, that, it, was, he, for, as, on, with, his, be, at, you, I, are, this, by, from, had, have, they, not, or, one.*

IN OTHER WORDS: SIMILES

Similes are comparisons of two things that use "as" or "like." Here are some to wrap your brain around.

fresh as a daisy = "alert and ready to go." A well-rested, energetic person is often compared to a daisy, which opens its petals in the morning.

graceful as a swan = "smooth and elegant." Swans are admired for their long necks and the way they quietly glide through the water. Ballerinas are often compared to swans, with their extended, smooth movements on the stage.

cold as ice = "very cold, freezing." If your friend has been outside during winter without wearing gloves, you might describe her hands as being cold as ice.

Getting to the ROOT

Many English words and parts of words can be traced back to Latin or Greek. If you know the meaning of parts of a word, you can probably guess what it means. A **root** (also called a stem) is the part of the word that gives its basic meaning but can't be used by itself. Roots need other word parts to complete them: either a **prefix** at the beginning, or a **suffix** at the end, or sometimes both. The following tables give some examples of Latin and Greek roots, prefixes, and suffixes.

Latin

root	basic meaning	example
-alt-	high	*altitude*
-dict-	to say	*dictate*
-port-	to carry	*transport*
-scrib-/ -script-	to write	*prescription*
-vert-	turn	*invert*

prefix	basic meaning	example
de-	away, off	*defrost*
in-/im-	not	*invisible*
non-	not	*nontoxic*
pre-	before	*prehistoric*
re-	again, back	*rewrite*
trans-	across, through	*transatlantic*

suffix	basic meaning	example
-ation	(makes verbs into nouns)	*invitation*
-fy/-ify	make or cause to become	*horrify*
-ly	like, to the extent of	*highly*
-ment	(makes verbs inton nouns)	*government*
-ty/-ity	state of	*purity*

Greek

root	basic meaning	example
-anthrop-	human	*anthropology*
-bio-	life	*biology*
-dem-	people	*democracy*
-phon-	sound	*telephone*
-psych-	soul	*psychology*

prefix	basic meaning	example
anti-/ant-	against	*antisocial*
auto-	self	*autopilot*
biblio-/ bibl-	book	*bibliography*
micro-	small	*microscope*
tele-	far off	*television*

suffix	basic meaning	example
-graph	write, draw, describe, record	*photograph*
-ism	act, state, theory of	*realism*
-ist	one who believes in, practices	*capitalist*
-logue/ -log	speech, to speak	*dialogue*
-scope	see	*telescope*

MILITARY

➔Who is buried in the Tomb of
he Unknowns? PAGE 123

AMERICAN REVOLUTION

Why? The British king sought to control American trade and tax the 13 colonies without their consent. The colonies wanted independence from Great Britain.

Who? British vs. Americans with French support

When? 1775–1783

Result? The colonies gained their independence.

WAR OF 1812

Why? Britain interfered with American commerce and forced American sailors to join the British navy.

Who? Britain vs. United States

When? 1812–1814

Result? There was no clear winner. The U.S. unsuccessfully invaded Canada, a British colony. The British burned Washington, D.C., but were defeated in other battles.

DID YOU KNOW? Because news traveled slowly in the early 1800s, the last big battle of the War of 1812—the Battle of New Orleans—was fought in January 1815, two weeks after the war was ended by the signing of the Treaty of Ghent.

MEXICAN WAR

Why? The U.S. annexed Texas and wanted control of California, a Mexican province.

Who? Mexico vs. United States

When? 1846–1848

Result? Mexico gave up its claim to Texas and ceded to the U.S. California and all or part of six other Western states.

CIVIL WAR

Why? Eleven Southern states seceded from the U.S. The U.S. fought to keep them.

Who? Confederacy vs. Union

When? 1861–1865

Result? The United States remained a unified country. Slavery was abolished.

DID YOU KNOW? Although far from the South, Vermont was the scene of a small battle when Confederate cavalry coming from Canada raided the town of St. Albans.

SPANISH-AMERICAN WAR

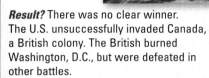

Why? The Americans supported Cuban independence from Spain.

Who? United States vs. Spain

When? 1898

Result? Spain lost the Philippines, Guam, and Puerto Rico to the U.S. Cuba became independent.

WORLD WAR I

Why? Colonial and military competition between European powers.

Who? Allies (including the U.S., Britain, France, Russia, Italy, and Japan) vs. Central Powers (including Germany, Austria-Hungary, and Turkey)

When? 1914–1918 (U.S. entered in 1917)

Result? The Allies defeated the Central Powers. An estimated 8 million soldiers and close to 10 million civilians were killed.

DID YOU KNOW? **World War I was the first conflict in which airplanes were used on a large scale. Flying "aces" (pilots) on both sides became famous for their boldness and bravery in combat.**

KOREAN WAR

Why? North Korea invaded South Korea. In many ways, the conflict was part of the Cold War between the Communist and non-Communist nations.

Who? North Korea with support from China and the Soviet Union vs. South Korea backed by the United States and its allies

When? 1950–1953

Result? The war ended in a stalemate. Korea remains divided.

DID YOU KNOW? **More than 5.7 million American troops served in the Korean War. Almost 140,000 of them were killed or wounded. And 136 people were awarded the Congressional Medal of Honor, the highest U.S. military award for bravery.**

WORLD WAR II

▲ ***U.S. troops land in France on D-Day***

Why? The Axis sought world domination.

Who? Axis (including Germany, Italy, and Japan) vs. Allies (including the U.S., Britain, France, and the Soviet Union). The U.S. did not enter the war until Japan attacked Pearl Harbor in 1941.

When? 1939–1945 (U.S. dropped atomic bombs on Hiroshima and Nagasaki in August 1945.)

Result? The Allies defeated the Axis. The Holocaust (the Nazi effort to wipe out the Jews and other minorities) was stopped. The U.S. helped rebuild Western Europe and Japan. The Soviet Union set up Communist governments in Eastern Europe.

VIETNAM WAR

Why? Communists (Viet Cong) backed by North Vietnam attempted to overthrow South Vietnam's government.

Who? North Vietnam and the Viet Cong with support from the Soviet Union and China vs. South Vietnam with support from the U.S. and its allies

When? 1959–1975

Result? The U.S. withdrew its troops in 1973. In 1975, South Vietnam surrendered. Vietnam became a unified Communist country.

DID YOU KNOW? **Ho Chi Minh, North Vietnam's leader for most of the war, had lived in the U.S. for a while in the early 1900s. Among other jobs, he worked as a baker at a Boston hotel.**

PERSIAN GULF WAR

Why? Iraq invaded and annexed Kuwait. It refused to withdraw despite United Nations demands.

Who? Iraq vs. U.S.-led coalition

When? 1991

Result? The coalition drove out Iraqi forces from Kuwait.

AFGHANISTAN WAR

Why? The U.S. demanded that the Taliban regime in Afghanistan turn over Osama bin Laden, the man who planned the 9/11 terrorist attacks in 2001.

Who? Taliban vs. Afghan forces, supported by the U.S. and its allies.

When? 2001–

Result? The Taliban was driven from power but later regained control over large parts of the country. In 2009 and 2010, President Barack Obama increased U.S. troop strength to around 100,000, but the U.S. announced plans to withdraw most troops by 2014.

IRAQ WAR

Why? The U.S. accused Iraq of hiding weapons of mass destruction (WMDs) and supporting terrorists.

Who? Iraq vs. United States, Great Britain, and their allies

When? 2003–2011

Result? Saddam Hussein's government was toppled. Hussein was captured, put on trial, and hanged. No WMDs were found. The U.S. withdrew the last American combat support troops in 2011, when the war was officially declared ended.

▲ ***Ceremony in Baghdad marking the end of the Iraq War***

DID YOU KNOW? **Between 2003 and 2011, more than one million members of the U.S. armed forces served in Iraq. Almost 4,500 U.S. troops were killed, and more than 32,000 were wounded. At the height of the war, the U.S. had more than 500 military bases around the country. That number had been reduced to two by the end of 2011.**

Top 10 Nations With Largest Armed Forces*

Rank	Country	Troops
1.	China	2,285,000
2.	United States	1,564,000
3.	India	1,325,000
4.	North Korea	1,190,000
5.	Russia	1,046,000
6.	South Korea	655,000
7.	Pakistan	617,000
8.	Iran	523,000
9.	Turkey	511,000
10.	Egypt	469,000

*Troops on active duty in 2011. Source: *The Military Balance*/International Institute for Strategic Studies.

The Military: *Mother of Inventions*

When you think about the military, you probably think of tanks, fighter planes, and submarines. But all kinds of inventions that have become part of everyday life were developed for use by the armed forces—to help the military carry out its missions or to help those who were injured while serving. Here are a few of those inventions.

ANESTHESIA Chloroform, an early anesthetic, was first widely used in the United States during the Civil War to keep wounded soldiers from suffering terrible pain as doctors treated their wounds. After the war, private civilian hospitals began using it. Soon the use of anesthesia during surgery and other medical procedures became widespread.

THE INTERNET An early version of the Internet—a system of connected computer networks—was developed for the U.S. military in the 1960s and 1970s. Called ARPAnet, it was used for military communications and transmission of information, and it was seen as a way to keep essential information from being destroyed in the event of an attack on any one military location.

PENICILLIN Although penicillin had been discovered in the 1920s, research on its ability to kill bacteria and on ways to make large amounts of it was spurred by World War II. Doctors were eager to find a drug that could prevent and treat infections in millions of wounded soldiers. By the end of the war, penicillin had saved the lives of countless soldiers, and soon after, it was widely being used by doctors worldwide.

MICROWAVE OVEN In World War II, a tube called a magnetron, which produces microwaves, was used by the Allies in radar to spot German planes. Soon after the war, a scientist working on improving radar systems noticed that a candy bar in his pocket had melted when he went near a magnetron. He experimented with other foods and found that they all got hot when near this type of tube. He created a metal box, fed the microwaves from the tube into it—and created the first microwave oven.

What Is the TOMB OF THE UNKNOWNS?

The Tomb of the Unknowns is in Arlington National Cemetery, just outside Washington, D.C. It was dedicated in 1921 to honor soldiers who had died fighting in World War I and whose remains could not be identified. One unidentified person is buried in the monument, sometimes called the Tomb of the Unknown Soldier. In later years, the remains of unidentified soldiers from World War II, the Korean War, and the Vietnam War were buried in nearby graves on the plaza in front of the monument. Advances in DNA testing enabled the Vietnam unknown to be identified in 1998. His remains have been removed.

MONEY

→Why have the pictures of people on paper money been made larger? PAGE 126

WORLD'S TEN RICHEST PEOPLE*

Name	Age	Country	Industry	Worth
Carlos Slim Helú†	72	Mexico	Communications	$69.0 billion
Bill Gates	56	United States	Software (Microsoft)	61.0 billion
Warren Buffett	81	United States	Investments	44.0 billion
Bernard Arnault	63	France	Luxury goods (LMVH)	41.0 billion
Amancio Ortega	75	Spain	Fashion	37.5 billion
Lawrence Ellison	67	United States	Data Management (Oracle)	36.0 billion
Eike Batista	55	Brazil	Mining, oil	30.0 billion
Stefan Persson	64	Sweden	Fashion (H&M stores)	26.0 billion
Li Ka-shing	83	Hong Kong	Diversified	25.5 billion
Karl Albrecht	92	Germany	Supermarkets (Aldi)	25.4 billion

*As of March 2012 (Source: www.forbes.com). †Includes other family members.

WORLD'S YOUNGEST BILLIONAIRES*

Name	Age	Country	Industry	Worth
Dustin Moskovitz	27	United States	Technology (Facebook, Asana)	$3.5 billion
Mark Zuckerberg	27	United States	Technology (Facebook)	17.5 billion
Prince Albert von Thurn und Taxis	28	Germany	Diversified investments	1.5 billion
Scott Duncan	29	United States	Inherited energy company	4.1 billion
Eduardo Saverin	30	United States	Technology (Facebook)	2.0 billion
Yang Huiyan	30	China	Property development	4.7 billion
Fahd Hariri	31	Lebanon	Technology, real estate	1.3 billion
Sean Parker	32	United States	Technology (Facebook)	2.1 billion
Ayman Hariri	33	Lebanon	Technology, real estate	1.3 billion
Robert Pera	34	United States	Technology (hardware developer)	1.5 billion

*As of March 2012 (Source: www.forbes.com).

WORLD CURRENCY

Most countries have their own currency. Sometimes two countries call their currency by the same name, but the money usually has different designs and may have different values. Most currency is decorated with cultural symbols and pictures of important people in the country's history. The designs are colorful and interesting, and they also make it harder to counterfeit the money.

An exchange rate is the price of a country's currency in terms of another. For example, one U.S. dollar cost, or could buy, 6.29 yuan in China in April 2012. These rates are based on a country's economy, the value of products it makes and buys, and inflation, the increase in how much money is needed to buy goods.

When people want to buy goods or services from someone in another country, they need to exchange their money for, or buy, some of the other country's currency.

THE EURO

Because Europe is so small and because many European countries wanted to make it easier for companies in one country to do business with companies in other countries, an organization was formed to find ways to eliminate barriers to trade. This organization, now called the European Union (EU), decided, among other things, to create one currency that could be used by many countries.

The euro, whose symbol is €, became the official currency of 12 EU members on January 1, 2002. As of mid-2012, the euro was used by 17 EU countries (see page 138). It was also used by agreement in six other countries.

HOW MUCH IS THE DOLLAR WORTH?

In April 2012, here is about how much one dollar could buy of 12 other currencies.

Amount	Currency	Amount	Currency
0.63	British pounds	82.25	Japanese yen
0.99	Canadian dollars	12.71	Mexican pesos ►
6.29	Chinese yuan	29.16	Russian rubles
0.75	euros	3.75	Saudi Arabian riyals
50.64	Indian rupees	1,122.85	South Korean won
3.72	Israeli new shekels	1.77	Turkish lira

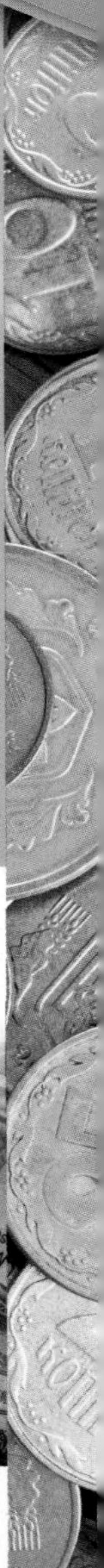

DID YOU KNOW? The first coins were made about 4,000 years ago. Because their value was determined by their weight, they weren't very convenient to carry around. Paper money was first used in China about 2,800 years ago.

What's New in Coins

The U.S. Mint is making one-dollar coins that show the faces of the presidents. The coins are being released in the order in which the presidents served in office. The Mint plans to issue four presidential $1 coins per year through 2016.

The new coins to be introduced in 2013 honor William McKinley, Theodore Roosevelt, William Howard Taft, and Woodrow Wilson. On the back of all the coins is an image of the Statue of Liberty.

The U.S. Mint is also releasing five new America the Beautiful quarters each year, honoring National Park Service sites and other "National Sites." The five quarters released in 2012 featured El Yunque National Forest, Chaco Culture National Historical Park, Acadia National Park, Hawaii Volcanoes National Park, and Denali National Park. ▶

For more information on all these coins, visit the U.S. Mint's website at *www.usmint.gov*

OUTSMARTING THE COUNTERFEITERS

In recent years, the U.S. government has increased its efforts to keep counterfeiters from making fake paper money that can pass for the real thing. Because today's laser printers and scanners have made it easier to make realistic copies of actual bills, the government has had to come up with new ways to stop counterfeiters. Among the techniques used by the government in $5, $10, $20, $50, and $100 bills made in recent years are watermarks that don't show up on scanned or copied bills and special inks that change color depending on the way light hits the money. The newer bills have fine lines in the background that copiers and scanners generally can't pick up. They also have enlarged portraits that include difficult-to-copy details. (The larger portraits have the added advantage of making it easier for visually impaired people to identify bills of different denominations.)

The U.S. $1 Bill: AN OWNER'S MANUAL

Everybody knows that George Washington is on the U.S. one-dollar bill, but did you ever wonder what all that other stuff is?

Plate position
Shows where on the 32-note plate this bill was printed.

The Treasury Department seal:
The balancing scales represent justice. The pointed stripe across the middle has 13 stars for the original 13 colonies. The key represents authority.

Serial number
Each bill has its own.

Plate serial number
Shows which printing plate was used for the face of the bill.

Federal Reserve District Number
Shows which district issued the bill.

Treasurer of the U.S. Signature

Series indicator
(year note's design was first used)

Secretary of the Treasury signature

(Since 1949, every Treasurer of the U.S. has been a woman.)

Federal Reserve District Seal

The name of the Federal Reserve Bank that issued the bill is printed in the seal. The letter tells you quickly where the bill is from. Here are the letter codes for the 12 Federal Reserve Districts:

A: Boston
B: New York
C: Philadelphia
D: Cleveland
E: Richmond
F: Atlanta
G: Chicago
H: St. Louis
I: Minneapolis
J: Kansas City
K: Dallas
L: San Francisco

Front of the Great Seal of the United States:
The bald eagle is the national bird. The shield has 13 stripes for the 13 original colonies. The eagle holds 13 arrows (symbol of war) and an olive branch (symbol of peace). Above the eagle is the motto "E Pluribus Unum," Latin for "out of many, one," and a constellation of 13 stars.

Plate serial number
Shows which plate was used for the back.

Back of the Great Seal of the United States:
The pyramid symbolizes something that lasts for ages. It is unfinished because the U.S. is always growing. The eye, known as the "Eye of Providence," probably comes from an ancient Egyptian symbol. The pyramid has 13 levels; at its base are the Roman numerals for 1776, the year of American independence. "Annuit Coeptis" is Latin for "God has favored our undertaking." "Novus Ordo Seclorum" is Latin for "a new order of the ages." Both phrases are from the works of the Roman poet Virgil.

MOVIES & TV

→Which actor will play Oz in 2013? PAGE 129

MOVIE & TV FACTS

SUPER RATINGS On February 5, 2012, more than 111 million Americans turned on their TVs to watch the New York Giants defeat the New England Patriots during Super Bowl XLVI. More than 114 million tuned in for the halftime special, which featured Madonna and Nicki Minaj. Super Bowl XLVI was the most-watched TV event in U.S. history.

BOX OFFICE *HUNGER* *The Hunger Games* hit theaters in March 2012. The film was a massive hit, becoming the first movie since 2009's *Avatar* to take the #1 spot at the box office for four weekends in a row. Its opening weekend made more money than any spring movie in history.

Madonna

ALL-TIME TOP ANIMATED MOVIES*

Rank	Title (Year released)	Gross (in millions)
1	*Shrek 2* (2004)	$436.7
2	*Toy Story 3* (2010)	415.0
3	*Finding Nemo* (2003)	339.7
4	*Shrek the Third* (2007)	322.7
5	*The Lion King* (1994)	312.9
6	*Up* (2009)	293.0
7	*Shrek* (2001)	267.7
8	*The Incredibles* (2004)	261.4
9	*Monsters, Inc.* (2001)	255.9
10	*Despicable Me* (2010)	251.5

ALL-TIME TOP MOVIES*

Rank	Title (Year released)	Gross (in millions)
1	*Avatar* (2009)	$760.5
2	*Titanic* (1997)	600.8
3	*The Avengers* (2012)	561.1
4	*The Dark Knight* (2008)	533.3
5	*Star Wars* (1977)	461.0
6	*Shrek 2* (2004)	436.7
7	*E.T. the Extra-Terrestrial* (1982)	435.0
8	*Star Wars: Episode I The Phantom Menace* (1999)	431.1
9	*Pirates of the Caribbean: Dead Man's Chest* (2006)	423.3
10	*Toy Story 3* (2010)	415.0

Source: © 2012 by Rentrak Corporation. Rankings are for movies rated G, PG, or PG-13.
*Through June 7, 2012, based on box office sales in the U.S. and Canada.

VIRAL VIDEO STARS

Many of today's stars, including Justin Bieber and Soulja Boy, first became famous through online videos. Anyone can upload videos to sites such as YouTube and Vimeo. Here are some examples of success stories.

Actor **LUCAS CRUIKSHANK** ▶ began putting videos on YouTube in 2008. His *Fred* video channel (based on a character named Fred Figglehorn) reached 1 million subscribers in its first year. The videos caught the attention of Nickelodeon producers. Cruikshank has now starred in three movies about Fred Figglehorn.

Professional dancer **MARQUESE SCOTT** has been posting videos online since 2003, but he saw his popularity explode when his dance to the song "Pumped Up Kicks" by Foster the People went viral in 2011. His videos have now received more than 45 million views. He has been featured in several commercials and performed on *The Ellen DeGeneres Show*.

MICHELLE PHAN began posting style and beauty tips on YouTube in 2006. Her videos—often featuring instructions set to music—caught on quickly. She has been featured in *Seventeen* magazine and on many popular fashion blogs. In 2010, she was hired as the official video makeup artist for Lancôme cosmetics.

HITTING THEATERS

IN THE SECOND HALF OF 2012

- Colin Farrell and Kate Beckinsale star in *Total Recall*. (August)
- Zachary Gordon stars in *Diary of a Wimpy Kid: Dog Days*, adapted from two books in the bestselling series. (August)
- Adam Sandler and Kevin James provide voices for the animated film *Hotel Transylvania*. (September)
- *Breaking Dawn: Part 2*, the final Twilight film, closes Edward and Bella's story. (November)
- Peter Jackson directs *The Hobbit: An Unexpected Journey*. (December)

...AND IN 2013

- James Franco plays the title role in *Oz: The Great and Powerful*, which hits theaters in March.
- Logan Lerman returns as Percy in *Percy Jackson: Sea of Monsters*, due in March. ▶
- Robert Downey Jr. and Gwyneth Paltrow star in *Iron Man 3*, coming in May.
- *The Hunger Games: Catching Fire* opens in November.

BOOKS to FILM

MOVIE: *The Hunger Games* (2012)
BOOK: *The Hunger Games* (2008)
by Suzanne Collins

Suzanne Collins is the author of three books known as The Hunger Games trilogy. The books are set slightly in the future and tell the story of a girl named Katniss Everdeen who must fight in a violent competition between kids. In 2012, the first book, *The Hunger Games*, was made into a movie starring Jennifer Lawrence and Liam Hemsworth. At least two more movies will follow.

MOVIE: *The Lorax* (2012)
BOOK: *The Lorax* (1971)
by Dr. Seuss

The Lorax is a picture book written and illustrated by beloved children's author Dr. Seuss. (Dr. Seuss was the pen name of Theodor Geisel.) The book tells the story of a small creature who "speaks for the trees." The movie version, released in 2012, expanded on the story to make it long enough for a full-length film. It featured the voices of Danny DeVito, Zac Efron, and Taylor Swift.

MOVIE: *Breaking Dawn: Part 1* and *Part 2* (2011 and 2012)
BOOK: *Breaking Dawn* (2008)
by Stephenie Meyer

Stephenie Meyer is the author of four books, known as the Twilight series, about Bella Swan, a girl who falls in love with a vampire named Edward Cullen. Each of Meyer's Twilight books has been made into a movie. As with the Harry Potter books, the last title in the series was made into two movies. Robert Pattinson, Kristen Stewart, and Taylor Lautner star in the films.

The Twilight Series

1 *Twilight* (book: 2005; movie: 2008)
2 *New Moon* (book: 2006; movie: 2009)
3 *Eclipse* (book: 2007; movie: 2010)
4 *Breaking Dawn* (book: 2008; movies: *Part 1*, 2011, and *Part 2*, 2012)

Top TV Shows in 2011-2012

FOR AGES 6-11

NETWORK	CABLE
1. *American Idol*	1. *Phineas & Ferb*
2. *The Voice*	2. *Kickin' It*
3. *The X Factor*	3. *Jessie*
4. *NBC Sunday Night Football*	4. *A.N.T. Farm*
5. *Wipeout*	5. *House of Anubis*

Glee

FOR AGES 12-17

NETWORK	CABLE
1. *The Voice*	1. *NFL on ESPN*
2. *American Idol*	2. *Family Guy*
3. *Glee*	3. *House of Anubis*
4. *Family Guy*	4. *Jessie*
5. *NBC Sunday Night Football*	5. *Victorious*

Source: © 2012, Nielsen. Top 5 programs with 10 telecasts or more, excluding motion pictures, September 19, 2011, through April 15, 2012.

MOVIES & TV WORD SEARCH

Find the name of each movie or TV show listed. The names may appear running up, down, forward, backward, or diagonally.

Names to Find:

- Total Recall
- American Idol
- Catching Fire
- Glee
- Victorious
- The Lorax
- Jessie
- Family Guy

X	Y	C	H	E	M	W	G	J	V	D	O	I	R	R
E	A	X	A	T	D	G	L	I	U	M	D	I	Q	R
I	Q	R	V	T	J	A	C	D	U	G	I	P	N	F
S	J	B	O	U	C	T	Q	M	R	H	K	S	T	B
S	C	U	G	L	O	H	M	N	V	H	D	O	W	T
E	B	J	C	R	E	U	I	E	T	G	R	S	X	O
J	A	D	I	C	N	H	Z	N	C	Z	V	G	R	T
H	D	O	W	K	Q	P	T	E	G	T	B	H	R	A
Y	U	G	Y	L	I	M	A	F	T	F	S	P	C	L
S	Y	G	E	T	L	R	B	S	T	K	I	X	D	R
A	M	E	R	I	C	A	N	I	D	O	L	R	T	E
P	L	X	W	X	M	N	I	P	K	E	N	T	E	C
G	D	S	Y	N	S	I	C	K	K	S	X	I	S	A
M	Q	L	C	U	W	O	K	E	A	K	B	V	D	L
R	W	H	V	P	H	Q	F	S	P	B	B	V	K	L

ANSWERS ON PAGES 334-336.

MUSIC & DANCE

→ Who is the youngest member of the Grand Ole Opry? PAGE 133

TOP ALBUMS OF 2011

1. *21* .... Adele
2. *Speak Now* .... Taylor Swift
3. *Born This Way* .... Lady Gaga
4. *My Kinda Party* .... Jason Aldean
5. *The Gift* .... Susan Boyle
6. *Tha Carter IV* .... Lil Wayne
7. *Pink Friday* .... Nicki Minaj
8. *Sigh No More* .... Mumford & Sons
9. *Loud* .... Rihanna
10. *Teenage Dream* .... Katy Perry

Source: *Billboard 200*/The Nielsen Company

All About AMERICAN IDOL

American Idol has been popular since the show's first season, which aired in 2002. The program's goal is to discover the best new singer in the country. Auditions are held across the United States. The show's judges select a group of semifinalists, who sing each week on the program. Then, viewers vote by phone or text message to decide who advances or who goes home. Eventually, only two finalists are left to compete for the title of American Idol. In 2012, the winner was **Phillip Phillips**. Many past winners, and also runners-up, have gone on to become stars. Winners from previous seasons are Kelly Clarkson, Ruben Studdard, Fantasia Barrino, Carrie Underwood, Taylor Hicks, Jordin Sparks, David Cook, Kris Allen, Lee DeWyze, and Scotty McCreery. Among the most successful runners-up are Katharine McPhee, Chris Daughtry, and Jennifer Hudson. *American Idol*'s host, Ryan Seacrest, has also gained international fame from the show.

WHO'S HOT NOW?

CARRIE UNDERWOOD

BORN: March 10, 1983, in Checotah, Oklahoma

ALBUMS: *Some Hearts* (2005), *Carnival Ride* (2007), *Play On* (2009), *Good Girl* (2012)

Singer-songwriter Carrie Underwood grew up in rural Oklahoma, where she sang in church and local talent competitions. She also played the guitar and piano. During her senior year at Northeastern State College, where she was studying journalism, she auditioned for *American Idol*. She went on to become the first country singer to win the competition. Her first album, *Some Hearts*, featured the hit songs "Jesus, Take the Wheel" and "Before He Cheats." *Some Hearts* was the best-selling solo female debut album in country music history. Underwood's success continued with *Carnival Ride, Play On*, and *Good Girl*. She also took on acting roles in *How I Met Your Mother* and the movie *Soul Surfer*. Underwood is currently the youngest member of country music's prestigious Grand Ole Opry.

JUSTIN BIEBER

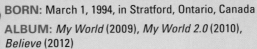

BORN: March 1, 1994, in Stratford, Ontario, Canada

ALBUM: *My World* (2009), *My World 2.0* (2010), *Believe* (2012)

Canadian-born Justin Bieber was interested in music from a very young age, and he taught himself to play several musical instruments. When he was 12 years old, he took second place in a local talent competition. His mother posted a video of his performance online, and she followed it with more clips as he began to build a fan following. R&B singer Usher signed Bieber to his record label and became a mentor to the young singer. Bieber's first album, *My World*, was a smash hit. He followed with the successful albums *My World 2.0* and *Believe*, along with a popular 3-D concert movie, *Justin Bieber: Never Say Never*. The video for his song "Baby" is one of the most watched YouTube clips of all time.

Dancing With the Stars

Dancing With the Stars is a popular reality-competition show that pairs celebrities with professional dancers. Each pair dances live on the show every week. The dancers receive scores and advice from three judges. Viewers also cast their votes. Past celebrity winners have included singer Nicole Scherzinger, racecar driver Hélio Castroneves, and figure skater Kristi Yamaguchi.

The winner of the show's 14th season were football player Donald Driver and professional dancer Peta Murgatroyd. ▶

Dancing Around the World

All over the world, different cultures enjoy dance in celebrations and performances, or just for recreation and to stay healthy—dancing can be great exercise. Here are just a few of the types of dance that trace their roots back to particular cultures.

◀ **STEP DANCING** is performed in many different cultures, but it is especially popular in Ireland. Irish step dancing involves quick movements of the feet and legs. The upper body is usually kept stiff. The dance can be seen in the touring show *Riverdance* and in the movie *Titanic*.

BALLET began in Italy in the 15th century. It quickly spread to France, where it became very popular. Ballet is a formal type of dancing, usually performed to classical music. The first ballet dancers did not wear the traditional tights and tutus seen today, but they did create the five basic positions of ballet that are still used.

TANGO dancing goes with a special type of music, also called tango. The exact origins of tango are not known, but it became popular in Argentina in the late 1800s. Tango is a type of ballroom dance involving quick, precise movements. It is typically performed by couples.

Musical INSTRUMENTS

There are many kinds of musical instruments. Instruments in an orchestra are divided into four groups, or sections: string, woodwind, brass, and percussion.

PERCUSSION instruments make sounds when they are struck. They include **drums**, cymbals, triangles, gongs, bells, and xylophones. Keyboard instruments, like the piano, are sometimes included in percussion instruments.

WOODWINDS are cylindrical and hollow inside. They make sounds when air is blown into them. The clarinet, **flute**, oboe, bassoon, and piccolo are woodwinds.

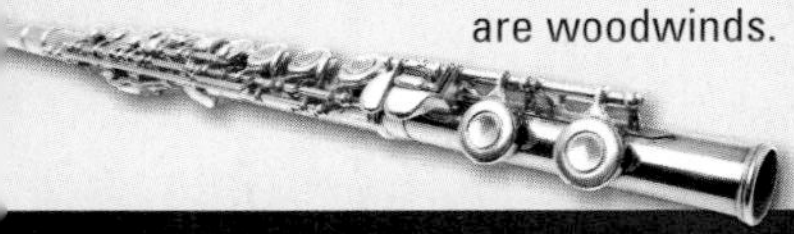

STRING instruments make sounds when the strings are either stroked with a bow or plucked with the fingers. The **violin**, viola, cello, bass, and harp are used in an orchestra. The guitar, banjo, and mandolin are other stringed instruments.

BRASSES are hollow inside. They make sounds when air is blown into a mouthpiece. The trumpet, French horn, trombone, and **tuba** are brasses.

DID YOU KNOW? Many of today's actors and actresses got their start singing and dancing in Broadway plays when they were kids. Actress Sarah Jessica Parker played the lead role in *Annie* when she was 13 years old. Because Broadway plays are usually shown eight times a week, several kids are often cast for the same part. This allows the actors to split up the performances and have more time for schoolwork.

MYTHOLOGY

→What was Hercules's most famous deed? PAGE 137

MYTHS OF THE GREEKS

Poseidon/Neptune

The Ancient Greeks believed that a big family of gods and goddesses watched over them from Mount Olympus. Farmers planting crops, sailors crossing the sea, and poets writing verses thought that these powerful beings could help or harm them. Stories about the gods and goddesses are called myths.

After the Romans conquered Greece, in 146 B.C., they adopted Greek myths but gave Roman names to the main gods and goddesses. Except for Earth, the planets in our solar system are named after Roman or Greek gods.

Greek & Roman Gods

The family of Greek and Roman gods and goddesses was large. Some of the most important gods, who lived on Mount Olympus, are listed here. Those with an * are children of Zeus (Jupiter).

Greek Name	Roman Name	Description
Aphrodite	Venus	Goddess of beauty and of love
*Apollo	Apollo	God of prophecy, music, and medicine
*Ares	Mars	God of war; protector of the city
*Artemis	Diana	Goddess of the Moon and of the hunt
*Athena	Minerva	Goddess of wisdom and of war
Cronus	Saturn	Father of Zeus (Jupiter), Poseidon (Neptune), Hades (Pluto), Hera (Juno), and Demeter (Ceres)
Demeter	Ceres	Goddess of crops and harvest, sister of Zeus (Jupiter)
*Dionysus	Bacchus	God of wine, dancing, and theater
Hades	Pluto	Ruler of the Underworld, brother of Zeus (Jupiter)
Hephaestus	Vulcan	God of fire
Hera	Juno	Queen of the gods, wife of Zeus (Jupiter), goddess of marriage
*Hermes	Mercury	Messenger god, had winged helmet and sandals
Poseidon	Neptune	God of the sea and of earthquakes, brother of Zeus (Jupiter)
Zeus	Jupiter	Sky god (grandson of Uranus), ruler of gods and mortals

DID YOU KNOW? **According to one legend about Apollo, he entered a music contest. One of the listeners thought Apollo did not play well enough to win. Apollo got so angry that he turned the listener's ears into donkey ears.**

MAKING SENSE OF THE WORLD

Re

Myths were once thought to be true. Most ancient peoples explained many things in nature by referring to gods and heroes with superhuman qualities. To the Greeks, a rough sea meant that **POSEIDON** was angry. Lightning was **THOR'S** hammer in Norse mythology. Egyptians worshipped the sun god **RE**, who sailed across the sky in a ship each day. In Japan, **AMATERASU** was the Shinto sun goddess who gave light to the land. Her brother **SUSANOO** was the storm god who ruled the sea.

There are even stories of gods or heroes who chose brain over brawn to get what they wanted. **COYOTE** was wild and cunning, a true trickster for many Native American tribes throughout the West. He was usually a loner and was never simply good or bad. **ANANSI** was a spider in the stories of the Akan tribes of West Africa. The tiny spider used his wits to capture the hornet, python, and leopard. In return, the sky god **NYAME** let him own every story ever told.

Myths have remained popular long after people knew they weren't true because the stories hold important life lessons and morals for cultures around the world. Myths have also inspired countless stories and works of art.

GREEK & ROMAN HEROES

Besides stories about the gods, Greek and Roman mythology has many stories about other heroes with amazing qualities.

ODYSSEUS, the king of Ithaca, was a hero of the Trojan War in the epic poem the *Iliad*. It was his idea to build a huge wooden horse, hide Greek soldiers inside, and smuggle them into the city of Troy to capture it. The long poem the *Odyssey* is the story of his long and magical trip home after the war.

PANDORA was the first woman created by the Greek gods. Zeus ordered Hephaestus to create a beautiful woman out of earth. All the gods on Olympus gave her gifts. Hera's gift was curiosity. When Pandora was finished, she received a box that she was never to open. But, because of her curiosity, Pandora could not resist. She opened the box and released all the evil spirits into the world.

JASON and the Argonauts set out on a quest to find the golden fleece so that Jason could reclaim his rightful throne. Among the Argonauts were Herakles and Orpheus. After many adventures and with the help of Medea, Jason slew the Minotaur and claimed the fleece. He later betrayed Medea and eventually died when a beam from his ship, the Argo, fell off and hit him on the head.

HERCULES, or Herakles, was said to have superhuman strength. The most famous of his deeds were his 12 labors. They included killing the **Hydra**, a many-headed monster, and capturing the three-headed dog **Cerberus**, who guarded the gates of the Underworld. Hercules was so great a hero that the gods granted him immortality. When his body lay on his funeral pyre, Athena came and carried him off to Mount Olympus in her chariot.

Pandora

NATIONS

→What are Canada's two national sports? PAGE 156

GOVERNMENTS

As of 2012, there were 196 independent nations, with various kinds of governments.

Totalitarianism In **totalitarian** countries, the rulers have strong power, and the people have little freedom. Elections are controlled, so that people do not have a real choice. North Korea is an example of a totalitarian country.

Monarchy A **monarchy** is a country headed by a king or queen (or occasionally by a ruler with a different title), who usually has inherited the title from a parent or other relative. There still are some monarchies in the world today. The United Kingdom (Great Britain) is one.

Democracy The word **democracy** comes from the Greek words *demos* ("people") and *kratos* ("rule"). In modern democracies, people govern themselves through the leaders they choose in elections. The United States and many other countries are democracies. Some monarchies, like the United Kingdom, are also democracies because the main decisions are actually made by elected leaders.

THE EUROPEAN UNION (EU)

The EU is a group of nations with a total population of over 500 million people. In 2012, the EU included 27 countries. It will have 28 members by 2013, if Croatia joins, as expected. Each nation is still independent, but the organization is like a super-government.

- The European Union has many policies all member nations must follow.
- The EU has its own flag and anthem.
- Leaders from the EU countries meet regularly to help set common policies.
- The Council of the European Union (with one representative from each nation) and the European Parliament (with 736 elected members) help make laws.
- A Court of Justice interprets laws and resolves disputes between members.
- Citizens can move freely from one EU country to another, to live and work.
- Goods can be traded freely between member countries.

As of mid-2012, 17 of the member nations had a common currency, known as the euro.

EU Members 2012

Austria*	Germany*	Netherlands*
Belgium*	Greece*	Poland
Bulgaria	Hungary	Portugal*
Cyprus*	Ireland*	Romania
Czech Republic	Italy*	Slovakia*
Denmark	Latvia	Slovenia*
Estonia*	Lithuania	Spain*
Finland*	Luxembourg*	Sweden
France*	Malta *	United Kingdom

***People in these countries used the euro as of mid-2012.**

A COMMUNITY OF NATIONS

The UN emblem shows the world surrounded by olive branches of peace.

The **United Nations** was founded after World War II to help promote peace and cooperation among nations. Representatives from 50 countries had met in San Francisco, California, in June 1945, to sign the UN Charter, and the world organization officially came into existence on October 24, 1945. By 2012, the UN had 193 member nations. Kosovo, Taiwan, and Vatican City were not members.

How the UN Is Organized

- **GENERAL ASSEMBLY** **What It Does:** Discusses world problems, admits new members, appoints the secretary-general, decides the UN budget. **Members:** All UN members; each country has one vote.
- **SECURITY COUNCIL** **What It Does:** Handles questions of peace and security. **Members:** Five permanent members (China, France, the United Kingdom, Russia, and the United States) who must all vote the same way before certain proposals can pass; ten elected by the General Assembly to two-year terms. In 2012, the ten temporary members were Colombia, Germany, India, Portugal, and South Africa (terms ending December 31, 2012) and Azerbaijan, Guatemala, Morocco, Pakistan, and Togo (terms ending December 31, 2013).
- **ECONOMIC AND SOCIAL COUNCIL** **What It Does:** Deals with issues related to economic development, population, education, health, and human rights. **Members:** 54 member countries elected to three-year terms.
- **INTERNATIONAL COURT OF JUSTICE (WORLD COURT)** located in The Hague, Netherlands. **What It Does:** UN court for disputes between countries. **Members:** 15 judges, each from a different country, elected to nine-year terms.
- **SECRETARIAT** **What It Does:** Carries out the UN's day-to-day operations. **Members:** UN staff, headed by the secretary-general.

For more information, go to ***www.un.org***

What Is WHO?

The World Health Organization (WHO) is part of the UN. It was created in 1948 to help promote the highest possible level of health for people around the world. One of its most important roles is to keep track of disease epidemics, get vaccines to people who may be in danger, and help countries treat those who get sick. WHO provides information and aid to countries so they can develop the best health policies and give people access to quality health care. The agency also tries to promote good health habits worldwide and help provide healthful living conditions, including access to clean water.

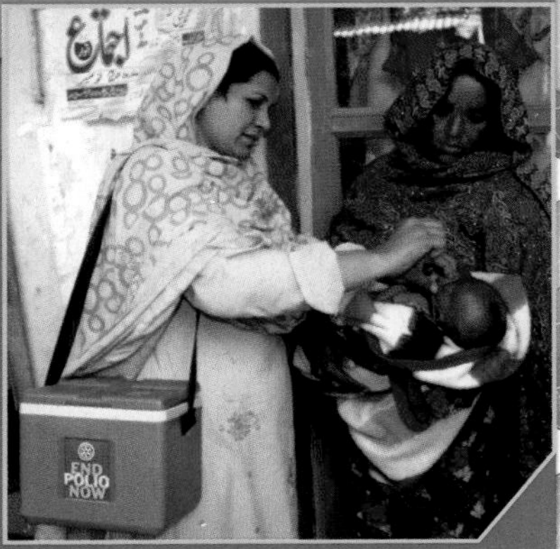

MAPS SHOWING NATIONS OF THE WORLD

Maps showing the continents and nations of the world appear on pages 140-151. Flags of the nations appear on pages 152-177. A map of the United States appears on pages 288-289.

PACIFIC ISLANDS

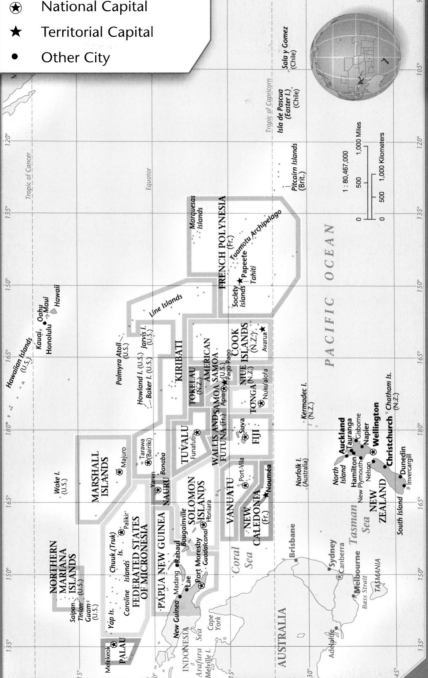

- ⍟ National Capital
- ★ Territorial Capital
- • Other City

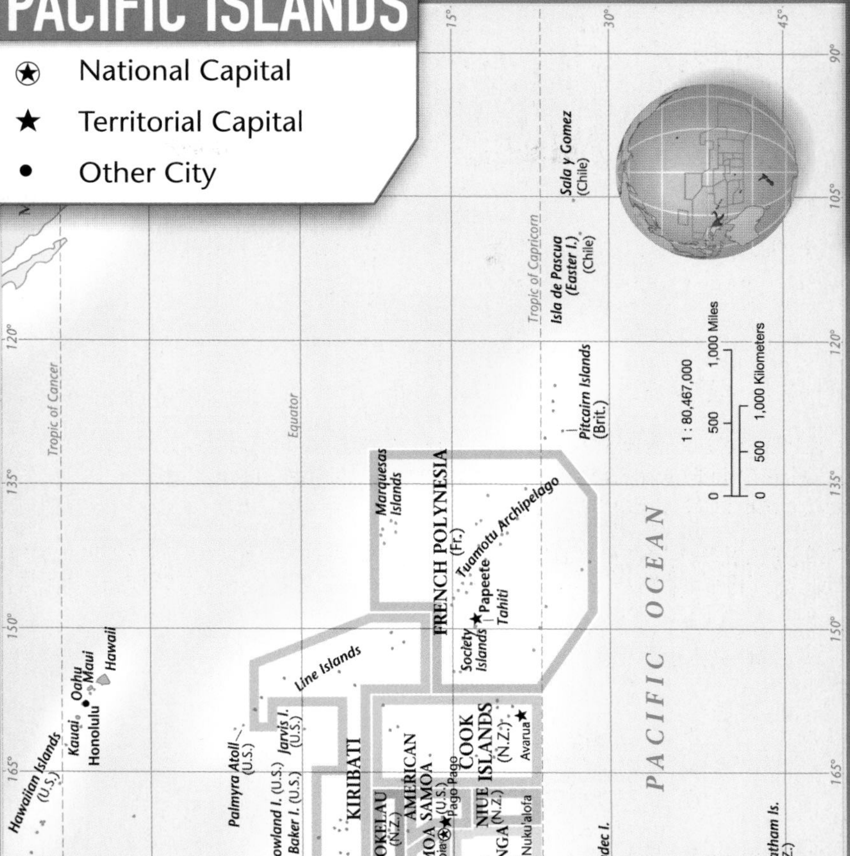

RUSSIA
SWEDEN
NORWAY
UNITED KINGDOM
ICELAND
Svalbard (Nor.)
Greenland Sea
Denmark Strait
GREENLAND (KALAALLIT NUNAAT) (Den.)
Nord
Cape Morris Jessup
Knud Rasmussen Land
Qaanaaq (Thule)
Tasiilaq
Nuuk
Cape Farewell
Arctic Circle
North Pole
Arctic Ocean
Baffin Bay
Davis Strait
Labrador Sea
Alert
Ellesmere I.
Grise Fiord
Queen Elizabeth Islands
Resolute
Arctic Bay
Pond Inlet
Baffin Island
Pangnirtung
Iqaluit
Hudson Strait
Ungava Peninsula
Povungnituk
Hebron
NEWFOUNDLAND AND LABRADOR
Happy Valley-Goose Bay
St. Anthony
Island of Newfoundland
St. John's
Corner Brook
St. Pierre & Miquelon (Fr.)
Anticosti I.
Sydney
Halifax
N.S.
P.E.I.
NEW BRUNS.
Saint John
MAINE
St. Lawrence
Sept-Iles
Schefferville
Labrador City
QUEBEC
Chicoutimi
Chibougamau
Quebec
Southampton I.
Repulse Bay
Hudson Bay
Belcher Is.
James Bay
Moosonee
Timmins
ONTARIO
CANADIAN SHIELD
Churchill
York Factory
MANITOBA
L. Winnipeg
Winnipeg
Thunder Bay
Thompson
Flin Flon
The Pas
NUNAVUT
CANADA
Victoria I.
Cambridge Bay
Holman
Banks I.
Sachs Harbour
Kugluktuk
Beaufort Sea
NORTHWEST TERRITORIES
Great Bear L.
Déline
Yellowknife
Great Slave L.
Fort Smith
Hay River
Ft. Simpson
Uranium City
L. Athabasca
SASK.
La Loche
La Ronge
Ft. McMurray
Prince Albert
Saskatchewan
Saskatoon
Regina
Brandon
ALBERTA
Athabasca
Peace River
Edmonton
Calgary
Inuvik
Fort McPherson
Mackenzie
Watson Lake
BRITISH COLUMBIA
Peace
Prince George
Jasper
Williams Lake
Fraser
Columbia
Spokane
WASH.
ROCKY RANGE
GREAT
YUKON
Dawson
Mayo
Carmacks
Whitehorse
COAST MOUNTAINS
Kitimat
Prince Rupert
Queen Charlotte Is.
Ketchikan
Juneau
Sitka
Skagway
Yakutat
Vancouver
Vancouver I.
Victoria
Seattle
ALASKA
BROOKS RANGE
Point Barrow
Barrow
Fort Yukon
Fairbanks
Yukon
Point Hope
Kotzebue
Nome
Bering Strait
Bering Sea
ALASKA RANGE
Mt. McKinley 6,194 m. (20,320 ft.)
Anchorage
Valdez
Kenai
Seward
Kodiak
Bethel
Mt. Logan 5,959 m. (19,551 ft.)
Gulf of Alaska

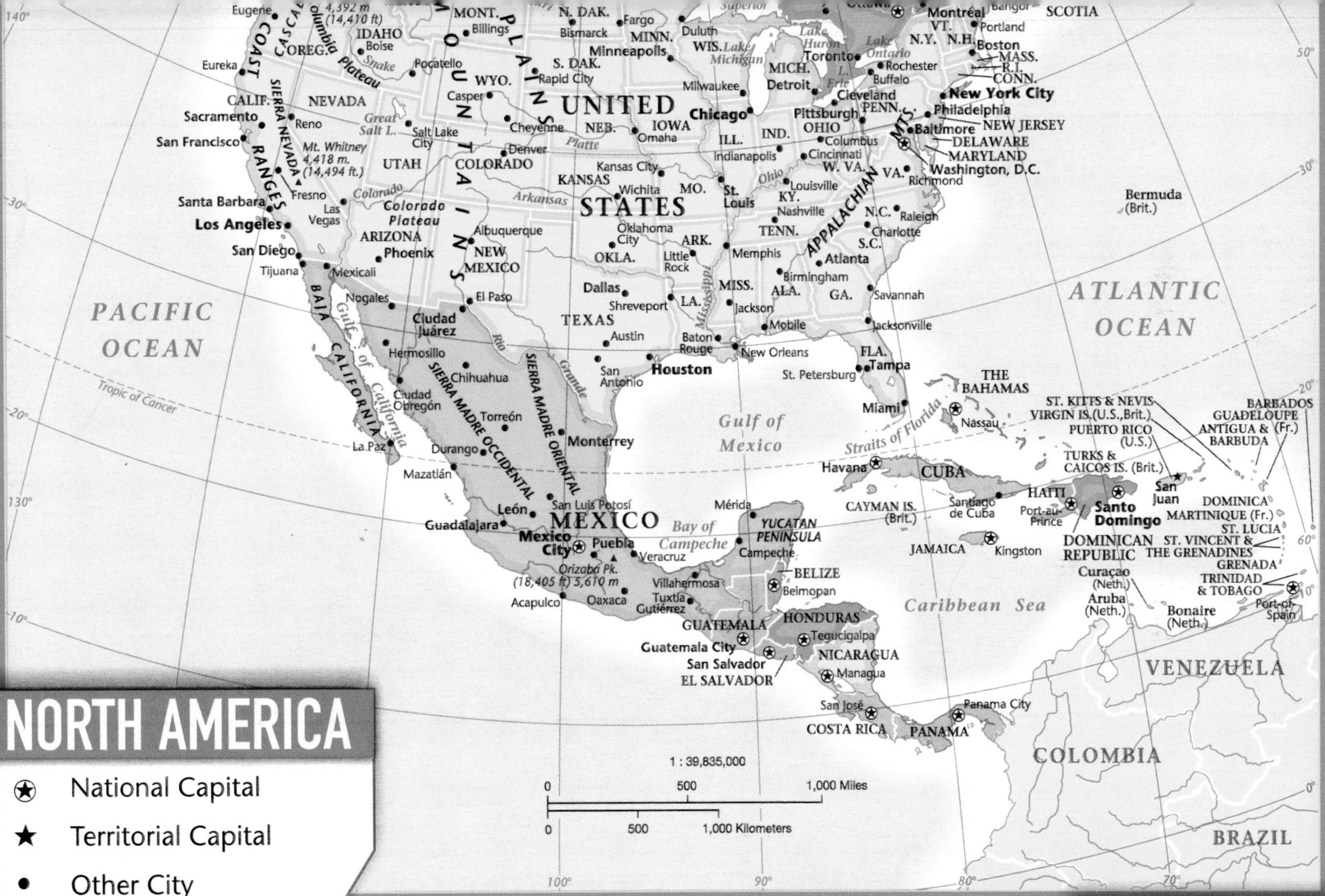

NORTH AMERICA

- ⍟ National Capital
- ★ Territorial Capital
- • Other City

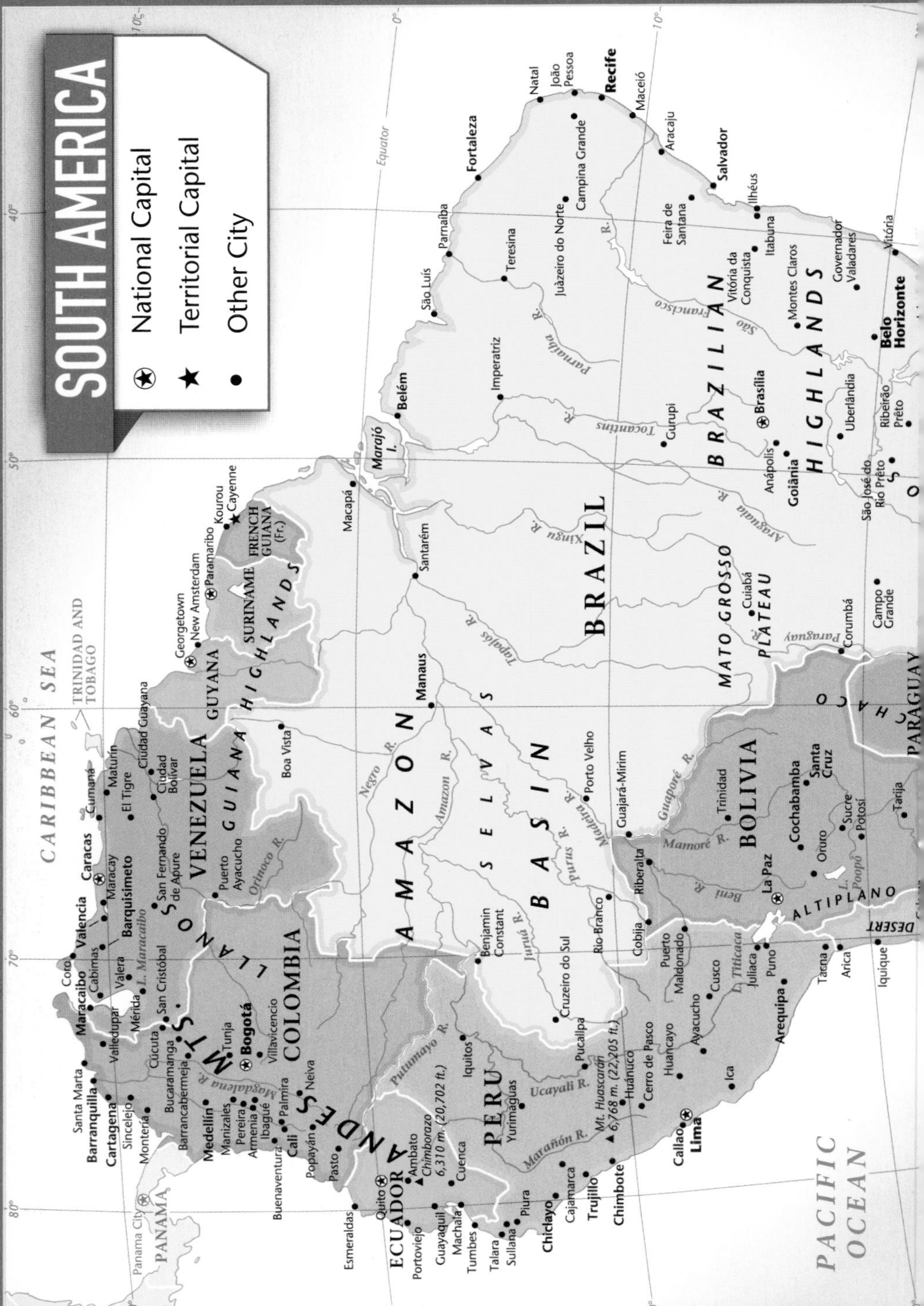
SOUTH AMERICA
National Capital
Territorial Capital
Other City
CARIBBEAN SEA
TRINIDAD AND TOBAGO
PACIFIC OCEAN
Equator
PANAMA
Panama City
VENEZUELA
Caracas
Maracaibo
Valencia
Barquisimeto
Maracay
Coro
Cabimas
Valera
Mérida
San Cristóbal
L. Maracaibo
Cumaná
Maturín
El Tigre
Ciudad Guayana
Ciudad Bolívar
San Fernando de Apure
Puerto Ayacucho
Orinoco R.
GUYANA
Georgetown
New Amsterdam
SURINAME
Paramaribo
FRENCH GUIANA (Fr.)
Kourou
Cayenne
GUIANA HIGHLANDS
LLANOS
COLOMBIA
Bogotá
Barranquilla
Santa Marta
Cartagena
Sincelejo
Montería
Valledupar
Cúcuta
Bucaramanga
Barrancabermeja
Tunja
Villavicencio
Medellín
Manizales
Pereira
Armenia
Ibagué
Neiva
Cali
Palmira
Buenaventura
Popayán
Pasto
Magdalena R.
ANDES MTS.
ECUADOR
Quito
Esmeraldas
Portoviejo
Guayaquil
Machala
Cuenca
Ambato
Chimborazo 6,310 m. (20,702 ft.)
Putumayo R.
PERU
Lima
Callao
Tumbes
Talara
Sullana
Piura
Chiclayo
Cajamarca
Trujillo
Chimbote
Iquitos
Yurimaguas
Pucallpa
Huánuco
Cerro de Pasco
Huancayo
Ayacucho
Cusco
Ica
Arequipa
Juliaca
Puno
Tacna
Puerto Maldonado
Mt. Huascarán 6,768 m. (22,205 ft.)
Marañón R.
Ucayali R.
L. Titicaca
BOLIVIA
La Paz
Cochabamba
Santa Cruz
Trinidad
Oruro
Sucre
Potosí
Tarija
Riberalta
L. Poopó
ALTIPLANO
Mamoré R.
Beni R.
Guaporé R.
CHACO
PARAGUAY
Arica
Iquique
DESERT
BRAZIL
AMAZON BASIN
SELVAS
Amazon R.
Negro R.
Juruá R.
Purus R.
Madeira R.
Tapajós R.
Xingu R.
Araguaia R.
Tocantins R.
Parnaíba R.
São Francisco R.
Paraguay R.
Manaus
Boa Vista
Benjamin Constant
Cruzeiro do Sul
Rio Branco
Cobija
Porto Velho
Guajará-Mirim
Santarém
Macapá
Marajó I.
Belém
São Luís
Parnaíba
Fortaleza
Teresina
Imperatriz
Natal
João Pessoa
Recife
Maceió
Campina Grande
Juàzeiro do Norte
Aracaju
Salvador
Feira de Santana
Ilhéus
Itabuna
Vitória da Conquista
Montes Claros
Governador Valadares
Vitória
Belo Horizonte
Brasília
Gurupi
Anápolis
Goiânia
Uberlândia
Ribeirão Prêto
São José do Rio Prêto
MATO GROSSO PLATEAU
Cuiabá
Campo Grande
Corumbá
BRAZILIAN HIGHLANDS

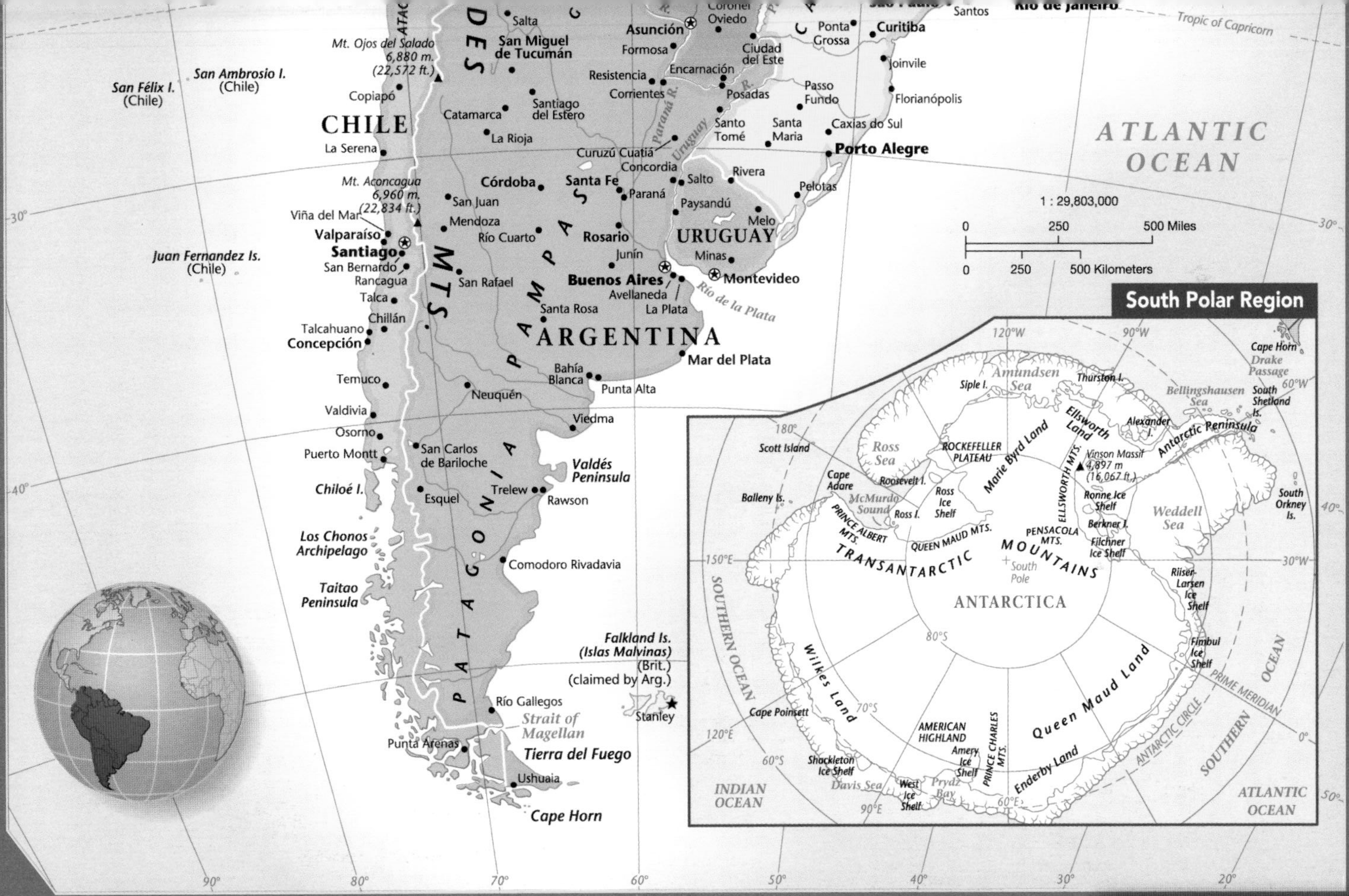

Tropic of Capricorn
Santos
Rio de Janeiro
Curitiba
Ponta Grossa
Joinvile
Florianópolis
Passo Fundo
Caxias do Sul
Porto Alegre
Pelotas
Santa Maria
Santo Tomé
Rivera
Ciudad del Este
Coronel Oviedo
Asunción
Formosa
Resistencia
Corrientes
Encarnación
Posadas
Paraná R.
Uruguay
Curuzú Cuatiá
Concordia
Salto
Paysandú
Melo
URUGUAY
Minas
Montevideo
Río de la Plata
Buenos Aires
Avellaneda
La Plata
Santa Fe
Paraná
Rosario
Junín
Córdoba
San Juan
Mendoza
Río Cuarto
San Rafael
Santa Rosa
ARGENTINA
Mar del Plata
Bahía Blanca
Punta Alta
Neuquén
Viedma
San Carlos de Bariloche
Valdés Peninsula
Trelew
Rawson
Esquel
Comodoro Rivadavia
PATAGONIA
PAMPAS
Salta
San Miguel de Tucumán
Santiago del Estero
Catamarca
La Rioja
ANDES MTS.
Mt. Ojos del Salado 6,880 m. (22,572 ft.)
Copiapó
CHILE
La Serena
Mt. Aconcagua 6,960 m. (22,834 ft.)
Viña del Mar
Valparaíso
Santiago
San Bernardo
Rancagua
Talca
Chillán
Talcahuano
Concepción
Temuco
Valdivia
Osorno
Puerto Montt
Chiloé I.
Los Chonos Archipelago
Taitao Peninsula
San Félix I. (Chile)
San Ambrosio I. (Chile)
Juan Fernandez Is. (Chile)
Falkland Is. (Islas Malvinas) (Brit.) (claimed by Arg.)
Stanley
Río Gallegos
Strait of Magellan
Punta Arenas
Tierra del Fuego
Ushuaia
Cape Horn
ATLANTIC OCEAN
1 : 29,803,000
0 250 500 Miles
0 250 500 Kilometers
30°
40°
50°
90° 80° 70° 60° 50° 40° 30° 20°
South Polar Region
Cape Horn
Drake Passage
South Shetland Is.
South Orkney Is.
Bellingshausen Sea
Antarctic Peninsula
Alexander I.
Thurston I.
Amundsen Sea
Siple I.
Ellsworth Land
Vinson Massif 4,897 m (16,067 ft.)
ELLSWORTH MTS.
Ronne Ice Shelf
Berkner I.
Filchner Ice Shelf
Weddell Sea
Marie Byrd Land
ROCKEFELLER PLATEAU
Ross Sea
Roosevelt I.
Ross Ice Shelf
Ross I.
McMurdo Sound
Cape Adare
Scott Island
Balleny Is.
PRINCE ALBERT MTS.
QUEEN MAUD MTS.
PENSACOLA MTS.
TRANSANTARCTIC MOUNTAINS
South Pole
ANTARCTICA
Riiser-Larsen Ice Shelf
Fimbul Ice Shelf
Queen Maud Land
Enderby Land
PRINCE CHARLES MTS.
AMERICAN HIGHLAND
Amery Ice Shelf
Prydz Bay
West Ice Shelf
Davis Sea
Shackleton Ice Shelf
Wilkes Land
Cape Poinsett
SOUTHERN OCEAN
INDIAN OCEAN
ATLANTIC OCEAN
PRIME MERIDIAN
ANTARCTIC CIRCLE
120°W 90°W 60°W 30°W 0° 60°E 90°E 120°E 150°E 180°
60°S 70°S 80°S

EUROPE
National Capital
Other City
1 : 22,667,000
0
250
500 Miles
0
250
500 Kilometers
Arctic Circle
Reykjavík
Akureyri
ICELAND
Tromsø
Kiruna
Bodø
Norwegian
Sea
Faroe Is.
(Den.)
Shetland Is.
(Brit.)
Trondheim
Sundsvall
NORWAY
SWEDEN
Bergen
Oslo
Orkney
Is.
Hebrides
Stavanger
Uppsala
Stockholm
Linköping
Aberdeen
Skagerrak
Kattegat
Gotland
Glasgow
Edinburgh
Göteborg
Belfast
UNITED KINGDOM
(GREAT BRITAIN)
Newcastle
Jutland
Århus
Öland
Dublin
Irish
Sea
Copenhagen
Helsingborg
IRELAND
Liverpool
Leeds
North
Sea
DENMARK
Odense
Malmö
Baltic
Cork
Manchester
Sheffield
Birmingham
Gdańsk
Cardiff
Bristol
NETHERLANDS
Amsterdam
Elbe
Hamburg
Szczecin
Vistula
Bremen
Hannover
ATLANTIC
OCEAN
Land's End
Portsmouth
London
Rotterdam
Antwerp
Berlin
Poznań
English Channel
Brussels
Essen
GERMANY
Channel Is.
(Brit.)
Lille
Cologne
Oder
Łódź
Le Havre
BELGIUM
Bonn
Liège
Leipzig
Dresden
Brest
Rouen
Frankfurt
Wrocław
LUXEMBOURG
Prague
Katowice
Paris
Luxembourg
Mannheim
CZECH REP.
Brno
Ostrava
Nantes
Loire
Strasbourg
Rhine
Stuttgart
Danube
SLOVAKIA
Bay
of
Biscay
FRANCE
Dijon
Munich
Linz
Vienna
Bratislava
Bern
Zürich
LIECHTENSTEIN
Cape Finisterre
Geneva
SWITZERLAND
AUSTRIA
Budapest
Gijón
Bordeaux
Lyon
ALPS
Graz
HUNGARY
Vigo
Mt. Blanc
4807 m
(15,771 ft)
Milan
SLOVENIA
Ljubljana
Pécs
Bilbao
Rhône
Turin
Verona
Zagreb
Porto
Ebro
Toulouse
Venice
DINARIC
Valladolid
PYRENEES
Genoa
Bologna
CROATIA
BOSNIA &
HERZEGOVINA
Marseille
Nice
MONACO
Florence
SAN
MARINO
Sarajevo
PORTUGAL
IBERIAN
Pico de Aneto
3404 m
(11,168 ft)
Zaragoza
Toulon
Ligurian Sea
APENNINES
Adriatic
ALPS
Lisbon
Madrid
ANDORRA
Split
MONTENEGRO
Tagus
Barcelona
Corsica
(Fr.)
Elba
Dubrovnik
Badajoz
PENINSULA
Podgorica
Valencia
Balearic Sea
VATICAN
CITY
Rome
Sea
SPAIN
Córdoba
Majorca
Minorca
ITALY
Bari
Cape
St. Vincent
Sevilla
Palma
Naples
Alicante
Balearic Is.
(Sp.)
Sardinia
(It.)
Salerno
Cádiz
Granada
Tyrrhenian
Sea
Corfu
Málaga
Cagliari
Ionian
Sea
Strait of
Gibraltar
GIBRALTAR
(Brit.)
Mediterranean
Palermo
Rabat
Algiers
Mt. Etna
3323 m
(10,902 ft)
Casablanca
Catania
Sicily
Tunis
MOUNTAINS
Valletta
MALTA
MOROCCO
ATLAS
ALGERIA
TUNISIA
Sea

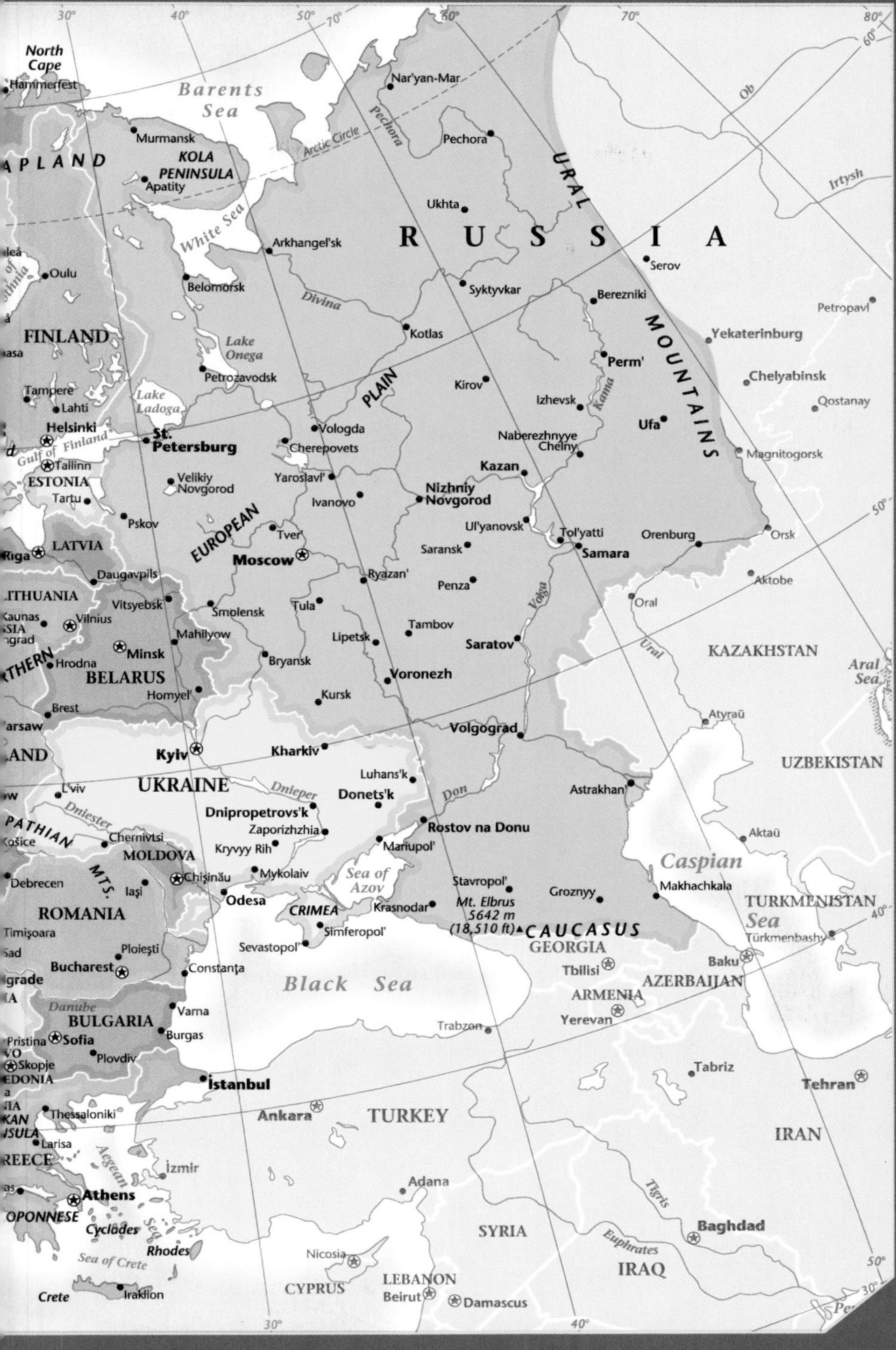
North Cape
Hammerfest
Barents Sea
Nar'yan-Mar
Pechora
Pechora
Murmansk
KOLA PENINSULA
Apatity
Arctic Circle
White Sea
Ukhta
URAL MOUNTAINS
Ob
Irtysh
Arkhangel'sk
RUSSIA
Serov
Oulu
Belomorsk
Divina
Syktyvkar
Berezniki
Petropavl
FINLAND
Lake Onega
Kotlas
Yekaterinburg
Perm'
Petrozavodsk
PLAIN
Kirov
Chelyabinsk
Tampere
Lahti
Lake Ladoga
Izhevsk
Kama
Qostanay
Helsinki
Vologda
Ufa
Gulf of Finland
St. Petersburg
Cherepovets
Naberezhnyye Chelny
Magnitogorsk
Tallinn
ESTONIA
Velikiy Novgorod
Yaroslavl'
Kazan
Tartu
Ivanovo
Nizhniy Novgorod
Pskov
EUROPEAN
Tver'
Ul'yanovsk
Tol'yatti
Orenburg
Orsk
Riga
LATVIA
Moscow
Saransk
Samara
Daugavpils
Ryazan'
Penza
Aktobe
LITHUANIA
Vitsyebsk
Smolensk
Tula
Oral
Kaunas
Vilnius
Mahilyow
Tambov
Volga
Lipetsk
Saratov
Ural
KAZAKHSTAN
Minsk
Hrodna
Bryansk
Aral Sea
BELARUS
Voronezh
Homyel'
Kursk
Brest
Atyraū
Volgograd
Kyiv
Kharkiv
UZBEKISTAN
Luhans'k
UKRAINE
Dnieper
Astrakhan'
L'viv
Donets'k
Don
Dniester
Dnipropetrovs'k
Zaporizhzhia
Rostov na Donu
Aktaū
Chernivtsi
Mariupol'
MOLDOVA
Kryvyy Rih
Caspian Sea
MTS.
Chişinău
Mykolaiv
Sea of Azov
Stavropol'
Makhachkala
Debrecen
Iaşi
Odesa
Krasnodar
Mt. Elbrus 5642 m (18,510 ft)
Groznyy
TURKMENISTAN
ROMANIA
CRIMEA
CAUCASUS
Timişoara
Simferopol'
GEORGIA
Türkmenbashy
Sevastopol'
Ploieşti
Bucharest
Constanţa
Tbilisi
Baku
Black Sea
AZERBAIJAN
ARMENIA
Danube
Varna
Yerevan
BULGARIA
Trabzon
Sofia
Burgas
Pristina
Skopje
Plovdiv
Tabriz
İstanbul
Tehran
Thessaloniki
Ankara
TURKEY
IRAN
Larisa
Aegean Sea
İzmir
Tigris
Athens
Adana
Cyclades
Baghdad
Rhodes
SYRIA
Euphrates
Sea of Crete
Nicosia
IRAQ
LEBANON
CYPRUS
Beirut
Damascus
Crete
Iraklion
30°
40°
50°
60°
70°
80°

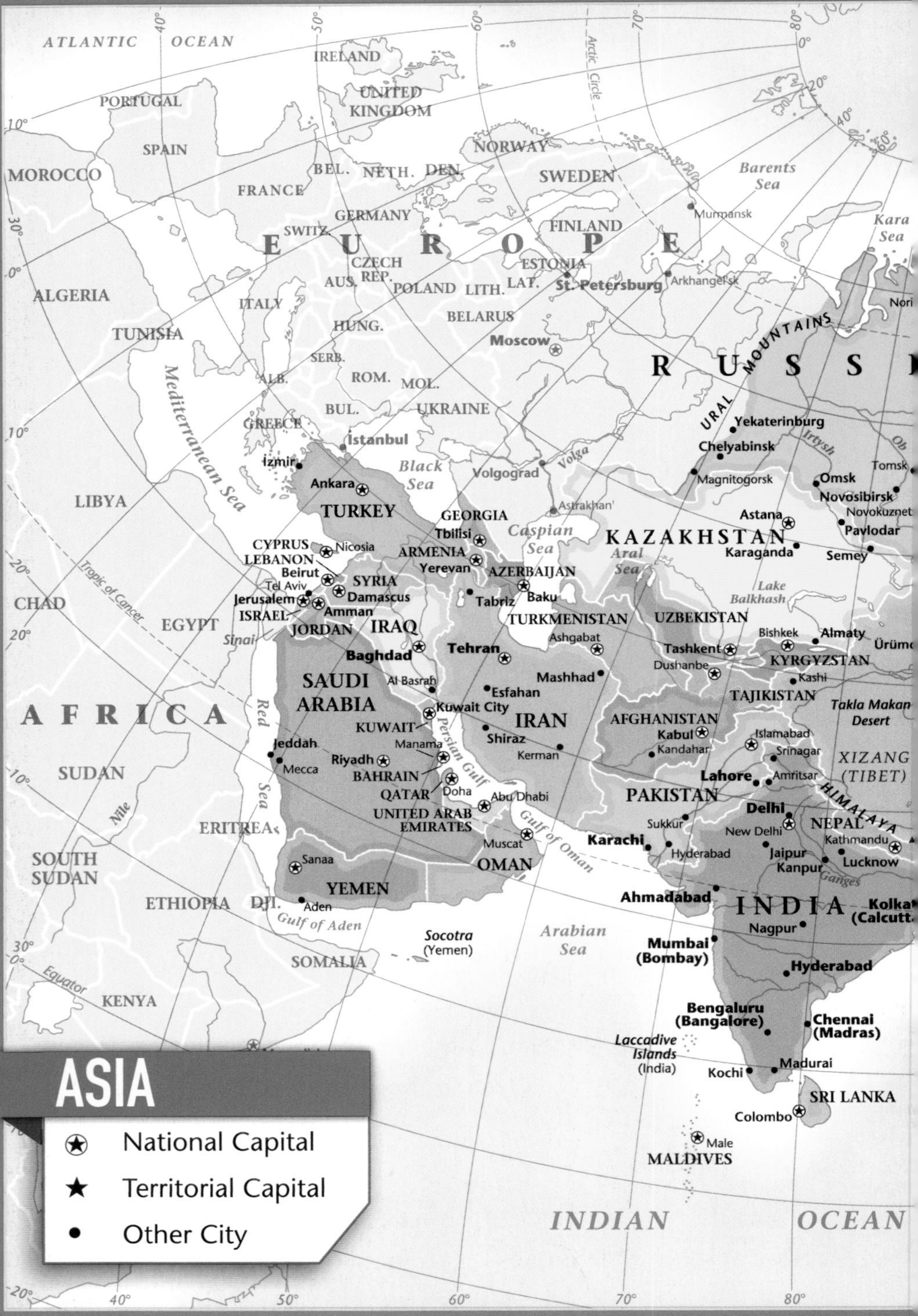
ASIA
National Capital
Territorial Capital
Other City
ATLANTIC OCEAN
IRELAND
UNITED KINGDOM
PORTUGAL
SPAIN
MOROCCO
FRANCE
BEL.
NETH.
DEN.
NORWAY
SWEDEN
FINLAND
GERMANY
SWITZ.
E U R O P E
CZECH REP.
AUS.
POLAND
LITH.
LAT.
ESTONIA
St. Petersburg
Arkhangel'sk
Murmansk
Barents Sea
Kara Sea
ALGERIA
TUNISIA
ITALY
HUNG.
BELARUS
Moscow
SERB.
ALB.
ROM.
MOL.
BUL.
UKRAINE
GREECE
Istanbul
Izmir
Mediterranean Sea
Black Sea
Ankara
TURKEY
Volgograd
Volga
Astrakhan'
GEORGIA
Tbilisi
ARMENIA
Yerevan
AZERBAIJAN
Baku
Caspian Sea
R U S S
URAL MOUNTAINS
Yekaterinburg
Chelyabinsk
Magnitogorsk
Irtysh
Omsk
Novosibirsk
Tomsk
Novokuznet
Pavlodar
Astana
KAZAKHSTAN
Karaganda
Semey
Aral Sea
Lake Balkhash
LIBYA
CYPRUS
Nicosia
LEBANON
Beirut
SYRIA
Damascus
Tel Aviv
Jerusalem
Amman
ISRAEL
JORDAN
IRAQ
Baghdad
Tabriz
Tehran
TURKMENISTAN
Ashgabat
Mashhad
UZBEKISTAN
Tashkent
Dushanbe
Bishkek
Almaty
KYRGYZSTAN
Kashi
TAJIKISTAN
Takla Makan Desert
CHAD
EGYPT
Sinai
Tropic of Cancer
SAUDI ARABIA
Al Basrah
Kuwait City
KUWAIT
Esfahan
IRAN
Shiraz
Kerman
AFGHANISTAN
Kabul
Kandahar
Islamabad
Srinagar
XIZANG (TIBET)
Lahore
Amritsar
PAKISTAN
HIMALAYA
A F R I C A
Red Sea
Jeddah
Mecca
Riyadh
Manama
BAHRAIN
Persian Gulf
QATAR
Doha
Abu Dhabi
UNITED ARAB EMIRATES
Gulf of Oman
Muscat
OMAN
SUDAN
Nile
ERITREA
SOUTH SUDAN
ETHIOPIA
DJI.
Sanaa
YEMEN
Aden
Gulf of Aden
SOMALIA
KENYA
Equator
Socotra (Yemen)
Arabian Sea
Sukkur
Karachi
Hyderabad
Delhi
New Delhi
NEPAL
Kathmandu
Jaipur
Kanpur
Lucknow
Ganges
Ahmadabad
INDIA
Kolka (Calcutt
Nagpur
Mumbai (Bombay)
Hyderabad
Bengaluru (Bangalore)
Chennai (Madras)
Laccadive Islands (India)
Kochi
Madurai
SRI LANKA
Colombo
Male
MALDIVES
INDIAN OCEAN
Arctic Circle
40°
50°
60°
70°
80°
0°
20°
10°
30°

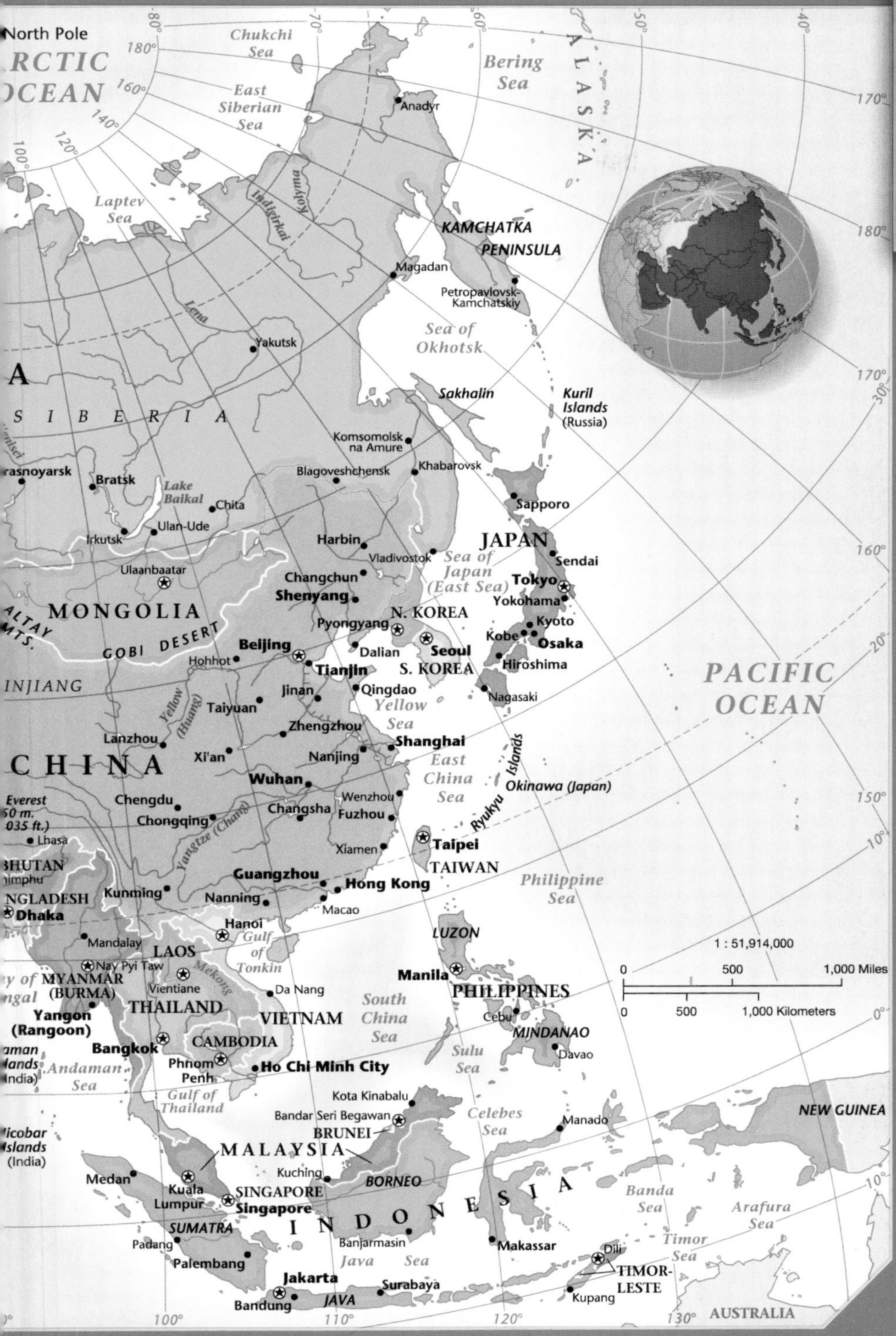
North Pole
ARCTIC OCEAN
Chukchi Sea
East Siberian Sea
Laptev Sea
Bering Sea
ALASKA
Anadyr
Kolyma
Indigirka
Lena
KAMCHATKA PENINSULA
Magadan
Petropavlovsk-Kamchatskiy
Sea of Okhotsk
Yakutsk
Sakhalin
Kuril Islands (Russia)
SIBERIA
Komsomolsk na Amure
Khabarovsk
Blagoveshchensk
Krasnoyarsk
Bratsk
Lake Baikal
Chita
Irkutsk
Ulan-Ude
Sapporo
JAPAN
Harbin
Vladivostok
Sea of Japan (East Sea)
Sendai
Ulaanbaatar
Changchun
Shenyang
Tokyo
Yokohama
MONGOLIA
ALTAY MTS.
GOBI DESERT
N. KOREA
Pyongyang
Kyoto
Kobe
Osaka
Beijing
Hohhot
Dalian
Seoul
S. KOREA
Hiroshima
Tianjin
XINJIANG
Jinan
Qingdao
Nagasaki
Yellow (Huang)
Taiyuan
Yellow Sea
PACIFIC OCEAN
Zhengzhou
Lanzhou
Shanghai
Xi'an
Nanjing
East China Sea
Ryukyu Islands
CHINA
Wuhan
Okinawa (Japan)
Everest
Chengdu
Wenzhou
Changsha
Fuzhou
Chongqing
Yangtze (Chang)
Lhasa
Taipei
Xiamen
TAIWAN
BHUTAN
Thimphu
Guangzhou
Hong Kong
Philippine Sea
BANGLADESH
Kunming
Nanning
Macao
Dhaka
Hanoi
Gulf of Tonkin
LUZON
Mandalay
LAOS
Nay Pyi Taw
Mekong
1 : 51,914,000
MYANMAR (BURMA)
Vientiane
Manila
0 500 1,000 Miles
Da Nang
PHILIPPINES
0 500 1,000 Kilometers
THAILAND
South China Sea
Yangon (Rangoon)
VIETNAM
Cebu
MINDANAO
CAMBODIA
Bangkok
Davao
Andaman Islands (India)
Andaman Sea
Phnom Penh
Ho Chi Minh City
Sulu Sea
Gulf of Thailand
Kota Kinabalu
Bandar Seri Begawan
Celebes Sea
NEW GUINEA
Nicobar Islands (India)
BRUNEI
Manado
MALAYSIA
Kuching
BORNEO
Medan
Kuala Lumpur
SINGAPORE
Singapore
INDONESIA
Banda Sea
Arafura Sea
SUMATRA
Padang
Banjarmasin
Makassar
Timor Sea
Palembang
Java Sea
Dili
Jakarta
Surabaya
TIMOR-LESTE
Bandung
JAVA
Kupang
AUSTRALIA
80°
70°
60°
50°
40°
180°
160°
140°
120°
100°
170°
30°
20°
10°
0°
150°
100°
110°
120°
130°

ATLANTIC OCEAN
AZORES (Port.)
MADEIRA (Port.)
CANARY IS. (Sp.)
Las Palmas
PORTUGAL
Lisbon
SPAIN
Madrid
FRANCE
Paris
GERMANY
CZECH REP.
SWITZ.
AUSTRIA
SLOVAKIA
HUNGARY
SLOVE.
CRO.
ITALY
Rome
BOS. & HER.
SERB.
KOS.
MONT.
MAC.
ALBANIA
GREECE
Athens
ROMANIA
Bucharest
BULGARIA
MOLDOVA
UKRAINE
RUSSIA
KAZAKHSTAN
Aral Sea
UZBEKISTAN
TURKMENISTAN
Caspian Sea
Black Sea
GEORGIA
ARMENIA
AZERBAIJAN
TURKEY
İstanbul
Ankara
CYPRUS
SYRIA
Damascus
LEBANON
ISRAEL
Jerusalem
JORDAN
IRAQ
Baghdad
IRAN
Tehran
KUWAIT
Persian Gulf
BAHRAIN
QATAR
SAUDI ARABIA
Riyadh
Tropic of Cancer
OMAN
YEMEN
Sanaa
Gulf of Aden
DJIBOUTI
Djibouti
MALTA
Mediterranean Sea
Gulf of Sidra
Tangier
Rabat
Casablanca
Safi
Marrakech
Fez
Oujda
Oran
Algiers
Constantine
Annaba
Bizerte
Tunis
Sfax
TUNISIA
MOROCCO
ATLAS MOUNTAINS
Béchar
Ghardaia
ALGERIA
I-n-Salah
AHAGGAR MTS.
Tamanrasset
Tripoli
Misratah
Benghazi
al-Bayda
Tobruk
LIBYA
al-Jawf
LIBYAN DESERT
Alexandria
Port Said
Cairo
Suez Canal
Siwa
EGYPT
Luxor
Aswan
L. Nasser
Red Sea
NUBIAN DESERT
Port Sudan
Atbara
Nile
SAHARA
Laayoune
WESTERN SAHARA (occ. by Morocco)
Nouadhibou
MAURITANIA
Nouakchott
MALI
Timbuktu
Niger
Senegal
NIGER
AIR
Agadez
Zinder
Niamey
SAHEL
TIBESTI
Faya-Largeau
CHAD
Abéché
L. Chad
N'Djamena
SUDAN
Omdurman
Khartoum
Kassala
Wad Medani
El Fasher
El Obeid
Blue Nile
ERITREA
Asmara
Assab
Gonder
L. Tana
ETHIOPIAN HIGHLANDS
Addis Ababa
Jima
Harer
Hargeysa
Berbera
GREAT RIFT VALLEY
ETHIOPIA
Kelafo
SOMALIA
L. Turkana
Dakar
SENEGAL
Kaolack
THE GAMBIA
Banjul
Bissau
GUINEA-BISSAU
Labé
GUINEA
Kankan
Kayes
Ségou
Bamako
Conakry
Freetown
SIERRA LEONE
Monrovia
LIBERIA
CÔTE D'IVOIRE
Bouaké
Yamoussoukro
Abidjan
BURKINA FASO
Ouagadougou
Bobo-Dioulasso
GHANA
Kumasi
Accra
Sekondi-Takoradi
TOGO
Lomé
BENIN
Porto-Novo
NIGERIA
Sokoto
Zaria
Kano
Maiduguri
Abuja
Ogbomosho
Ibadan
Lagos
Enugu
Onitsha
Port Harcourt
Benue
Maroua
Garoua
CAMEROON
Douala
Malabo
Yaoundé
Sarh
CENTRAL AFRICAN REPUBLIC
Bouar
Bangui
Ubangi
SOUTH SUDAN
Malakal
Wau
Juba
White Nile

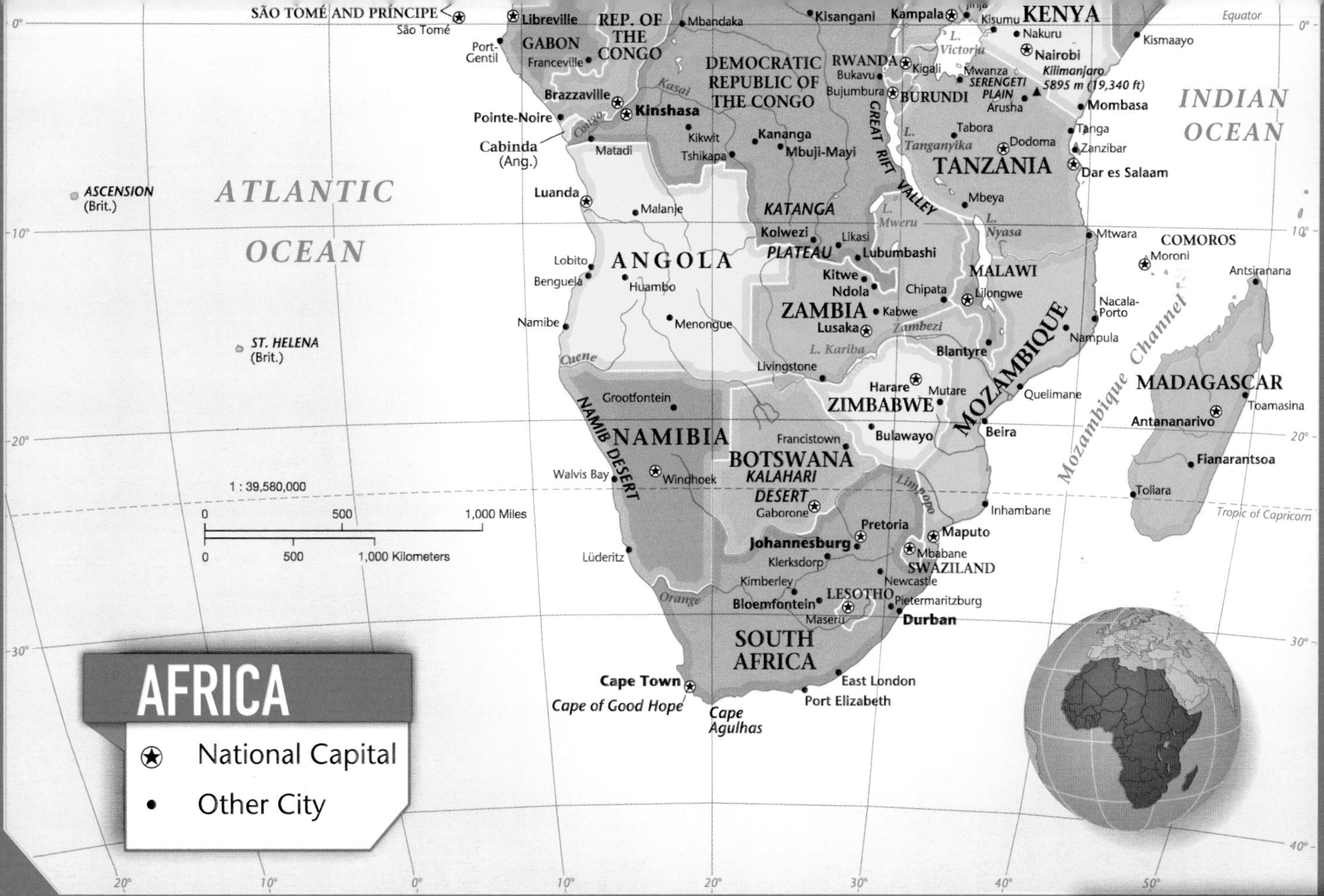

AFRICA
National Capital
Other City
1 : 39,580,000
0
500
1,000 Miles
0
500
1,000 Kilometers
ATLANTIC OCEAN
INDIAN OCEAN
ASCENSION (Brit.)
ST. HELENA (Brit.)
SÃO TOMÉ AND PRÍNCIPE
São Tomé
Port-Gentil
Libreville
GABON
Franceville
REP. OF THE CONGO
Brazzaville
Pointe-Noire
Cabinda (Ang.)
Kinshasa
Matadi
Mbandaka
Kasai
Congo
DEMOCRATIC REPUBLIC OF THE CONGO
Kikwit
Tshikapa
Kananga
Mbuji-Mayi
Kisangani
KATANGA
Kolwezi
Likasi
PLATEAU
Lubumbashi
RWANDA
Kigali
Bukavu
Bujumbura
BURUNDI
GREAT RIFT VALLEY
Kampala
Kisumu
KENYA
Nakuru
Nairobi
L. Victoria
Mwanza
SERENGETI PLAIN
Arusha
Kilimanjaro 5895 m (19,340 ft)
Mombasa
Kismaayo
Equator
L. Tanganyika
Tabora
Dodoma
Tanga
Zanzibar
TANZANIA
Dar es Salaam
Mbeya
L. Mweru
L. Nyasa
Mtwara
COMOROS
Moroni
Antsiranana
MALAWI
Lilongwe
Chipata
Kitwe
Ndola
ZAMBIA
Kabwe
Lusaka
Zambezi
L. Kariba
Livingstone
Blantyre
MOZAMBIQUE
Nacala-Porto
Nampula
Quelimane
Beira
Mozambique Channel
MADAGASCAR
Toamasina
Antananarivo
Fianarantsoa
Toliara
Luanda
Malanje
ANGOLA
Lobito
Benguela
Huambo
Menongue
Namibe
Cuene
Harare
Mutare
ZIMBABWE
Bulawayo
Francistown
Grootfontein
NAMIBIA
NAMIB DESERT
Walvis Bay
Windhoek
BOTSWANA
KALAHARI DESERT
Gaborone
Limpopo
Inhambane
Tropic of Capricorn
Pretoria
Maputo
Johannesburg
Mbabane
SWAZILAND
Klerksdorp
Newcastle
Kimberley
LESOTHO
Pietermaritzburg
Bloemfontein
Maseru
Durban
Lüderitz
Orange
SOUTH AFRICA
Cape Town
Cape of Good Hope
Cape Agulhas
East London
Port Elizabeth
0°
10°
20°
30°
40°
50°

FACTS ABOUT NATIONS

Here are basic facts about the world's independent nations. The color of the heading for each country tells you what continent it belongs in. The population is an estimate for 2012. The area includes both land and inland water. The language entry gives official languages and other common languages.

Afghanistan

Capital: Kabul
Population: 30,419,928
Area: 250,001 sq mi (647,500 sq km)
Language: Afghan Persian (Dari), Pashtu
Did You Know? Afghanistan has both high mountains and desert valleys. Summer temperatures in some areas may hit 120°F. Winter temperatures in the mountains can fall to –15°F.

Albania

Capital: Tirana
Population: 3,002,859
Area: 11,100 sq mi (28,748 sq km)
Language: Albanian, Greek
Did You Know? Some twenty years after the fall of its Communist government, Albania is attracting tourists with its beautiful beaches and historic cities.

Algeria

Capital: Algiers (El Djazair)
Population: 35,406,303
Area: 919,595 sq mi (2,381,740 sq km)
Language: Arabic, French, Berber dialects
Did You Know? Turkey ruled Algeria for more than 300 years, until France took control in 1830. But the Algerian people revolted against French rule and won independence in the early 1960s.

ALGIERS, ALGERIA

Andorra

Capital: Andorra la Vella
Population: 85,082
Area: 181 sq mi (468 sq km)
Language: Catalan, French, Castilian
Did You Know? Tiny Andorra is ruled by two "co-princes" from neighboring countries: the president of France and the bishop of Urgel in Spain.

Angola

Capital: Luanda
Population: 18,056,072
Area: 481,354 sq mi (1,246,700 sq km)
Language: Portuguese, African languages
Did You Know? Angola has more oil reserves than any other country in Sub-Saharan Africa except Nigeria.

Antigua and Barbuda

Capital: St. John's
Population: 89,018
Area: 171 sq mi (443 sq km)
Language: English
Did You Know? Most of the people in this former British colony are descended from African slaves who worked on sugar plantations. Every year in August the country has a lively ten-day carnival to celebrate the end of slavery there on August 1, 1834.

COLOR KEY

- Africa
- Asia
- Australia
- Europe
- North America
- Pacific Islands
- South America

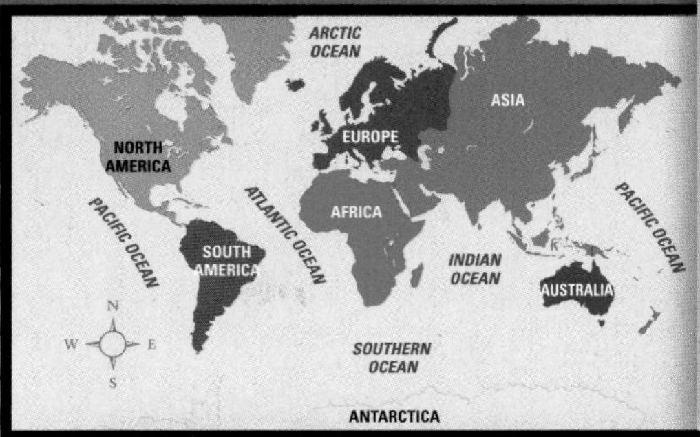

Argentina

Capital: Buenos Aires
Population: 42,192,494
Area: 1,068,302 sq mi (2,766,890 sq km)
Language: Spanish, English, Italian, German, French
Did You Know? Ushuaia, at the tip of Argentina, is the world's southernmost city. It lies about 700 miles away from the continent of Antarctica.

Armenia

Capital: Yerevan
Population: 2,970,495
Area: 11,484 sq mi (29,743 sq km)
Language: Armenian, Russian
Did You Know? On September 21, 1991, Armenians voted overwhelmingly to drop out of what was then the Soviet Union. This day is now known in Armenia as Independence Day. It is celebrated each year with parades and other festive events.

Australia

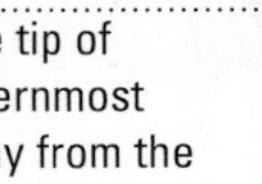

Capital: Canberra
Population: 22,015,576
Area: 2,967,909 sq mi (7,686,850 sq km)
Language: English, Aboriginal languages
Did You Know? Uluru, or Ayers Rock, in central Australia, is the biggest monolith, or single rock, in the world. It is over 2 miles long and about 1.5 miles wide.

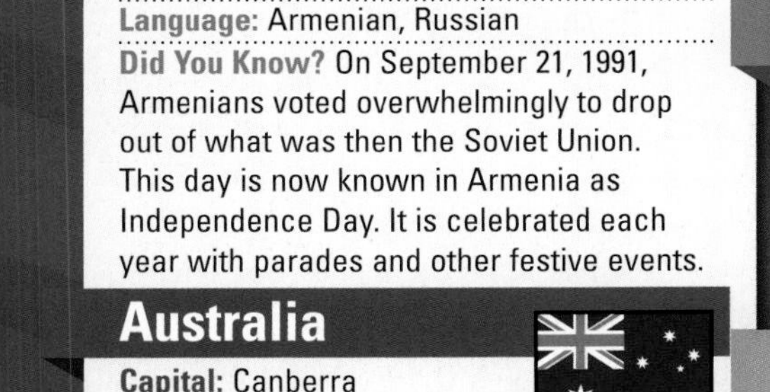

ULURU (AYERS ROCK), AUSTRALIA

Austria

Capital: Vienna
Population: 8,219,743
Area: 32,382 sq mi (83,870 sq km)
Language: German, Slovene, Croatian, Hungarian
Did You Know? Austria is one of the few countries in the world where people can vote when they reach the age of 16.

Azerbaijan

Capital: Baku
Population: 9,493,600
Area: 33,436 sq mi (86,600 sq km)
Language: Azeri, Russian, Armenian
Did You Know? Azerbaijan is about the same size as the U.S. state of Maine.

The Bahamas

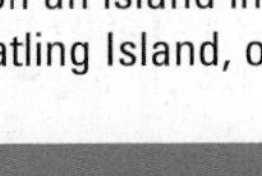

Capital: Nassau
Population: 316,182
Area: 5,382 sq mi (13,940 sq km)
Language: English, Creole
Did You Know? Columbus first set foot in America when he landed on an island in the Bahamas, probably Watling Island, on October 12, 1492.

Bahrain

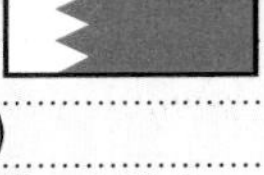

Capital: Manama
Population: 1,248,348
Area: 257 sq mi (665 sq km)
Language: Arabic, English, Farsi, Urdu
Did You Know? Most of the people in this small island kingdom in the Persian Gulf are Shiite Muslims. However, Sunni Muslims have most of the power in the government.

Bangladesh

Capital: Dhaka

Population: 161,083,804

Area: 55,599 sq mi (144,000 sq km)

Language: Bangla, English

Did You Know? The saltwater crocodile, found mainly in India and Bangladesh, can measure more than 20 feet long.

Barbados

Capital: Bridgetown

Population: 287,733

Area: 166 sq mi (431 sq km)

Language: English

Did You Know? The so-called green monkeys of Barbados arrived about 350 years from West Africa. Their fur looks greenish in certain light.

GREEN MONKEYS OF BARBADOS

Belarus

Capital: Minsk

Population: 9,542,883

Area: 80,155 sq mi (207,600 sq km)

Language: Belarusian, Russian

Did You Know? Much of southern Belarus is a part of the Pripyat, or Pripet, Marshes, a vast swampy region of Eastern Europe that is also about one-third forest. Elk, lynx, wolves, foxes, and beavers live there, along with many kinds of birds.

Belgium

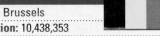

Capital: Brussels

Population: 10,438,353

Area: 11,787 sq mi (30,528 sq km)

Language: Dutch, French, German

Did You Know? Belgium is known for its waffles, baked goods, and chocolates, as well as for its deep-fried chipped potatoes.

Belize

Capital: Belmopan

Population: 327,719

Area: 8,867 sq mi (22,966 sq km)

Language: English, Spanish, Mayan, Garifuna, Creole

Did You Know? Belize—a neighbor of Mexico and Guatemala—was a British colony before it became independent in 1981.

Benin

Capital: Porto-Novo (constit.); Cotonou (admin.)

Population: 9,598,787

Area: 43,483 sq mi (112,620 sq km)

Language: French, Fon, Yoruba

Did You Know? Most of present-day Benin was part of the Kingdom of Abomey for almost 300 years.

Bhutan

Capital: Thimphu

Population: 716,896

Area: 18,147 sq mi (47,000 sq km)

Language: Dzongkha, Tibetan dialects

Did You Know? People in Bhutan must wear traditional clothes when in public.

Bolivia

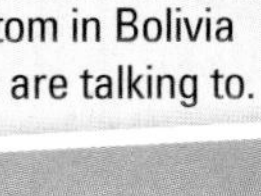

Capital: La Paz (admin.); Sucre (legislative/judicial)

Population: 10,290,003

Area: 424,164 sq mi (1,098,580 sq km)

Language: Spanish, Quechua, Aymara

Did You Know? It is a polite custom in Bolivia to stand close to the person you are talking to.

LA PAZ OUTSKIRTS, BOLIVIA

Bosnia and Herzegovina

Capital: Sarajevo
Population: 4,622,292
Area: 19,772 sq mi (51,209 sq km)
Language: Bosnian, Croatian, Serbian
Did You Know? On June 28, 1914, Archduke Franz Ferdinand of Austria and his wife were shot and fatally wounded as they rode in an open car in Sarajevo. The event helped set off World War I.

Botswana

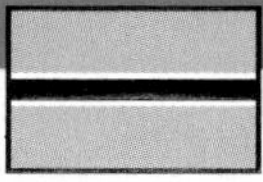

Capital: Gaborone
Population: 2,098,018
Area: 231,804 sq mi (600,370 sq km)
Language: Setswana, English
Did You Know? After diamond deposits were discovered in 1967, Botswana became one of Africa's most prosperous countries.

Brazil

Capital: Brasília
Population: 205,716,890
Area: 3,286,488 sq mi (8,511,965 sq km)
Language: Portuguese, Spanish, English, French
Did You Know? About 180 million people in the world speak Portuguese. Most of them live in Brazil.

RIO DE JANEIRO, BRAZIL

Brunei

Capital: Bandar Seri Begawan
Population: 408,786
Area: 2,228 sq mi (5,770 sq km)
Language: Malay, English, Chinese
Did You Know? Brunei lies on the north coast of Borneo. Other parts of this big tropical island belong to Malaysia and Indonesia. Brunei is ruled by a sultan who is one of the richest people in the world.

Bulgaria

Capital: Sofia
Population: 7,037,935
Area: 42,823 sq mi (110,910 sq km)
Language: Bulgarian, Turkish
Did You Know? Plovdiv, Bulgaria's second largest city, is very old. There is evidence that people were living at the site as early as 6,000 years ago.

Burkina Faso

Capital: Ouagadougou
Population: 17,275,115
Area: 105,869 sq mi (274,200 sq km)
Language: French, indigenous languages
Did You Know? Many of the people in Burkina Faso belong to the Mossi ethnic group. The Mossi are mostly farmers. They live in villages ruled by chiefs. Above all the chiefs is a "Morho Naba," or big lord.

Burundi

Capital: Bujumbura
Population: 10,557,259
Area: 10,745 sq mi (27,830 sq km)
Language: Kirundi, French, Swahili
Did You Know? The Twa, a Pygmy group (men average 5 feet tall), are thought to be Burundi's original inhabitants.

Cambodia

Capital: Phnom Penh
Population: 14,952,665
Area: 69,900 sq mi (181,040 sq km)
Language: Khmer, French, English
Did You Know? The powerful Khmer Empire that flourished from the 9th to the 13th centuries included large parts of present-day Laos, Thailand, and Vietnam, as well as Cambodia.

COLOR KEY

- Africa
- Asia
- Australia
- Europe
- North America
- Pacific Islands
- South America

Cameroon

Capital: Yaoundé
Population: 20,129,878
Area: 183,568 sq mi (475,440 sq km)
Language: English, French, African languages
Did You Know? The most popular sport in Cameroon is soccer. Teams from Cameroon have won the Africa Cup of Nations soccer championship four times.

Canada

Capital: Ottawa
Population: 34,300,083
Area: 3,855,103 sq mi (9,984,670 sq km)
Language: English, French
Did You Know? In 1994, Canada's Parliament declared ice hockey the country's national winter sport and lacrosse the national summer sport.

Cape Verde

Capital: Praia
Population: 523,568
Area: 1,557 sq mi (4,033 sq km)
Language: Portuguese, Crioulo
Did You Know? More Cape Verdeans live abroad than live on the nation's islands.

Central African Republic

Capital: Bangui
Population: 5,057,208
Area: 240,535 sq mi (622,984 sq km)
Language: French, Sangho
Did You Know? In 1976, Jean-Bedel Bokassa proclaimed himself emperor, but he was overthrown a few years later.

COLOR KEY

- Africa
- Asia
- Australia
- Europe
- North America
- Pacific Islands
- South America

Chad

Capital: N'Djamena
Population: 10,975,648
Area: 495,755 sq mi (1,284,000 sq km)
Language: French, Arabic, Sara
Did You Know? There are some 200 native ethnic groups living in Chad.

Chile

Capital: Santiago
Population: 17,067,369
Area: 292,260 sq mi (756,950 sq km)
Language: Spanish
Did You Know? The Atacama Desert in northern Chile is one of the earth's driest places. In some areas, rain has never been recorded.

China

Capital: Beijing
Population: 1,343,239,923
Area: 3,705,407 sq mi (9,596,960 sq km)
Language: Mandarin, and many dialects
Did You Know? The Forbidden City, in the heart of Beijing, was the home of Chinese emperors for centuries. Most ordinary people were forbidden to enter its walls. It is now visited by thousands of tourists every day.

FORBIDDEN CITY, BEIJING, CHINA

Colombia

Capital: Bogotá
Population: 45,239,079
Area: 439,736 sq mi (1,138,910 sq km)
Language: Spanish
Did You Know? The town of Lloro, in the Andes Mountains, may be the world's rainiest place. It gets an average of more than 500 inches of rain each year.

Comoros

Capital: Moroni
Population: 737,284
Area: 838 sq mi (2,170 sq km)
Language: Arabic, French, Shikomoro
Did You Know? On Grande Comore, the largest of the islands in the Comoros, land is owned and inherited by women, and people take their mothers' last names.

Congo, Democratic Republic of the

Capital: Kinshasa
Population: 73,599,190
Area: 905,568 sq mi (2,345,410 sq km)
Language: French, Lingala, Kingwana, Kikongo, Tshiluba
Did You Know? This country in the heart of Africa was ruled by Belgium for about 80 years, until it won independence in 1960.

Congo, Republic of the

Capital: Brazzaville
Population: 4,366,266
Area: 132,047 sq mi (342,000 sq km)
Language: French, Lingala, Monokutuba, Kikongo
Did You Know? The Bantu people of the Congo have lived in the region since before A.D. 1000.

Costa Rica

Capital: San José
Population: 4,636,348
Area: 19,730 sq mi (51,100 sq km)
Language: Spanish, English
Did You Know? Almost one-fourth of the land in Costa Rica has been set aside as protected areas for the nation's many kinds of plants and animals.

Côte d'Ivoire (Ivory Coast)

Capital: Yamoussoukro
Population: 21,952,093
Area: 124,503 sq mi (322,460 sq km)
Language: French, Dioula
Did You Know? The largest Christian church in the world is in Côte d'Ivoire's capital city of Yamoussoukro.

Croatia

Capital: Zagreb
Population: 4,480,043
Area: 21,831 sq mi (56,542 sq km)
Language: Croatian, Serbian
Did You Know? Croatians enjoy the *kolo,* a Slavic folk dance performed in a circle, with music from violins and a *tambura*, or Croatian mandolin.

Cuba

Capital: Havana
Population: 11,075,244
Area: 42,803 sq mi (110,860 sq km)
Language: Spanish
Did You Know? One of the world's few remaining Communist countries, Cuba lies just 90 miles away from the tip of Florida.

Cyprus

Capital: Nicosia
Population: 1,138,071
Area: 3,571 sq mi (9,250 sq km)
Language: Greek, Turkish, English
Did You Know? The island of Cyprus is divided into two parts, one mostly Greek, the other almost entirely Turkish. The Turkish North declared independence in 1983 but no other country except Turkey recognizes it as an independent nation.

RAIN FOREST, COSTA RICA

Czech Republic

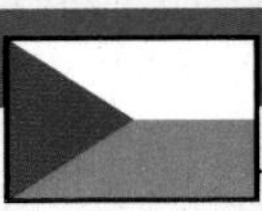

Capital: Prague
Population: 10,177,300
Area: 30,450 sq mi (78,866 sq km)
Language: Czech, Slovak
Did You Know? Many Czechs eat pork and lentils on New Year's Day. Some people say that eating pork may bring good luck in the coming year and that eating lentils may bring health and prosperity.

Denmark

Capital: Copenhagen
Population: 5,543,453
Area: 16,639 sq mi (43,094 sq km)
Language: Danish, Faroese
Did You Know? The statue of the Little Mermaid in Copenhagen's harbor was created in honor of the Danish fairy tale author Hans Christian Andersen.

Djibouti

Capital: Djibouti
Population: 774,389
Area: 8,880 sq mi (23,000 sq km)
Language: French, Arabic, Somali, Afar
Did You Know? Common foods in Djibouti include chicken, lentils, flat bread, and baked fish with a spicy sauce.

Dominica

Capital: Roseau
Population: 73,126
Area: 291 sq mi (754 sq km)
Language: English, French patois
Did You Know? The Sisserou parrot, seen on Dominica's flag, is the national bird. Dominica's tropical rain forests are its only home in the world.

Dominican Republic

Capital: Santo Domingo
Population: 10,088,598
Area: 18,815 sq mi (48,730 sq km)
Language: Spanish
Did You Know? More than 500 athletes who have played major league baseball over the years were born in the Dominican Republic.

Ecuador

Capital: Quito
Population: 15,223,680
Area: 109,483 sq mi (283,560 sq km)
Language: Spanish, Quechua
Did You Know? The tortoises in Ecuador's Galapagos Islands can weigh more than 500 pounds and live for 150 years or more.

Egypt

Capital: Cairo
Population: 83,688,164
Area: 386,662 sq mi (1,001,450 sq km)
Language: Arabic, English, French
Did You Know? The Great Pyramid of Giza, built around 2250 B.C., is made up of more than 2 million stone blocks.

PYRAMID AT GIZA, EGYPT

El Salvador

Capital: San Salvador
Population: 6,090,646
Area: 8,124 sq mi (21,040 sq km)
Language: Spanish, Nahua
Did You Know? El Salvador, the smallest country in Central America, is known as the "Land of Volcanoes" because it has so many of them. The massive San Salvador volcano lies on the edge of the nation's capital city.

COLOR KEY

- Africa
- Asia
- Australia
- Europe
- North America
- Pacific Islands
- South America

Equatorial Guinea

Capital: Malabo
Population: 685,991
Area: 10,831 sq mi (28,051 sq km)
Language: Spanish, French, Fang, Bubi
Did You Know? Equatorial Guinea is the only African country in which Spanish is an official language.

Eritrea

Capital: Asmara
Population: 6,086,495
Area: 46,842 sq mi (121,320 sq km)
Language: Afar, Arabic, Tigre, Kunama, Tigrinya
Did You Know? Spicy stews are a popular food in Eritrea. At meals, it is a sign of politeness to take some of your own food and feed it to the person next to you.

Estonia

Capital: Tallinn
Population: 1,274,709
Area: 17,462 sq mi (45,226 sq km)
Language: Estonian, Russian
Did You Know? In 1991, Estonia became independent, and it joined the European Union in 2004. In January 2011, Estonia became the 17th nation of the EU to adopt the euro as its currency.

Ethiopia

Capital: Addis Ababa
Population: 93,815,992
Area: 435,186 sq mi (1,127,127 sq km)
Language: Amharic, Tigrinya, Oromigna, Guaragigna, Somali, Arabic
Did You Know? Ethiopia was taken over by Italy in 1936 but was freed by British forces five years later during World War II.

Fiji

Capital: Suva
Population: 890,057
Area: 7,054 sq mi (18,270 sq km)
Language: English, Fijian, Hindustani
Did You Know? This country is made up of more than 300 islands in the South Pacific Ocean. Some of them are very tiny, and most of them have no people living there.

Finland

Capital: Helsinki
Population: 5,262,930
Area: 130,559 sq mi (338,145 sq km)
Language: Finnish, Swedish
Did You Know? In Finland, fines for speeding are based on income. One of Finland's richest citizens was fined $216,900 for driving too fast.

France

Capital: Paris
Population: 65,630,692
Area: 248,429 sq mi (643,427 sq km)
Language: French
Did You Know? Every year more than 70 million tourists visit France, making it the world's top tourist destination.

NOTRE DAME CATHEDRAL, PARIS, FRANCE

Gabon

Capital: Libreville
Population: 1,608,321
Area: 103,347 sq mi (267,667 sq km)
Language: French, Fang, Myene, Nzebi
Did You Know? Gabon lies on the equator and stays hot year round. But there are rainy seasons and dry seasons. The rainiest month is November, while July is usually the driest, with little or no rain.

The Gambia

Capital: Banjul
Population: 1,840,454
Area: 4,363 sq mi (11,300 sq km)
Language: English, Mandinka, Wolof
Did You Know? The River Gambia splits The Gambia in two as it flows west to the Atlantic Ocean.

Georgia

Capital: T'bilisi
Population: 4,570,934
Area: 26,911 sq mi (69,700 sq km)
Language: Georgian, Russian, Armenian, Azeri, Abkhaz
Did You Know? Forests in the mountains of Georgia provide a habitat for deer, boar, lynxes, and wolves. In all, Georgia has more than 100 kinds of mammals.

Germany

Capital: Berlin
Population: 81,305,856
Area: 137,847 sq mi (357,021 sq km)
Language: German
Did You Know? Sauerbraten, a favorite German dish, used to be made with horse meat. Today, it is usually made with beef.

Ghana

Capital: Accra
Population: 25,241,998
Area: 92,456 sq mi (239,460 sq km)
Language: English, Akan, Moshi-Dagomba, Ewe, Ga
Did You Know? On Fridays, schoolchildren in Ghana are often invited to share folktales and other stories told to them by their parents and grandparents.

COLOR KEY

- Africa
- Asia
- Australia
- Europe
- North America
- Pacific Islands
- South America

Greece

Capital: Athens
Population: 10,767,827
Area: 50,942 sq mi (131,940 sq km)
Language: Greek, English, French
Did You Know? More than 2,000 islands are part of the country of Greece. Many are quite small, and fewer than 200 are inhabited.

FISHING VILLAGE, GREECE

Grenada

Capital: Saint George's
Population: 109,011
Area: 133 sq mi (344 sq km)
Language: English, French patois
Did You Know? Spring in Grenada is often sunny, dry, and windy. It's a great time to fly kites. On the day after Easter, there are kite flying competitions all across the country.

Guatemala

Capital: Guatemala City
Population: 14,099,032
Area: 42,043 sq mi (108,890 sq km)
Language: Spanish, Amerindian languages
Did You Know? Before the arrival of the Spanish, the Mayan Indian empire flourished for more than 1,000 years in what is today Guatemala.

Guinea

Capital: Conakry
Population: 10,884,958
Area: 94,926 sq mi (245,857 sq km)
Language: French, Susu, Pulaar, Malinke
Did You Know? Much of Guinea is covered by wooded grassland and dense forests. The many kinds of animals found in these habitats include snakes, crocodiles, parrots, leopards, monkeys, wild boar, elephants, and hippopotamuses.

Guinea-Bissau

Capital: Bissau
Population: 1,628,603
Area: 13,946 sq mi (36,120 sq km)
Language: Portuguese, Crioulo, African languages
Did You Know? At carnival time, the people of Guinea-Bissau wear masks to make them look like sharks, hippos, and bulls.

Guyana

Capital: Georgetown
Population: 741,908
Area: 83,000 sq mi (214,970 sq km)
Language: English, Amerindian dialects, Creole, Hindi
Did You Know? Christopher Columbus explored the coast of Guyana in 1498, and almost 100 years later, Sir Walter Raleigh searched for gold there.

Haiti

Capital: Port-au-Prince
Population: 9,801,664
Area: 10,714 sq mi (27,750 sq km)
Language: French, Creole
Did You Know? Michel Martelly, a popular musician who pioneered the Haitian style of dance music called *kompas*, was elected president of Haiti in 2011.

Honduras

Capital: Tegucigalpa
Population: 8,296,693
Area: 43,278 sq mi (112,090 sq km)
Language: Spanish, Amerindian dialects
Did You Know? Popular foods in Honduras include tacos, tortillas, and tamales, along with conch soup and fried plantains. These are often served with rice and beans.

Hungary

Capital: Budapest
Population: 9,958,453
Area: 35,919 sq mi (93,030 sq km)
Language: Hungarian (Magyar)
Did You Know? In the course of Hungary's history, large parts of the country have been part of the Roman Empire, the Mongol Empire, and Turkey's Ottoman Empire.

Iceland

Capital: Reykjavik
Population: 313,183
Area: 39,769 sq mi (103,000 sq km)
Language: Icelandic, English
Did You Know? Glaciers, lakes, and a lava desert cover about three-fourths of Iceland's surface area.

India

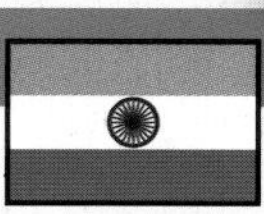

Capital: New Delhi
Population: 1,205,073,612
Area: 1,269,346 sq mi (3,287,590 sq km)
Language: Hindi, English, Bengali, Urdu
Did You Know? By around the year 2025, India is expected to have the largest population of any country in the world.

GANGES RIVER, VARANASI, INDIA

Indonesia

Capital: Jakarta
Population: 248,216,193
Area: 741,100 sq mi (1,919,440 sq km)
Language: Bahasa Indonesian, English, Dutch, Javanese
Did You Know? In Indonesia, there are over 200 million Muslims, more than in any other country.

Iran

Capital: Tehran

Population: 78,868,711

Area: 636,296 sq mi (1,648,000 sq km)

Language: Farsi (Persian), Turkic, Kurdish

Did You Know? The Persians settled in Iran around 1500 B.C. and made it the center of a vast empire in the 6th century B.C. But the empire fell to Alexander the Great.

Iraq

Capital: Baghdad

Population: 31,129,225

Area: 168,754 sq mi (437,072 sq km)

Language: Arabic, Kurdish

Did You Know? The Sumerians settled in the region more than 5,000 years ago. They built walled cities and an advanced civilization that lasted for 3,000 years.

Ireland

Capital: Dublin

Population: 4,722,028

Area: 27,135 sq mi (70,280 sq km)

Language: English, Irish

Did You Know? Over the years, many people from Ireland have immigrated to the United States. The number of Irish Americans today (almost 35 million) is more than 7 times the population of Ireland.

Israel

Capital: Jerusalem

Population: 7,590,758

Area: 8,019 sq mi (20,770 sq km)

Language: Hebrew, Arabic, English

Did You Know? When Romans destroyed the Second Temple in Jerusalem, in A.D. 70, an outer wall of the Temple Mount was left standing. This Western Wall, sometimes called the Wailing Wall, is sacred to Jews around the world. It is common for visitors to slip written prayers into the cracks.

COLOR KEY

- Africa
- Asia
- Australia
- Europe
- North America
- Pacific Islands
- South America

Italy

Capital: Rome

Population: 61,261,254

Area: 116,306 sq mi (301,230 sq km)

Language: Italian, German, French, Slovenian

Did You Know? Alessandro Volta of Italy is credited with inventing an early version of the battery. The electrical unit *volt* is named for him.

Jamaica

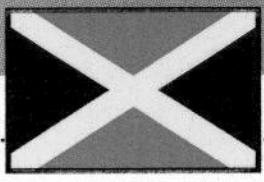

Capital: Kingston

Population: 2,889,187

Area: 4,244 sq mi (10,991 sq km)

Language: English, Jamaican Creole

Did You Know? Reggae, a mixture of native, rock, and soul music, was developed in Jamaica.

Japan

Capital: Tokyo

Population: 127,368,088

Area: 145,883 sq mi (377,835 sq km)

Language: Japanese

Did You Know? Sumo wrestling is Japan's national sport. Other popular sports include judo and other martial arts, as well as baseball and soccer.

Jordan

Capital: Amman

Population: 6,508,887

Area: 35,637 sq mi (92,300 sq km)

Language: Arabic, English

Did You Know? Philadelphia was the name in ancient times for the city that is now Amman.

Kazakhstan

Capital: Astana
Population: 17,522,010
Area: 1,049,155 sq mi (2,717,300 sq km)
Language: Kazakh, Russian
Did You Know? Kazakhstan, the world's biggest landlocked country in area, is located mostly in Central Asia. Like Russia, and unlike the other former Soviet republics, Kazakhstan has large oil reserves.

Kenya

Capital: Nairobi
Population: 43,013,341
Area: 224,962 sq mi (582,650 sq km)
Language: Kiswahili, English
Did You Know? A worldwide ban on ivory trading in 1989 helped save Kenya's elephants from becoming extinct. But illegal hunting of elephants continues to be a problem.

Kiribati

Capital: Tarawa
Population: 101,998
Area: 313 sq mi (811 sq km)
Language: English, I-Kiribati
Did You Know? Tarawa is one of many tiny Pacific islands that are part of Kiribati. It was the site of a fierce battle between Japanese forces and U.S. Marines during World War II.

Korea, North

Capital: Pyongyang
Population: 24,589,122
Area: 46,541 sq mi (120,540 sq km)
Language: Korean
Did You Know? When North Korea's "supreme leader," Kim Jong Il, died in December 2011, his youngest son, Kim Jong Un, took over his position. Still in his twenties, Kim Jong Un became the world's youngest head of state.

Korea, South

Capital: Seoul
Population: 48,860,500
Area: 38,023 sq mi (98,480 sq km)
Language: Korean
Did You Know? About 10 million people, more than one in five South Koreans, live in Seoul.

SEOUL, SOUTH KOREA

Kosovo

Capital: Pristina
Population: 1,836,529
Area: 4,203 sq mi (10,887 sq km)
Language: Albanian, Serbian, Bosnian, Turkish, Roma
Did You Know? Kosovo declared its independence from Serbia in 2008 and has its own government, but some countries do not accept it as an independent nation.

Kuwait

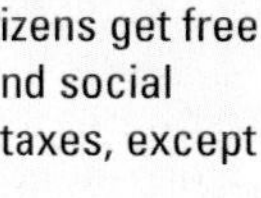

Capital: Kuwait City
Population: 2,646,314
Area: 6,880 sq mi (17,820 sq km)
Language: Arabic, English
Did You Know? Because of the money Kuwait gets from oil, its citizens get free medical care, education, and social security. And there are no taxes, except for customs duties.

Kyrgyzstan

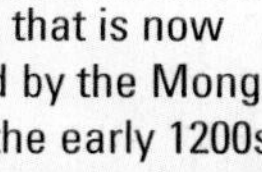

Capital: Bishkek
Population: 5,496,737
Area: 76,641 sq mi (198,500 sq km)
Language: Kyrgyz, Russian
Did You Know? The region that is now Kyrgyzstan was conquered by the Mongol emperor Genghis Khan in the early 1200s.

Laos

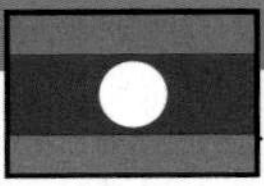

Capital: Vientiane

Population: 6,586,266

Area: 91,429 sq mi (236,800 sq km)

Language: Lao, French, English

Did You Know? The first kingdom in what is now Laos was called *Lan Xang*, or "Kingdom of the Million Elephants."

Latvia

Capital: Riga

Population: 2,191,580

Area: 24,938 sq mi (64,589 sq km)

Language: Latvian, Russian, Lithuanian

Did You Know? The president's official home is a castle built in the early 1300s.

Lebanon

Capital: Beirut

Population: 4,140,289

Area: 4,015 sq mi (10,400 sq km)

Language: Arabic, French, English, Armenian

Did You Know? Beirut's history goes back about 5,000 years. It was founded as early as 3000 B.C., before Jerusalem, Athens, Damascus, or any other capital city in the world.

Lesotho

Capital: Maseru

Population: 1,930,493

Area: 11,720 sq mi (30,355 sq km)

Language: English, Sesotho, Zulu, Xhosa

Did You Know? The high, rugged mountains of Lesotho attract many tourists from South Africa and other countries. Hiking and bird watching are very popular. Visitors often ride ponies to get to remote areas.

Liberia

Capital: Monrovia

Population: 3,887,886

Area: 43,000 sq mi (111,370 sq km)

Language: English, ethnic languages

Did You Know? Liberia was founded in the early 1820s as a colony for freed African slaves from the U.S. It became an independent republic in 1847.

Libya

Capital: Tripoli

Population: 6,733,620

Area: 679,362 sq mi (1,759,540 sq km)

Language: Arabic, Italian, English

Did You Know? Most of Libya is desert. Only about 1 percent of the land is naturally suitable for farming.

Liechtenstein

Capital: Vaduz

Population: 36,713

Area: 62 sq mi (160 sq km)

Language: German, Alemannic dialect

Did You Know? Nearly half of all the workers in tiny Liechtenstein commute there each day from their homes in Austria, Switzerland, or Germany.

Lithuania

Capital: Vilnius

Population: 3,525,761

Area: 25,213 sq mi (65,300 sq km)

Language: Lithuanian, Russian, Polish

Did You Know? Lithuania and France rely on nuclear power for their energy needs more than any other countries in the world.

MALETSUNYANE FALLS, LESOTHO

COLOR KEY

- Africa
- Asia
- Australia
- Europe
- North America
- Pacific Islands
- South America

Luxembourg

Capital: Luxembourg
Population: 509,074
Area: 998 sq mi (2,586 sq km)
Language: French, German, Luxembourgish
Did You Know? Tiny Luxembourg has been ruled by Burgundy, Spain, Austria, and France, and it was overrun by Germany in two world wars.

OLD QUARTER, LUXEMBOURG

Macedonia

Capital: Skopje
Population: 2,082,370
Area: 9,781 sq mi (25,333 sq km)
Language: Macedonian, Albanian, Turkish
Did You Know? Skopje was rebuilt after an earthquake in 1963 destroyed more than half of the city.

Madagascar

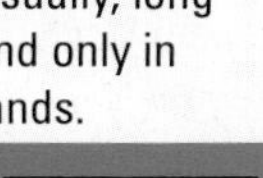

Capital: Antananarivo
Population: 22,585,517
Area: 226,657 sq mi (587,040 sq km)
Language: Malagasy, French, English
Did You Know? Lemurs are monkey-like animals with big eyes and, usually, long bushy tails. They can be found only in Madagascar and nearby islands.

Malawi

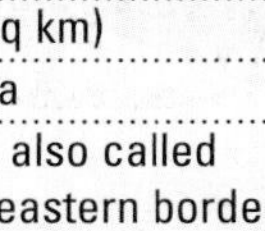

Capital: Lilongwe
Population: 16,323,044
Area: 45,745 sq mi (118,480 sq km)
Language: English, Chichewa
Did You Know? Lake Nyasa, also called Lake Malawi, lies along the eastern border of Malawi. One of the world's biggest and deepest lakes, it is a popular vacation spot and has more kinds of fish than any other lake in the world.

Malaysia

Capital: Kuala Lumpur
Population: 29,179,952
Area: 127,317 sq mi (329,750 sq km)
Language: Malay, English, Chinese, Tamil
Did You Know? During the late 20th century, Malaysia grew into a major industrial power.

Maldives

Capital: Male
Population: 394,451
Area: 116 sq mi (300 sq km)
Language: Maldivian Divehi, English
Did You Know? An island nation that is officially part of Asia, Maldives is that continent's smallest country in area.

Mali

Capital: Bamako
Population: 14,533,511
Area: 478,767 sq mi (1,240,000 sq km)
Language: French, Bambara
Did You Know? Until the 15th century, this area was part of the great Mali Empire in Africa.

Malta

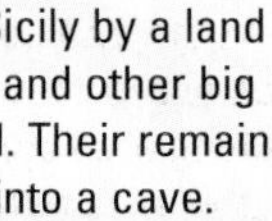

Capital: Valletta
Population: 409,836
Area: 122 sq mi (316 sq km)
Language: Maltese, English
Did You Know? Some 200,000 years ago, Malta was connected to Sicily by a land bridge. Elephants, hippos, and other big animals lived on the island. Their remains have been found washed into a cave.

MAKUZI BAY, LAKE MALAWI

Marshall Islands

Capital: Majuro
Population: 68,480
Area: 70 sq mi (181 sq km)
Language: English, Marshallese
Did You Know? Hiking, swimming, snorkeling, and fly fishing are among popular activities on these islands in the Pacific Ocean.

Mauritania

Capital: Nouakchott
Population: 3,359,185
Area: 397,955 sq mi (1,030,700 sq km)
Language: Arabic, Wolof, Pulaar
Did You Know? Ben Amera, one of the biggest monoliths (large single rocks) in the world, lies in the desert sands of Mauritania.

Mauritius

Capital: Port Louis
Population: 1,313,095
Area: 788 sq mi (2,040 sq km)
Language: Creole, Bhojpuri, French, English
Did You Know? The island of Mauritius is the longtime home of dodo birds. For many centuries, these birds had no enemies. They lost their fear of danger and their ability to fly. When humans came in large numbers in the 1600s, the birds were easily hunted and soon became extinct.

Mexico

Capital: Mexico City
Population: 114,975,406
Area: 761,606 sq mi (1,972,550 sq km)
Language: Spanish, Mayan languages
Did You Know? Near Mexico City lie the ruins of an ancient city. It was abandoned in the eighth century A.D., and even its name was lost. The Aztecs later called it Teotihuacán, or "City of the Gods."

BEACH IN MEXICO

Micronesia

Capital: Palikir
Population: 106,487
Area: 271 sq mi (702 sq km)
Language: English, Trukese, Pohnpeian, Yapese
Did You Know? Micronesia is made up of 607 separate islands in the Pacific Ocean, spread over a path about 2,000 miles long.

Moldova

Capital: Chisinau
Population: 3,656,843
Area: 13,067 sq mi (33,843 sq km)
Language: Moldovan, Russian
Did You Know? Romania is Moldova's next-door neighbor. The Moldavian language is almost the same as Romanian, and about four-fifths of the people in Moldova belong to the Romanian ethnic group.

Monaco

Capital: Monaco
Population: 30,510
Area: 0.76 sq mi (1.96 sq km)
Language: French, English, Italian, Monegasque
Did You Know? Children born in Monaco today can be expected to live to be almost 90 years old. That is longer than in any other country.

Mongolia

Capital: Ulaanbaatar
Population: 3,179,997
Area: 603,909 sq mi (1,564,116 sq km)
Language: Khalkha Mongolian
Did You Know? There is plenty of space in Mongolia. It is the most thinly populated country in the world.

COLOR KEY

- Africa
- Asia
- Australia
- Europe
- North America
- Pacific Islands
- South America

Montenegro

Capital: Cetinje; Podgorica (admin.)

Population: 657,394

Area: 5,415 sq mi (14,026 sq km)

Language: Serbian, Bosnian, Albanian, Croatian

Did You Know? *Montenegro* means "black mountain." The country gets its name from the dark mountain forests that cover much of the land.

Morocco

Capital: Rabat

Population: 32,309,239

Area: 172,414 sq mi (446,550 sq km)

Language: Arabic, Berber dialects, French

Did You Know? Part of Morocco is close to the tropics, but in some regions of the country, it can get very cold. On February 11, 1935, the temperature in a mountainous area of Morocco fell to –11°F, a record low for any place in Africa.

Mozambique

Capital: Maputo

Population: 23,515,934

Area: 309,496 sq mi (801,590 sq km)

Language: Portuguese, Bantu languages

Did You Know? For many years, Mozambique was a colony of Portugal. The first Portuguese settlement was set up in 1505, as a stopping place for Portuguese ships sailing around Africa to reach Asia.

Myanmar (Burma)

Capital: Nay Pyi Taw

Population: 54,584,650

Area: 261,970 sq mi (678,500 sq km)

Language: Burmese

Did You Know? In 1989, the military rulers of this country changed its name from Burma to Myanmar. The UN and most countries use the new name, but some nations that oppose the regime, including the United States, have not accepted it.

Namibia

Capital: Windhoek

Population: 2,165,828

Area: 318,696 sq mi (825,418 sq km)

Language: Afrikaans, English, German

Did You Know? The largest naturally occurring piece of iron on Earth is a meteorite that fell in Namibia.

Nauru

Capital: Yaren district

Population: 9,378

Area: 8 sq mi (21 sq km)

Language: Nauruan, English

Did You Know? In the 1920s, a flu epidemic left Nauru with only about 1,000 people. The birth of a baby girl on October 26, 1932, brought the number to 1,500, a milestone. Nauru celebrates that day each year, with great rejoicing.

Nepal

Capital: Kathmandu

Population: 29,890,686

Area: 56,827 sq mi (147,181 sq km)

Language: Nepali, Maithali, Bhojpuri, English

Did You Know? More than 3,000 people have climbed to the top of Mount Everest, on the Nepal-China border. Over 200 have died in the attempt.

MOUNT EVEREST, NEPAL

Netherlands

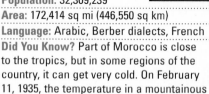

Capital: Amsterdam; The Hague (admin.)

Population: 16,730,632

Area: 16,033 sq mi (41,526 sq km)

Language: Dutch, Frisian

Did You Know? For breakfast, many Dutch people like to eat bread with different kinds of toppings, as well as cheeses and cold meats.

New Zealand

Capital: Wellington
Population: 4,327,944
Area: 103,738 sq mi (268,680 sq km)
Language: English, Maori
Did You Know? The first European to see the New Zealand coast was the 17th-century Dutch navigator Abel Tasman. The Maori natives did not let him land.

Nicaragua

Capital: Managua
Population: 5,727,707
Area: 49,998 sq mi (129,494 sq km)
Language: Spanish, Miskito, indigenous languages
Did You Know? Uncle Rabbit, or Tio Conejo, is a popular figure from Nicaraguan folktales. He is known for playing tricks on Uncle Tiger (Tio Tigre) and other animal neighbors.

Niger

Capital: Niamey
Population: 17,078,839
Area: 489,192 sq mi (1,267,000 sq km)
Language: French, Hausa, Djerma
Did You Know? Horse racing and camel racing are popular sports in Niger, along with wrestling and soccer.

Nigeria

Capital: Abuja
Population: 170,123,740
Area: 356,669 sq mi (923,768 sq km)
Language: English, Hausa, Yoruba, Ibo
Did You Know? Nigeria has more people than any other African country. It also exports the most oil of any nation on the continent.

COLOR KEY

- Africa
- Asia
- Australia
- Europe
- North America
- Pacific Islands
- South America

Norway

Capital: Oslo
Population: 4,707,270
Area: 125,021 sq mi (323,802 sq km)
Language: Norwegian, Sami
Did You Know? The UN ranks Norway as the nation with the highest "quality of life."

Oman

Capital: Muscat
Population: 3,090,150
Area: 82,031 sq mi (212,460 sq km)
Language: Arabic, English, Indian dialects
Did You Know? The Sultan Qaboos Grand Mosque in Muscat can hold 20,000 worshippers. It has a hand-woven prayer rug that's about 230 feet long and 200 feet wide. It took 600 women to weave the rug, over a period of 4 years.

SULTAN QABOOS GRAND MOSQUE, MUSCAT, OMAN

Pakistan

Capital: Islamabad
Population: 190,291,129
Area: 310,403 sq mi (803,940 sq km)
Language: Urdu, English, Punjabi, Sindhi
Did You Know? The British brought the sport of cricket to Pakistan when it was under British rule. Cricket has become the nation's most popular sport.

Palau

Capital: Melekeok
Population: 21,032
Area: 177 sq mi (458 sq km)
Language: English, Palauan, Sonsoral, Tobi, Angaur
Did You Know? Palau has coral reefs, sea caves, shipwrecks, and a wide variety of sea creatures—including giant clams that may weigh as much as 500 pounds.

Panama

Capital: Panama City
Population: 3,510,045
Area: 30,193 sq mi (78,200 sq km)
Language: Spanish, English
Did You Know? El Camino Real was a road across Panama used by Spanish conquerers in the 1500s to bring gold from the Pacific to the Atlantic coast, where it was loaded onto ships to be brought to Spain.

Papua New Guinea

Capital: Port Moresby
Population: 6,310,129
Area: 178,704 sq mi (462,840 sq km)
Language: English, Motu, Melanesian pidgin
Did You Know? There are only six species of poisonous birds in the world, and they all live in Papua New Guinea.

Paraguay

Capital: Asunción
Population: 6,541,591
Area: 157,047 sq mi (406,750 sq km)
Language: Spanish, Guarani
Did You Know? Paraguay and Bolivia are the only countries in South America that do not have a seacoast.

Peru

Capital: Lima
Population: 29,549,517
Area: 496,226 sq mi (1,285,220 sq km)
Language: Spanish, Quechua, Aymara
Did You Know? More than 16,700 feet above sea level, the mining town of La Rinconada, in the Andes Mountains of Peru, is said to be the highest town in the world.

Philippines

Capital: Manila
Population: 103,775,002
Area: 115,831 sq mi (300,000 sq km)
Language: Filipino, English
Did You Know? The martial art of *arnis*, also called *escrima* or *kali*, has a long history in the Philippines. In 2009, it was named the national sport.

Poland

Capital: Warsaw
Population: 38,415,284
Area: 120,726 sq mi (312,679 sq km)
Language: Polish, Ukrainian, German
Did You Know? Famous people born in Poland include composer Frederic Chopin, Nobel Prize-winning scientist Marie Curie, and Pope John Paul II.

WAWEL CASTLE, POLAND

Portugal

Capital: Lisbon
Population: 10,781,459
Area: 35,672 sq mi (92,391 sq km)
Language: Portuguese
Did You Know? The city of Guimarães in northern Portugal has a medieval castle dating back to the 12th century and many well preserved buildings from the time when Portugal was the seat of an empire.

Qatar

Capital: Doha

Population: 1,951,591

Area: 4,416 sq mi (11,437 sq km)

Language: Arabic, English

Did You Know? Qatar and Liechtenstein are the two richest countries in the world, as measured by economic output per person.

Romania

Capital: Bucharest

Population: 21,848,504

Area: 91,699 sq mi (237,500 sq km)

Language: Romanian, Hungarian, German

Did You Know? At the Pharmaceutical Museum in the city of Cluj-Napoca, you can enter a centuries-old drugstore, learn about medieval medicine and alchemy, and view old scales, prescriptions, and glass cases of mummy dust.

Russia

Capital: Moscow

Population: 138,082,178

Area: 6,592,772 sq mi (17,075,200 sq km)

Language: Russian, many minority languages

Did You Know? The Trans-Siberian Railroad, the world's longest, stretches almost 5,800 miles across Russia, from Moscow's Yaroslavl Station to the port city of Vladivostok.

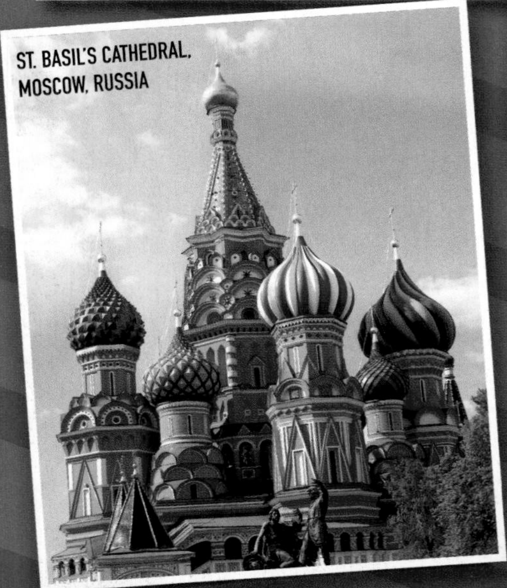

ST. BASIL'S CATHEDRAL, MOSCOW, RUSSIA

Rwanda

Capital: Kigali

Population: 11,689,696

Area: 10,169 sq mi (26,338 sq km)

Language: French, English, Kinyarwanda, Kiswahili

Did You Know? Nyungwe National Park in Rwanda is Africa's biggest protected mountain rain forest. It is home to large numbers of monkeys and chimpanzees and to more than 300 species of birds.

Saint Kitts and Nevis

Capital: Basseterre

Population: 50,726

Area: 101 sq mi (261 sq km)

Language: English

Did You Know? The island of St. Kitts was named in honor of St. Christopher, patron saint of Christopher Columbus. "Kitt" is actually a nickname for "Christopher." Columbus sighted the island in November 1493, becoming the first European to do so.

COAST OF SAINT LUCIA

Saint Lucia

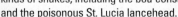

Capital: Castries

Population: 162,178

Area: 238 sq mi (616 sq km)

Language: English, French patois

Did You Know? This tropical island has several kinds of snakes, including the boa constrictor and the poisonous St. Lucia lancehead.

Saint Vincent and the Grenadines

Capital: Kingstown
Population: 103,537
Area: 150 sq mi (389 sq km)
Language: English, French patois
Did You Know? The Pirates of the Caribbean movies, starring Johnny Depp, were filmed mostly at Wallilabou Bay on the island of St. Vincent.

Samoa (formerly Western Samoa)

Capital: Apia
Population: 194,320
Area: 1,137 sq mi (2,944 sq km)
Language: English, Samoan
Did You Know? This Pacific island nation has temperatures in the 70s and 80s (Fahrenheit) all year round.

San Marino

Capital: San Marino
Population: 32,140
Area: 24 sq mi (61 sq km)
Language: Italian
Did You Know? San Marino, a tiny nation surrounded entirely by Italy, claims to be the oldest country in Europe, dating back to the fourth century.

São Tomé and Príncipe

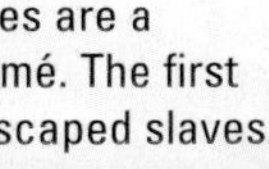

Capital: São Tomé
Population: 183,176
Area: 386 sq mi (1,001 sq km)
Language: Portuguese, Creole
Did You Know? The Angolares are a small ethnic group in São Tomé. The first Angolares may have been escaped slaves.

COLOR KEY

- Africa
- Asia
- Australia
- Europe
- North America
- Pacific Islands
- South America

Saudi Arabia

Capital: Riyadh
Population: 26,534,504
Area: 830,000 sq mi (2,149,960 sq km)
Language: Arabic
Did You Know? Saudi Arabia is the birthplace of Islam, and just about all Saudis today are Muslims. Only Muslim services are permitted in public.

Senegal

Capital: Dakar
Population: 12,969,606
Area: 75,749 sq mi (196,190 sq km)
Language: French, Wolof, Pulaar
Did You Know? Visiting family and friends is very popular in Senegal, and it is not considered impolite to just drop by without warning. When you do stop in, you are nearly always invited to stay for a meal or for tea.

Serbia

Capital: Belgrade
Population: 7,276,604
Area: 29,913 sq mi (77,474 sq km)
Language: Serbian, Albanian, Romanian
Did You Know? In Serbian weddings, it is common for the groom's brother to walk down the aisle with the bride. Towels are a traditional wedding present in Serbia. Many Serbians consider them a symbol of closeness.

BELGRADE, SERBIA

Seychelles

Capital: Victoria

Population: 90,024

Area: 176 sq mi (455 sq km)

Language: Creole, English, French

Did You Know? The colors of Seychelles' flag represent the sky and sea (blue), the sun (yellow), the people and their work (red), social justice and harmony (white), and the environment (green).

Sierra Leone

Capital: Freetown

Population: 5,485,998

Area: 27,699 sq mi (71,740 sq km)

Language: English, Mende, Temne, Krio

Did You Know? The lakes and rivers of Sierra Leone are home to crocodiles and hippos.

Singapore

Capital: Singapore

Population: 5,353,494

Area: 269 sq mi (697 sq km)

Language: Chinese, Malay, Tamil, English

Did You Know? In Singapore you can be given a big fine for spitting in public, carrying chewing gum, or bringing a toy weapon or toy money into the country.

Slovakia

Capital: Bratislava

Population: 5,483,088

Area: 18,859 sq mi (48,845 sq km)

Language: Slovak, Hungarian

Did You Know? Slovakia and the Czech Republic were joined together after World War I (as the country of Czechoslovakia), but they broke up into separate nations in 1993.

Slovenia

Capital: Ljubljana

Population: 1,996,617

Area: 7,827 sq mi (20,273 sq km)

Language: Slovenian, Serbo-Croatian

Did You Know? Slovenia was part of Yugoslavia from 1918 to 1991, when it declared independence. It later became a member of the European Union and the UN.

Solomon Islands

Capital: Honiara

Population: 584,578

Area: 10,985 sq mi (28,450 sq km)

Language: English, Melanesian pidgin

Did You Know? These islands got their name from a Spanish explorer who found gold in 1568 at the mouth of a river. He thought the site could be one of the places where King Solomon got the gold for his temple in Jerusalem.

Somalia

Capital: Mogadishu

Population: 10,085,638

Area: 246,201 sq mi (637,657 sq km)

Language: Somali, Arabic, Italian, English

Did You Know? Former British and Italian colonies combined to form the independent nation of Somalia in 1960.

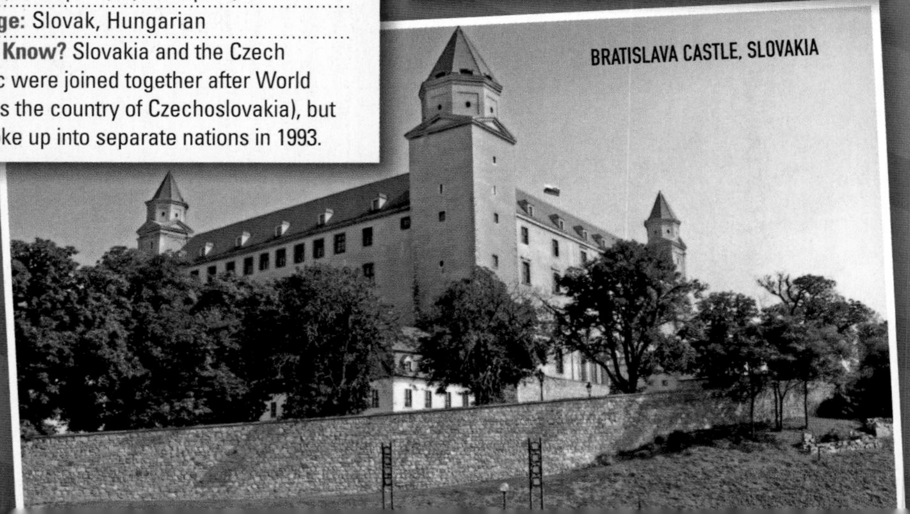

BRATISLAVA CASTLE, SLOVAKIA

South Africa

Capital: Pretoria (admin.); Cape Town (legis.); Bloemfontein (judicial)
Population: 48,810,427
Area: 471,011 sq mi (1,219,912 sq km)
Language: Afrikaans, English, Ndebele, Sotho, Zulu, Xhosa
Did You Know? South Africa is a leading source of valuable minerals, such as gold, diamonds, and platinum.

GAME RESERVE, SOUTH AFRICA

South Sudan

Capital: Juba
Population: 10,625,176
Area: 248,777 sq mi (644,329 sq km)
Language: English, Arabic, Dinka, Nuer
Did You Know? In a few years, the new nation of South Sudan will have a new capital. Plans are to build it at a place called Ramciel, in the center of the country.

Spain

Capital: Madrid
Population: 47,042,984
Area: 194,897 sq mi (504,782 sq km)
Language: Castilian Spanish, Catalan, Galician
Did You Know? The Prado in Madrid is one of the world's leading art museums. It opened 1819.

Sri Lanka

Capital: Colombo
Population: 21,481,334
Area: 25,332 sq mi (65,610 sq km)
Language: Sinhala, Tamil, English
Did You Know? Sri Lanka is known for precious gems such as rubies, sapphires, and moonstones.

Sudan

Capital: Khartoum
Population: 34,206,710
Area: 718,723 sq mi (1,861,484 sq km)
Language: Arabic, English, Nubian, Ta Bedawie
Did You Know? Khartoum is located where the White Nile and the Blue Nile rivers meet to form the main Nile River.

Suriname

Capital: Paramaribo
Population: 560,157
Area: 63,039 sq mi (163,270 sq km)
Language: Dutch, English, Sranang Tongo
Did You Know? Suriname is the smallest country in South America.

Swaziland

Capital: Mbabane
Population: 1,386,914
Area: 6,704 sq mi (17,363 sq km)
Language: English, siSwati
Did You Know? Only one out of five people in Swaziland lives in a city.

Sweden

Capital: Stockholm
Population: 9,103,788
Area: 173,732 sq mi (449,964 sq km)
Language: Swedish, Sami, Finnish
Did You Know? In Kiruna, Sweden's northernmost city, the Sun does not rise in January, and does not set in June.

COLOR KEY

- Africa
- Asia
- Australia
- Europe
- North America
- Pacific Islands
- South America

THE MATTERHORN, SWITZERLAND

Switzerland

Capital: Bern (admin.); Lausanne (judicial)

Population: 7,655,628

Area: 15,942 sq mi (41,290 sq km)

Language: German, French, Italian, Romansch

Did You Know? The Gotthard Base tunnel will be the world's longest railway tunnel when it opens for operation in a few years. It extends for 35 miles through the Alps.

Syria

Capital: Damascus

Population: 22,530,746

Area: 71,498 sq mi (185,180 sq km)

Language: Arabic, Kurdish, Armenian

Did You Know? The Syrian city of Aleppo got its name from the Arabic word for "fresh milk." The name came about because of a belief that the biblical figure Abraham milked his cow there.

Taiwan

Capital: Taipei

Population: 23,113,901

Area: 13,892 sq mi (35,980 sq km)

Language: Mandarin Chinese, Taiwanese

Did You Know? Beef noodle soup is a traditional dish from mainland China that is very popular in Taiwan. It is often made with very hot red chili peppers.

Tajikistan

Capital: Dushanbe

Population: 7,768,385

Area: 55,251 sq mi (143,100 sq km)

Language: Tajik, Russian

Did You Know? Tajikistan is a landlocked country in Central Asia. Mountains cover more than 90 percent of the land, and the glaciers there are the biggest in Asia.

Tanzania

Capital: Dar es Salaam; Dodoma (legislative)

Population: 43,601,796

Area: 364,900 sq mi (945,087 sq km)

Language: Kiswahili (Swahili), English, Arabic

Did You Know? Mount Kilimanjaro, the tallest mountain in Africa, stands by itself in Tanzania. There are no other mountains around it.

Thailand

Capital: Bangkok

Population: 67,091,089

Area: 198,457 sq mi (514,000 sq km)

Language: Thai, English

Did You Know? The king of Thailand is said to be the richest royal person in the world, worth about $30 billion.

BANGKOK, THAILAND

Timor-Leste (East Timor)

Capital: Dili

Population: 1,201,255

Area: 5,743 sq mi (14,874 sq km)

Language: Tetum, Portuguese, Indonesian, English

Did You Know? Evidence found in 2006 at a cave site at the eastern tip of the island of Timor indicates that people lived there more than 42,000 years ago, eating turtles, tuna, and giant rats.

Togo

Capital: Lomé

Population: 6,961,049

Area: 21,925 sq mi (56,785 sq km)

Language: French, Ewe, Mina, Kabye, Dagomba

Did You Know? Foods popular in Togo include fried yams, grilled chicken with chili sauce, and snails.

Tonga

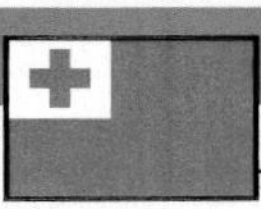

Capital: Nuku'alofa

Population: 106,146

Area: 289 sq mi (748 sq km)

Language: Tongan, English

Did You Know? Children in Tonga enjoy playing *lanita*, a simplified form of cricket, and various traditional games that involve tossing sticks. Friendliness is a big part of Tonga's culture, and many of these games stress cooperation rather than competition.

Trinidad and Tobago

Capital: Port-of-Spain

Population: 1,226,383

Area: 1,980 sq mi (5,128 sq km)

Language: English, Hindi, French, Spanish

Did You Know? Many people from India came to Trinidad in the 1800s to work on sugar cane plantations. Today, about 40 percent of Trinidad's population is of Indian descent.

Tunisia

Capital: Tunis

Population: 10,732,900

Area: 63,170 sq mi (163,610 sq km)

Language: Arabic, French

Did You Know? The ancient city Carthage was located in what is now Tunisia.

Turkey

Capital: Ankara

Population: 79,749,461

Area: 301,384 sq mi (780,580 sq km)

Language: Turkish, Kurdish, Arabic

Did You Know? The Bosporus Bridge, in Istanbul, spans two continents, linking Asia with Europe. About 3% of Turkey is in Europe, and the rest is in Asia.

BOSPORUS BRIDGE, ISTANBUL, TURKEY

Turkmenistan

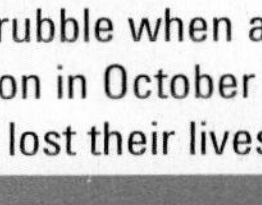

Capital: Ashgabat

Population: 5,054,828

Area: 188,456 sq mi (488,100 sq km)

Language: Turkmen, Russian, Uzbek

Did You Know? Much of the city of Ashgabat was turned into rubble when an earthquake struck the region in October 1948. Some 110,000 people lost their lives.

Tuvalu

Capital: Funafuti

Population: 10,619

Area: 10 sq mi (26 sq km)

Language: Tuvaluan, English

Did You Know? Some scientists predict that because of global warming and rising sea levels these nine small islands could disappear within the next fifty years.

COLOR KEY

- Africa
- Asia
- Australia
- Europe
- North America
- Pacific Islands
- South America

Uganda

Capital: Kampala
Population: 35,873,253
Area: 91,136 sq mi (236,040 sq km)
Language: English, Ganda, Swahili
Did You Know? A recent study found that red colobus monkeys in Uganda's Kibale National Park have been dying out, mostly because of being hunted by chimpanzees.

Ukraine

Capital: Kiev (Kyiv)
Population: 44,854,065
Area: 233,090 sq mi (603,700 sq km)
Language: Ukrainian, Russian
Did You Know? Ukraine has the biggest area of any country in Europe, except Russia. Both Ukraine and Russia were once part of the Soviet Union.

United Arab Emirates

Capital: Abu Dhabi
Population: 5,314,317
Area: 32,278 sq mi (83,600 sq km)
Language: Arabic, Persian, English, Hindi, Urdu
Did You Know? The world's biggest indoor theme park is located in Abu Dhabi, United Arab Emirates. The park's Formula Rossa roller coaster, which starts indoors and travels outside, is the world's fastest roller coaster. It reaches a top speed of 149 miles an hour.

TRAFALGAR SQUARE, LONDON, UNITED KINGDOM

United Kingdom (Great Britain)

Capital: London
Population: 63,047,162
Area: 94,526 sq mi (244,820 sq km)
Language: English, Welsh, Scottish Gaelic
Did You Know? Queen Elizabeth I, Sir Isaac Newton, Charles Darwin, and Charles Dickens are among many famous people buried in London's Westminster Abbey.

United States

Capital: Washington, D.C.
Population: 313,847,465
Area: 3,795,951 sq mi (9,831,513 sq km)
Language: English, Spanish
Did You Know? The United States uses more energy than any other country—about one-fifth of the world's total energy consumption.

FORMULA ROSSA ROLLER COASTER, ABU DHABI

Uruguay

Capital: Montevideo
Population: 3,316,328
Area: 68,039 sq mi (176,220 sq km)
Language: Spanish, Portunol
Did You Know? Despite its relatively small population, Uruguay has had big success in soccer. Uruguay won the first-ever men's World Cup in 1930 and has won the Copa America soccer championship a record 15 times.

Uzbekistan

Capital: Tashkent

Population: 28,394,180

Area: 172,742 sq mi (447,400 sq km)

Language: Uzbek, Russian, Tajik

Did You Know? Uzbekistan and Liechtenstein are the only two countries that are "doubly landlocked." They are surrounded entirely by other countries that also have no seacoast.

Vanuatu

Capital: Port-Vila

Population: 227,574

Area: 4,710 sq mi (12,200 sq km)

Language: French, English, Bislama, local languages

Did You Know? Pigs have lived on the islands of Vanuatu for over 3,000 years. Owning, or giving away, pigs is a sign of wealth and prestige. Even today, pigs are often traded in place of cash.

Vatican City

Population: 836

Area: 0.17 sq mi (0.44 sq km)

Language: Italian, Latin, French

Did You Know? For many centuries, popes ruled over a large part of central Italy. The "Papal States" once had a population of about 3 million people.

Venezuela

Capital: Caracas

Population: 28,047,938

Area: 352,144 sq mi (912,050 sq km)

Language: Spanish, indigenous dialects

Did You Know? Some Venezuelans consider handkerchiefs to be unlucky and could be insulted to receive one as a gift.

COLOR KEY

- Africa
- Asia
- Australia
- Europe
- North America
- Pacific Islands
- South America

OLD CITADEL IN HUÉ, VIETNAM ▶

Vietnam

Capital: Hanoi

Population: 91,519,289

Area: 127,244 sq mi (329,560 sq km)

Language: Vietnamese, English, French, Chinese

Did You Know? The ancient city of Hué, in central Vietnam, served as the nation's capital for more than 100 years, beginning in the early 1800s.

Yemen

Capital: Sana'a

Population: 24,771,809

Area: 203,850 sq mi (527,970 sq km)

Language: Arabic

Did You Know? In some parts of Yemen, it rains only once every five or ten years. Based on weather records over the past 50 years, the port city of Aden gets less rainfall than any other city or town in Asia.

Zambia

Capital: Lusaka

Population: 14,309,466

Area: 290,586 sq mi (752,614 sq km)

Language: English, indigenous languages

Did You Know? Victoria Falls, on Zambia's border with Zimbabwe, are also known by the name Mosi-oa-Tunya, which means "the smoke that thunders." They are said to be one of the "seven wonders of the natural world."

Zimbabwe

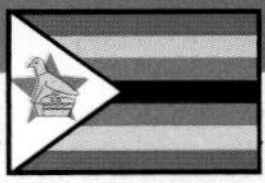

Capital: Harare

Population: 12,619,600

Area: 150,804 sq mi (390,580 sq km)

Language: English, Shona, Sindebele

Did You Know? The nation takes its name from the famous stone ruins of Great Zimbabwe, a city built between the 13th and 14th centuries.

NUMBERS

→What number cannot be written in Roman numerals? PAGE 179

The symbol for infinity looks like an eight lying on its side.

To...Infinity

The set of numbers includes all different types—positive and negative numbers, fractions and decimals, and even irrational numbers that cannot be expressed as fractions. In math, numbers are thought of as infinite because you can always imagine a larger number. For example, what's the biggest number you know? Add 1 to that number and you have a bigger number! Both positive and negative numbers go on to infinity.

PRIME TIME

All numbers—except 0 and 1—are either prime numbers or composite numbers. A **prime number** is a number that can be divided only by itself and the number 1. So, prime numbers include 2, 3, 5, 7, 11, 13, 17, and so on. All other positive numbers (other than 1) are called **composite numbers**, because they have at least two factors (numbers they can be divided by evenly) other than 1. For example, 6 is a composite number. Its factors are 1, 2, 3, and 6.

INTEGERS

Integers are whole numbers, both positive and negative. Zero is an integer. Fractions, decimals, and percentages are not.

THE PREFIX TELLS THE NUMBER

The table below shows prefixes that stand for various numbers from 1 to 1 billion. Knowing what each prefix means can help you figure out the meanings of words it is part of. For example, a **pent**agon has **five** sides.

Number	Prefix(es)	Word(s)
1	uni-, mono-	unicorn, monorail
2	bi-	binoculars
3	tri-	triangle
4	quadr-, tetr-	quadrangle, tetrahedron
5	pent-, quint-	pentagon, quintuplet
6	hex-, sext-	hexagon, sextuplet
7	hept-, sept-	heptathlon, septuplet

Number	Prefix(es)	Word(s)
8	oct-	octopus
9	non-	nonagon
10	dec-	decade
100	cent-	century
1,000	kilo-	kilometer
million	mega-	megabyte
billion	giga-	gigabyte

DID YOU KNOW?

Some people, known as "savants," have very unusual mental skills in a certain area, even while they may lack more common abilities. For example, two twins named John and Michael, who could not do simple arithmetic, became famous in the 1960s for being able to call out prime numbers at random. Some of these prime numbers were as many as 20 digits long. The twins said they could "see" such numbers in their minds and enjoyed sharing them with each other.

ROMAN NUMERALS

Numerals

Arabic	Roman	Arabic	Roman
1	I	16	XVI
2	II	17	XVII
3	III	18	XVIII
4	IV	19	XIX
5	V	20	XX
6	VI	30	XXX
7	VII	40	XL
8	VIII	50	L
9	IX	60	LX
10	X	70	LXX
11	XI	80	LXXX
12	XII	90	XC
13	XIII	100	C
14	XIV	500	D
15	XV	1,000	M

The numerals we use today are called Arabic, or Hindu Arabic, numerals, after the ancient peoples who first used them. The ancient Romans had a different system, based on letters, as shown in the table to the left.

If one Roman numeral is followed by one with a greater value, the first is subtracted from the second. For example, IX means 10 – 1 = 9. Think of it as "one less than ten." On the other hand, if a Roman numeral is followed by one or more others that are equal or of lesser value, add them together. Thus, LXI means 50 + 10 + 1 = 61.

A Roman numeral can be repeated only three times to express a number. For example, XXX equals 30. You would have to write XL (50 minus 10) to show the number 40.

Roman numerals are still sometimes used today, such as in the names for Super Bowls. In 2012, the New York Giants won Super Bowl XLVI. What number was that? Can you write 2012 in Roman numerals?

Super Bowl I was played in 1967. So when was Super Bowl XXI played? (This was the first year the New York Giants won.)

ANSWERS ON PAGES 334-336.

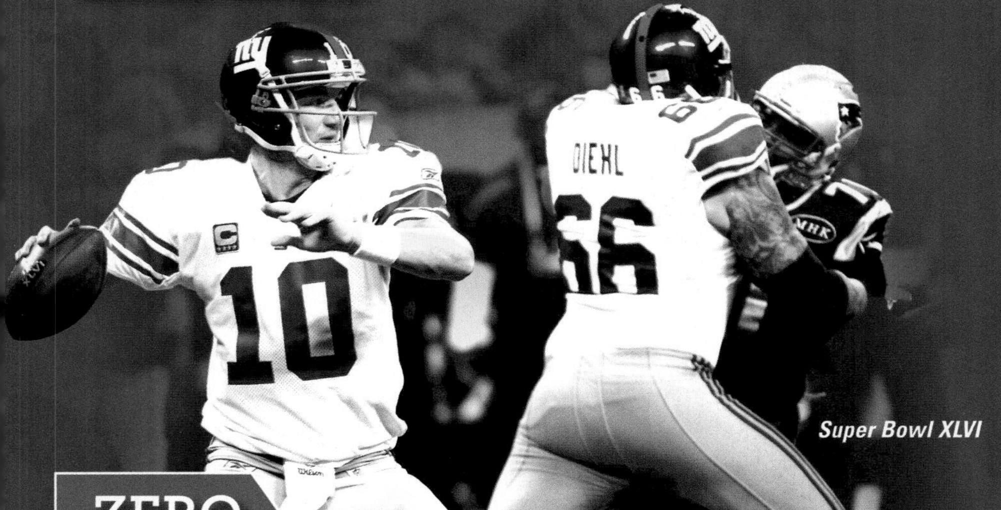

Super Bowl XLVI

ZERO

Do you know the Roman numeral for 0? Probably not, because there isn't one! The Babylonians in Asia, Hindus in India, and Mayans in the Americas were among the first peoples to use the idea of zero as a "placeholder." In our number system "10" means 1 "ten" and 0 "ones." The 0 in 10 is a placeholder in the ones column.

Zero has some interesting properties. Any number multiplied by 0 equals 0. Any number added to 0 equals the original number.

FRACTIONS, PERCENTS, AND DECIMALS

FRACTIONS

A fraction is part of a whole. It helps to think of a fraction as a slice of a circle, with the circle being the whole (represented by the number 1). Check out the common fractions at right.

1/2 **2/3** **7/8**

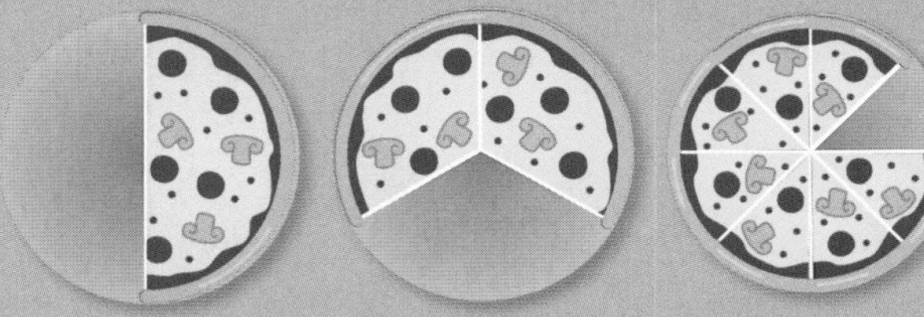

1/2 is missing ***1/3 is missing*** ***1/8 is missing***

HOMEWORK TIP

To reduce a fraction to its lowest terms, divide both the numerator (top number) and the denominator (bottom number) by the largest number by which both can be divided evenly. For example, to reduce 8/16 to its lowest terms, divide the numerator and denominator by 8. You end up with 1/2.

PERCENTS

Percents also represent part of a whole. The word *percent* means "per hundred." So, a percent is like a fraction with a denominator of 100. You see percents every day. If you scored 80 percent on a test at school, you received 80 points out of a possible 100. Changing percents to fractions is not hard. Here are two examples:

80% = 80/100; reduced to its lowest terms, 80/100 becomes 4/5
23% = 23/100, which cannot be reduced

DECIMALS

Decimals are also part of a whole. They are represented with numerals placed to the right of a decimal point. Each position—or place—in a decimal has its own name.

7.75

ones place (7) **tenths place** (7) **hundredths place** (5)

HOMEWORK TIP

To convert a decimal to a fraction or a percent, you have to pay attention to the placement after the decimal point. For example, 0.2 means 2 tenths, or 2/10, which can be reduced to 1/5. And think of 0.25 as 25 hundredths, or 25/100, which can be reduced to 1/4. To convert a decimal to a percent, just move the decimal point to the right of the hundredths place:
0.25 = 25% and 0.025 = 2.5%

Can you change these decimals to fractions that are reduced to lowest terms?
0.5 0.6 0.75

ANSWERS ON PAGES 334-336.

Cross-*Number* Puzzle

This is not exactly a crossword puzzle, but it's a good way to put your number skills to the test. See if you can fill in all the squares in the grid, using the correct numbers, based on the clues below. We filled in **1 Across** for you. You may be able to do a lot of the calculations in your head. But you can use pencil and paper or a calculator when you need to. This puzzle should be as easy as 1-2-3. Or maybe not.

ANSWERS ON PAGES 334-336.

ACROSS

1. 21 x 0 – 0 + 21

5. Jack is half as old as Jill, and Gus is 4 years older than Jack. Jill is 16. How old is Gus?

7. VIII times itself, in Arabic numbers.

9. CXLVII in Arabic numerals.

11. The total number of sides in two hexagons.

14. 2,601 divided by 3.

15. You are writing a secret letter in code, using 1 for A, 2 for B, 3 for C, and so on. Put in your first word, which is "Hi."

16. You just took a math test, and there were 20 questions for 5 points each. You got 2 wrong. What was your score?

17. XLI + LXI + XIX (Write the answer in Arabic numerals.)

19. 3, 7, 12, ___? What number is next?

21. 500 – 350 – 125 + 50 = ___.

23. If Bert has $11 to spend on buying music and Ernie has twice as much, how many dollars do they have altogether?

25. Emma gets to watch TV for 2 hours today. She has been watching for 1 hour and 5 minutes. How many minutes are left?

27. 1,000 divided by 10.

28. The next 6 integers after 1.

DOWN

2. The *lowest* (positive) prime number that fits into the spaces for this clue.

3. The *highest* prime number that fits.

4. Help! It's two octopuses! How many tentacles do they have altogether?

6. The lowest 7 (positive) prime numbers.

8. The lowest 5 (positive) composite numbers.

10. It's a pizza party! Each pizza has 8 slices. Five kids have 2 slices each, 6 kids eat 3 slices each, and 1½ pizzas are left. How many slices were there to begin with?

12. M plus M, in Arabic numbers.

13. 11 x 9?

15. Fred just spent 3 quarters, 3 nickels, and 3 dimes on a snack. He started with $2 in coins. How many cents are left?

18. Tom is 11 years old. His brother is 4 years older than he is and 2 years younger than their sister. How old is their sister?

20. 680, 340, 170, ___? What number is next?

22. Take 2/3 of 900 and subtract 76.

24. Jessica's new bike would have cost $200, but she got it at a 15% discount (15% off). How many dollars did she save?

26. 14 x 3 + 10.

POPULATION

→ How many people live in Texas? PAGE 185

Where Do People Live?

In 2012, there were more than 7 billion people in the world. Six out of every ten lived in Asia. Only one out of twenty people in the world lived in North America. China, the world's second-biggest country in land area, ranked first in population, with India close behind. Russia, by far the largest country in area, ranked only ninth in population. The United States is the world's third-biggest country, in both land area and population.

COUNTRY POPULATIONS, 2012

LARGEST COUNTRIES

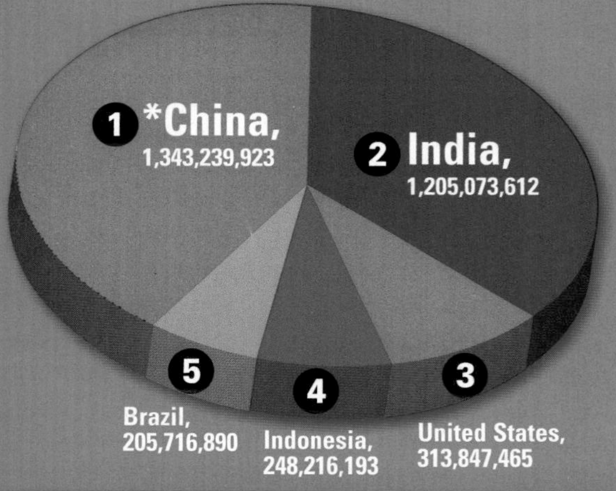

SMALLEST COUNTRIES

	COUNTRY	POPULATION
1.	Vatican City	836
2.	Nauru	9,378
3.	Tuvalu	10,619
4.	Palau	21,032
5.	Monaco	30,510

*Excluding Taiwan, pop. 23,113,901; Hong Kong, pop. 7,153,519; and Macau, pop. 578,025

Note: These and most other statistics in this chapter come from the U.S. Census Bureau.

MOST SPARSELY POPULATED

	COUNTRY	PERSONS PER SQ MI
1.	Mongolia	5.3
2.	Namibia	6.8
3.	Australia	7.4
4.	Iceland	8.1
5.	Mauritania	8.4

To get the population density, the country's population is divided by its land area.

MOST DENSELY POPULATED

	COUNTRY	PERSONS PER SQ MI*
1.	Monaco	39,623
2.	Singapore	20,202
3.	Vatican City	4,918
4.	Bahrain	4,261
5.	Maldives	3,430

* For comparison, New Jersey is the most densely populated U.S. state, with 1,196 people per square mile in 2010.

The *Growing* World Population

Partly because of better living conditions, the world population has increased rapidly since the 1700s. Since the early 1900s it has grown even faster, from fewer than 2 billion people in 1927 to what it is today.

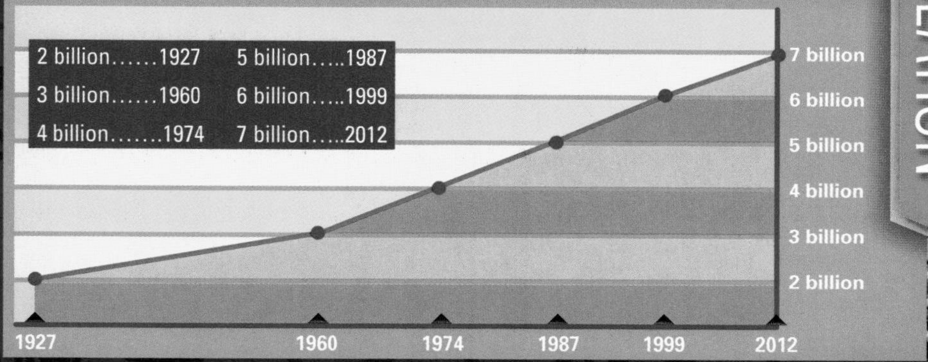

Looking to the Future

If current trends continue, the world's population is expected to reach 8 billion around 2023 and 9 billion well before 2050. The population is growing fastest in the developing countries of Africa. In Europe, the population is falling.

	Population (in millions)	
Continent	**2012**	**2050**
Africa	1,077	2,270
Asia	4,223	5,206
Europe	736	679
Latin America and the Caribbean	603	773
Northern America	348	464
Australia and Oceania	36	48

The World's BIGGEST MEGA-CITIES

Many people live in and around cities, in a large area sometimes called a "mega-city" or an "urban agglomeration." The area may include more than one city when the cities are close together. These are the biggest mega-cities according to United Nations estimates for 2010.

CITY, COUNTRY	POPULATION
1. Tokyo, Japan	36,669,000
2. Delhi, India	22,157,000
3. Sao Paulo, Brazil	20,262,000
4. Mumbai, India	20,041,000
5. Mexico City, Mexico	19,460,000
6. New York/Newark, U.S.	19,425,000

Sao Paulo, Brazil

The *Growing* U.S. Population

The number of Americans has grown from under 4 million in 1790 to over 300 million today. By 2050, it is expected to pass 420 million.

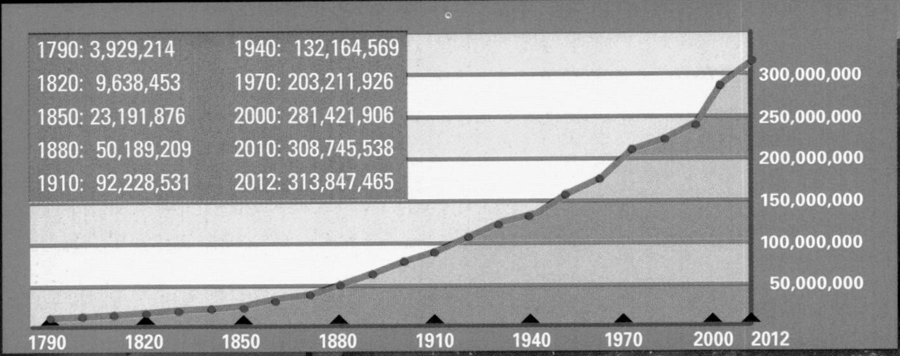

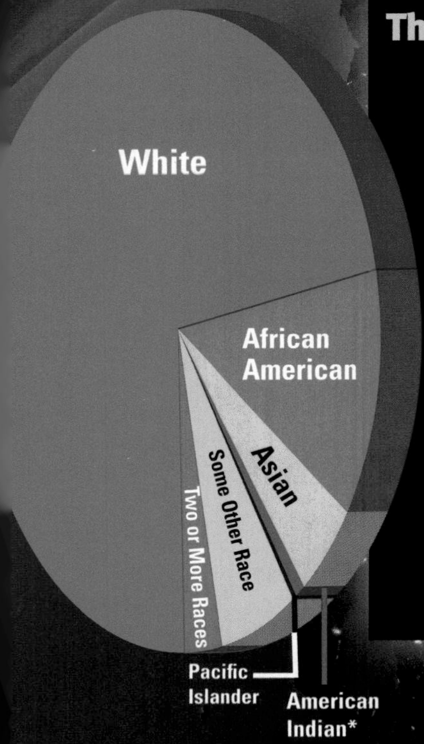

The U.S. Population by Race, 2010

Most Americans today are white, but African Americans make up a large minority group, and the number of Asian Americans is growing.

Race	Number	Percent of Population
White	223,553,265	72.4%
African American	38,929,319	12.6%
Asian	14,674,252	4.8%
American Indian*	2,932,248	0.9%
Pacific Islander	540,013	0.2%
Some Other Race	19,107,368	6.2%
Two or More Races	9,009,073	2.9%

*Also includes Alaska Natives

Note: Hispanic Americans, or Latinos, are not listed separately here, since they may be of any race. In 2010, they made up 16.3% of the population.

DID YOU KNOW? As compared to a century ago, Americans today come from a greater variety of backgrounds. They have smaller families and live longer lives. More of the nation's people live in the South and West, where cities such as Charlotte, North Carolina, and Austin, Texas (shown here), have grown very fast.

Population of the United States, 2011

as of July, based on U.S. Census Bureau estimates

RANK & STATE NAME	POPULATION	RANK & STATE NAME	POPULATION
1. California (CA)	37,691,912	27. Oregon (OR)	3,871,859
2. Texas (TX)	25,674,681	28. Oklahoma (OK)	3,791,508
3. New York (NY)	19,465,197	29. Connecticut (CT)	3,580,709
4. Florida (FL)	19,057,542	30. Iowa (IA)	3,062,309
5. Illinois (IL)	12,869,257	31. Mississippi (MS)	2,978,512
6. Pennsylvania (PA)	12,742,886	32. Arkansas (AR)	2,937,979
7. Ohio (OH)	11,544,951	33. Kansas (KS)	2,871,238
8. Michigan (MI)	9,876,187	34. Utah (UT)	2,817,222
9. Georgia (GA)	9,815,210	35. Nevada (NV)	2,723,322
10. North Carolina (NC)	9,656,401	36. New Mexico (NM)	2,082,224
11. New Jersey (NJ)	8,821,155	37. West Virginia (WV)	1,855,364
12. Virginia (VA)	8,096,604	38. Nebraska (NE)	1,842,641
13. Washington (WA)	6,830,038	39. Idaho (ID)	1,584,985
14. Massachusetts (MA)	6,587,536	40. Hawaii (HI)	1,374,810
15. Indiana (IN)	6,516,922	41. Maine (ME)	1,328,188
16. Arizona (AZ)	6,482,505	42. New Hampshire (NH)	1,318,194
17. Tennessee (TN)	6,403,353	43. Rhode Island (RI)	1,051,302
18. Missouri (MO)	6,010,688	44. Montana (MT)	998,199
19. Maryland (MD)	5,828,289	45. Delaware (DE)	907,135
20. Wisconsin (WI)	5,711,767	46. South Dakota (SD)	824,082
21. Minnesota (MN)	5,344,861	47. Alaska (AK)	722,718
22. Colorado (CO)	5,116,796	48. North Dakota (ND)	683,932
23. Alabama (AL)	4,802,740	49. Vermont (VT)	626,431
24. South Carolina (SC)	4,679,230	50. Wyoming (WY)	568,158
25. Louisiana (LA)	4,574,836	District of Columbia (DC)	617,996
26. Kentucky (KY)	4,369,356	Puerto Rico	3,706,690

LARGEST CITIES in the United States

Cities grow and shrink in population. Below is a list of the largest U.S. cities in 2010. Their 1950 populations are shown for comparison. Populations are for people living within the city limits only.

RANK & CITY	2010	1950
1. New York, NY	8,175,133	7,891,957
2. Los Angeles, CA	3,792,621	1,970,358
3. Chicago, IL	2,695,598	3,620,962
4. Houston, TX	2,099,451	596,163
5. Philadelphia, PA	1,526,006	2,071,605
6. Phoenix, AZ	1,445,632	106,818
7. San Antonio, TX	1,327,407	408,442
8. San Diego, CA	1,307,402	434,462
9. Dallas, TX	1,197,816	334,387
10. San Jose, CA	945,942	95,280

The Many Faces of America: IMMIGRATION

The number of Americans who were born in another country (foreign-born) has risen since the 1970s. In 2010 there were some 40 million foreign-born Americans, accounting for about 13% of the population. In contrast to the early 1900s, when most immigrants came from Europe, most now come from other parts of the world. In 2010, 53% of foreign-born Americans could trace their origins to Latin America, and 28% to Asia. Only 12% were born in Europe.

Immigrants come for various reasons, such as to escape poverty or oppression and to make better lives for themselves and their children. The figures below, from the Department of Homeland Security, cover legal immigrants only. Each year, many people enter the U.S. illegally or overstay a temporary visa. (Visas are official government documents that grant permission for a person to visit, work in, or attend school in another country.) The U.S. government estimated there were a total of about 11.5 million unauthorized immigrants in the country in early 2011, including almost 7 million from Mexico. However, there are signs that illegal immigration from Mexico has declined in the past few years.

What Countries Do Immigrants Come From?

A total of 694,193 immigrants were naturalized—that is, were sworn in—as U.S. citizens in the 12-month period ending September 30, 2011. The table below shows the countries where the largest numbers of these immigrants came from.

COUNTRY	Number	Percent of total
Mexico	94,783	13.7
India	45,985	6.6
Philippines	42,520	6.1
China*	32,864	4.7
Colombia	22,693	3.3
Cuba	21,071	3.0
Vietnam	20,922	3.0
Dominican Republic	20,508	3.0
Jamaica	14,591	2.1
Haiti	14,191	2.0
El Salvador	13,834	2.0
South Korea	12,664	1.8
Pakistan	10,655	1.5
Peru	10,266	1.5
Brazil	10,251	1.5

*Excluding Taiwan, Hong Kong, and Macau.

Where Do Immigrants Settle?

In the 12 months ending September 30, 2011, 1,062,040 people from foreign countries became "legal permanent residents" of the U.S. One out of five, including many from Vietnam, Mexico, and the Philippines, settled in California. Many of those born in the Dominican Republic settled in New York. Florida was the destination for most Haitian immigrants and the vast majority of those from Cuba.

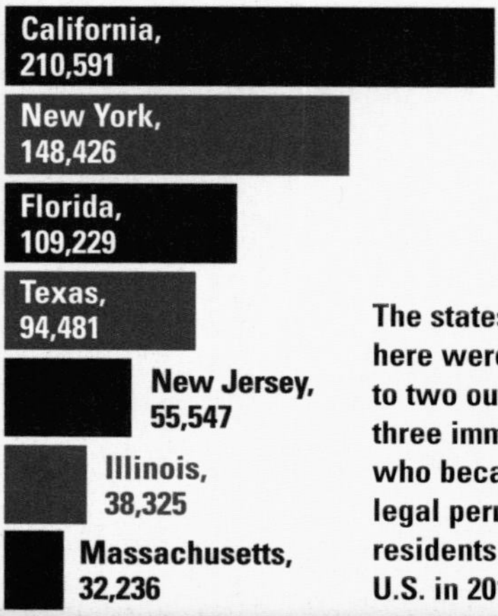

The states shown here were home to two out of three immigrants who became legal permanent residents of the U.S. in 2011.

Fast-Growing POPULATIONS

Hispanic Americans by Background

Origin	Percent of All Hispanics
Mexico	64.9%
Puerto Rico	9.2%
Cuba	3.7%
El Salvador	3.6%
Dominican Rep.	3.0%
Guatemala	2.3%
Colombia	1.9%
Honduras	1.4%
Ecuador	1.3%
Peru	1.2%
All Other or Unknown	7.5%

HISPANIC AMERICANS

About 50 million Americans trace their heritage back to a Spanish-speaking country, making Hispanic Americans the biggest minority group in the United States. Between 2000 and 2010, the Hispanic-American population grew by 43%. By 2050, if current trends continue, three out of every ten Americans will be Hispanic. There are about 14 million Hispanic Americans living in California, more than in any other state. New Mexico has the highest proportion of Hispanic residents (46% in 2010).

ASIAN AMERICANS

Some 15 million Americans are Asian, not counting those of two or more races. Between 2000 and 2010 alone, the Asian American population grew by 43.3%—faster than any other racial group, and a little faster than Hispanic Americans. In comparison, the number of whites who are not Hispanic grew by only 1.2%. About 5 million Asians live in California, more than in any other state.

▲ *Korean-American festival*

Asian Americans by Background

Origin	Percent of All Asians
China*	22.3%
India	18.8%
Philippines	17.1%
Vietnam	11.0%
South Korea	9.9%
Japan	5.3%
Pakistan	2.4%
Cambodia	1.8%
Hmong**	1.7%
Laos	1.4%
All Other or Unknown	8.3%

*Not including Taiwan.
**The Hmong are an ethnic group from China and Southeast Asia.

PRIZES & CONTESTS

→ Who won the Kids' Choice Award for Movie Actor? PAGE 189

NOBEL PRIZES

The Nobel Prizes are named after Alfred B. Nobel (1833–1896), a Swedish scientist who invented dynamite and who left money for most of the prizes. They are given every year for promoting peace, as well as for achievements in physics, chemistry, physiology or medicine, literature, and economics.

◀ In 2011, the Nobel Peace Price was shared by three people—(left to right) Leymah Gbowee from Liberia, Tawakkol Karman from Yemen, and Ellen Johnson Sirleaf, also from Liberia—"for their non-violent struggle for the safety of women and for women's rights to full participation in peace-building work."

SOME PAST WINNERS OF THE NOBEL PEACE PRIZE

YEAR	NAME	POSITION AND ACTIONS
2009	Barack Obama	U.S. president, for his efforts in international diplomacy
2007	Al Gore Jr.	Former U.S. vice president, and the International Panel on Climate Change, for their efforts in educating the world about global warming
2004	Wangari Maathai	Kenyan environmentalist and social reformer
2002	Jimmy Carter	Former U.S. president and peace negotiator ▶
1993	Nelson Mandela F. W. de Klerk	Leader of South African blacks and South African president, for working to end apartheid
1991	Aung San Suu Kyi	Activist for democracy in Myanmar (Burma)
1989	Dalai Lama	Tibetan Buddhist leader, forced into exile in 1959
1986	Elie Wiesel	Holocaust survivor and author
1979	Mother Teresa	Leader of the order of the Missionaries of Charity, who cared for the sick and dying in India
1964	Martin Luther King Jr.	Civil rights leader who used only peaceful means to achieve change
1954	Albert Schweitzer	Missionary, surgeon
1919	Woodrow Wilson	President who played a key role in founding the League of Nations
1906	Theodore Roosevelt	U.S. president who helped negotiate a peace treaty between Japan and Russia

2012 KIDS' CHOICE AWARDS

The 2012 Kids' Choice Awards were held March 31, 2012, and hosted by Will Smith. More than 220 million votes were cast by kids to choose the winners. For more information, go to: ***www.nick.com***

Award	Winner
Music Group	Big Time Rush
Movie	*Alvin and the Chipmunks: Chipwrecked*
Book	Diary of a Wimpy Kid series
Video Game	*Just Dance 3*
Favorite Buttkicker	Taylor Lautner
Reality TV Show	*Wipeout*
TV Show	*Victorious*
Cartoon	*SpongeBob SquarePants*
TV Actor	Jake Short
TV Actress	Selena Gomez ▶
TV Sidekick	Jennette McCurdy
Movie Actor	Adam Sandler
Movie Actress	Kristen Stewart
Animated Movie	*Puss in Boots*
Voice from an Animated Movie	Katy Perry (*The Smurfs*)
Male Singer	Justin Bieber
Female Singer	Selena Gomez
Male Athlete	Tim Tebow
Female Athlete	Danica Patrick
Big Help Award	Taylor Swift

THE ACADEMY AWARDS

The Academy Awards—sometimes called the Oscars—have been held every year since 1929. Winners are chosen by the Academy of Motion Picture Arts and Sciences, a group made up of actors and other people involved in the film industry. Winners at the 2012 Academy Awards ceremony, honoring 2011 movies, included:

Award	Winner
Best Picture	*The Artist*
Actress in a Leading Role	Meryl Streep (*The Iron Lady*)
Actor in a Leading Role	Jean Dujardin (*The Artist*)
Actress in a Supporting Role	Octavia Spencer (*The Help*)
Actor in a Supporting Role	Christopher Plummer (*Beginners*)
Animated Feature Film	*Rango*
Original Song	"Man or Muppet" (*The Muppets*) ▶
Visual Effects	*Hugo*

BEE INVOLVED

If you have a knack for spelling or an interest in world geography, then these two national contests may be for you.

NATIONAL SPELLING BEE

The National Spelling Bee was started in Louisville, Kentucky, by the *Courier-Journal* newspaper in 1925. Today, winners of local spelling bees may qualify for the Scripps National Spelling Bee, held in Washington, D.C., in late May or early June. If you are interested, ask your school principal about enrolling your school.

Snigdha Nandipati, 14, from San Diego, California, won the 85th annual Scripps National Spelling Bee on May 31, 2012. She won the bee by correctly spelling the word "guetapens," which means a trap or ambush. "Whenever I encounter an interesting word, I spend 15 minutes or so looking up its background," she said. "It kind of helps me relax."

Here are some of the words used in the 2012 spelling bee. Some of them are just a little bit difficult!

schwarmerei
ericeticolous
ingluvies
schwannoma
ridotto
vetiver
geistlich
dirigible
pejerrey
theophylline

For more information, visit: *www.spellingbee.com*

NATIONAL GEOGRAPHIC BEE

The 2012 winner is...

Rahul Nagvekar, a 14-year-old from Sugar Land, Texas. Nagvekar won the 24th National Geographic Bee by answering this question: "Which Bavarian city located on the Danube River was a legislative seat of the Holy Roman Empire from 1663 to 1806?" (The answer: Regensburg.) Nagvekar won a $25,000 scholarship for college, a trip to the Galapagos Islands, and a lifetime membership in the National Geographic Society. "I think it's very important for people to know more about the world," Nagvekar said. "That helps with world conflict. It helps people understand others better. It helps people understand why problems happen and how to solve those problems."

The National Geographic Bee draws 4 million contestants from nearly 12,000 schools in all parts of the United States. To enter, you must be in grades 4-8. School-level bees are followed by state-level bees and then the nationals (which are moderated by *Jeopardy!* host Alex Trebek).

For more information, visit: *www.nationalgeographic.com/geobee*

ODD CONTESTS

It just seems to be part of human nature to find out who is the best at something, no matter what it is! There are state, national, and international competitions in a wide variety of events. Most of them are commonplace ones such as foot races or trivia contests. But then there are others that are more unusual. Here are a few contests that are not very ordinary.

Jarrid Scott and Lindsay Ashby

DUCT TAPE PROM OUTFITS

Couples entering the Duck® Brand Duct Tape Stuck on Prom Contest must attend a high school prom wearing complete outfits and accessories made from duct tape. The winning couple is chosen based on originality, workmanship, quantity of Duck Tape used, use of colors, and creative use of accessories. The first place couple each receives a $5,000 scholarship and a $5,000 cash prize is awarded to the school that hosted the prom.

For more information, visit: *www.stuckatprom.com*

ROTTEN SNEAKER CONTEST

The National Odor-Eaters® Rotten Sneaker Contest is held annually in Montpelier, Vermont. In 2012, the panel of judges included NASA "Master Sniffer" George Aldrich, a chemical specialist for space missions. Each year, the winner's sneakers are added to the Odor-Eaters "Hall of Fumes." The 2012 winner, Mason Bennett, was awarded $2,500, the Golden Sneaker Award trophy, a supply of Odor-Eaters products, and a trip to see the play *The Lion King* on Broadway in New York City.

For more information, visit: *www.odor-eaters.com*

MILK MUSTACHE OF THE YEAR

The Scholar Athlete Milk Mustache of the Year (SAMMY) competition awards college scholarships to high school student athletes. Candidates are judged on academic and athletic achievement, community service, and an essay about how milk has helped them compete in sports and do well in school. Winners are awarded a $7,500 scholarship and a chance to appear in a "milk mustache" ad.

Mackenzie Chojnacky

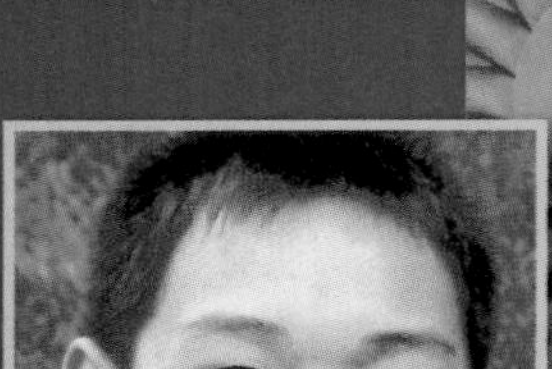

Victor Hsiao

For more information, visit: *www.sammyapplication.com*

RELIGION

→When do Hindus celebrate the festival of Holi? PAGE 195

How did the universe begin? Why are we here on Earth? What happens to us after we die? For many people, religion provides answers to questions like these. Believing in a God or gods, or in a higher power, is one way people make sense of the world around them. Religion can also help guide people's lives.

Different religions have different beliefs. For example, Christians, Jews, and Muslims are monotheists, meaning they believe in only one God. Hindus are polytheists, meaning they believe in many gods. On this page and the next are some facts about the world's major religions.

Christianity

WHO STARTED CHRISTIANITY? Christianity is based on the teachings of Jesus Christ. He was born in Bethlehem between 8 B.C. and 4 B.C. and died about A.D. 29.

WHAT WRITINGS ARE THERE? The **Bible**, consisting of the Old Testament and New Testament, is the main spiritual text in Christianity.

WHAT DO CHRISTIANS BELIEVE?
There is only one God. God sent his Son, Jesus Christ, to Earth. Jesus died to save humankind but later rose from the dead.

HOW MANY ARE THERE?
Christianity is the world's biggest religion. In 2010, there were about 2.3 billion Christians worldwide.

WHAT KINDS ARE THERE?
About 1.2 billion Christians are **Roman Catholics**, who follow the Pope's leadership. **Orthodox Christians** accept similar teachings but follow different leadership. **Protestants** disagree with many Catholic teachings. They believe in the Bible's authority.

Buddhism

WHO STARTED BUDDHISM?
Siddhartha Gautama (the Buddha), around 525 B.C.

WHAT WRITINGS ARE THERE?
The Tripitaka, or "Three Baskets," contains three collections of teachings, rules, and commentaries. There are also other texts, many of which are called sutras.

WHAT DO BUDDHISTS BELIEVE?
Buddha taught that life is filled with suffering. Through meditation and deeds, one can end the cycle of endless birth and rebirth and achieve a state of perfect peace known as nirvana.

HOW MANY ARE THERE?
In 2010, there were about 463 million Buddhists in the world, 98% of them in Asia.

WHAT KINDS ARE THERE?
There are two main kinds. Theravada ("Way of the Elders") Buddhism, the older kind, is more common in countries such as Sri Lanka, Myanmar, and Thailand. Mahayana ("Great Vehicle") Buddhism is more common in China, Korea, Japan, and Tibet.

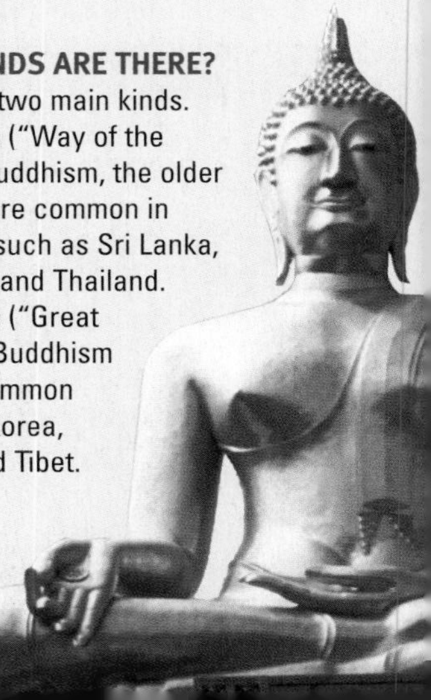

Hinduism

WHO STARTED HINDUISM? The beliefs of Aryans, who migrated to India around 1500 B.C., intermixed with the beliefs of the people who already lived there.

WHAT WRITINGS ARE THERE? The **Vedas** ("Knowledge") collect the most important writings, including the ancient hymns in the **Samhita** and the teachings in the **Upanishads.** Also important are the stories the **Bhagavad-Gita** and the **Ramayana**.

WHAT DO HINDUS BELIEVE? There is one divine principle, known as **brahman**; the various gods are only aspects of it. Life is an aspect of, yet separate from the divine. To escape a meaningless cycle of birth and rebirth (**samsara**), one must improve one's **karma** (the purity or impurity of one's past deeds).

HOW MANY ARE THERE? In 2010, there were about 943 million Hindus, mainly in India and in places that people from India have immigrated to.

WHAT KINDS ARE THERE? Most Hindus are primarily devoted to a single deity, the most common being the gods **Vishnu** and **Shiva** and the goddess **Shakti**.

Islam

WHO STARTED ISLAM? Muhammad, the Prophet, about A.D. 622.

WHAT WRITINGS ARE THERE? The **Koran** (*al-Qur'an* in Arabic) is regarded as the word of God. The **Sunna**, or example of the Prophet is recorded in the **Hadith**.

WHAT DO MUSLIMS BELIEVE? People who practice Islam are known as Muslims. There is only one God. God revealed the Koran to Muhammad so he could teach humankind truth and justice. Those who "submit" (literal meaning of "Islam") to God will attain salvation.

HOW MANY ARE THERE? In 2010, there were about 1.6 billion Muslims, mostly in parts of Africa and Asia.

WHAT KINDS ARE THERE? There are two major groups: the Sunnis, who make up about 84% of the world's Muslims, and the Shiites, who broke away in a dispute over leadership after Muhammad died in 632.

Judaism

WHO STARTED JUDAISM? Abraham is thought to be the founder of Judaism, one of the first monotheistic religions. He probably lived between 2000 B.C. and 1500 B.C.

WHAT WRITINGS ARE THERE? The most important is the **Torah** ("Law"), the five books of Moses. The **Nevi'im** ("Prophets") and **Ketuvim** ("Writings") are also part of the Hebrew Bible.

WHAT DO JEWS BELIEVE? There is one God who created the universe. One should be faithful to God and observe God's laws.

HOW MANY ARE THERE? In 2010, there were about 14.8 million Jews around the world. Many live in Israel or the United States.

WHAT KINDS ARE THERE? In the U.S. there are three main forms: **Orthodox**, **Conservative**, and **Reform**. Orthodox Jews are the most traditional, following strict laws about dress and diet. Reform Jews are the least traditional. Conservative Jews are somewhere in-between.

MAJOR HOLY DAYS

FOR CHRISTIANS, JEWS, MUSLIMS, BUDDHISTS, AND HINDUS

CHRISTIAN HOLY DAYS

	2013	2014	2015
Ash Wednesday	February 13	March 5	February 18
Good Friday	March 29	April 18	April 3
Easter Sunday	March 31	April 20	April 5
Easter for Orthodox Churches	May 5	April 20	April 12
Christmas*	December 25	December 25	December 25

*Russian and some other Orthodox churches celebrate Christmas in January.

JEWISH HOLY DAYS

The Jewish holy days begin at sundown the night before the first full day of the observance. The dates of first full days are listed below.

	2013–2014 (5774)	2014–2015 (5775)	2015–2016 (5776)
Rosh Hashanah (New Year)	September 5, 2013	September 25, 2014	September 14, 2015
Yom Kippur (Day of Atonement)	September 14, 2013	October 4, 2014	September 23, 2015
Hanukkah (Festival of Lights)	November 28, 2013	December 17, 2014	December 7, 2015
Passover	April 15, 2014	April 4, 2015	April 23, 2016

ISLAMIC (MUSLIM) HOLY DAYS

The Islamic holy days begin at sundown the night before the first full day of the observance. The dates of first full days are listed below.

	2012–2013 (1434)	2013–2014 (1435)	2014–2015 (1436)
Muharram 1 (New Year)	November 15, 2012	November 4, 2013	October 25, 2014
Mawlid (Birthday of Muhammad)	January 24, 2013	January 13, 2014	January 3, 2015
Ramadan (Month of Fasting)	July 9, 2013	June 28, 2014	June 18, 2015
Eid al-Fitr (End of Ramadan)	August 8, 2013	July 28, 2014	July 17, 2015
Eid al-Adha	October 15, 2013	October 4, 2014	September 23, 2015

BUDDHIST HOLY DAYS

Not all Buddhists use the same calendar to determine holidays and festivals. A few well-known Buddhist observances and the months in which they may fall are listed below.

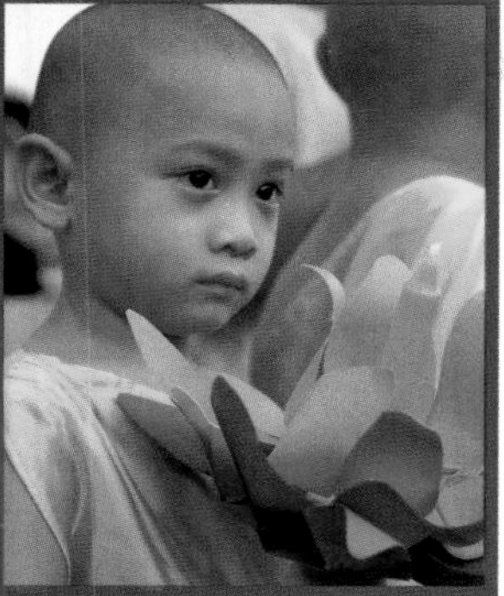

NIRVANA DAY, February: Marks the death of Siddhartha Gautama (the Buddha).

◄ **VESAK OR VISAKAH PUJA (BUDDHA DAY), April/May:** Celebrates the birth, enlightenment, and death of the Buddha.

ASALHA PUJA (DHARMA DAY), July: Commemorates the Buddha's first teaching.

MAGHA PUJA OR SANGHA DAY, February: Commemorates the day when 1,250 of Buddha's followers (**sangha**) visited him without his calling them.

VASSA (RAINS RETREAT), July-October: A three-month period during Asia's rainy season when monks travel little and spend more time on meditation and study.

HINDU HOLY DAYS

Different Hindu groups use different calendars. A few of the many Hindu festivals and the months in which they may fall are listed below.

MAHA SHIVARATRI, February/March: Festival dedicated to Shiva, creator and destroyer.

◄ **HOLI, February/March:** Festival of spring

RAMANAVAMI, March/April: Celebrates the birth of Rama, the seventh incarnation of Vishnu.

DIWALI, October/November: Festival of Lights

All About MORMONISM

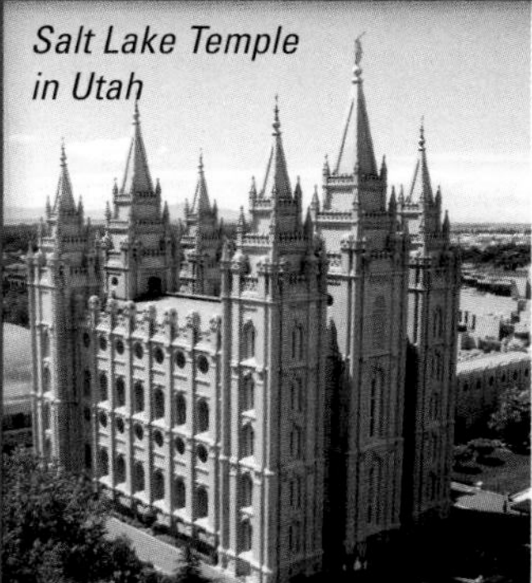
Salt Lake Temple in Utah

The Mormon faith, also known as the Church of Jesus Christ of Latter-day Saints, was founded in the 1830s. Its founder was Joseph Smith Jr. Smith said he was inspired to start the Mormon faith by a vision in which he saw God the Father and Jesus Christ, as well as by other revelations. After Smith died, Brigham Young became the leader of the group. In the 1840s, Young led thousands of Mormons from the Midwest to the church's new base in Utah, where many Mormons still live. Mormons believe that their faith returns Christianity to Christ's own teachings. In addition to the Christian Bible, Mormons accept the *Book of Mormon*, written by Smith, as a religious text. Mormons have often faced discrimination, partly because Mormonism in the past accepted some controversial practices, including polygamy (the marriage of one man to more than one woman at a time).

SCIENCE

→ Who is the founder of modern astronomy? PAGE 204

THE WORLD OF SCIENCE

The Latin root of the word "science" is *scire*, meaning "to know." There are many kinds of knowledge, but when people use the word *science* they usually mean a kind of knowledge that can be discovered and backed up by observation or experiments.

The branches of scientific study can be loosely grouped into four main branches: Physical Science, Life Science (Biology), Earth Science, and Social Science. Each branch has more specific areas of study. For example, zoology includes entomology (study of insects), which in turn includes lepidopterology (the study of butterflies and moths).

In answering questions about our lives, our world, and our universe, scientists must often draw from more than one discipline. Biochemists, for example, deal with the chemistry that happens inside living things. Paleontologists study fossil remains of ancient plants and animals. Astrophysicists study matter and energy in outer space. And mathematics, considered by many to be both an art and a science, is used by all scientists.

Physical Science

ASTRONOMY: stars, planets, outer space

CHEMISTRY: properties and behavior of substances

PHYSICS: matter and energy

Life Science (Biology)

ANATOMY: structure of the human body

BOTANY: plants

ECOLOGY: living things in relation to their environment

GENETICS: heredity

PATHOLOGY: diseases and their effects on the human body

PHYSIOLOGY: the body's biological processes

ZOOLOGY: animals

Earth Science

GEOGRAPHY: Earth's surface and its relationship to humans

GEOLOGY: Earth's structure

HYDROLOGY: water

METEOROLOGY: Earth's atmosphere and weather

MINERALOGY: minerals

OCEANOGRAPHY: the sea, including currents and tides

PETROLOGY: rocks

SEISMOLOGY: earthquakes

VOLCANOLOGY: volcanoes

Social Science

ANTHROPOLOGY: human cultures and physical characteristics

ECONOMICS: production and distribution of goods and services

POLITICAL SCIENCE: governments

PSYCHOLOGY: mental processes and behavior

SOCIOLOGY: human society and community life

HOW DO SCIENTISTS MAKE DISCOVERIES?

THE SCIENTIFIC METHOD

The scientific method was developed over many centuries. You can think of it as having five steps:

→ ❶ **Ask a question.**

→ ❷ **Gather information through observation.**

→ ❸ **Based on that information, make an educated guess (hypothesis) about the answer to your question.**

→ ❹ **Design an experiment to test that hypothesis.**

→ ❺ **Evaluate the results.**

If the experiment shows that your hypothesis is wrong, make up a new hypothesis. If the experiment supports your hypothesis, then your hypothesis may be correct! However, it is usually necessary to test a hypothesis with many different experiments before it can be accepted as a scientific law—something that is generally accepted as true.

You can apply the **scientific method** to problems in everyday life. For example, suppose you plant some seeds and they fail to sprout. You would probably **ask** yourself, "Why didn't they sprout?"—and that would be step one of the scientific method. The next step would be to make **observations**; for example, you might take note of how deep the seeds were planted, how often they were watered, and what kind of soil was used. Then, you would make an **educated guess** about what went wrong—for example, you might hypothesize that the seeds didn't sprout because you didn't water them enough. After that, you would **test** your hypothesis—perhaps by trying to grow the seeds again, under the exact same conditions as before, except that this time you would water them more frequently.

Finally, you would wait and **evaluate** the results of your experiment. If the seeds sprouted, then you could conclude that your hypothesis may be correct. If they didn't sprout, you'd continue to use the method to find a scientific answer to your original question.

DID YOU KNOW?

Scientists have discovered what may be the world's oldest fleas, and they're much bigger than the ones we know today. Working in northeastern China, paleontologists—scientists who study fossils—found the remains of two ancient flea species from more than 150 million years ago. The fossil fleas were up to one-half inch long—about ten times the size of today's pests. Moreover, while today's fleas feast on dogs, cats, and other mammals, the ancient fleas may have fed on dinosaurs. They had sharp claws to fasten onto their prey and long, pointed mouth parts, called siphons, that could pierce a dinosaur's tough reptile skin.

WHAT EVERYTHING IS MADE OF

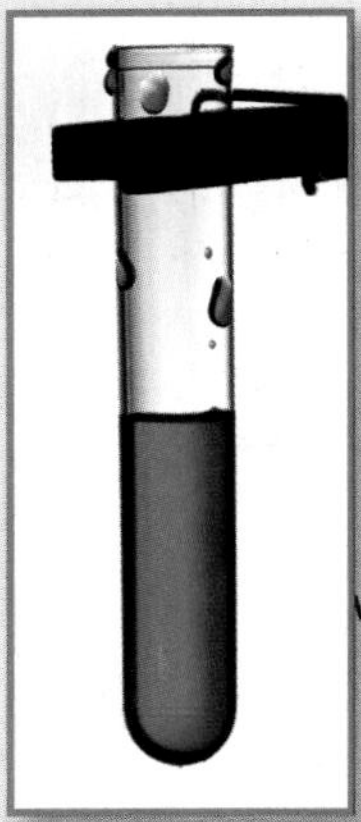

Everything we see and use is made of basic ingredients called elements. There are more than 100 elements. They are found in nature or made by scientists.

Elements in Earth's Crust
(percent by weight)

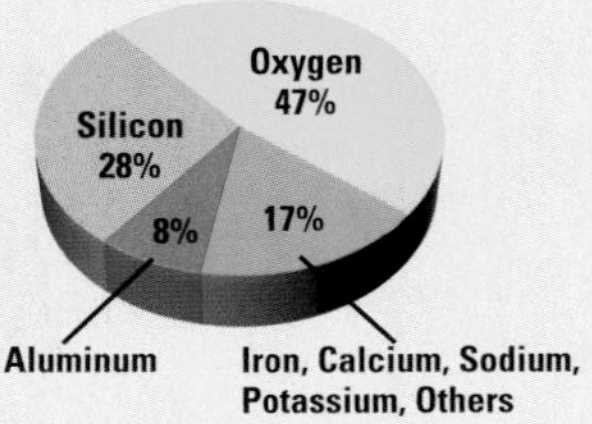

Elements in the Atmosphere
(percent by volume)

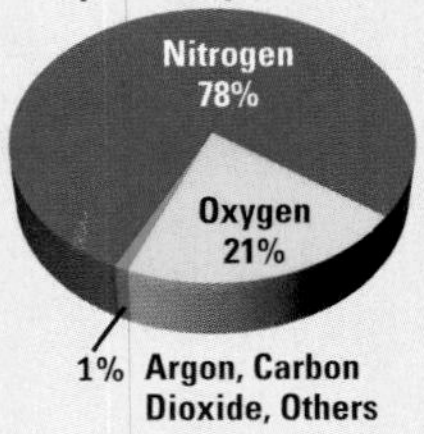

HOW ELEMENTS ARE NAMED

Elements are named after places, scientists, figures in mythology, or properties of the element. But no element gets a name until the International Union of Pure and Applied Chemistry (IUPAC) accepts it. In 2009, the IUPAC officially accepted the 112th element, later given the name copernicium and the symbol Cn. In 2011, two more new elements were accepted: No. 114 and No. 116. In 2012, the IUPAC officially approved the name flerovium (honoring the Flerov Laboratory of Nuclear Reactions), and the symbol Fl, for No. 114. The IUPAC also approved the name livermorium (honoring the Lawrence Livermore National Laboratory), and the symbol Lv, for No. 116.

NAME	SYMBOL	WHAT IT IS	WHEN FOUND	NAMED FOR
Argon	**Ar**	**gas**	**1894**	**the Greek word *argos*, which means inactive or lazy; it is among the least reactive of all elements**
Californium	**Cf**	**radioactive metal**	**1950**	**state of California and the University of California**
Hydrogen	**H**	**non-metal**	**1766**	**the Greek words *hydro* and *genes*, which mean water and forming**
Iodine	**I**	**nonmetallic solid**	**1811**	**the Greek word *iodes*, which means violet**
Iridium	**Ir**	**transitional metal**	**1804**	**the Latin word *iridis*, which means rainbow**
Nickel	**Ni**	**transitional metal**	**1774**	**the German word *kupfernickel*, meaning devil's copper**
Tungsten	**W**	**transitional metal**	**1783**	**the Swedish words *tung sten*, meaning heavy stone**

ALL ABOUT... Compounds

Carbon, hydrogen, nitrogen, and oxygen are the most common chemical elements in the human body. Many other elements may be found in small amounts. These include calcium, iron, phosphorus, potassium, and sodium.

When elements join together, they form compounds. Water is a compound made up of hydrogen and oxygen. Salt is a compound made up of sodium and chlorine.

COMMON NAME	CONTAINS THE COMPOUND	CONTAINS THE ELEMENTS
Chalk	calcium carbonate	calcium, carbon, oxygen
Fool's Gold	iron disulfide	iron, sulfur
Marble	calcium carbonate	calcium, carbon, oxygen
Rust	iron oxide	iron, oxygen
Sugar	sucrose	carbon, hydrogen, oxygen
Toothpaste	sodium fluoride	sodium, fluorine
Vinegar	acetic acid	carbon, hydrogen, oxygen

CHEMICAL SYMBOLS ARE SCIENTIFIC SHORTHAND

When scientists write the names of elements, they often use a symbol instead of spelling out the full name. The symbol for each element is one or two letters. Scientists write O for oxygen and He for helium. The symbols usually come from the English name for the element (C for carbon). The symbols for some of the elements come from the element's Latin name. For example, the symbol for gold is Au, which is short for *aurum*, the Latin word for gold.

WHAT MAKES THE COLORS IN NEON LIGHTS?

Neon signs are displays made of glass tubes filled with gas. The tubes emit light and give off a glow when an electrical current is passed through the gas. But neon lights don't always use neon gas! Neon gas produces red light. To make blue light, argon gas is used, sometimes mixed with a bit of mercury. Xenon, krypton, and helium gases can be used in neon lights as well. Sometimes, gases can be combined to create more colors and effects.

PHYSICAL SCIENCE

What Is SOUND?

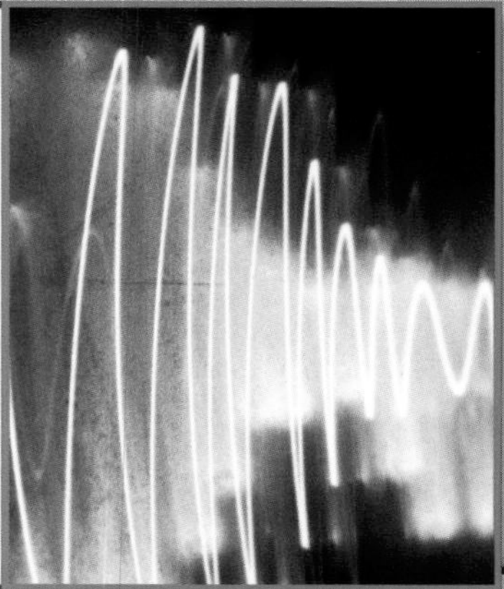

Sound is a form of energy that is made up of waves traveling through matter. When you "hear" a sound, it is actually your ear detecting the vibrations of molecules as the sound wave passes through. To understand sound, you first have to understand waves. Take a bowl full of water and drop a penny into the middle of it. You'll see little circular waves move away from the area where the penny hit, spread out toward the bowl's edges, and bounce back. Sound moves in the same way. The waves must travel through a gas, a liquid, or a solid. In the vacuum of space, there is no sound because there are no molecules to vibrate. When you talk, your vocal cords vibrate to produce sound waves.

What Is LIGHT?

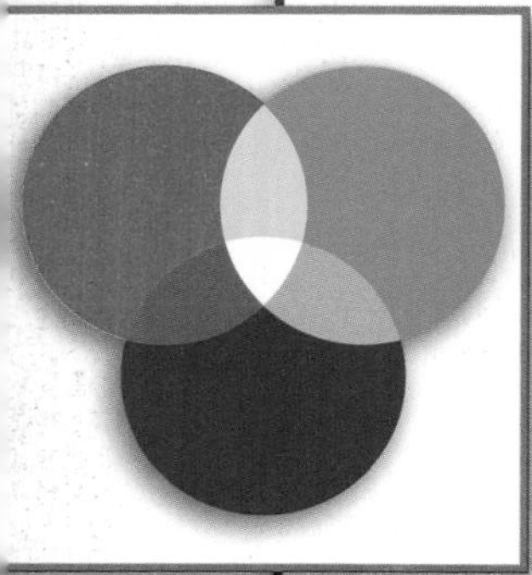

Light is a little tricky. It is a form of energy known as electromagnetic radiation that is emitted from a source. It travels as waves in straight lines and spreads out over a larger area the farther it goes. Scientists also think it goes along as particles known as photons. Light is produced in many ways. They generally involve changes in the energy levels of electrons inside atoms.

Regular white light is made up of all the colors of the spectrum from red to violet. Each color has its own frequency and wavelength. When you see a color on something, such as a red apple, that means that the apple absorbed all other colors of the spectrum and reflected the red light. Things that are white reflect almost all the light that hits them. Things that are black, on the other hand, absorb all the light that hits them.

LIGHT vs. SOUND

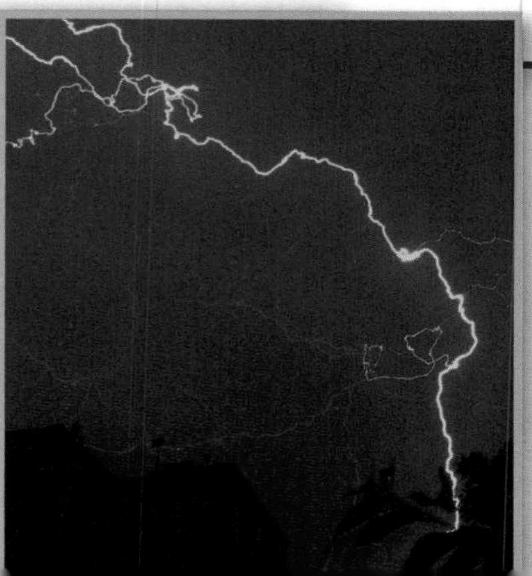

Sound travels fast but light travels a whole lot faster. You've probably noticed that when you see lightning, you don't hear thunder until several seconds later. That's because the light reaches you before the sound. The speed of sound in air varies depending mainly on temperature (sound also travels faster through liquids and many solids). A jet traveling at about 761 miles per hour is considered to be flying at the "speed of sound." But this is nothing compared to light. In a vacuum, such as in space, it goes 186,000 miles per *second*! Scientists don't think anything in the universe can travel faster.

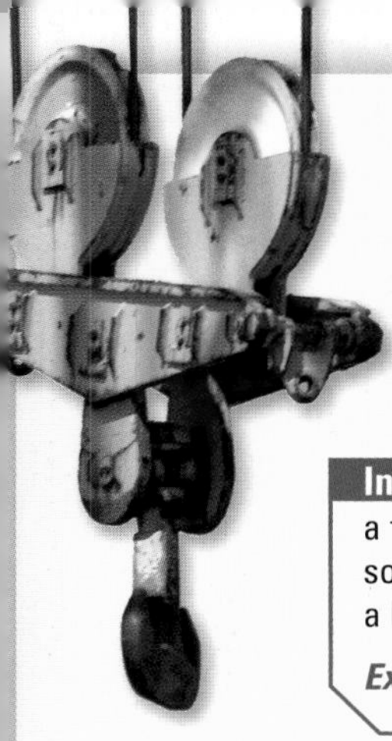

What Are Simple Machines?

Simple machines are devices that make our lives easier. They increase the magnitude or change the direction of a force. Using simple machines makes it easier to do many kinds of work.

Inclined Plane When trying to get a refrigerator onto the back of a truck, a worker will use a ramp, or inclined plane. Instead of lifting something heavy a short distance, we can more easily push it over a longer distance, but to the same height.

Examples: escalators, staircases, slides

Lever Any kind of arm, bar, or plank that can pivot on something (known as a fulcrum) is a lever.

Examples: shovel, seesaw, bottle opener, "claw" part of a hammer used for prying out nails

Wedge A wedge is two inclined planes fastened onto each other to make a point. Wedges are used to pull things apart and even cut.

Examples: axes, knives

Wheel and Axle This is another kind of lever, but instead of going up and down, it goes around. The wheel is the lever, and the axle on which it turns is the fulcrum.

Examples: cars, bicycles, wagons

Pulley A pulley is similar to a wheel and axle, except that there's no axle. It can be used to change both the direction and level of force needed to move an object.

Examples: a block and tackle, a flag pole, tow trucks

Screw A screw is an inclined plane wrapped around a cylinder. In the case of a wood screw, as it is turned it travels deeper into the piece of wood.

Examples: drills, corkscrews

Forces and Acceleration

In physics, **acceleration** is a change in an object's speed or direction. To scientists, a car accelerates when it speeds up—and when it slows down or makes a turn. **Force** is whatever causes an object to accelerate, since an object cannot begin to move on its own. Force can be thought of as a push or pull. When you kick a soccer ball lying still on the ground, your foot applies a force that pushes the ball and makes it start moving (accelerate).

Biological Science

WHAT ARE LIVING THINGS MADE OF?

Cells are sometimes called the "building blocks" of living things. Complex life forms have many cells. There are trillions of them in the human body.

There are two main kinds of cells: **eukaryotic** and **prokaryotic**. All the cells in your body—along with the cells of other animals, plants, and fungi—are eukaryotic. These contain several different structures called **organelles**. Like tools in a toolbox, each kind of organelle has its own function. The **nucleus**, for example, contains most of the cell's DNA, while the **mitochondria** provide energy for the cell. The ribosomes are involved in making proteins.

Plant and animal cells differ in a few ways. Animal cells rely on mitochondria for energy, but plant cells also have an organelle called a **chloroplast**. This contains chlorophyll, a green chemical plants use to get oxygen and energy from sunlight and water, a process called **photosynthesis**. Unlike animal cells, plant cells have a rigid cell wall made largely of **cellulose**.

Prokaryotes (living things, or organisms, with prokaryotic instead of eukaryotic cells) are all around you—and even inside of you. For example, bacteria are prokaryotes. Most prokaryotes are single-celled. They don't have the variety of organelles that eukaryotic cells do.

WHAT IS DNA?

Every cell has **DNA**, a molecule that holds all the information about the organism containing the cell. The structure of DNA was discovered in 1953 by the British scientist Francis Crick and the American scientist James Watson.

Lengths of connected bits of a DNA molecule, called **genes**, are tiny pieces of code. They determine what each organism is like. Almost all the DNA and genes come packaged in thread-like structures called **chromosomes**. Humans have 46. There are 22 almost identical pairs, plus the X and Y chromosomes, which determine whether a human is male (one X chromosome and one Y chromosome) or female (two X chromosomes).

Genes are passed on from parents to children, and no two organisms (except clones or identical twins) have the same DNA.

Many things—the color of our eyes or hair, whether we're tall or short, our chances of getting certain diseases—depend on our genes.

WHAT IS THE HUMAN GENOME?

A genome is all the DNA in an organism, including its genes. The human genome contains 20,000 to 25,000 genes. That's fewer than the 50,000-plus genes of a rice plant! Human genes can produce more than one kind of protein. Proteins perform most life functions and make up a large part of cellular structures.

The structure of DNA ▶

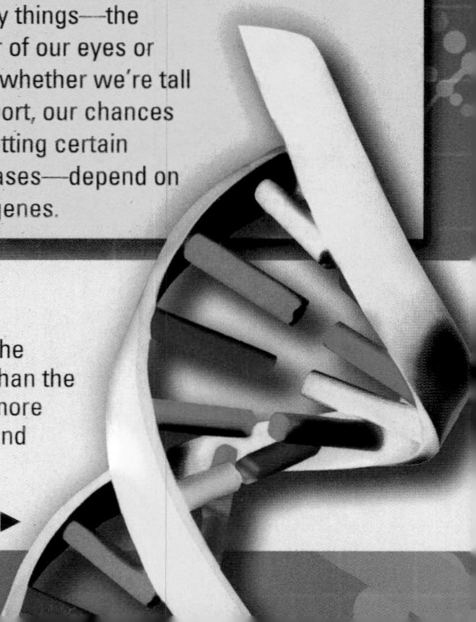

TINY CREATURES

Microbes Anton van Leeuwenhoek (pronounced Lay-wen-ook) made the first practical microscope in 1674. When he looked through it, he saw tiny bacteria, plant cells, and fungi, among other things. When he wrote about his findings, Leeuwenhoek called the creatures "wee beasties." We call them **microorganisms** ("micro" means *little*), or microbes. Before the microscope, people had no idea that there were millions of tiny living things crawling all over them.

Amoebas Amoebas (uh-ME-buhz) are eukaryotic jelly-like blobs of protoplasm that ooze through their microscopic world. They eat by engulfing their food and slowly digesting it. To move around, the cell extends a part of its goo to create something called a **pseudopod** (SOO-doh-pod), which means "false foot." The amoeba uses this to pull the rest of its "body" along. Amoebas normally live in water or on moist surfaces. In humans, most kinds of amoebas are harmless, but some cause diseases.

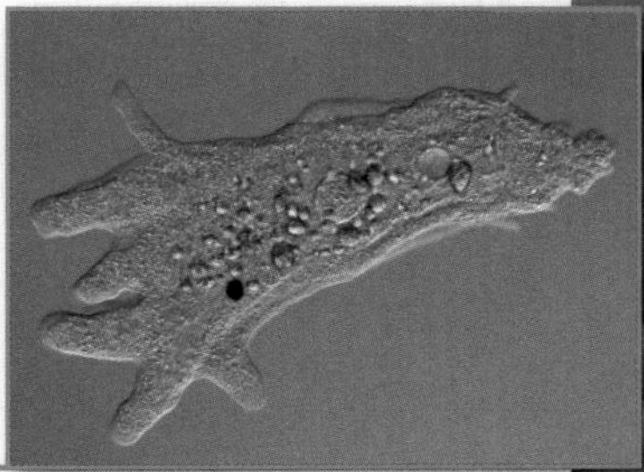

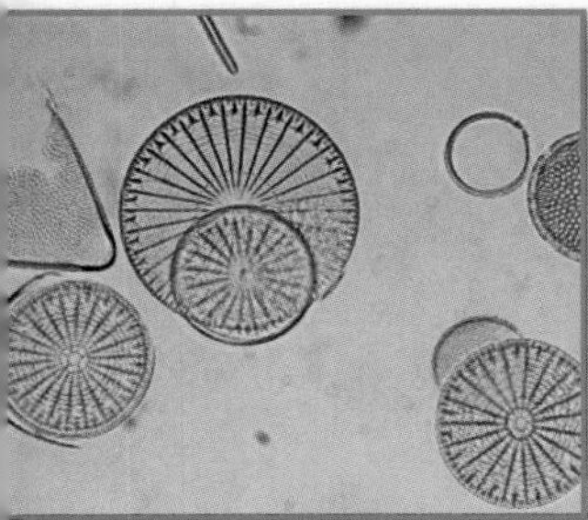

Diatoms Diatoms are one-celled algae that make glass shells to protect themselves. When they die, their shells collect at the bottom of the ocean in great numbers and form something called **diatomaceous earth**. It's gritty like sandpaper. Diatomaceous earth was once used in toothpaste to help scrape plaque off teeth. Nowadays, among other things, it is used as a pesticide—when sprayed in the air, it gets caught in the lungs of insects and slowly suffocates them.

WHAT ABOUT VIRUSES?

Viruses are often thought of as not really alive. But it depends on how you define life. Tiny in size and lacking cells, viruses consist of genetic material—either DNA or the similar RNA—and a protein coat. They don't grow. They don't appear to react to the environment. They don't do anything—unless they are located inside a living thing, in which case they can reproduce, by borrowing the living thing's genetic machinery. In recent years super-sized viruses, dubbed the mimivirus and mamavirus, have been discovered in amoebas. They are as big as small bacteria. Scientists have also found a very tiny virus that appears to use the mamavirus's genetic machinery to reproduce.

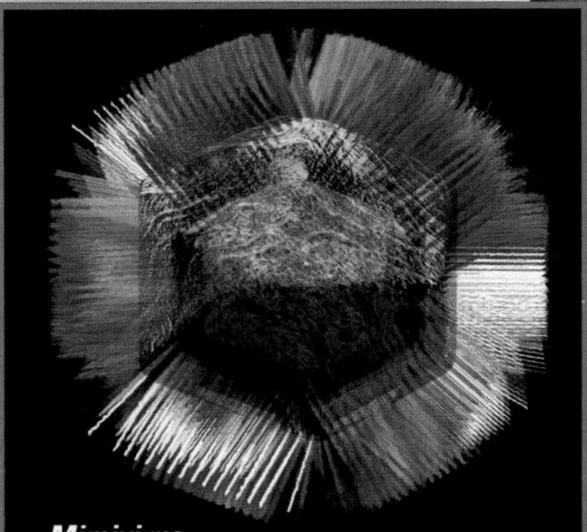

Mimivirus

SOME FAMOUS

SCIENTISTS

1473–1543 NICOLAUS COPERNICUS

Polish scientist known as the founder of modern astronomy. He came up with the theory that Earth and other planets revolve around the Sun. But most thinkers continued to believe that Earth was the center of the universe.

1571–1630 JOHANNES KEPLER

German astronomer who developed three laws of planetary motion. He was the first to propose a force (later named gravity) that governs planets' orbits around the Sun.

1749–1823 EDWARD JENNER

British physician who discovered the process of vaccination, exposing someone to a killed or weakened disease-causing microorganism to protect against that disease. His experiments—conducted on healthy individuals, including his own son—succeeded in protecting people against smallpox.

1867–1934 MARIE CURIE

Polish-born French physicist who discovered the radioactive elements polonium and radium with her husband, Pierre, and later carried out important research on radium. Marie and Pierre Curie shared the Nobel Prize for Physics in 1903, and Marie by herself won the Nobel Prize for Chemistry in 1911. She was the first person to receive two Nobel prizes. She was also the first woman to become a professor at the University of Paris.

1879–1955 ALBERT EINSTEIN

German-American physicist who developed a number of revolutionary theories about the relationships between time, space, matter, and energy. Probably the most famous and influential scientist of the 20th century, he won a Nobel Prize in 1921.

1881–1955 ALEXANDER FLEMING

Scottish bacteriologist who discovered the life-saving antibiotic penicillin. The development came about as a lucky accident. He failed to clean up some laboratory culture dishes and found that the mold that grew there, which he named penicillin, had microbe-killing power. He shared a Nobel Prize in 1945.

1906–1972 MARIA GOEPPERT MAYER

German-born physicist who developed the shell model of the atomic nucleus, to explain the arrangement of protons and neutrons. In 1963, she became only the second woman to be honored with the Nobel Prize for Physics.

1959– NEIL deGRASSE TYSON

American astrophysicist who heads the Hayden Planetarium at New York's American Museum of Natural History but is best known for his popular books and TV programs on science. He has received the NASA Distinguished Public Service Medal, and an asteroid has been named after him. His 2012 book *Space Chronicles: Facing the Ultimate Frontier* talked about the importance and benefits of space exploration and research.

On the JOB ▸ Biologist

Biologists are scientists who study life and living things. **Richard King** is a professor of biology at Northern Illinois University. His special interests are conservation and herpetology—the study of reptiles and amphibians. He agreed to talk to *The World Almanac for Kids* about his work.

What do you do in a typical day?

In my job, I have two kinds of days—office days and field-work days. On field-work days, my students and I travel to one of our study locations to find snakes. When we find a snake, we identify what kind it is, measure and weigh it, and mark it before letting it go. That way, if we see the snake again, we know who it is. Office days are spent analyzing the data we collect. I also write reports, teach classes, and help students with their projects.

What interests and strengths of yours make this job right for you?

I have always been interested in wildlife and the outdoors, so biology was a natural job area for me. I also enjoy teaching and working with students. I have learned to manage multiple projects at the same time—something that teachers and researchers have to do daily.

What kind of education or training did you need to get in order to do your job?

I have an undergraduate degree in zoology and a Ph.D. emphasizing ecology (the study of living things and their environment) and evolution. I also have on-the-job training in conservation biology and statistics.

What do you like best about your job? What is most challenging?

Each day is a little different, and I get to do the sorts of things I enjoy: spending time outdoors, training students, and discovering new things about the animals I study. My job has given me the opportunity to travel to nature preserves and natural areas throughout the Midwest. Challenges include managing my time and explaining to people how the work I do can further our understanding of biology and help protect biological diversity.

SPACE

→Which two planets have no moons? PAGE 207

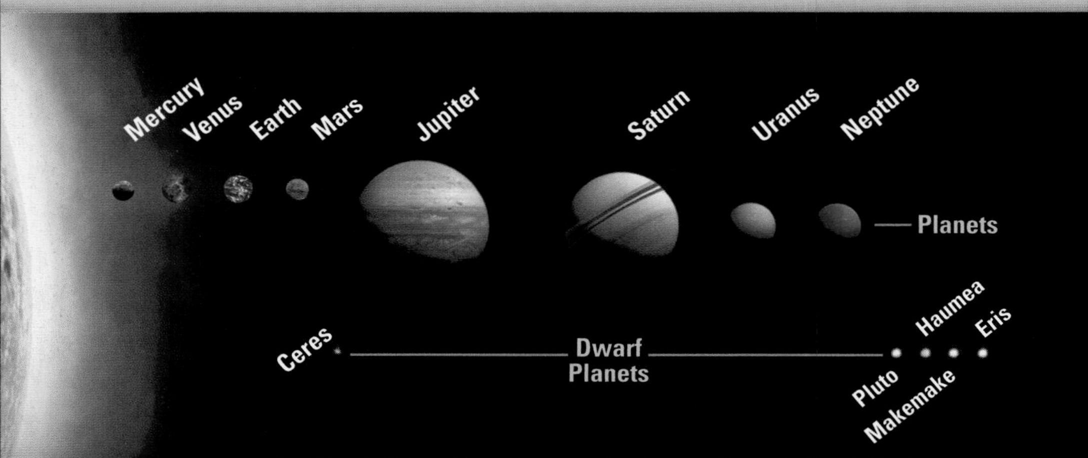

>>THE SOLAR SYSTEM

The Sun Is a Star

Did you know that the Sun is a star, like the other stars you see at night? It is a typical, medium-size star. But because the Sun is much closer to our planet than any other star, we can study it in great detail. The diameter of the Sun is 865,000 miles—more than 100 times Earth's diameter. The gravity of the Sun at its surface is nearly 28 times the gravity of Earth.

> **How hot is the Sun?** The surface temperature of the Sun is close to 10,000° F, and it is believed that the Sun's inner core may reach temperatures around 28 million degrees! The Sun provides enough light and heat energy to support life on our planet.

HOMEWORK TIP

Here's a useful way to remember the names of planets in order of their distance from the Sun. Think of this sentence: My Very Excellent Mother Just Sent Us Nachos.

M = Mercury, **V** = Venus, **E** = Earth, **M** = Mars, **J** = Jupiter,
S = Saturn, **U** = Uranus, **N** = Neptune

The Planets Are in Motion

The planets in the solar system move around the Sun in oval-shaped paths called **orbits**. One complete trip around the Sun is called a **revolution**. Earth takes one year, or 365¼ days, to make one revolution. Planets farther away from the Sun take longer. Most planets have one or more moons. A moon orbits a planet in much the same way that the planets orbit the Sun. Each planet also spins, or rotates, on its axis. An axis is an imaginary line running through the center of a planet. The time it takes Earth to rotate on its axis equals one day.

PLANET CHAMPIONS

→**Largest planet:**
Jupiter (88,846 miles diameter)

→**Smallest planet:**
Mercury (3,032 miles diameter)

→**Shortest orbit:**
Mercury (88 days)

→**Longest orbit:**
Neptune (164.8 years)

→**Tallest mountain:**
Mars (Olympus Mons, 16.8 miles high)

→**Hottest planet:**
Venus (867° F)

→**Coldest planet:**
Neptune (–330° F)

→**Shortest day:**
Jupiter (9 hours, 55 minutes, 33 seconds)

→**Longest day:**
Mercury (175.94 days)

→**No moons:**
Mercury, Venus

→**Most moons:**
Jupiter (63 known satellites)

What Is an Eclipse?

During a solar eclipse, the Moon casts a shadow on part of Earth. A total solar eclipse is when the Sun is completely blocked out. When this happens, the halo of gas around the Sun, called the **corona**, can be seen.

The next total solar eclipse is predicted to take place on November 13, 2012. It will be seen in northern Australia and the South Pacific Ocean. After this, another total solar eclipse will not take place until March 20, 2015. An annular eclipse—in which only the central portion of the Sun is blocked out—will be visible in Australia and the Pacific on May 20, 2013.

Sometimes Earth casts a shadow on the Moon. During a total lunar eclipse, the Moon remains visible, but it looks dark.

The next total lunar eclipses will not occur until 2014, when two are predicted.

Solar Eclipse

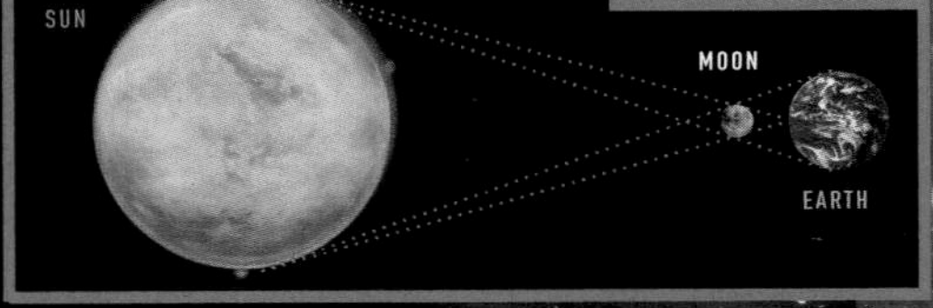

Lunar Eclipse

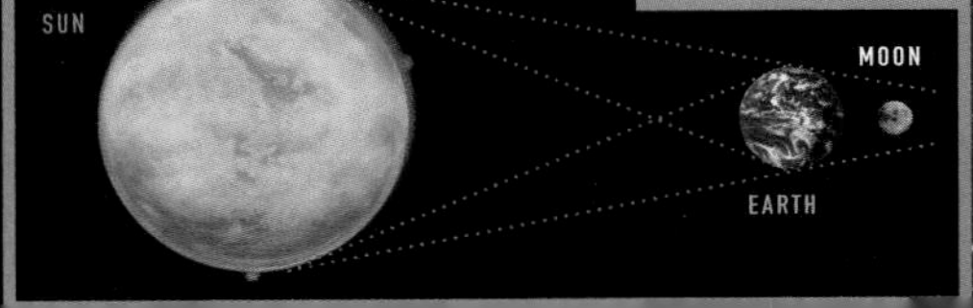

THE PLANETS

1 MERCURY

Average distance from the Sun: 36 million miles

Diameter: 3,032 miles

Average temp.: 333°F

Surface: silicate rock

Time to revolve around the Sun: 88 days

Day (synodic—midday to midday): 175.94 days

Number of moons: 0

DID YOU KNOW? Mercury has the most extreme differences in temperature in the solar system.

2 VENUS

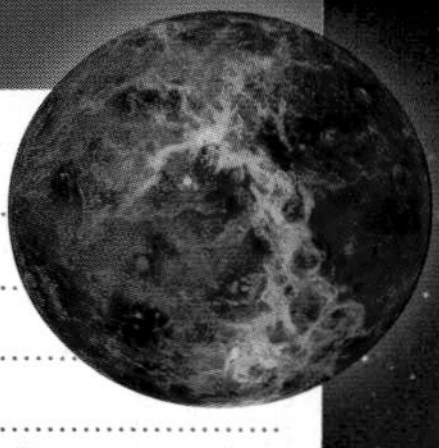

Average distance from the Sun: 67 million miles

Diameter: 7,521 miles

Average temp.: 867°F

Surface: silicate rock

Time to revolve around the Sun: 224.7 days

Day (synodic): 116.75 days

Number of moons: 0

DID YOU KNOW? From Earth, Venus usually appears brighter than any other planet or star.

3 EARTH

Average distance from the Sun: 93 million miles

Diameter: 7,926 miles

Average temp.: 59°F

Surface: water, basalt, and granite rock

Time to revolve around the Sun: 365¼ days

Day (synodic): 24 h.

Number of moons: 1

DID YOU KNOW? The huge earthquake that shook Japan in 2011 caused Earth to rotate faster, shortening the day 1.8 millionths of a second.

4 MARS

Average distance from the Sun: 142 million miles

Diameter: 4,222 miles

Average temp.: –81°F

Surface: iron-rich basaltic rock

Time to revolve around the Sun: 687 days

Day (synodic): 24 h., 39 min., 35 s.

Number of moons: 2

DID YOU KNOW? NASA's Mars Reconnaissance Orbiter went into orbit around the Red Planet in 2006. Since then, it has sent more data to Earth than all other interplanetary spacecraft put together.

5 JUPITER

Average distance from the Sun: 484 million miles

Diameter: 88,846 miles

Average temp.: –162°F

Surface: liquid hydrogen

Time to revolve around the Sun: 11.9 years

Day (synodic): 9 h., 55 min., 33 s.

Number of moons: 63

DID YOU KNOW? Io, one of Jupiter's many moons, has hundreds of volcanoes. It is the most volcanically active body in the solar system.

6 SATURN

Average distance from the Sun: 887 million miles

Diameter: 74,898 miles

Average temp.: –218°F

Surface: liquid hydrogen

Time to revolve around the Sun: 29.5 years

Day (synodic): 10 h., 34 min., 13 s.

Number of moons: 62

DID YOU KNOW? Saturn is the only planet in the solar system that is less dense than water. If Saturn were placed in a huge pool of water, it would float.

7 URANUS

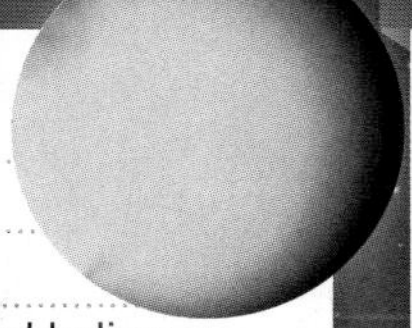

Average distance from the Sun: 1.8 billion miles

Diameter: 31,763 miles

Average temp.: –323°F

Surface: liquid hydrogen and helium

Time to revolve around the Sun: 84 years

Day (synodic): 17 h., 14 min., 23 s.

Number of moons: 27

DID YOU KNOW? Most planets turn on an axis that is close to vertical, compared to the planet's path around the Sun. Uranus's axis, though, is tipped so far that the planet basically spins on its side.

8 NEPTUNE

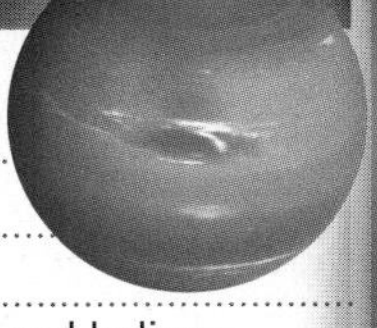

Average distance from the Sun: 2.8 billion miles

Diameter: 30,775 miles

Average temp.: –330°F

Surface: liquid hydrogen and helium

Time to revolve around the Sun: 164.8 years

Day (synodic): 16 h., 6 min., 36 s.

Number of moons: 13

DID YOU KNOW? Neptune, Jupiter, Saturn, and Uranus are often called gas-giant planets because they consist largely of gas (and liquid). But they all also are thought to have rocky cores.

DWARF PLANETS AND PLUTOIDS

In 2006 the International Astronomical Union (IAU) officially changed the definition of "planet." It decided that a planet must "clear the neighborhood" around its orbit. In other words, a planet has to have strong enough gravity that nearby bodies either merge with it or orbit around it. As a result, Pluto, an object that travels around the Sun in an orbit lying mostly past Neptune's, lost planet status. Pluto is rather small—smaller even than Earth's Moon—and it does not clear its neighborhood, which happens to be part of a collection of objects called the Kuiper Belt. The IAU put Pluto in a new category called **dwarf planet**.

Like a planet, a dwarf planet orbits the Sun. It doesn't have enough gravity to clear its neighborhood, but the gravity must be strong enough to give the dwarf a rounded shape. The first objects to be officially classified as dwarf planets were Pluto, Ceres, and Eris in 2006 and Haumea and Makemake in 2008. Ceres orbits the Sun in the asteroid belt between Mars and Jupiter. Dwarf planets with orbits beyond Neptune's are called **plutoids** by the IAU. Pluto, Eris, Haumea, and Makemake are all plutoids.

>CERES

Average distance from the Sun: 257 million miles

Diameter: 592 miles

Number of moons: 0

>PLUTO

Average distance from the Sun: 3.67 billion miles

Diameter: 1,430 miles

Number of moons: 4

DID YOU KNOW? Pluto was discovered by American astronomer Clyde Tombaugh in 1930.

>HAUMEA

Average distance from the Sun: 4 billion miles

Diameter: roughly 900 miles

Number of moons: 2

>MAKEMAKE

Average distance from the Sun: 4.2 billion miles

Diameter: 930 miles

Number of moons: 0

>ERIS

Average distance from the Sun: 6.3 billion miles

Diameter: 1,600 miles

Number of moons: 1

PLANET EARTH SEASONS

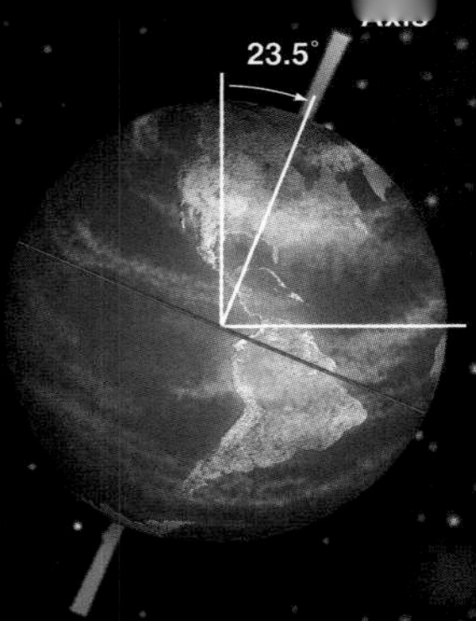

Earth spins on its axis of rotation. That's how we get day and night. But Earth's axis isn't straight up and down. It is tilted about 23½ degrees. Because of this tilt, different parts of the globe get different amounts of sunlight during the year as Earth orbits the Sun. This is why we have seasons.

↓SPRING

At the vernal equinox (around March 21), daylight is 12 hours long throughout the world because Earth is not tilted toward or away from the Sun. Days continue to get longer and the sunlight gets more direct in the Northern Hemisphere during spring.

↓WINTER

Winter begins at the winter solstice (around December 21) in the Northern Hemisphere (north of the equator, where we live). Our hemisphere is tilted away from the Sun, so the Sun's rays reach us less directly. While days get longer during winter, they are still shorter than in spring and summer, so it's cold. Everything is reversed in the Southern Hemisphere, where it's summer!

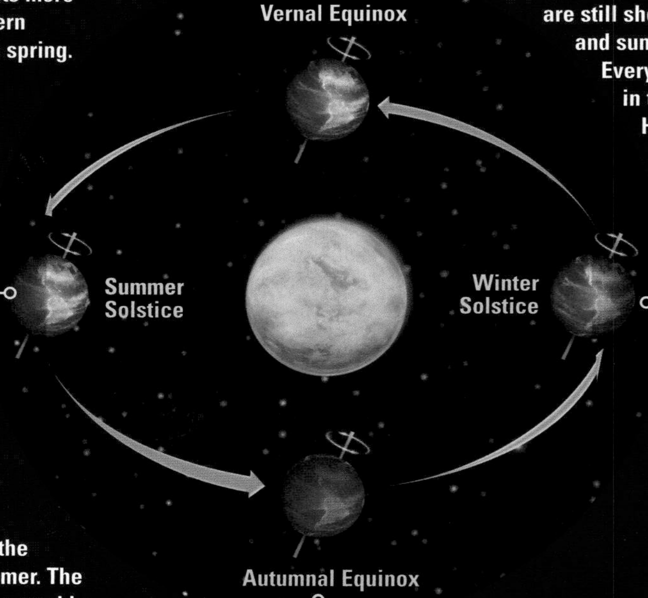

The summer solstice (around June 21) marks the longest day of the year in the Northern Hemisphere and the beginning of summer. The build-up of heat caused by more-direct sunlight during the long late spring and early summer days in the Northern Hemisphere makes summer our warmest season.

↑SUMMER

After the autumnal equinox (around September 21) the Northern Hemisphere tilts away from the Sun; sunlight is less direct and lasts less than 12 hours. The hemisphere cools off as winter approaches.

↑FALL

THE MOON

The Moon is about 238,900 miles from Earth. It is 2,160 miles in diameter and has almost no atmosphere. The dusty surface is covered with craters. The Moon takes the same time to rotate on its axis as it does to orbit Earth (27 days, 7 hours, 43 minutes). This is why one side of the Moon is always facing Earth. The Moon has no light of its own but reflects light from the Sun. The lighted part of the Moon that we see changes in a regular cycle, waxing (growing) and waning (shrinking). It takes the Moon about 29½ days to go through all the "phases" in this cycle. This is called a lunar month.

PHASES OF THE MOON

MOON Q&A

Has the Moon always been the same size?
Actually, evidence indicates that the Moon is shrinking, but its diameter has gotten only a few feet smaller over the past billion years. High-resolution images released by NASA in late 2010 showed ridges, called lobate scarps, on the Moon's surface. According to astronomers, the Moon has been slowly cooling. As it cools, it shrinks, causing cracks and scarps to form on the surface.

How did the Moon form?
There are different theories about the Moon's formation. According to one theory, a protoplanet—a young planet that had not yet fully formed—may have collided with Earth more than 4 billion years ago. The collision produced debris that eventually came together, as a result of gravitational forces, to form the Moon.

Are there any plans to go back to the Moon?
Countries such as the U.S., China, Russia, and India plan to use unmanned spacecraft to explore the Moon in coming years. In October 2010, China put *Chang'e-2* (named for a mythical moon goddess) into orbit around the Moon. *Chang'e-3*, expected to launch in 2013, will try to place a rover on the lunar surface. The U.S. launched two spacecraft in late 2011 on a mission, called GRAIL, to learn about the Moon's inner structure by studying its gravity. The U.S. and some other countries have also talked about sending humans to the Moon in the future.

SOME UNMANNED MISSIONS IN THE SOLAR SYSTEM

LAUNCH DATE

1959 — **Luna 2** First spacecraft to hit the surface of the Moon

1962 — **Mariner 2** First successful flyby of Venus ▶

1964 — **Mariner 4** First probe to reach Mars, 1965

1972 — **Pioneer 10** First probe to reach Jupiter, 1973

1973 — **Mariner 10** First probe to reach Mercury, 1974

1975 — **Viking 1 and 2** Landed on Mars in 1976

1977 — **Voyager 2** Reached Jupiter in 1979, Saturn in 1981, Uranus in 1986, Neptune in 1989

1989 — **Magellan** Orbited Venus and mapped its surface

1989 — **Galileo** Reached Jupiter in 1995

1997 — **Cassini** Reached Saturn in June 2004

2003 — **Mars rovers Spirit and Opportunity** Landed on Mars in early 2004

2004 — **Messenger** Flew past Mercury in 2008 and 2009 and entered into orbit around the planet in 2011. Sent back first up-close data since 1975

2006 — **New Horizons** Due to reach Pluto in 2015 ▶

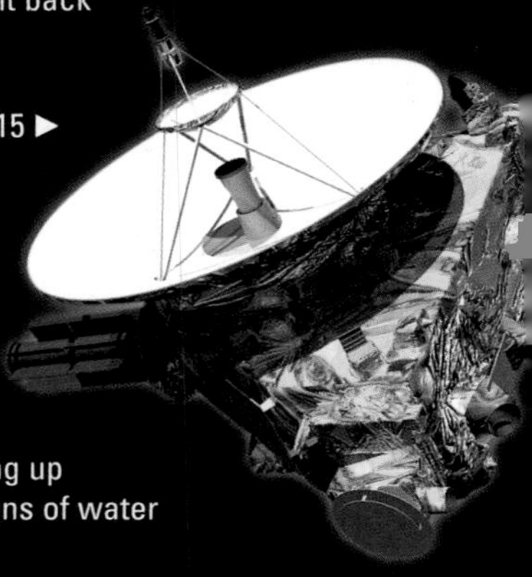

2007 — **Phoenix** Landed in 2008 to search for signs that Mars once held life

2007 — **Dawn** Reached asteroid Vesta in July 2011; due to reach Ceres in 2015

2009 — **LCROSS** Slammed into the Moon, kicking up debris for study. Scientists detected signs of water

2011 — **Mars rover Curiosity** Due to land in August 2012 to assess whether Mars ever supported microbial life

2012 — **Dragon** First privately owned (by the SpaceX company) spacecraft to journey to the International Space Station

MILESTONES
N HUMAN SPACEFLIGHT

e U.S. formed NASA in 1958. It was in response to the Soviet Union's
nching of the first artificial satellite *Sputnik I* on October 4, 1957. Since
n, more than 500 astronauts have made trips into space to conduct
earch, visit orbiting space stations, and explore the Moon. Below are
ne of the biggest moments in human spaceflight.

- On April 12, Soviet cosmonaut Yuri Gagarin, in *Vostok 1*, became the first person to orbit Earth. On May 5, U.S. astronaut Alan B. Shepard Jr. during the *Mercury 3* mission became the first American in space.
- On February 20, U.S. astronaut John H. Glenn Jr. during the *Mercury 6* mission became the first American to orbit Earth.
- From June 16 to 19, the Soviet spacecraft *Vostok 6* carried the first woman into space, Valentina V. Tereshkova.
- On March 18, Soviet cosmonaut Aleksei A. Leonov became the first person to "walk" in space.
- On March 16, U.S. *Gemini 8* became the first craft to dock with (become attached to) another vehicle (an unmanned Agena rocket).
- On July 20, U.S. *Apollo 11*'s lunar module *Eagle* landed on the Moon's surface in the area known as the Sea of Tranquility. Neil Armstrong was the first person ever to walk on the Moon.
- In April, *Apollo 13* astronauts returned safely to Earth after an explosion damaged their spacecraft and prevented them from landing on the Moon.
- On May 14, the U.S. put its first space station, *Skylab*, into orbit. The last *Skylab* crew left in February 1974.
- American and Soviet spacecraft docked in July, and for several days their crews worked and spent time together in space.
- *Columbia* was launched on April 12 and became the first space shuttle to reach space.
- On January 28, space shuttle *Challenger* exploded 73 seconds after takeoff. All seven astronauts, including teacher Christa McAuliffe, died. In February, the Soviet space station *Mir* was launched into orbit, where it remained for 15 years.
- In December, space shuttle *Endeavour* carried into orbit *Unity*, a U.S.-built part of the International Space Station (ISS). *Unity* was linked up to the Russian-built *Zarya* control module, which had been carried into orbit the preceding month. The first ISS crew arrived in November 2000.
- In April, U.S. businessman Dennis Tito rode a Russian Soyuz rocket to the ISS, becoming the first paying space tourist.
- On February 1, space shuttle *Columbia* disintegrated during its reentry into the Earth's atmosphere, killing the seven-member crew. China launched its first manned spacecraft on October 15.
- On June 21, Mike Melvill piloted *SpaceShipOne*, the first privately funded spacecraft, into space.
- A May mission by space shuttle *Atlantis* repaired and enhanced the aging Hubble Space Telescope, which was launched in 1990.
- On July 8, space shuttle *Atlantis* began the final flight of the shuttle program; *Atlantis* landed July 21.

SPACE NEWS 2013

Spaceport America's terminal hangar

NEW SPACEPORT GETS READY FOR BUSINESS

In southern New Mexico, work continued at Spaceport America, described as the world's "first purpose-built commercial spaceport." With the first phase of construction nearing completion, the facility was declared open in October 2011. The spaceport was expected to be fully operational some time in 2013, when the second phase of construction is completed.

Spaceport America is owned by the state of New Mexico. Virgin Galactic—a company that plans to provide suborbital spaceflights for a price—announced in 2006 that it would make its world headquarters in the state. At least initially, Virgin Galactic is expected to be the spaceport's main tenant, taking advantage of the first terminal, hangar, and runway ever built completely for commercial space travel.

SHUTTLES FIND NEW HOMES

With the end of the space shuttle program, NASA in April 2011 announced permanent homes for the retired crafts. More than 20 institutions around the United States competed to get one of the shuttles, but only four emerged victorious. *Endeavour* was awarded to the California Science Center in Los Angeles, and *Atlantis* was slated for the Kennedy Space Center in Florida. Meanwhile, *Discovery* was awarded to the Smithsonian Institution in Washington, D.C. Since the Smithsonian was getting *Discovery*, it sent *Enterprise*, on display there since 2004, to the Intrepid Sea, Air and Space Museum in New York City. Unlike the other three shuttles, *Enterprise* never went into orbit—it was used only for tests. All of the shuttles were expected to be in their new permanent homes by the end of 2012.

THE MOON AND BEYOND

NASA launched two spacecraft in late 2011, in the GRAIL mission, to orbit the Moon. NASA's upcoming Moon missions include LADEE ("Lunar Atmosphere and Dust Environment Explorer"), set to take off in 2013. Mars is the goal of two other NASA missions. The Mars Science Laboratory, which launched in November 2011, involves landing a rover named Curiosity on the Red Planet. The landing is expected in August 2012. MAVEN ("Mars Atmosphere and Volatile EvolutioN") is slated for launch in late 2013. NASA's Juno, which launched in August 2011, will take five years to travel to Jupiter and then will go into orbit around the giant planet to study its atmosphere, gravity, and magnetic field.

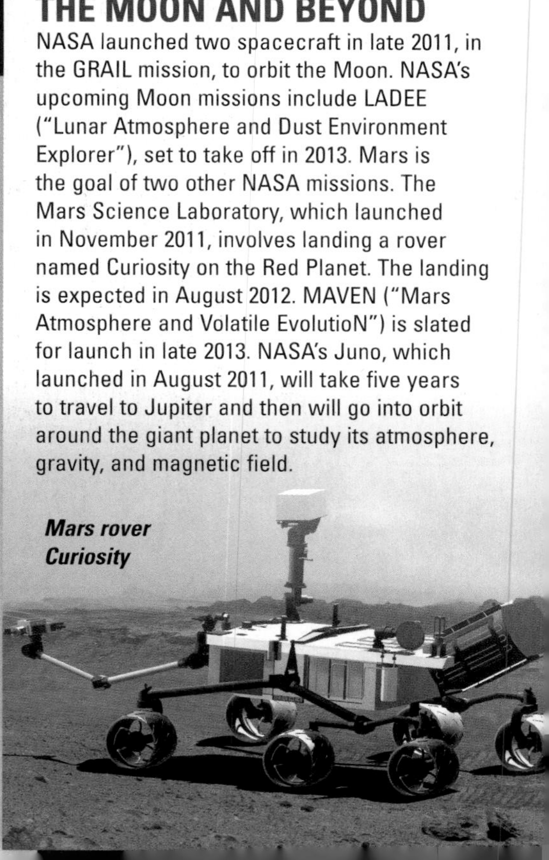

Mars rover Curiosity

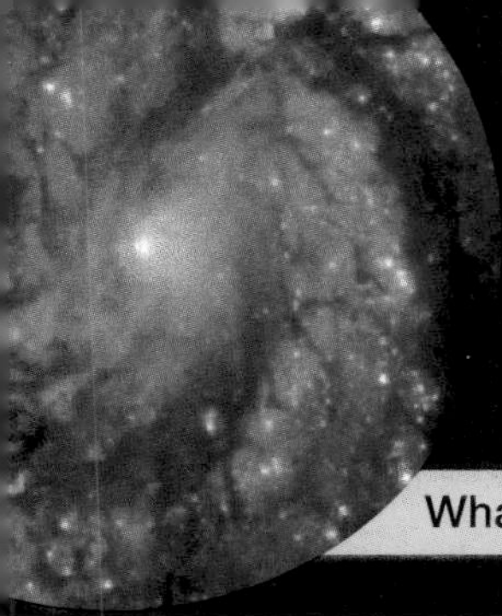

WHAT'S OUT THERE?

What else is in space besides planets?

▲ **A GALAXY** is a group of billions of stars held close together by gravity. The universe may have more than 100 billion galaxies! The one we live in is called the Milky Way.

NEBULA is the name astronomers give to any fuzzy patch in the sky, even galaxies and star clusters. Planetary nebulas come from the late stages of some stars, while star clusters and galaxies are groups of stars. Emission nebulas, reflection nebulas, and dark dust clouds are regions of gas and dust that may be hundreds of light-years wide and are often birthplaces of stars.

BLACK HOLE is the name given to a region in space with gravity so strong that nothing can get out—not even light. Many black holes are probably formed when giant stars at least 20 times as massive as our Sun burn up their fuel and collapse, creating very dense cores. Scientists think bigger, "supermassive" black holes may form from the collapse of many stars, or from the merging of smaller black holes, in the centers of galaxies. Black holes can't be seen, because they do not give off light. Astronomers watch for signs, such as effects on the orbits of nearby stars or X-ray bursts from matter being sucked into the black hole.

SATELLITES are objects that move in an orbit around a planet. Moons are natural satellites. Artificial satellites, launched into orbit by humans, are used as space stations and observatories. They are also used to take pictures of Earth's surface and to transmit communications signals.

ASTEROIDS are solid chunks of rock or metal that range in size from small boulders to hundreds of miles across. Some asteroids orbit other asteroids. Hundreds of thousands of asteroids orbit the Sun in the main asteroid belt between Mars and Jupiter.

COMETS are chunks of ice, dust, and rock that form long tails as they move nearer to the Sun. One of the most well-known is Halley's Comet. It can be seen about every 76 years and will appear again in the year 2061.

METEOROIDS are small pieces of stone or metal. Most meteoroids are fragments from comets or asteroids that broke off from crashes in space with other objects. A few are actually chunks that blew off the Moon or Mars after an asteroid hit. When a meteoroid enters Earth's atmosphere, it usually burns up completely. This streak of light is called a **meteor**, or **shooting star**. If a piece of a meteoroid manages to land on Earth, it is called a **meteorite**.

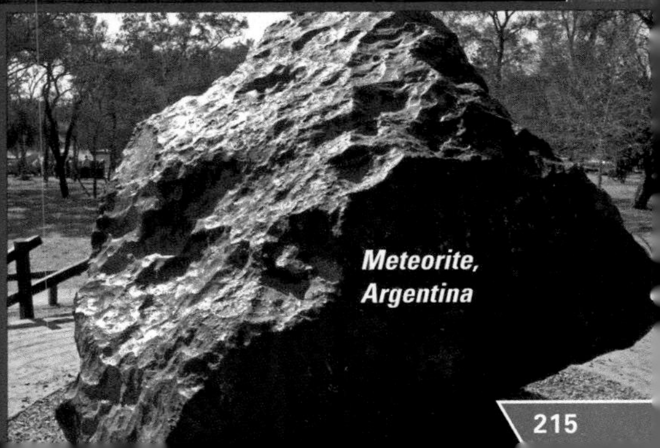

Meteorite, Argentina

SPORTS

→Which country has won the most Davis Cup championships? PAGE 237

You don't have to ski like Lindsey Vonn or pitch like Justin Verlander to enjoy playing sports. Indoors or out, there are plenty of ways to have fun and get a workout.

FAVORITE SPORTS*

In the U.S., these are the most popular sports played by high school students.

BOYS

Rank/Sport		Athletes
1.	Football	1,108,441
2.	Track and Field	579,302
3.	Basketball	545,844
4.	Baseball	471,025
5.	Soccer	398,351
6.	Wrestling	273,732
7.	Cross Country	246,948
8.	Tennis	161,367
9.	Golf	156,866
10.	Swimming and Diving	133,900

GIRLS

Rank/Sport		Athletes
1.	Track and Field	475,265
2.	Basketball	438,933
3.	Volleyball	409,332
4.	Softball—Fast Pitch	373,535
5.	Soccer	361,556
6.	Cross Country	204,653
7.	Tennis	182,074
8.	Swimming and Diving	160,881
9.	Competitive Spirit Squads	96,718
10.	Lacrosse	74,927

*In 2010–2011
Source: National Federation of State High School Associations

Getting Inline

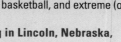

The earliest known roller skates, made in the 1760s, had three wheels in a row. Inline skates went out of fashion in the 1800s. They made a huge comeback in the 1980s when a company called Rollerblade began selling a stylish skate with four inline wheels, which resembled an ice skate. Other companies began producing similar skates, and by the 1990s, inline skating had gained worldwide popularity as a sport. Speed skating, figure skating, and roller hockey tournaments featured inline skaters. Competitions also were organized for inline dancing, inline soccer, inline basketball, and extreme (or aggressive) inline skating.

Visit the National Museum of Roller Skating in Lincoln, Nebraska, or find out more at *www.rollerskatingmuseum.com*

GLOBAL GAMES

Football, baseball, and auto racing are among the most popular professional sports in the U.S. But around the world, soccer (called football in other countries) rules. What other sports do kids in other countries love to watch and play? Here are a few of them.

Badminton In the sport of badminton, players use racquets to hit a shuttlecock (often called a birdie in the U.S.) back and forth over a net on a court. Badminton can be played indoors or outdoors, but official competitions are held indoors to minimize the effects of wind. At the highest levels of play, the game is extremely fast-paced. Badminton has been a medal sport at the Summer Olympics since 1992.

Cricket Cricket started in England in the 16th century. Today it is most popular in Great Britain and in former British colonies, such as India, Pakistan, and Australia. Cricket is similar to baseball. A pitcher, called a bowler, throws a ball (on a bounce) toward a target, called a wicket. A batsman guards the wicket by hitting the ball in any direction. The batting team scores runs and makes outs, and the matches are divided into innings. Major international matches are four innings, but they can take up to five days to complete.

Rugby Rugby is similar to football but with a bigger ball and much less protective equipment. Teams score a try (similar to a touchdown) by crossing the goal line with the ball. They also score by kicking the ball through goalposts. Players cannot pass the ball forward—only backward or sideways. They advance the ball mainly by running with it while trying to avoid being tackled by defenders. The two main types are rugby union, with 15 players on a team, and rugby league, with 13 players on a team. Rugby sevens, a variation of rugby union featuring seven-player teams, will debut as an Olympic sport in 2016.

Who Am I?

I was born in 1943 in Terre Haute, Indiana. I pitched in my first Major League Baseball (MLB) game when I was 20. During 26 seasons in the big leagues, I had 288 regular-season wins, which ranks 7th all-time among left-handers. I hurled 162 regular-season complete games and 46 shutouts. While pitching for the Dodgers in July 1974, my left elbow went bad. I couldn't throw the ball with any force and thought my career might be over. But it wasn't, thanks to the Dodgers' team doctor, Frank Jobe. He worked out a new type of surgery to repair my elbow. After a year of rehab, I returned as a starter for the Dodgers in 1976. Before my surgery, I had won 124 regular-season games. After my surgery, I won 164. At least 50 pitchers in the big leagues right now have had the surgery that carries my name.

Answer: Tommy John

The OLYMPIC GAMES

The first Olympics were held in Greece in 776 B.C. They featured one event—a footrace. For more than 1,000 years, the Olympic Games were held every four years. In 393 A.D., the Roman emperor Theodosius put an end to the Olympics. The first modern Games were held in Athens, Greece, in 1896. Since then, the Summer Olympics have taken place every four years at a different location. (The Games were canceled due to world wars in 1916, 1940, and 1944.)

2012 Summer Olympics

Olympic Stadium, London

In 2012, London was scheduled to host the Olympics for a record third time. (The United Kingdom's capital also was the site of the Summer Games in 1908 and 1948.) About 10,500 athletes from 205 countries or territories were expected to participate in the 2012 Games, from July 27 to August 12.

Most of the 2012 Olympic facilities were located in and around London, but many other parts of the United Kingdom expected to get in on the action. The new Olympic Park complex in London's East End section was planned as the main site of the Games. It included the 80,000-seat Olympic Stadium, where the track and field competitions and the opening and closing ceremonies were scheduled to take place.

2012 Summer Olympic Sports

Aquatics (diving, swimming, synchronized swimming, water polo)	Equestrian (dressage, eventing, jumping)	Sailing
	Fencing	Shooting
Archery	Field Hockey	Table Tennis
Athletics (track and field)	Football (soccer)	Taekwondo
Badminton	Gymnastics (artistic, rhythmic, trampoline)	Tennis
Basketball	Handball	Triathlon
Boxing	Judo	Volleyball (beach, indoor)
Canoe (slalom, sprint)	Modern Pentathlon	Weightlifting
Cycling (BMX, mountain bike, road, track)	Rowing	Wrestling

New in 2012

For the first time in Olympic history, women were scheduled to compete in the ring for a chance to win a medal in boxing. Another new event on the 2012 schedule was mixed-doubles tennis, which features teams made up of one man and one woman. Two sports included in the 2008 Olympics were eliminated from the 2012 schedule: baseball and softball.

Winter Youth Olympic Games

The first-ever Winter Youth Olympic Games took place January 13-22, 2012, in and around the Austrian city of Innsbruck. A total of 1,059 athletes ages 14 to 18 represented 70 countries in 63 medal events in 15 winter sports. Athletes from Germany won the most medals, 17, followed by China with 15 and host country Austria with 13. The International Olympic Committee (IOC) holds the Youth Olympic Games every two years, alternating between summer and winter events. The next Summer Youth Olympic Games will be held August 16-28, 2014, in Nanjing, China.

LOOKING AHEAD

2014 Winter Olympics | Sochi, Russia | February 7-23, 2014

Sochi, a city on the coast of the Black Sea in southern Russia, will host the 22nd Winter Olympics. For these Games, the IOC voted to add men's and women's medal competitions in slopestyle skiing, slopestyle snowboarding, and snowboarding parallel slalom.

2016 Summer Olympics | Rio de Janeiro, Brazil | August 5-21, 2016

Rio de Janeiro, Brazil, will host the 2016 Summer Games. They will be the first ever held in South America. The Games will include two new sports: golf and rugby sevens.

2018 Winter Olympics | Pyeongchang, South Korea | February 9-25, 2018

The IOC voted to make South Korea a Winter Olympics host nation for the first time.

The Winter Olympics

The first Winter Olympics were held in Chamonix, France, in 1924. Sixteen countries were represented by 258 athletes. Only 11 were women. Originally, the winter and summer games were both held every four years during the same year. Starting in 1994, the schedule changed, and now the winter and summer games alternate every two years.

2010 Winter Games

Vancouver, British Columbia, Canada, hosted the 21st Winter Games, which took place February 12-28, 2010. More than 2,500 athletes from a record 82 countries competed for 86 gold medals in 15 different sports. A total of 26 countries won at least one medal in Vancouver. The U.S.'s 37 medals were the most in Winter Olympic history. Germany finished second, with 30 medals, and Canada finished third, with 26. The Canadians' medal count included 14 golds—a Winter Olympic record for any country.

Shaun White, who took home the gold medal in the men's half-pipe, was a standout U.S. performer in Vancouver. White wowed the crowds with a new signature move, the Double McTwist 1260, which included two flips and three-and-a-half spins. U.S. ski star Bode Miller won three medals, including a gold in the super-combined event. Lindsey Vonn, who skied with a shin injury, became the first U.S. woman to win gold in the downhill event. She later added a silver in the super G.

Apolo Ohno, who entered the Vancouver Games as the most successful short-track speed skater in Olympic history, added three medals to his total: a silver in the 1,500 meters and bronze medals in the 1,000 meters and 5,000-meter relay. He now has more Winter Olympic medals than any other U.S. athlete.

OLYMPIANS OVERCOMING OBSTACLES

Over the years, Olympians have overcome various obstacles during their careers. Here are a few of their remarkable stories.

Born on an Indian reservation in Oklahoma in 1887, **Jim Thorpe** starred in baseball, football, basketball, and track and field. In the 1912 Summer Olympics in Stockholm, Sweden, he won gold medals in the decathlon and pentathlon, and he was hailed as the "world's greatest athlete." A year later, however, his gold medals were taken away because he had played semipro baseball. (Olympians were not permitted then to accept money as athletes.) Finally, in 1982, long after Thorpe had died, the International Olympic Committee (IOC) returned the medals to his family.

Wilma Rudolph (117)

Jesse Owens, born in Alabama in 1913, was the grandson of black slaves. At a single college track meet in 1935, he set three different world records. The next year, Owens competed in the Olympics in Berlin, Germany. There, he embarrassed German ruler Adolf Hitler (who talked of a white "master race") by winning four gold medals—in the 100-meter and 200-meter dashes, in the long jump, and on the U.S. 400-meter relay team.

Wilma Rudolph overcame more obstacles in her early years than most people do in a whole lifetime. She suffered from many diseases, including polio. She wore a brace for several years to support a twisted leg. This African-American sprinter won three gold medals in track and field at the Summer Olympics in Rome, Italy, in 1960.

PARALYMPICS

The Paralympic Games are the official Olympic Games for athletes with physical, mental, or sensory disabilities. The Games got their start in 1948, when Sir Ludwig Guttman organized a competition in England for World War II veterans with spinal-cord injuries. When athletes from the Netherlands joined in 1952, the movement went international.

Olympic-style competition began in Rome in 1960, and the first Winter Paralympics were held in Sweden in 1976. Since 1988, the Paralympics have been held just after the Winter and Summer Olympic competitions. Following the 2010 Winter Olympics in Vancouver, about 500 athletes from 44 countries took part in the Paralympic Games at the Vancouver Olympic venues. Athletes from around the world were scheduled to compete in the 2012 Summer Paralympic Games in London.

OFFICIAL PARALYMPIC SPORTS

Summer: archery, boccia, cycling, equestrian, goalball, judo, powerlifting, rowing, sailing, shooting, soccer (5-a-side and 7-a-side), swimming, table tennis, track and field, sitting volleyball, wheelchair basketball, wheelchair fencing, wheelchair rugby, wheelchair tennis

Winter: alpine skiing, biathlon, cross-country skiing, ice sledge hockey, wheelchair curling

Find out more at *www.paralympic.org*

SPECIAL OLYMPICS

The Special Olympics is the world's largest program of sports training and athletic competition for children and adults with intellectual disabilities. Founded in 1968, Special Olympics has offices in all 50 states, Washington, D.C., and throughout the world. The organization offers training and competition to about 3.4 million athletes in more than 170 countries.

Special Olympics holds World Games every two years. These alternate between summer and winter sports. The next World Winter Games are scheduled to be held in 2013 in Pyeongchang, South Korea. The next World Summer Games are planned for 2015 in Los Angeles, California.

Volunteer or find out more at ***www.specialolympics.org***

Auto Racing

NASCAR

Bill France founded the National Association for Stock Car Auto Racing (NASCAR) in 1947. Stock cars look a lot like the cars that are "in stock" at a car dealership. In 1949, Red Byron won the first NASCAR championship as the top driver of the season. Since 2008, the championship has been known as the Sprint Cup. Races in the Sprint Cup series include the Daytona 500 and the Brickyard 400.

Tony Stewart

NASCAR CHAMPIONS

Year	Winner	Year	Winner	Year	Winner
1985	Darrell Waltrip	1994	Dale Earnhardt	2003	Matt Kenseth
1986	Dale Earnhardt	1995	Jeff Gordon	2004	Kurt Busch
1987	Dale Earnhardt	1996	Terry Labonte	2005	Tony Stewart
1988	Bill Elliott	1997	Jeff Gordon	2006	Jimmie Johnson
1989	Rusty Wallace	1998	Jeff Gordon	2007	Jimmie Johnson
1990	Dale Earnhardt	1999	Dale Jarrett	2008	Jimmie Johnson
1991	Dale Earnhardt	2000	Bobby Labonte	2009	Jimmie Johnson
1992	Alan Kulwicki	2001	Jeff Gordon	2010	Jimmie Johnson
1993	Dale Earnhardt	2002	Tony Stewart	2011	Tony Stewart

DAYTONA 500

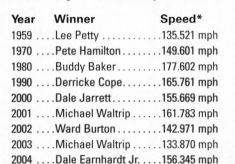

Trevor Bayne

In 1959, the first Daytona 500 auto race was held at the new Daytona International Speedway. More than 50 years later, the Daytona 500 remains one of the top races in the NASCAR season. The youngest driver to capture the Daytona 500 was Trevor Bayne, who won the race a day after celebrating his 20th birthday in 2011.

Year	Winner	Speed*
1959	Lee Petty	135.521 mph
1970	Pete Hamilton	149.601 mph
1980	Buddy Baker	177.602 mph
1990	Derricke Cope	165.761 mph
2000	Dale Jarrett	155.669 mph
2001	Michael Waltrip	161.783 mph
2002	Ward Burton	142.971 mph
2003	Michael Waltrip	133.870 mph
2004	Dale Earnhardt Jr.	156.345 mph
2005	Jeff Gordon	135.173 mph
2006	Jimmie Johnson	142.667 mph
2007	Kevin Harvick	149.335 mph
2008	Ryan Newman	152.672 mph
2009	Matt Kenseth	132.816 mph
2010	Jamie McMurray	137.284 mph
2011	Trevor Bayne	130.326 mph
2012	Matt Kenseth	140.256 mph

*Average lap speed

INDIANAPOLIS 500

The Indianapolis 500 is the biggest event in open-wheel racing. Open-wheel cars have narrow bodies and big uncovered tires. The first Indy 500 was held in 1911.

Year	Winner	Speed*
1911	Ray Harroun	74.602 mph
1920	Gaston Chevrolet	88.618 mph
1930	Billy Arnold	100.448 mph
1940	Wilbur Shaw	114.277 mph
1950	Johnnie Parsons	124.002 mph
1960	Jim Rathmann	138.767 mph
1970	Al Unser	155.749 mph
1980	Johnny Rutherford	142.862 mph
1990	Arie Luyendyk	185.981 mph**
2000	Juan Montoya	167.607 mph
2001	Helio Castroneves	131.294 mph
2002	Helio Castroneves	166.499 mph
2003	Gil de Ferran	156.291 mph
2004	Buddy Rice	138.518 mph
2005	Dan Wheldon	157.603 mph
2006	Sam Hornish Jr.	157.085 mph
2007	Dario Franchitti	151.774 mph
2008	Scott Dixon	143.567 mph
2009	Helio Castroneves	150.318 mph
2010	Dario Franchitti	161.623 mph
2011	Dan Wheldon	170.265 mph
2012	Dario Franchitti	167.734 mph ▼

*Average lap speed **Race record

NEED FOR SPEED

North American race-car fans feed their need for speed mostly with NASCAR and Indy events. Around the world, however, other types of auto races are also popular.

Formula One racing has a large international following. Formula One cars have a single seat and open wheels. A Formula One championship race is usually called a Grand Prix (pronounced *grahn pree*), a French term that means "grand prize." In 2012, Grand Prix races were scheduled for Australia, Brazil, Canada, China, India, the U.S., and several European countries. The most famous Formula One race in Europe is the Grand Prix de Monaco in Monte Carlo.

Rallying is also popular worldwide. Rally cars, which resemble road cars, generally have full-size seats and covered wheels. Rally races are not held on a closed track. Instead, they are run, rain or shine, on many different types of roads, sometimes alongside regular traffic. Typically, a rally is divided into several different stages, with their own start times. The International Automobile Federation conducts an annual World Championship Rally series. Most of the events in this series take place in Europe, but the 2012 calendar also featured rallies in Argentina, Mexico, and New Zealand.

DID YOU KNOW?

NASCAR, Indy, Formula One, and rally racing are types of motor sports. Other popular motor sports include motorcycle, truck, and snowmobile racing. Find out more at *www.motorsports.com*

BASEBALL

The first known game of baseball with rules similar to those of the modern game was played at Elysian Fields in Hoboken, New Jersey, on June 19, 1846. The current National League (NL) was formed in 1876. The American League (AL) was established in 1901. Since the early 1900s, the champions of the NL and AL have met in the World Series.

EARLY 2012 NO-HITTERS

From mid-April through mid-June 2012, baseball fans saw five games in which no batter on one team got a hit. On April 21, Philip Humber of the Chicago White Sox pitched the season's first no-hitter—and only the 21st perfect game (no opposing batter got on base) in Major League Baseball history. Less than two months later, on June 13, Matt Cain of the San Francisco Giants captured headlines with yet another perfect game.

WILD-CARD CHAMPIONS

In 2011, after a long slump nearly killed their playoff chances, the St. Louis Cardinals rallied to snag a wild-card spot on the final day of the regular season. In the first two National League playoff rounds, they got past the Philadelphia Phillies and the Milwaukee Brewers. Then, in the World Series, they fell behind the American League champions, the Texas Rangers, three games to two. Facing elimination in the seesaw sixth game, they came back to win, 10-9, in 11 innings. Series MVP David Freese blasted a clutch two-run triple to send the game into extra innings and a walkoff home run to win it. In the seventh and deciding game, Freese led his team to a 6-2 victory.

David Freese

2011 AWARD WINNERS

	MVP	CY YOUNG (top pitcher)	ROOKIE OF THE YEAR
AL	Justin Verlander, Detroit Tigers	Justin Verlander, Detroit Tigers	Jeremy Hellickson, Tampa Bay Rays
NL	Ryan Braun, Milwaukee Brewers	Clayton Kershaw, Los Angeles Dodgers	Craig Kimbrel, Atlanta Braves

DID YOU KNOW? Little League Baseball and Softball is one of the largest youth sports programs in the world. It began in 1939 in Williamsport, Pennsylvania, with 30 boys playing on three teams. Today, more than 2.8 million boys and girls ages 4 to 18 play on Little League baseball and softball teams in more than 100 countries. Find out more at *www.littleleague.org*

MODERN MAJOR LEAGUE RECORDS*

BATTERS

Most Home Runs

Career: 762, Barry Bonds (1986–2007)
Season: 73, Barry Bonds (2001)
Game: 4, by 15 different players

Most Hits

Career: 4,256, Pete Rose (1963–86)
Season: 262, **Ichiro Suzuki** (2004)
Game: 7, Rennie Stennett (1975)

Most Stolen Bases

Career: 1,406, Rickey Henderson (1979–2003)
Season: 130, Rickey Henderson (1982)
Game: 6, by four different players

PITCHERS

Most Strikeouts

Career: 5,714, Nolan Ryan (1966–93)
Season: 383, Nolan Ryan (1973)
Game: 20, Roger Clemens (1986, 1996); **Kerry Wood** (1998)

Most Wins

Career: 511, Cy Young (1890–1911)
Season: 41, Jack Chesbro (1904)

Most Saves

Career: 608, **Mariano Rivera** (1990–2011)
Season: 62, **Francisco Rodriguez** (2008)

*Records set in seasons from 1901 through 2011. Players in **bold** played in 2011. Single-game records are for nine-inning games only.

LEAPING FROM LEAGUE TO LEAGUE

When the 2012 Major League Baseball season began, the National League (NL) had 16 teams, while the American League (AL) had 14. Each league had three divisions. Each division had five teams except for the NL Central, which had six teams, and the AL West, which had only four. That will change soon, because the Houston Astros have agreed to switch from the NL Central to the AL West "as early as the 2013 season." The move would equalize the two leagues, giving them 15 teams each, with six divisions having five teams apiece. In addition, the switch would put the Astros in the same division with the Texas Rangers. League officials and team owners believe fans will welcome more in-division games between the same-state rivals.

SANTO, LARKIN ELECTED TO HALL OF FAME

Two infielders, Ron Santo and Barry Larkin, were elected in 2012 to the National Baseball Hall of Fame and Museum in Cooperstown, New York. Santo (who died in 2010) spent most of his big-league career in the 1960s and 1970s as a third baseman with the Chicago Cubs. Larkin played shortstop for the Cincinnati Reds (1986–2004). Their election raised the total number of Baseball Hall of Fame members to 297. Of that total, 207 Hall of Famers were elected based on their big-league playing careers. Another 35 were Negro leaguers, who played pro baseball at a time when African Americans were barred from playing alongside white ballplayers in the American and National leagues. The Hall of Fame also includes baseball executives, team managers, and umpires.

Find out more about baseball's legends at *www.baseballhall.org*

BASKETBALL

Dr. James Naismith

Dr. James Naismith invented basketball in Springfield, Massachusetts, in 1891. He used peach baskets as hoops. At first, each team had nine players instead of five. Big-time pro basketball started in the late 1940s, when the National Basketball Association (NBA) was formed. The Women's National Basketball Association (WNBA) began play in 1997.

Heat Defeats Thunder

The 2011–2012 NBA season ended in June with a commanding win by the Miami Heat in the Finals. Led by a red-hot LeBron James, the Heat outplayed the Oklahoma City Thunder and rising star Kevin Durant, taking the series four games to one. James, long considered one of the best players in basketball, finally earned the championship that had eluded him in eight other pro seasons. Named the Finals MVP, James put up 26 points and had 11 rebounds and 13 assists in the Heat's decisive 121-106 victory in game 5. He also was the MVP of the regular season.

LeBron James ▶

HALL OF FAME

The Naismith Memorial Basketball Hall of Fame in Springfield, Massachusetts, honors great players, coaches, and others who have had a big impact on the game. The 2012 inductees included shooting guard Reggie Miller, a five-time NBA All-Star who spent his pro career (1987–2005) with the Indiana Pacers and ranks among all-time NBA leaders in total points scored. Other members of the Hall of Fame class of 2012 were the All American Red Heads, the first American women's pro basketball team, who toured the United States from 1936 to 1986; two-time Olympic gold medalist Katrina McClain; and former Celtics player Don Nelson, who retired as a coach in 2010 with 1,335 wins and 1,063 losses.

Find out more about the legends of basketball at *www.hoophall.com*

Some 2012 Hall of Fame inductees

NBA Season Leaders*

Statistic	Number	Player	Team
Points per Game	28.0	Kevin Durant	Oklahoma City Thunder
Rebounds per Game	14.5	Dwight Howard	Orlando Magic
Blocks per Game	3.65	Serge Ibaka	Oklahoma City Thunder
Field Goal Average**	.679	Tyson Chandler	New York Knicks
Steals per Game	2.53	Chris Paul	Los Angeles Clippers
Free Throw Average**	.933	Anthony Morrow	New Jersey Nets
3-Point Field Goal Average**	472	Steve Novak	New York Knicks

*2011–2012 season. **Among players with 100 or more attempts.

Some All-Time NBA Records*

POINTS	ASSISTS	REBOUNDS	3-POINTERS
Career: 38,387, Kareem Abdul-Jabbar (1969–1989)	**Career:** 15,806, John Stockton (1984–2003)	**Career:** 23,924, Wilt Chamberlain (1959–1973)	**Career:** 2,716, **Ray Allen** (1996–2012)
Season: 4,029, Wilt Chamberlain (1961–1962)	**Season:** 1,164, John Stockton (1990–1991)	**Season:** 2,149, Wilt Chamberlain (1960–1961)	**Season:** 269, **Ray Allen** (2005–2006)
Game: 100, Wilt Chamberlain (1962)	**Game:** 30, Scott Skiles (1990)	**Game:** 55, Wilt Chamberlain (1960)	**Game:** 12, **Kobe Bryant** (2003); Donyell Marshall (2005)

*Through the 2011–2012 season. Players in **bold** played in 2011–2012.

The WNBA

Since the Minnesota Lynx began playing in the WNBA in 1999, the team hadn't given hometown fans much to cheer about. The Lynx failed to qualify for the playoffs their first four seasons. Then when they reached the playoffs in 2003 and 2004, they were knocked out in the first round. Six more years of frustration followed before the Lynx, with 27 wins and 7 losses, were able to compile the best record of any WNBA team during the 2011 season. Minnesota rolled past the San Antonio Silver Stars and the Phoenix Mercury in the first two playoff rounds, then swept the Atlanta Heat in three games to win the championship in October.

Three-time WNBA All-Star Seimone Augustus, who had played guard and forward for the Lynx since 2006, when she was a first-round draft pick, averaged 22 points per game in the playoffs and was named the Finals MVP.

Seimone Augustus (33)

COLLEGE BASKETBALL

The men's National Collegiate Athletic Association (NCAA) Tournament began in 1939. Today, it is a spectacular 65-team extravaganza known as March Madness. Games on the Final Four weekend, when the semifinals and finals are played, are watched by millions of viewers. The Women's NCAA Tournament began in 1982 and has soared in popularity.

THE 2012 NCAA TOURNAMENTS

Wildcats Win It All

The heavily favored University of Kentucky Wildcats won their eighth men's NCAA college basketball championship in 2012, defeating the University of Kansas Jayhawks, 67-59. In the championship game, played at the Superdome in New Orleans, Louisiana, on April 2, back-to-back 3-point field goals by Kentucky sophomore Doron Lamb helped the Wildcats withstand the Jayhawks' fourth-quarter comeback effort. Kentucky's freshman center Anthony Davis was named the Most Outstanding Player of the Final Four. The NCAA men's title was a first for Kentucky coach John Calipari, who had fallen short on three previous trips to the Final Four.

Anthony Davis (23) ▶

Baylor Perfect

Capping a 33-0 regular season, the Lady Bears of Baylor University stormed through the NCAA playoffs, crushing Notre Dame, 80-61, in the women's championship game in Denver, Colorado, on April 3, 2012. Touted as a number-one team even before the start of the 2011–2012 season, the Lady Bears lived up to their reputation as one of the most talented squads in the history of women's hoops. Baylor center Brittney Griner was voted Most Outstanding Player of the Final Four. Griner scored 26 points and had 13 rebounds and 5 blocked shots in the championship game. Guard Odyssey Sims scored 19 points.

SUMMITT RETIRES AT THE TOP

At the end of her 38th season as head coach of the University of Tennessee Lady Vols, Pat Summitt retired from active coaching in April 2012. When she stepped down, Summitt had led the team to 1,098 victories—the most wins by any major-college basketball coach ever. Before the 2011–2012 season, Summitt announced that she had symptoms of Alzheimer's disease. On her retirement, the university gave Summitt, 58, the honorary title of Head Coach Emeritus.

Pat Summitt ▶

COLLEGE FOOTBALL

Football began as a college sport in the 1800s. In 1998, the National Collegiate Athletic Association (NCAA) introduced the Bowl Championship Series (BCS), which pits many of the top-ranked college football teams against each other to determine a national champion.

The Crimson Tide of the University of Alabama won the Bowl Championship Series title game January 9, 2012, rolling over Louisiana State University (LSU), 21-0, at the Superdome in New Orleans. The Crimson Tide victory made up, in part, for the lone blemish on the team's 11-1 regular-season record, a 9-6 overtime loss to the LSU Tigers in December 2011 at Tuscaloosa, Alabama. In the title game, the Tide defense held the Tiger offense to only 92 total yards, as Alabama won its second national championship in three years. The two title game MVPs both played for Alabama: quarterback A. J. McCarron on offense and linebacker Courtney Upshaw on defense. The game's leading scorer was placekicker Jeremy Shelley, who nailed five of seven field goal attempts.

A. J. McCarron

More 2012 Bowls!

Here are the results of other major bowl games played in January 2012.

Game	Location	Score
Rose Bowl	Pasadena, CA	Oregon 45, Wisconsin 38
Sugar Bowl	New Orleans, LA	Michigan 23, Virginia Tech 20
Fiesta Bowl	Glendale, AZ	Oklahoma State 41, Stanford 38
Orange Bowl	Miami, FL	West Virginia 70, Clemson 33

HEISMAN TROPHY

Baylor University's junior quarterback Robert Griffin III (nicknamed RG3) won the Heisman Trophy in December 2011 as the year's outstanding player in college football. The first Baylor player ever to win the Heisman, RG3 led the Bears to a 9–3 regular-season record, the team's best since 1986.

ALL-TIME DIVISION I NCAA LEADERS*

RUSHING

YARDS

Career: 6,559, Adrian Peterson, Georgia Southern (1998–2001)
Season: 2,628, Barry Sanders, Okla. St. (1988)
Game: 406, LaDainian Tomlinson, TCU (1999)

TOUCHDOWNS

Career: 84, Adrian Peterson, Georgia Southern (1998–2001)
Season: 39, Omar Cuff, Delaware (2007)

PASSING

YARDS

Career: 19,217, **Case Keenum**, Houston (2006–2011)
Season: 5,631, **Case Keenum**, Houston (2009)
Game: 624, Jamie Martin, Weber State (1991)

TOUCHDOWNS

Career: 155, **Case Keenum**, Houston (2006–2011)
Season: 56, Willie Totten, Mississippi Valley State (1984); Bruce Eugene, Grambling (2005)

*Through the 2011 season. Players in **bold** played in 2011.

NATIONAL FOOTBALL LEAGUE

The professional league that became the modern National Football League (NFL) started in 1920. The rival American Football League began in 1960. The two leagues played the first Super Bowl in 1967. In 1970, the leagues merged to become the NFL as we know it today.

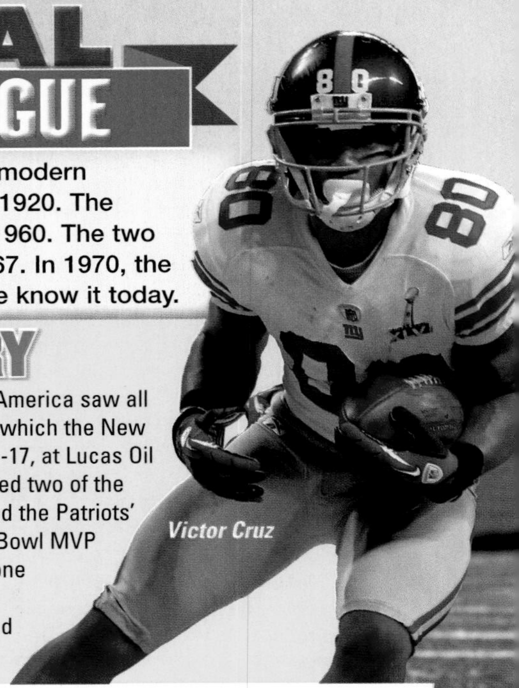

Victor Cruz

CRUZ-ING TO VICTORY

A record 111.3 million television viewers in North America saw all or part of Super Bowl XLVI on February 5, 2012, in which the New York Giants defeated the New England Patriots, 21-17, at Lucas Oil Stadium in Indianapolis, Indiana. The game matched two of the NFL's top quarterbacks, the Giants' Eli Manning and the Patriots' Tom Brady. Manning, who won his second Super Bowl MVP trophy, completed 30 passes in 40 attempts, with one touchdown and no interceptions. His lone passing TD went to wide receiver Victor Cruz, who also had a handful of other key receptions.

A CAM-TASTIC ROOKIE YEAR!

Although Cam Newton won the Heisman Trophy and quarterbacked the Auburn Tigers to a national college football championship during the 2010–2011 season, some experts were skeptical when the Carolina Panthers made him the first pick in the April 2011 NFL draft. But in his first year as a pro, Newton set rookie marks for passing yardage in a game (432) and in a season (4,051). His 14 rushing touchdowns smashed an all-time record for NFL quarterbacks, and he was the first player in NFL history to pass for more than 4,000 yards and run for more than 500 yards in the same season. The Associated Press named him the NFL Rookie of the Year on offense.

2011 NFL Leaders

Rushing Yards: 1,606, Maurice Jones-Drew, Jacksonville Jaguars

Receptions: 122, Wes Welker, New England Patriots

Receiving Yards: 1,681, Calvin Johnson, Detroit Lions

Touchdown Receptions: 17, Rob Gronkowski, New England Patriots

Passing Yards: 5,476, Drew Brees, New Orleans Saints

Touchdown Passes: 46, Drew Brees, New Orleans Saints

Points Scored: 166, David Akers, San Francisco 49ers

Interceptions: 7, Charles Woodson, Green Bay Packers; Eric Weddle, San Diego Chargers; Kyle Arrington, New England Patriots

Sacks: 22, Jared Allen, Minnesota Vikings

Charles Woodson (21)

NFL All-Time Record Holders*

RUSHING YARDS
- Career: 18,355, Emmitt Smith (1990–2004)
- Season: 2,105, Eric Dickerson (1984)
- Game: 296, **Adrian Peterson** (2007)

RECEIVING
- Career receptions: 1,549, Jerry Rice (1985–2004)
- Career yardage: 22,895, Jerry Rice (1985–2004)
- Game yardage: 336, Willie "Flipper" Anderson (1989)

PASSING
- Career completions: 6,300, Brett Favre (1991–2010)
- Career touchdowns passing: 508, Brett Favre (1991–2010)
- Season completions: 468, **Drew Brees** (2011)
- Season touchdowns passing: 50, **Tom Brady** (2007)

POINTS SCORED
- Career: 2,544, Morten Andersen (1982–2004, 2006–2007)
- Season: 186, **LaDainian Tomlinson** (2006)
- Game: 40, Ernie Nevers (1929)

*Through the 2011 season. Players in **bold** played in 2011.

LUCK OF THE DRAFT

The 77th annual NFL Draft was held April 26-28, 2012, in New York City. The Indianapolis Colts, with the first pick, chose Stanford quarterback Andrew Luck. To make way for Luck, the Colts released 14-year veteran and Super Bowl winner Peyton Manning, who had missed almost the whole 2011–2012 season because of neck problems.

NFL teams have been holding a draft to select top college players since 1936. That year, with the first pick in NFL Draft history, the Philadelphia Eagles selected Jay Berwanger of the University of Chicago. Over the years, many future NFL superstars were taken first overall in the draft. That list includes Peyton Manning (1998) and Eli Manning (2004), as well as Hall of Fame quarterbacks Terry Bradshaw (1970), John Elway (1983), and Troy Aikman (1989). Many high draft picks have had short NFL careers, however. And many players selected in late rounds became stars. The New England Patriots' star quarterback Tom Brady was the 199th overall pick in 2000.

PRO FOOTBALL HALL OF FAME

The Pro Football Hall of Fame in Canton, Ohio, was founded in 1963 to honor outstanding players, coaches, and contributors to the NFL. New members announced in February 2012 included Pittsburgh Steelers cornerback Jack Butler, one of the best pass interceptors in NFL history; running back Curtis Martin, who played for the Steelers, New England Patriots, and New York Jets; and Willie Roaf, an All-Pro offensive tackle first with the New Orleans Saints and then with the Kansas City Chiefs.
Other members of the Class of 2012 were center Dermontti Dawson, defensive end/linebacker Chris Doleman, and defensive tackle Cortez Kennedy.

Curtis Martin

Learn more about football's biggest names at *www.profootballhof.com*

GOLF

Golf began in Scotland as early as the 1400s. The first golf course in the U.S. opened in 1888 in Yonkers, New York. The sport has grown to include both men's and women's professional tours. And millions of other golfers play just for fun.

The men's tour in the U.S. is run by the Professional Golfers' Association (PGA). The four major championships (with the year first played) are:
- British Open (1860)
- U.S. Open (1895)
- PGA Championship (1916)
- Masters Tournament (1934)

The women's tour in the U.S. is guided by the Ladies Professional Golf Association (LPGA). The four major championships are:
- U.S. Women's Open (1946)
- LPGA Championship (1955)
- Kraft Nabisco Championship (1972)
- Ricoh Women's British Open (1976)

The All-Time "Major" Players

These pro golfers have won the most major championships through April 2012.

MEN
1. Jack Nicklaus, 18
2. Tiger Woods, 14
3. Walter Hagen, 11
4. Ben Hogan, 9
   Gary Player, 9

WOMEN
1. Patty Berg, 15
2. Mickey Wright, 13
3. Louise Suggs, 11
4. Babe Didrikson Zaharias, 10
   Annika Sorenstam, 10

DID YOU KNOW? ▲Rory McIlroy, age 22, of Northern Ireland, won the U.S. Open in June 2011. He was the youngest winner in 88 years.

GYMNASTICS

Gymnastics as a sport goes back to ancient Egypt. But it was only in the early 1800s that the modern-day sport became popular in Europe. Gymnastics became an Olympic sport in 1896, and the first World Gymnastic Championships were held in Belgium in 1903.

Artistic gymnastics is the most popular form of gymnastics. Men compete in the high bar, parallel bars, rings, vault, pommel horse, floor exercise, individual all-around, and team events, while women compete in the uneven parallel bars, vault, balance beam, floor exercise, individual all-around, and team events. Only women compete in rhythmic gymnastics, which includes the rope, hoop, ball, clubs, ribbon, and all-around events.

At the 2011 World Artistic Gymnastics Championships, held in October in Tokyo, Japan, Jordyn Wieber of the U.S. won the women's individual all-around title, and American Alexandra Raisman placed fourth. Gabrielle Douglas of the U.S., age 14, was the youngest competitor at the meet. For the second year in a row, Kohei Uchimura of Japan won the men's individual all-around competition. John Orozco of the U.S. placed fourth.

Gabrielle Douglas

ICE HOCKEY

Ice hockey began in Canada in the mid-1800s. The National Hockey League (NHL) was formed in 1917. Today the NHL has 30 teams. In the 2011–2012 season, there were 23 U.S. teams and 7 Canadian teams.

LOS ANGELES KINGS ARE CROWNED

In 2012, the Los Angeles Kings made history by winning their first Stanley Cup title. One of the youngest NHL teams, with an average player age of 26.5 years, the Kings defeated the New Jersey Devils, four games to two, in the finals. The Conn Smythe Trophy, awarded to the playoffs' Most Valuable Player, went to Kings goaltender Jonathan Quick.

STANLEY CUP CHAMPIONS

SEASON	WINNER	RUNNER-UP
2000–2001	Colorado Avalanche	New Jersey Devils
2001–2002	Detroit Red Wings	Carolina Hurricanes
2002–2003	New Jersey Devils	Anaheim Mighty Ducks
2003–2004	Tampa Bay Lightning	Calgary Flames
2004–2005	Season canceled	
2005–2006	Carolina Hurricanes	Edmonton Oilers
2006–2007	Anaheim Ducks	Ottawa Senators
2007–2008	Detroit Red Wings	Pittsburgh Penguins
2008–2009	Pittsburgh Penguins	Detroit Red Wings
2009–2010	Chicago Blackhawks	Philadelphia Flyers
2010–2011	Boston Bruins	Vancouver Canucks
2011–2012	Los Angeles Kings	New Jersey Devils

SOME ALL-TIME NHL RECORDS*

GOALS SCORED

Career: 894, Wayne Gretzky (1979–1999)

Season: 92, Wayne Gretzky (1981–1982)

Game: 7, Joe Malone (1920)

GOALIE WINS

Career: 656, **Martin Brodeur** (1992–2012)

Season: 48, **Martin Brodeur** (2006–2007)

POINTS

Career: 2,857, Wayne Gretzky (1979–1999)

Season: 215, Wayne Gretzky (1985–1986)

Game: 10, Darryl Sittler (1976)

GOALIE SHUTOUTS

Career: 119, **Martin Brodeur** (1992–2012)

Season: 22, George Hainsworth (1928–1929)

*Through the 2011–2012 season. Players in **bold** played in 2011–2012.

2011-2012 NHL League Leaders

Points: 109, Evgeni Malkin, Pittsburgh Penguins

Goals: 60, Steven Stamkos, Tampa Bay Lightning

Assists: 67, Henrik Sedin, Vancouver Canucks

Save Percentage: .940, Brian Elliott, St. Louis Blues

Wins: 43, Pekka Rinne, Nashville Predators ▼

HALL OF FAME

Located in Toronto, Ontario, Canada, the Hockey Hall of Fame honors former players, referees, and other people who have contributed to the game. There are also exhibits celebrating the history of ice hockey and the NHL.

Learn more at *www.hhof.com*

SOCCER

WORLD CUP

The men's FIFA World Cup, held every four years, is one of the most popular sporting events in the world. The FIFA Women's World Cup is also held every four years, one year after the men's tournament.

A First for Japan

The most recent FIFA Women's World Cup kicked off in Germany in June 2011. In the final, Japan beat the U.S., 3-1, on penalty kicks, becoming the first Asian nation to win the World Cup. The dramatic victory helped rebuild national pride just months after Japan's devastating tsunami.

For some fans, the U.S.'s unforgettable triumph over Brazil in the quarterfinals overshadowed its loss in the finals. The U.S. team included Abby Wambach, who has scored more than 130 goals in international play; star goalkeeper Hope Solo; and super subs Alex Morgan and Megan Rapinoe. Down a player for 55 minutes, the U.S. team scored to tie the game on a header by Wambach in the 122nd minute—the latest goal in World Cup history—and beat Brazil, 5-3, on penalty kicks.

Women's World Cup

Year	Winner
1991	U.S.
1995	Norway
1999	U.S.
2003	Germany
2007	Germany
2011	Japan

Men's World Cup

Year	Winner
1930	Uruguay
1934	Italy
1938	Italy
1942	not held
1946	not held
1950	Uruguay
1954	West Germany
1958	Brazil
1962	Brazil
1966	England
1970	Brazil
1974	West Germany
1978	Argentina
1982	Italy
1986	Argentina
1990	West Germany
1994	Brazil
1998	France
2002	Brazil
2006	Italy
2010	Spain

Abby Wambach (20)

Looking Ahead

Brazil will host the men's FIFA World Cup in 2014. Future men's World Cups will be hosted by Russia (2018) and Qatar (2022).

The next women's World Cup will be held in Canada in 2015.

Major League Soccer

In 2011, Major League Soccer (MLS) expanded to 18 teams with the addition of the Portland Timbers and the Vancouver Whitecaps FC. The playoffs were expanded to 10 teams. The 2011 season ended with the LA Galaxy beating the Houston Dynamos, 1-0, for the MLS Cup. Landon Donovan, who in the 72nd minute scored the only goal, was named the MLS Cup's Most Valuable Player. DC United star Dwayne De Rosario received the regular-season MVP honor. One of the top scorers of 2011 was Californian Chris Wondolowski, who put 16 balls in the net for the San Jose Earthquakes.

Chris Wondolowski (left)

Women's Professional Soccer

Women's Professional Soccer (WPS) held its 2011 championship game in Rochester, New York. The Western New York Flash beat the Philadelphia Independence in a close final that came down to a penalty shootout, 5-4. WNY Flash player and regular-season leading scorer Marta of Brazil was awarded the WPS Gold Boot award in 2011. Subsequently, the league folded in 2012, citing financial difficulties. The top players on the U.S. women's national team, however, were called into several training camps to prepare for the 2012 Summer Olympics.

Marta (10)

U.S. YOUTH SOCCER

The U.S. Youth Soccer Association began in 1974 with 100,000 players. Today, more than 3 million young soccer enthusiasts from ages 5 to 19 are registered to participate. U.S. Youth Soccer seeks to inspire a lifelong passion for the game while promoting physical, emotional, and intellectual growth in its participants.

Find out more at *www.usyouthsoccer.org*

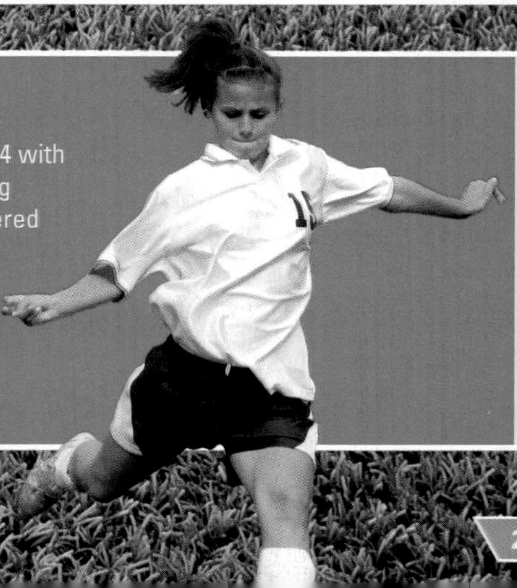

TENNIS

Modern tennis began in 1873. The first championships were held in Wimbledon, near London, England, four years later. In 1881, the first official U.S. men's championships were held at Newport, Rhode Island. Six years later, the first U.S. women's championships took place in Philadelphia, Pennsylvania. Today, the four most important tournaments, or Grand Slam events, are the Australian Open, the French Open, the All-England (Wimbledon) Championships, and the U.S. Open.

ALL-TIME GRAND SLAM SINGLES WINS

MEN	Australian	French	Wimbledon	U.S.	Total
Roger Federer (b. 1981)	4	1	6	5	16
Pete Sampras (b. 1971)	2	0	7	5	14
Roy Emerson (b. 1936)	6	2	2	2	12
Bjorn Borg (b. 1956)	0	6	5	0	11
Rod Laver (b. 1938)	3	2	4	2	11
Rafael Nadal (b. 1986)	1	7	2	1	11
Bill Tilden (1893–1953)	*	0	3	7	10

WOMEN					
Margaret Smith Court (b. 1942)	11	5	3	5	24
Steffi Graf (b. 1969)	4	6	7	5	22
Helen Wills Moody (1905–1998)	*	4	8	7	19
Chris Evert (b. 1954)	2	7	3	6	18
Martina Navratilova (b. 1956)	3	2	9	4	18

*Never played in tournament. Athletes in **bold** competed in 2012. Wins through June 2012.

SLAMMIN' GOOD TENNIS

Serbian star Novak Djokovic dominated men's tennis in the second half of 2011 and early 2012, winning three Grand Slam events in a row. After defeating Spain's Rafael Nadal in the Wimbledon and U.S. Open finals in 2011, Djokovic again came out on top against Nadal at the 2012 Australian Open. In Australia, the pair battled it out in the longest Grand Slam singles final in the history of professional tennis—5 hours, 53 minutes. In the 2012 French Open finals, however, Nadal defeated Djokovic and set a new record (7) for most career singles titles at the event.

As for the women, a different player won each Grand Slam event in 2011. Kim Clijsters of Belgium triumphed at the Australian Open, Li Na of China took the French Open to become the first Asian player to win a Grand Slam singles title, the Czech Petra Kvitova won at Wimbledon, and Australia's Samantha Stosur took the top prize at the U.S. Open. In 2012, Victoria Azarenka of Belarus prevailed at the Australian Open, and the French Open champion was Russia's Maria Sharapova, who earned a career Grand Slam with the win.

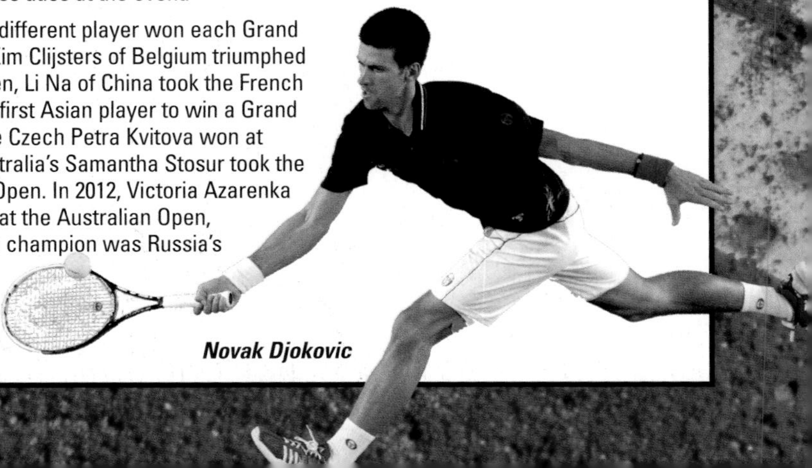

Novak Djokovic

Davis Cup

The Davis Cup is an international team tennis competition for men. It began in 1900 as a contest between just the U.S. and Great Britain called the International Lawn Tennis Challenge. Now more than 120 countries participate. Teams face off in a best-of-five series of singles and doubles matches to determine who advances. The U.S. has won the most Davis Cup championships (32), followed by Australia (28), France and Great Britain (9), and Sweden (7). Here are the results of the Davis Cup finals since 2000.

Year	Results
2000	Spain 3, Australia 1
2001	France 3, Australia 2
2002	Russia 3, France 2
2003	Australia 3, Spain 1
2004	Spain 3, U.S. 2
2005	Croatia 3, Slovakia 2
2006	Russia 3, Argentina 2
2007	U.S. 4, Russia 1
2008	Spain 3, Argentina 1
2009	Spain 5, Czech Republic 0
2010	Serbia 3, France 2
2011	Spain 3, Argentina 1

FAMILY MATTERS

You know how parents are always telling their children to play nicely together? Well, here are two pairs of siblings who play very well together.

Twin brothers Bob and Mike Bryan have been the most successful men's doubles team in recent years. Since 2003, Bob—a lefty with a big serve—and Mike—a right-handed player with a great service return—have collected 11 Grand Slam doubles championships. And back in their college days at Stanford University, the Bryans also won the 1998 NCAA doubles title. As junior players, however, they didn't play each other in singles tournaments. Their parents wouldn't allow it.

Of course, on the women's side, Williams sisters Serena and Venus have been an unstoppable team through the years. From 1999 through 2011, they won 12 Grand Slam doubles titles. As singles players, they have famously competed against each other in Grand Slam finals. As of mid-2012, Serena was ahead, 6-2.

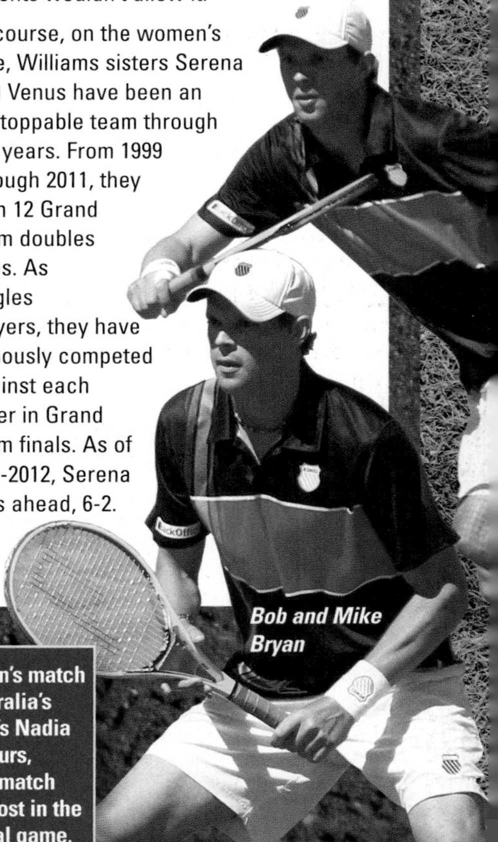

Bob and Mike Bryan

DID YOU KNOW? **The longest U.S. Open women's match ever took place in 2011. Australia's Samantha Stosur and Russia's Nadia Petrova battled it out for 3 hours, 16 minutes in the third round. After fighting off two match points, Petrova went on to win the second set but lost in the third. Stosur won on her fifth match point of the final game.**

X Games

ESPN held the first X Games (originally called the Extreme Games) in 1995. The first Winter X Games followed two years later. Considered the Olympics of action sports, the X Games showcase fearless athletes who are always looking for new ways to go higher and faster and invent more exciting tricks.

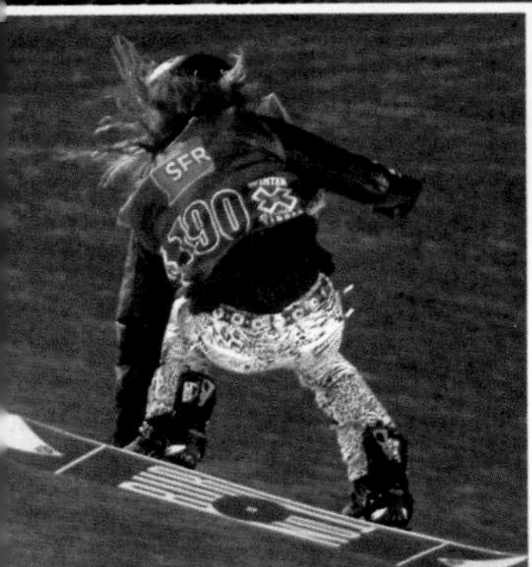

Shaun White

WINTER X GAMES The Winter X Games feature events in snowboarding, skiing, and snowmobiling. The 16th Winter X Games took place in Aspen, Colorado, January 26-29, 2012. Two of the top performances belonged to repeat winners: snowboard cross champion Nate Holland and snowboarder Shaun White. At the games, White set two records—for winning five consecutive men's snowboard superpipe gold medals and for earning the first perfect score in Winter X Games history.

Travis Pastrana

SUMMER X GAMES The Summer X Games feature events in Moto X (motocross), BMX, skateboarding, and rally car racing. The 18th Summer X Games were set to be held in downtown Los Angeles, June 28-July 1, 2012, one month earlier than previous years. More than 35 million Americans watched the 2011 Summer X Games on television, and outside the U.S., live coverage was delivered to almost 200 countries and territories.

Find out more about extreme sports at *espn.go.com/action*

ALL-TIME X GAMES GOLD MEDALISTS

Here are the X Games competitors who have won the most events at the annual action sports championships.

WINTER X GAMES		
Competitor	**Sport(s)**	**Medals***
Shaun White	snowboarding	12
Tanner Hall	skiing	7
Nate Holland	snowboarding	7
Lindsey Jacobellis	snowboarding	7
Shaun Palmer	skiing, snowboarding	6
Tucker Hibbert	snowmobiling	6
Tara Dakides	snowboarding	5
Blair Morgan	snowmobiling	5

*Through 2012. Athletes in **bold** competed in 2012 X Games.

SUMMER X GAMES		
Competitor	**Sport(s)**	**Medals***
Dave Mirra	BMX, rally car	14
Travis Pastrana	motocross, rally car	11
Tony Hawk	skateboarding	10
Jamie Bestwick	BMX	9
Bob Burnquist	skateboarding	8
Andy Macdonald	skateboarding	8
Fabiola de Silva	inline skating	7
Pierre-Luc Gagnon	skateboarding	7

*Through 2011. Athletes in **bold** competed in 2011 X Games.

SPORTS PUZZLES

SPORTS STAR Challenge

Find the names of the following people discussed in the Sports section. The names are all hidden in the puzzle. The letters of the names may run up, down, forward, backward, or diagonally. Two names may share the same letter.

NAMES TO FIND

Griner	Santo
Heisman	Shaun
John	Solo
Luck	Venus
Naismith	Verlander
Nelson	Vonn

A	V	E	N	U	S	H	A	U	N
H	E	I	S	M	A	N	R	V	Q
T	R	M	M	Y	J	J	O	H	N
W	L	K	J	O	H	L	S	C	E
K	A	M	U	K	O	A	B	E	L
C	N	A	I	S	M	I	T	H	S
U	D	W	Z	K	S	A	N	T	O
L	E	V	O	N	N	F	R	E	N
X	R	E	N	I	R	G	X	J	D

ANSWERS ON PAGES 334-336.

MATCH IT!

Match the sporting event with the organization that sponsors it.

Sporting Events

1. Super Bowl ○

2. Soccer World Cup ○

3. Wimbledon ○

4. Stanley Cup Finals ○

5. Ryder Cup ○

6. March Madness ○

7. Daytona 500 ○

8. Olympic Games ○

Organizations

a All England Lawn Tennis Club

b NHL

c IOC

d FIFA

e NFL

f NASCAR

g PGA

h NCAA

TECHNOLOGY & COMPUTERS

→What is cloud computing? PAGE 241

Computer Highlights Timeline

100 B.C.	The Antikythera Mechanism, which used gears to predict the positions of astronomical bodies, was built by the ancient Greeks. It was the first known mechanical computer.
1623	Wilhelm Schickard built the first machine that could automatically add, subtract, multiply, and divide. He called it a "calculating clock."
1946	The first electronic, programmable, general-purpose computer was invented. It was called ENIAC, for "Electronic Numerical Integrator and Computer." ▶
1967	The Advanced Research Projects Agency (ARPA) allotted money toward creating a computer network. It became ARPAnet, which evolved into the Internet.
1971	The "floppy disk" was introduced by IBM as a means of affordable portable storage.
1975	The Altair 8800 entered the market. It was the first widely sold personal microcomputer.
1975	Bill Gates and Paul Allen founded Microsoft. Later came the first version of Windows.
1990	The World Wide Web was first launched by British physicist Tim Berners-Lee.
1996	Google, the Internet's most popular search engine, began as a graduate student project at Stanford University called BackRub.
2004	Facebook, the popular social networking site, was launched by Harvard University student Mark Zuckerberg.
2005	YouTube, a popular video sharing service, was founded.
2006	Twitter, a Web service letting people send or post short messages, was founded.
2010	Apple introduced the iPad, a tablet computer.
2011	More than 400 million smartphones were sold during the year, exceeding annual personal computer sales for the first time. ▶

DID YOU KNOW? Among people who use the Internet, the most popular activities are searching for information and using e-mail. About 92 percent of users go online for each of these reasons. About 65 percent of Internet users go to social networking sites.

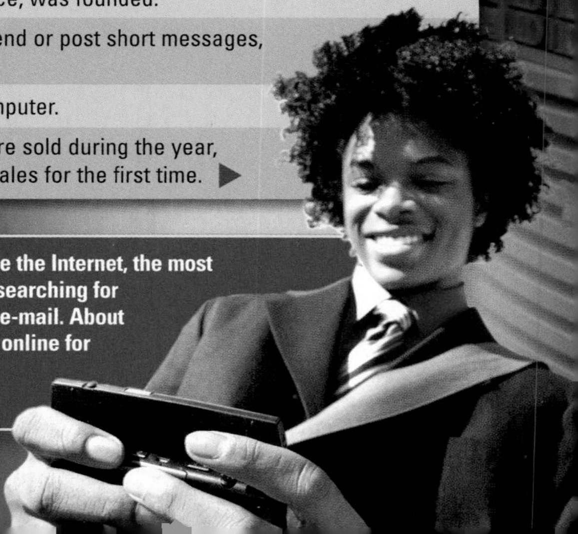

Playing It Safe ONLINE

Social networking websites can be a lot of fun. But they can also be a source of problems. To be on the safe side, you should always keep an eye out for risks.

Protect against cyberbullying. Cyberbullying refers to e-mails or posts sent over the Internet that are intended to embarrass or hurt another person. These posts often spread lies or tell secrets the victim shared in confidence. If you are a victim of a cyberbully, save the posts or e-mails and show them to an adult you trust. Often the person behind the bullying can be found. To help keep cyberbullying from spreading, refuse to pass along bullying e-mails about someone else, express disapproval of cyberbullying messages, and report them to an adult.

Be careful about what personal information you make public. Carefully guard your password, birthday, address, phone number, and other personal information.

Take advantage of the website's security features. Pick a unique, hard-to-guess password. Keep your profile viewable only by friends. If the website allows your username to be different from your real name, make sure yours is different—and does not include personal information, such as your age or town.

Beware of viruses. Antivirus software may not recognize new viruses. For this reason it is important to think twice before downloading an app or any other file from a source that you don't know or don't have reason to trust.

DID YOU KNOW? The number of American teenagers using smartphones in 2011 was about 5 million, almost triple the number just two years earlier.

HEADS IN THE CLOUD?

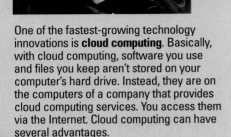

One of the fastest-growing technology innovations is **cloud computing**. Basically, with cloud computing, software you use and files you keep aren't stored on your computer's hard drive. Instead, they are on the computers of a company that provides cloud computing services. You access them via the Internet. Cloud computing can have several advantages.

- **What you can do is not limited by what software your computer has or how much speed and power it has.** Even if you don't have a video-editing program, through a service provider, you can edit videos—whether for a school project or just for fun.
- **What you save is not limited by how much storage space your computer has.** Many companies allow people to store photos, music, movies, e-books, and other large files in the cloud.
- **When you can use software and stored files is not limited by where you are.** Even if you're away from your own computer, as long as you have access to the Internet, you can use programs and retrieve files.

Cloud computing has some possible problems. Some people are concerned about the security of information that is stored in the cloud. And if your service provider has a service interruption, or your Internet connection is lost, then you can't get to software or stored files until the problem is fixed.

Still, many experts think cloud computing will become more widespread as time goes by. Even NASA uses the cloud computing services of companies like Microsoft and Google for data storage and complex calculations.

FINDING FACTS ONLINE

Limit the Keyword Search

Before you start researching a topic with a search engine, decide exactly what you need. Knowing what you're looking for makes it easier to find sites that have the information you need. It can also help you evaluate the source.

As you search the Internet, keep the following tips in mind:

- Make your search terms as specific as possible. Suppose you have an assignment that asks you to describe three famous inventions of Thomas Edison. You can search for: famous inventions Thomas Edison.
- Put words in quotes when you are searching for a specific phrase. To find out which president said, "I cannot live without books," type the exact phrase in quotation marks (as shown) in the search box. Some search engines have an "Advanced Search" tool so that you can search for particular combinations of terms.
- Try using a synonym if you are having trouble with your search. Suppose you are searching for the different ways in which moisture, or water, reaches the ground. Try searching for "forms of precipitation."
- Try different search engines if one isn't producing results. The three most popular general search engines—Google (www.google.com), Yahoo (www.yahoo.com), and Bing (www.bing.com)—usually come up with slightly different sets of results.

Identify the Website

Huge amounts of information are on the Internet. While this makes the Internet great for research, not all sources are reliable. A wide variety of information is available, from facts and data to stories and opinions.

The ending of the main part of a web page's address may offer clues to the type of page. Government sites in the U.S. generally end in **.gov** or **.us**. These sites are reliable sources for data and objective reports. Nonprofit organizations often end in **.org**. Educational institutions end in **.edu**. Business sites usually end in **.com** or **.net**. Many international organizations end in **.int**.

DID YOU KNOW? **The Internet address of a website is called its domain name. As of early 2012, there were about 140 million domain names in active use.**

On the JOB ▸ Systems Engineer

Systems engineers are responsible for supporting, installing, and maintaining different computer systems, including e-mail systems. **Chris Robley** is a senior systems engineer in the IT (information technology) department of a worldwide fashion company. He agreed to talk to *The World Almanac for Kids* about his work.

What do you do in a typical day?

My typical day includes checking all of the company's computer systems and making sure that they're functioning properly. Company employees who are working from home or are traveling on business have to be able to access their work e-mail and reach work-related Internet sites. I help people who work for my company all around the world and who are having computer-related problems. My department is also responsible for updating the company's computer systems so that they run faster and so that our users can do more work from home or other remote locations.

What interests and strengths of yours make this job right for you?

The main interest and strength that suits me for this job is my desire to fix things that are broken. This started when I was young. As a kid, I would break my toy train in an attempt to figure out how it worked. Then I would have to fix it. Later, I started playing with bigger toys, like computers, and my curiosity for figuring out how thing worked and fixing them grew.

What kind of education or training did you need to get in order to do your job?

I have a bachelor's degree in mechanical engineering. I have also taken various specialized Microsoft classes.

What do you like best about your job? What is most challenging?

The best thing about my job is being able to help my company's employees with their computer problem anywhere in the world. Our company, like most, has become dependent on e-mails and other computer systems. This makes IT jobs important, but it can also be challenging because users need their problems fixed right away, and sometimes that just isn't possible.

TRANSPORTATION

→When was subway service first introduced in the U.S.? PAGE 246

GETTING FROM THERE TO HERE
A SHORT HISTORY OF TRANSPORTATION

5000 B.C. People harness **animal power**. Oxen and donkeys carry heavy loads.

3500 B.C. Egyptians create the first **sailboat**. Before this, people made rafts or canoes and paddled them with poles or their hands.

3500 B.C. In Mesopotamia (modern-day Iraq), vehicles with **wheels** are invented. But the first wheels are made of heavy wood, and the roads are terrible.

A.D. 800 Fast, shallow-draft **longships** make Vikings a powerful force in Europe from 800 to 1100.

983 First **locks** to raise water level are built on China's Grand Canal. By 1400, a 1,500-mile water highway system is developed.

Around 1000 Using **magnetic compasses**, Chinese are able to sail long distances in flat-bottomed ships called junks.

1450s Portuguese build **fast ships** with three masts. These, plus the compass, usher in an age of exploration.

1660s **Horse-drawn stagecoaches** begin running in France. They stop at "stages" to switch horses and passengers—the first mass transit system.

1681 France's 150-mile **Canal du Midi** connects the Atlantic Ocean with the Mediterranean Sea.

1730s **Stagecoach service** begins in the U.S.

1769 James Watt patents the first successful **steam engine**.

1783 In Paris, the Montgolfier brothers fly the first **hot air balloon**.

1807 Robert Fulton patents a highly efficient **steamboat**.

1825 The 363-mile **Erie Canal** connects the Hudson River with Lake Erie, opening up the U.S. frontier and making New York City the nation's top port.

1830 **Inter-city passenger rail service** begins in England. Trains are powered by a steam engine built by George Stephenson. They go about 24 miles per hour.

1832 The first U.S. **horse-drawn streetcar** is driven up and down the Bowery in New York City.

1839 Kirkpatrick Macmillan of Scotland invents the first **pedaled bicycle**.

1860s
Paddle-wheel steamboats dominate U.S. river travel.

1862
Etienne Lenoir of Belgium builds the **first car** with an internal-combustion engine.

1863
Using steam locomotives, the **London subway** (known as the "tube") opens.

1869
Transcontinental railroad is completed at Promontory Point, Utah. The Suez Canal in Egypt opens, saving ships a long trip around Africa.

1873
San Francisco's **cable car** system begins service.

1887
First practical electric street railway system opens in the U.S. in Richmond, Virginia. Suburbs soon grow around cities as **trolley** systems let people live farther away from the workplace.

1897
The first U.S. **subway service** begins in Boston. New York City follows in 1904.

1903
At Kitty Hawk, North Carolina, the Wright brothers fly the first powered **heavier-than-air machine**.

1908
Henry Ford builds the first **Model T**, a practical car for the general public.

1914
The 50-mile **Panama Canal** opens, saving ships a nearly 6,000-mile trip around South America.

1927
Charles A. Lindbergh makes the first **nonstop solo flight** across the Atlantic, flying from Long Island, New York, to Paris, France, in 33 hours, 30 minutes.

1939
The first practical **helicopter** and **first jet plane** are invented. The jet flies up to 434 mph. (Jet passenger service begins in 1952.)

1964
Shinkansen "**bullet train**" service (124 mph) begins in Japan.

1969
U.S. astronauts aboard ***Apollo 11*** land on the Moon.

1981
The first **space shuttle** is launched on April 12, 1981.

1994
Trains cross under the English Channel in the new **Channel Tunnel**, or "Chunnel."

2010
China reports that one of its **high-speed trains** travels at more than 300 mph.

2012
The Nissan Leaf becomes the world's best-selling **all-electric car**.

TRAVEL

→What was the world's first national park? PAGE 252

In the late 13th century, famed Italian adventurer Marco Polo took a winding 5,600-mile journey overland from Venice, Italy, to Beijing, China. When he returned to Venice, Polo published a chronicle of his travels. The stories were so fantastic that many people didn't believe his tales.

You may not be taking a journey of thousands of miles on your next trip, but the excitement of traveling is the same. People always have the desire to stretch their legs, explore new places, and have great adventures.

The 10 Most Visited Countries*

1.	France
2.	United States
3.	China
4.	Spain
5.	Italy
6.	United Kingdom
7.	Turkey
8.	Germany
9.	Malaysia
10.	Mexico

*2010

The 10 Most Visited U.S. Tourist Sites*

1.	Times Square, New York, NY
2.	Las Vegas Strip, Las Vegas, NV
3.	National Mall and Memorials, Washington, D.C.
4.	Faneuil Hall, Boston, MA
5.	Magic Kingdom, Lake Buena Vista, FL
6.	Golden Gate National Recreation Area, San Francisco, CA
7.	Disneyland, Anaheim, CA
8.	Fisherman's Wharf, San Francisco, CA
9.	Hollywood Walk of Fame, Los Angeles, CA
10.	Great Smoky Mountains National Park, NC and TN

*2010

World's Five Most-Visited Amusement Parks*

1. Magic Kingdom, Walt Disney World (Lake Buena Vista, Florida), 16.9 million
2. Disneyland (Anaheim, California), 15.9 million
3. Tokyo Disneyland (Japan), 14.4 million
4. Tokyo Disney Sea (Japan), 12.6 million
5. Epcot, Walt Disney World (Lake Buena Vista, Florida), 10.8 million

*2010

Amusement Parks

The first amusement parks appeared in Europe more than 400 years ago. Attractions included flower gardens and a few simple rides. Today's amusement parks are much more impressive, with super-fast roller coasters, parades, shows, and other attractions. Here's a look at some of the most popular amusement parks in the U.S.

FABULOUS PARK FACTS

Biggest Park: Walt Disney World, Lake Buena Vista, Florida, 30,500 acres

Most Rides: 74, Cedar Point, Sandusky, Ohio

Most Roller Coasters: 17, Cedar Point, Sandusky, Ohio

Fastest Roller Coaster: 128 mph, Kingda Ka, Six Flags Great Adventure, Jackson, New Jersey

Tallest Roller Coaster: 456 feet, Kingda Ka, Six Flags Great Adventure, Jackson, New Jersey

Cedar Point (Sandusky, Ohio)

One of the oldest amusement parks in the U.S., Cedar Point (on Lake Erie) opened in 1870. Today at Cedar Point, the most exciting ride is the Top Thrill Dragster roller coaster, which reaches a height of 420 feet, while the cars zip along at a top speed of 120 mph! There are also plenty of other attractions, including the maxAir, which spins and swings 140 feet above the ground. ▼

Water World (Denver, Colorado)

One of the largest water parks in the United States, Water World opened in 1982. There are 49 attractions on its 64 acres, including more family tube rides than at any other water park in the U.S. and Wally World for young children. The park also has some of the highest water slides in the world, where riders can reach speeds of up to 40 miles per hour.

Universal Studios Florida/Islands of Adventure (Orlando, Florida)

Universal Studios opened in 1990, and visitors have been "riding the movies" there ever since. Rides, shows, and many other attractions feature favorite movie and TV characters. A major new attraction, The Wizarding World of Harry Potter, has three rides, as well as shops and a restaurant.

DID YOU KNOW?

Ferrari World Abu Dhabi, the world's largest indoor theme park, opened in late 2010. Located on Yas Island in the Persian Gulf, it has more than 20 Ferrari-inspired rides and attractions. They include advanced racing simulations and Formula Rossa, the world's fastest roller coaster, with a top speed of 149 mph.

SOME MUST SEE MUSEUMS

As you travel to new places, you can learn a lot—and have a lot of fun—by visiting local museums. Some museums have exhibits about space, the history of life on Earth, and other areas of science. Some display great art. Some focus on American history. And there are museums about almost any subject you can imagine. Here is a small sampling of some of the leading museums in the United States.

√ The **EXPLORATORIUM**, in San Francisco, California, weaves together science and art to encourage experimentation, curiosity, and creativity. Hundreds of interactive exhibits let visitors touch a tornado, use a joystick to land a lunar spacecraft, and dig through a pile of decay to feel the heat generated when organisms decompose.

For more information, see: ***www.exploratorium.edu***

√ The **KENNEDY SPACE CENTER**, near Daytona Beach, Florida, gives visitors the chance to meet real astronauts, experience "liftoff" at the beginning of a space flight, and imagine what the future of space travel will be like. There's an IMAX theater and a real Saturn V rocket like the one that launched the astronauts who landed on the Moon. Soon, the center will display the retired space shuttle *Atlantis*.

For more information, see: ***www.kennedyspacecenter.com***

√ The **METROPOLITAN MUSEUM OF ART**, in New York City, is among the largest museums of fine art in the world. Its collection covers art from all parts of the world and includes works by the most important artists in history. The Met also has collections of furniture from past centuries, medieval arms and armor, and a beautiful, peaceful Chinese garden.

For more information, see: ***www.metmuseum.org***

THE 7 WONDERS OF THE WORLD

These 7 Wonders of the World were chosen in 2007 through an online poll in which over 100 million people from 200 countries cast votes. The 7 Wonders are all equal in rank.

THE GREAT WALL OF CHINA
(begun 221 B.C.; completed A.D. 1368–1644), China

THE PYRAMID AT CHICHÉN ITZÁ
(before A.D. 1200), Yucatan Peninsula, Mexico

PETRA
(1st century B.C.), Jordan

THE ROMAN COLOSSEUM
(A.D. 70–82), Rome, Italy

MACHU PICCHU
(A.D. 1460–1470), Peru

CHRIST THE REDEEMER
(A.D. 1931), Rio de Janiero, Brazil

THE TAJ MAHAL
(A.D. 1630), Agra, India

DID YOU KNOW?

The Musical Instrument Museum, located in Phoenix, Arizona, aims to collect musical instruments and music from every nation in the world. Visitors can hear each instrument played in its original cultural context. The museum collection currently numbers 15,000 instruments and artifacts, with the oldest being a Chinese *paigu* (hourglass drum) from 5000 to 4000 B.C.

NATIONAL PARKS

The world's first national park was Yellowstone, established in 1872. Today in the U.S., there are 58 national parks, including parks in the Virgin Islands, Guam, Puerto Rico, and American Samoa. The National Park Service manages 397 units in all, including national monuments, memorials, battlefields, military parks, historic parks, historic sites, lakeshores, seashores, recreation areas, scenic rivers and trails, wilderness areas, and the White House—more than 84 million acres in all! For more information, go to: ***www.nps.gov/parks.html***

CRATER LAKE NATIONAL PARK

OR

This park of 183,000 acres, established in 1902 in southwestern Oregon, is home to spectacular Crater Lake, which at 1,958 feet is the deepest lake in the United States and one of the deepest in the world. The lake was created by the eruption of a volcano, Mount Mazama, more than 7,000 years ago. Surrounding glaciers filled the caldera (the volcano's basin) with clear blue water. The lake is not all there is to see. The park boasts 680 plant species, 74 types of mammals, and 158 kinds of birds. Since snow generally falls from October to June, cross-country skiing and snowshoeing are among the most popular pastimes.

GRAND CANYON NATIONAL PARK

AZ

This national park, established in 1919, has one of the world's most spectacular landscapes, covering more than a million acres in northwestern Arizona. The canyon is 6,000 feet deep at its deepest point and 15 miles wide at its widest. Its 277-mile-long walls display a cross section of Earth's crust from as far back as 2 billion years ago. The Colorado River—which carved out the giant canyon—still runs through the park, which is a valuable wildlife preserve. The pine and fir forests, painted deserts, plateaus, caves, and sandstone canyons offer a wide range of habitats.

ACADIA NATIONAL PARK

Acadia National Park is located in eastern Maine. It offers spectacular views of the rocky Maine coast, the tallest mountain on the U.S. Atlantic seaboard (Cadillac Mountain), and 120 miles of hiking trails. Its 47,000 acres include lakes, ponds, and Mount Desert Island, which was first settled 5,000 years ago by American Indians. In the 1800s, the region became popular as a summer resort. Concerned that the land would be ruined, conservationist George B. Dorr started buying up thousands of acres. He donated this land to the U.S. government, and in 1919 the park was created.

EVERGLADES NATIONAL PARK

Located in southern Florida, the Everglades is the largest subtropical wilderness in the U.S. More than 1.5 million acres of this wilderness are now protected in Everglades National Park. More than 350 species of birds, 40 species of mammals, and 50 kinds of reptiles live in the park's varied ecosystems, which include swamps, saw grass prairies, and mangrove forests. The park's different habitats allow a huge variety of life forms to thrive. As you move from place to place, you may see all kinds of animals, from tiny frogs to free-roaming alligators and crocodiles, graceful herons, and lots of snakes. You can visit a mahogany forest and pine forests, and you can walk along raised boardwalks to get beautiful views of miles of swaying saw grass marshes full of wildlife.

YELLOWSTONE NATIONAL PARK

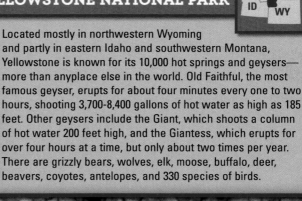

Located mostly in northwestern Wyoming and partly in eastern Idaho and southwestern Montana, Yellowstone is known for its 10,000 hot springs and geysers—more than anyplace else in the world. Old Faithful, the most famous geyser, erupts for about four minutes every one to two hours, shooting 3,700-8,400 gallons of hot water as high as 185 feet. Other geysers include the Giant, which shoots a column of hot water 200 feet high, and the Giantess, which erupts for over four hours at a time, but only about two times per year. There are grizzly bears, wolves, elk, moose, buffalo, deer, beavers, coyotes, antelopes, and 330 species of birds.

UNITED STATES

→Which state has the most seats in the U.S. House of Representatives? PAGE 259

FACTS & FIGURES

AREA	50 states and Washington, D.C.
LAND	3,531,905 square miles
WATER	264,837 square miles
TOTAL	3,796,742 square miles

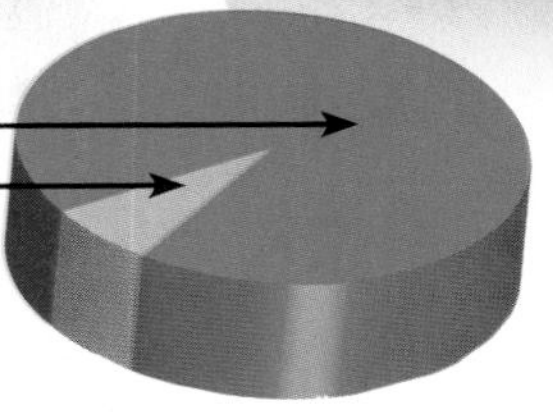

POPULATION (JULY 2012 ESTIMATE): 313,847,465

CAPITAL: WASHINGTON, D.C.

LARGEST, *HIGHEST*, AND OTHER STATISTICS

Largest state:	Alaska (665,384 square miles)
Smallest state:	Rhode Island (1,545 square miles)
Northernmost city:	Barrow, Alaska (71°17′ north latitude)
Southernmost city:	Hilo, Hawaii (19°44′ north latitude)
Easternmost city:	Eastport, Maine (66°59′ west longitude)
Westernmost city:	Adak Station, Alaska (173°11′ east longitude)
Highest settlement:	Tordal Estates, Colorado (10,653 feet)
Lowest settlement:	Bombay Beach, California (223 feet below sea level)
Oldest national park:	Yellowstone National Park (Idaho, Montana, Wyoming), 2,219,791 acres, established 1872
Largest national park:	Wrangell-St. Elias, Alaska (8,323,148 acres)
Highest mountain:	Mount McKinley, Alaska (20,320 feet) ▶
Lowest point:	Death Valley, California (258 feet below sea level)
Longest river system:	Mississippi-Missouri-Red Rock (3,710 miles)
Deepest lake:	Crater Lake, Oregon (1,958 feet)
Tallest building:	(as of 2012) Willis Tower, Chicago, Illinois (1,450 feet)
Tallest structure:	TV tower, Blanchard, North Dakota (2,063 feet)
Longest bridge span:	Verrazano-Narrows Bridge, New York (4,260 feet)
Highest bridge:	Royal Gorge, Colorado (1,053 feet above water)

DID YOU KNOW? **Harvard University, in Cambridge, Massachusetts, is the oldest college or university in the United States. It was founded in 1636.**

SYMBOLS OF THE UNITED STATES

THE GREAT SEAL

The Great Seal of the United States shows an American bald eagle with a ribbon in its mouth bearing the Latin words *e pluribus unum* (out of many, one). In its talons are the arrows of war and an olive branch of peace. On the back of the Great Seal is an unfinished pyramid with an eye (the eye of Providence) above it. The seal was approved by Congress on June 20, 1782.

THE FLAG

The flag of the United States has 50 stars (one for each state) and 13 stripes (one for each of the original 13 states). It is unofficially called the "Stars and Stripes."

The first U.S. flag was commissioned by the Second Continental Congress in 1777 but did not exist until 1783, after the American Revolution. Historians are not certain who designed the Stars and Stripes. Many different flags are believed to have been used during the American Revolution.

The flag of 1777 was used until 1795. In that year, Congress passed an act ordering that a new flag have 15 stripes, alternate red and white, and 15 stars on a blue field. In 1818, Congress directed that the flag have 13 stripes and that a new star be added for each new state of the Union. The last star was added in 1960 for the state of Hawaii.

There are many customs for flying the flag and treating it with respect. For example, it should not touch the floor and no other flag should be flown above it, except for the UN flag at UN headquarters. When the flag is raised or lowered, when it passes in a parade, or during the Pledge of Allegiance, people should face it and stand at attention. Those in military uniform should salute. Others should put their right hand over their heart. The flag is flown at half-staff as a sign of mourning.

1777

1795

1818

Pledge of Allegiance to the Flag

"I pledge allegiance to the flag of the United States of America and to the republic for which it stands, one nation under God, indivisible, with liberty and justice for all."

THE NATIONAL ANTHEM

"The Star-Spangled Banner" was a poem written in 1814 by Francis Scott Key after he watched British ships bombard Fort McHenry, Maryland, during the War of 1812. It became the National Anthem by an act of Congress in 1931. The music to "The Star-Spangled Banner" was originally a tune called "Anacreon in Heaven."

THE U.S. CONSTITUTION

The Foundation of American Government

The Constitution is the document that created the present government of the United States. It was written in 1787 and went into effect in 1789. It establishes the three branches of the U.S. government—the legislative (Congress), the executive (headed by the president), and the judicial (the Supreme Court and other federal courts). The first 10 amendments to the Constitution (the **Bill of Rights**) explain the basic rights of all American citizens.

You can find the Constitution online at:
www.archives.gov/exhibits/charters/constitution.html

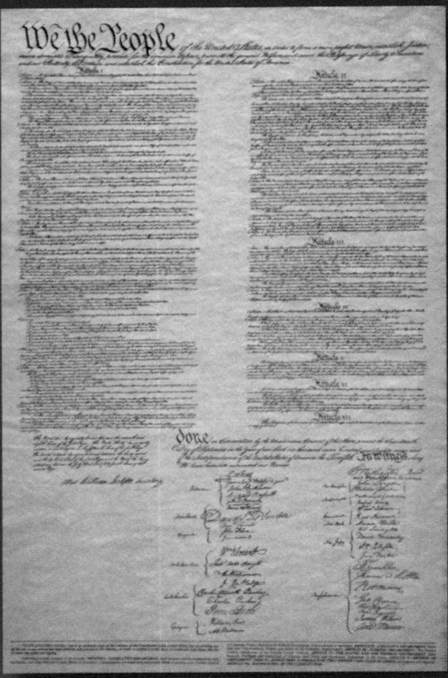

The Preamble to the Constitution

The Constitution begins with a short statement called the Preamble. The Preamble states that the government of the United States was established by the people.

"We the people of the United States, in order to form a more perfect union, establish justice, insure domestic tranquility, provide for the common defense, promote the general welfare, and secure the blessings of liberty to ourselves and our posterity, do ordain and establish this Constitution for the United States of America."

THE ARTICLES

The original Constitution contained seven articles. The first three articles of the Constitution establish the three branches of the U.S. government.

Article 1, Legislative Branch Creates the Senate and House of Representatives and describes their functions and powers.

Article 2, Executive Branch Creates the office of the President and the Electoral College and lists their powers and responsibilities.

Article 3, Judicial Branch Creates the Supreme Court and gives Congress the power to create lower courts. The powers of the courts and certain crimes are defined.

Article 4, The States Discusses the relationship of the states to one another and to the citizens. Defines the states' powers.

Article 5, Amending the Constitution Describes how the Constitution can be amended (changed).

Article 6, Federal Law Makes the Constitution the supreme law of the land over state laws and constitutions.

Article 7, Ratifying the Constitution Establishes how to ratify (approve) the Constitution.

AMENDMENTS TO THE CONSTITUTION

The writers of the Constitution understood that it might need to be amended, or changed, in the future, but they wanted to be careful and made it hard to change. Article 5 describes how the Constitution can be amended.

In order to take effect, an amendment must be approved by a two-thirds majority in both the House of Representatives and the Senate. It must then be approved (ratified) by three-fourths of the states (38 states). So far, there have been 27 amendments. One of them (the 18th, ratified in 1919) banned the manufacture or sale of liquor. It was canceled by the 21st Amendment, in 1933.

The Bill of Rights: The First Ten Amendments

The first ten amendments were adopted in 1791 and contain the basic freedoms Americans enjoy as a people. These amendments are known as the Bill of Rights.

1 **Guarantees freedom of religion, speech, and the press.**

2 **Guarantees the right to have firearms.**

3 **Guarantees that soldiers cannot be lodged in private homes unless the owner agrees.**

4 **Protects people from being searched or having property searched or taken away by the government without reason.**

5 **Protects rights of people on trial for crimes.**

6 **Guarantees people accused of crimes the right to a speedy public trial by jury.**

7 **Guarantees the right to a trial by jury for other kinds of cases.**

8 **Prohibits "cruel and unusual punishments."**

9 **Says specific rights listed in the Constitution do not take away rights that may not be listed.**

10 **Establishes that any powers not given specifically to the federal government belong to states or the people.**

OTHER IMPORTANT AMENDMENTS

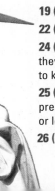

13 (1865): Ends slavery in the United States.

14 (1868): Bars states from denying rights to citizens; guarantees equal protection under the law for all citizens.

15 (1870): Guarantees that a person cannot be denied the right to vote because of race or color.

19 (1920): Gives women the right to vote.

22 (1951): Limits the president to two four-year terms of office.

24 (1964): Outlaws the poll tax (a tax people had to pay before they could vote) in federal elections. (The poll tax had been used to keep African Americans in the South from voting.)

25 (1967): Specifies presidential succession; also gives the president the power to appoint a new vice president if one dies or leaves office during a term.

26 (1971): Lowers the voting age to 18 from 21.

THE LEGISLATIVE BRANCH

CONGRESS

Congress is the legislative branch of the federal government. Congress's major responsibility is to pass the laws that govern the country and determine how money collected in taxes is spent. Congress consists of two parts—the Senate and the House of Representatives.

THE SENATE

The Senate has 100 members, two from each state. The Constitution says that the Senate will have equal representation (the same number of representatives) from each state. Thus, small states have the same number of senators as large states. Senators are elected for six-year terms. There is no limit on the number of terms a senator can serve.

The Senate also has the responsibility of approving people the president appoints for certain jobs: for example, cabinet members and Supreme Court justices. The Senate must approve all treaties by at least a two-thirds vote. It also has the responsibility under the Constitution of putting on trial high-ranking federal officials who have been impeached (accused of wrongdoing) by the House of Representatives.

For more information, see: ***www.senate.gov***

THE HOUSE OF REPRESENTATIVES

The number of members of the House of Representatives for each state depends on its population according to a recent census. But each state has at least one representative, no matter how small its population. A term lasts two years.

The first House of Representatives in 1789 had 65 members. As the country's population grew, the number of representatives increased. Since 1911, however, the total membership has been kept at 435.

For more information, see: ***www.house.gov***

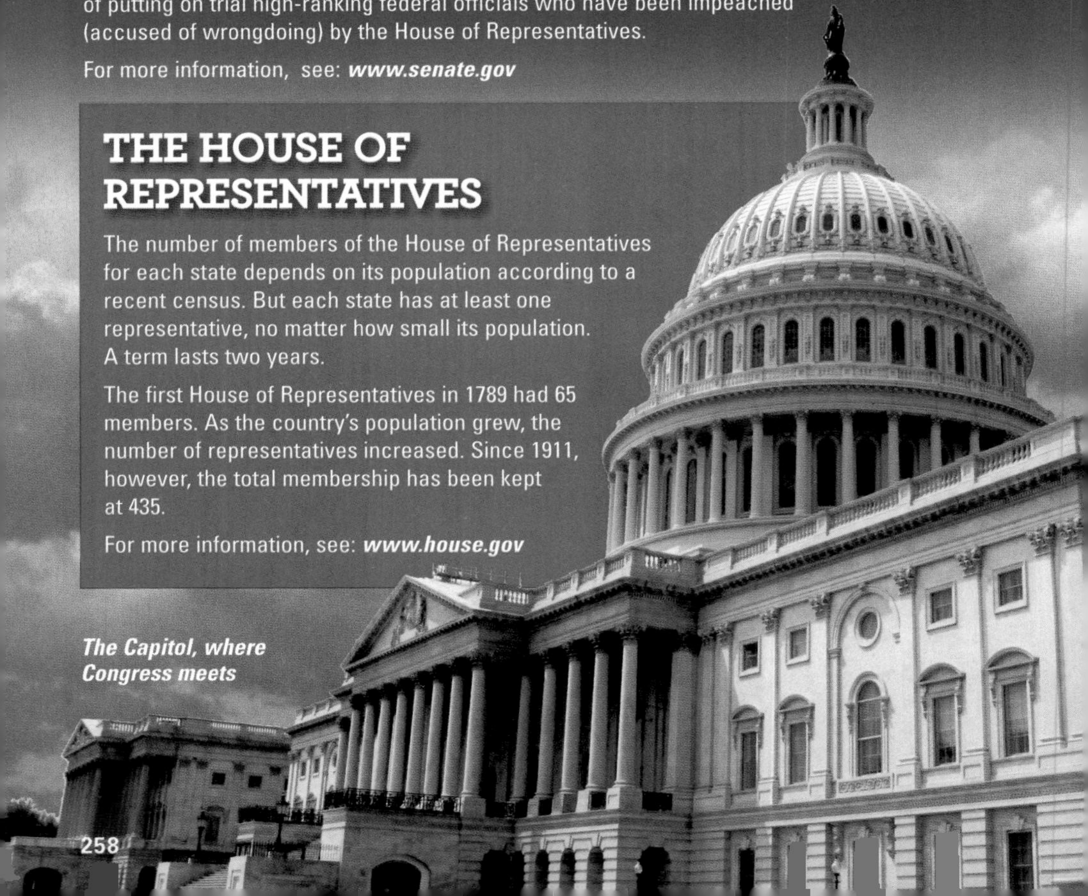

The Capitol, where Congress meets

The House of Representatives, by State

As a result of the 2010 Census, some states gained or lost House members (or "seats"), starting in 2013, because of population changes. The table shows how many seats each state gained or lost.

State	Seats 2013	Seats 2003–2012	Change in Seats
Alabama	7	7	0
Alaska	1	1	0
Arizona	9	8	+1
Arkansas	4	4	0
California	53	53	0
Colorado	7	7	0
Connecticut	5	5	0
Delaware	1	1	0
Florida	27	25	+2
Georgia	14	13	+1
Hawaii	2	2	0
Idaho	2	2	0
Illinois	18	19	-1
Indiana	9	9	0
Iowa	4	5	-1
Kansas	4	4	0
Kentucky	6	6	0
Louisiana	6	7	-1
Maine	2	2	0
Maryland	8	8	0
Massachusetts	9	10	-1
Michigan	14	15	-1
Minnesota	8	8	0
Mississippi	4	4	0
Missouri	8	9	-1
Montana	1	1	0
Nebraska	3	3	0
Nevada	4	3	+1
New Hampshire	2	2	0
New Jersey	12	13	-1
New Mexico	3	3	0
New York	27	29	-2
North Carolina	13	13	0
North Dakota	1	1	0
Ohio	16	18	-2
Oklahoma	5	5	0
Oregon	5	5	0
Pennsylvania	18	19	-1
Rhode Island	2	2	0
South Carolina	7	6	+1
South Dakota	1	1	0
Tennessee	9	9	0
Texas	36	32	+4
Utah	4	3	+1
Vermont	1	1	0
Virginia	11	11	0
Washington	10	9	+1
West Virginia	3	3	0
Wisconsin	8	8	0
Wyoming	1	1	0

Washington, D.C., Puerto Rico, American Samoa, Guam, and the Virgin Islands each has one nonvoting member of the House of Representatives.

How a Bill Becomes a Law

A proposed law is called a bill. To become a law, a bill must first be approved by both houses, or chambers, of Congress. Most kinds of bills can start in either chamber.

Let's assume that a bill starts in the House of Representatives. It is introduced by one or more members and then assigned to one of the many House committees, where it is studied and possibly changed. The committee may get advice from outside experts and hold public hearings, or meetings, on the proposal. Then the committee votes on the bill. If a majority of the committee members support the bill, it goes to the full House. The House will then debate the bill, perhaps make changes to it, and then vote on the bill. If a majority of the full House votes for the bill, it is approved. It then goes to the Senate, where the process is repeated.

If the two chambers approve different versions of the same bill, usually a committee made up of members from the House and the Senate tries to work out the disagreements and come up with one revised bill. If both chambers of Congress pass this new version, the bill goes to the president. The president can either sign the bill, making it a law, or veto it (turn it down). If the president vetoes the bill, it can still become law if it is passed again by a two-thirds majority in both chambers of Congress.

THE EXECUTIVE BRANCH

The **executive branch** of the federal government is headed by the president, who enforces the laws passed by Congress and is commander in chief of the U.S. armed forces. It also includes the vice president, people who work for the president or vice president, the major departments of the government, and special agencies. The **cabinet** is made up of the vice president, heads of major departments, and other officials. It meets when the president chooses. The chart at right shows cabinet departments in the order in which they were created.

President

Vice President

Cabinet Departments

1. State
2. Treasury
3. Defense
4. Justice
5. Interior
6. Agriculture
7. Commerce
8. Labor
9. Health and Human Services
10. Housing and Urban Development
11. Transportation
12. Energy
13. Education
14. Veterans Affairs
15. Homeland Security

Who Can Be President?

To be eligible to serve as president, a person must be a native-born U.S. citizen, must be at least 35 years old, and must have been a resident of the United States for at least 14 years.

How Long Does the President Serve?

The president serves a four-year term, starting on January 20. No president can be elected more than twice, or more than once if he or she had served two years as president filling out the term of a president who left office.

What Happens If the President Dies in Office?

If the president dies in office or cannot complete the term, the vice president becomes president. If the president is temporarily unable to perform his or her duties, the vice president can become acting president.

The White House has a web site. It is:
www.whitehouse.gov

You can send e-mail to the president at:
president@whitehouse.gov

Voter Turnout in Presidential Elections, 1972–2008

Percent of voting age population who actually voted.

Year	Percent	Year	Percent
1972	55.1%	1992	55.2%
1976	53.6%	1996	49.0%
1980	52.8%	2000	50.3%
1984	53.3%	2004	55.5%
1988	50.3%	2008	58.2%

Source: U.S. Census Bureau

THE JUDICIAL BRANCH

Above are the nine justices who were on the Supreme Court in the 2011–2012 term (October 2011 to June 2012). The justices are (standing from left to right) Sonia Sotomayor, Stephen Breyer, Samuel Alito, and Elena Kagan; (seated from left to right) Clarence Thomas, Antonin Scalia, Chief Justice John Roberts, Anthony Kennedy, and Ruth Bader Ginsburg.

THE SUPREME COURT

The highest court in the United States is the Supreme Court. It has nine justices who are appointed for life by the president with the approval of the Senate. Eight of the nine members are called associate justices. The ninth is the Chief Justice, who presides over the Court's meetings.

What Does the Supreme Court Do?

The Supreme Court's major responsibilities are to judge cases that involve reviewing federal laws, actions of the president, treaties of the United States, and laws passed by state governments to be sure they do not conflict with the U.S. Constitution. If the Supreme Court finds that a law or action violates the Constitution, the law is struck down or the action is reversed.

The Supreme Court's Decision Is Final.

Most cases must go through other state courts or federal courts before they reach the Supreme Court. The Supreme Court is the final court for a case, and the justices generally can decide which cases they will review. After the Supreme Court hears a case, it may agree or disagree with the decision by a lower court. Each justice has one vote, and the majority rules. When the Supreme Court makes a ruling, its decision is final, so each of the justices has a very important job.

PRESIDENTS OF THE UNITED STATES

As the nation's chief executive, the president has one of the hardest jobs in the world and can have a big impact on people's lives.

What Does the President Do?

Here are some of the roles the president has, under the U.S. Constitution.

- Suggest measures for Congress to pass.
- Send Congress a budget, which recommends how the government should raise and spend money.
- Approve or veto (reject) bills that are passed by Congress.
- Act as the commander-in-chief of the U.S. armed forces.
- Make treaties, or agreements, with other countries.
- Appoint justices to the U.S. Supreme Court and judges to other federal courts.

The president has many responsibilities but also must share power with the other two branches of the federal government. They are the legislative branch, or Congress, and the judicial branch, which is headed by the Supreme Court.

President Barack Obama

The U.S. Constitution describes how each of the three branches of government checks, or limits, the powers of the other branches. This system of "checks and balances" helps to prevent any one branch from becoming too powerful.

What Does the Vice President Do?

According to the U.S. Constitution, the vice president has only two major duties. First, the vice president takes over as president if the president dies, resigns, or is removed from office. Second, the vice president presides over the Senate and can cast the deciding vote in case of a tie. John Adams, the first vice president, called his job "the most insignificant office that ever the imagination of man contrived."

However, in recent times, the vice president has usually been given other important duties by the president.

Vice President Joe Biden

★★★★ Presidential ★★★★
Firsts and Records

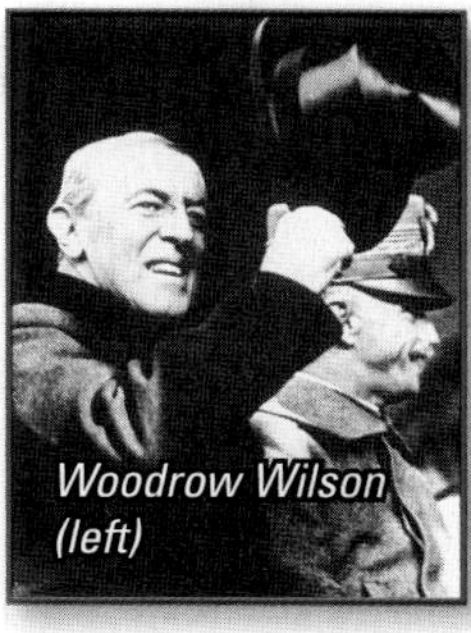
Woodrow Wilson (left)

There have been 43 different presidents from George Washington up to and including Barack Obama. (However, Obama is counted as the 44th president. This is because Grover Cleveland served two terms that were not in a row. He is counted as both the 22nd and the 24th president.) Presidents have been distinctive in many ways. Here are some of them.

★ Tallest President: Abraham Lincoln (6 feet, 4 inches)

◀★ First President to Cross the Atlantic Ocean While in Office: Woodrow Wilson, in 1918

★ Shortest President: James Madison (5 feet, 4 inches)

★ Oldest to Become President: Ronald Reagan (69 years old when he took office in 1981) ▶

★ Youngest to Become President: Theodore Roosevelt (42 years old when he was sworn in after William McKinley was assassinated in 1901)

★ Youngest to Get Elected: John F. Kennedy (43 years old when he won the November 1960 election)

★ First President to Live in the White House: John Adams (moved in when the building was completed in 1800)

★ First President to Die in Office: William Henry Harrison, in 1841

★ First President to Be Assassinated: Abraham Lincoln, in 1865

★ First President to Have a Phone in the White House: Rutherford B. Hayes, in 1879

★ First President to Go to a Foreign Country While in Office: Theodore Roosevelt (visited the Panama Canal site in 1906)

◀★ First President to Give a Press Conference on TV: John F. Kennedy, in 1961

★ First President to Hold an Internet Chat: Bill Clinton, in 1999

★ Only President Who Never Married: James Buchanan

★ Only Divorced President: Ronald Reagan

★ Only African American President: Barack Obama

★ Heaviest President: William Howard Taft (332 pounds)

★ Only Left-Handed Presidents: James Garfield, Herbert Hoover, Harry Truman, Gerald Ford, Ronald Reagan, George H. W. Bush, Bill Clinton, Barack Obama

★ Only President to Resign: Richard Nixon, in 1974 (because of the Watergate scandal)

DID YOU KNOW? **President Taft, a big baseball fan, was the first president to throw out the first pitch on opening day (on April 14, 1910). He began a tradition followed by every later president.**

ELECTING A PRESIDENT

? Who elects the president?

The president is actually elected by a group of "electors" known as the Electoral College. Members of this group from each state meet in December in their state capitals to cast their votes.

? But I thought Election Day was in November!

It is, but on Election Day voters don't directly vote for president. Instead, they vote for a group of presidential electors who have pledged to support whichever candidate wins that state's popular vote.

? What's the total number of electoral votes?

There are 538 total votes. A presidential candidate must win at least 270 of those (a majority).

? How many electoral votes does each state get?

Each state gets one vote for each of its senators (2) and one for each of its members in the House of Representatives. Also, Washington, D.C., has 3 electoral votes.

? What if no candidate gets a majority of electoral votes?

Then the election is decided by the U.S. House of Representatives. That's what happened after the 1800 and 1824 elections.

? Can a candidate who didn't get the most votes on Election Day still win a majority of electoral votes?

Yes. That happened in the 1876, 1888, and 2000 elections.

Who **CAN** Vote?

Voting rules vary from state to state, but they must agree with the Constitution. No state can deny the right to vote because of a person's race or gender, or because of age if the voter is at least 18 years old.

All voters must be U.S citizens. In most states voters must already be registered, or signed up to vote in elections, by some time before Election Day. However, under a 1993 federal law, states took steps to allow people to register in many different locations or by mail.

Who **DOES** Vote?

Voter turnout is generally highest in presidential elections, and recent presidential elections have shown some increase. But even in the 2008 election, only about 58 percent of the voting age population actually voted.

Sometimes only a few votes can make a big difference. In 2000, for example, George W. Bush defeated Al Gore in Florida by only 537 votes and became president!

The 2012 Presidential Election

★ During the first half of 2012 there were primary elections or caucuses (political gatherings) in the 50 states, Washington, D.C., and U.S. territories. These contests helped pick delegates to go to the Democratic and Republican conventions in the summer and select their parties' candidates for president and vice president.

★ On the Democratic side, no major candidate challenged Barack Obama, who wanted to run for a second term as president.

★ On the Republican side, many candidates campaigned in key states and appeared in debates on TV, starting well before the year 2012 even began. By late January 2012, several leading candidates had dropped out, including Minnesota Representative Michele Bachmann, Texas Governor Rick Perry, and businessman Herman Cain. Former House Speaker Newt Gingrich ended his campaign in the spring.

Mitt Romney

★ Former Massachusetts Governor Mitt Romney won the first primary election of 2012, in New Hampshire on January 10, and remained the frontrunner. His chief remaining rival, former Pennsylvania Senator Rick Santorum, dropped out in April.

★ The Republicans scheduled their national convention for August 27-30, 2012, in Tampa, Florida. The Democrats planned theirs for September 3-6, 2012, in Charlotte, North Carolina.

★ At the conventions, most delegates are already pledged to vote for a particular candidate for president. For vice president, delegates usually pick the person the presidential candidate wants.

★ The conventions give each party the chance to kick off the fall campaign. Then, on November 6, 2012, voters get to decide.

2012 Electoral College Map

This map shows how many electoral votes each state has in the 2012 election.

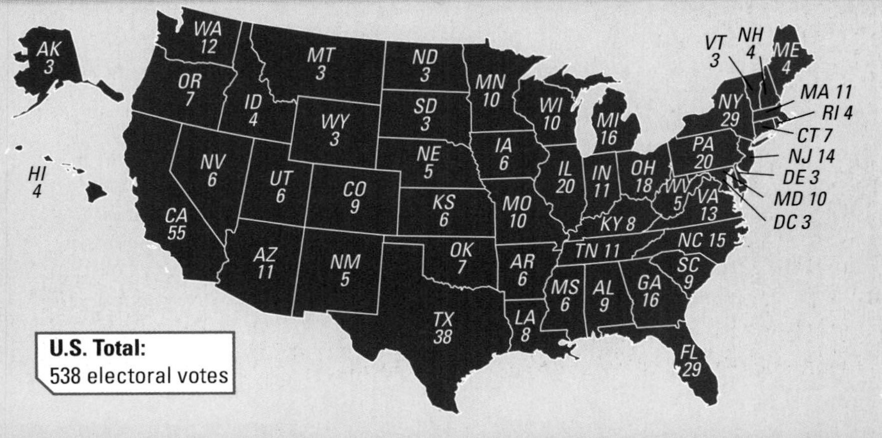

Facts about the PRESIDENTS

1 GEORGE WASHINGTON
Federalist Party, 1789–1797

Born: Feb. 22, 1732, at Wakefield, Westmoreland County, Virginia

Married: Martha Dandridge Custis (1731–1802); no children

Died: Dec. 14, 1799; buried at Mount Vernon, Virginia

Vice President: John Adams (1789–1797)

2 JOHN ADAMS
Federalist Party, 1797–1801

Born: Oct. 30, 1735, in Braintree (now Quincy), Massachusetts

Married: Abigail Smith (1744–1818); 3 sons, 2 daughters

Died: July 4, 1826; buried in Quincy, Massachusetts

Vice President: Thomas Jefferson (1797–1801)

3 THOMAS JEFFERSON
Democratic-Republican Party, 1801–1809

Born: Apr. 13, 1743, at Shadwell, Albemarle County, Virginia

Married: Martha Wayles Skelton (1748–1782); 1 son, 5 daughters

Died: July 4, 1826; buried at Monticello, Virginia

Vice President: Aaron Burr (1801–1805), George Clinton (1805–1809)

4 JAMES MADISON
Democratic-Republican Party, 1809–1817

Born: Mar. 16, 1751, at Port Conway, King George County, Virginia

Married: Dolley Payne Todd (1768–1849); no children

Died: June 28, 1836; buried at Montpelier Station, Virginia

Vice President: George Clinton (1809–1813), Elbridge Gerry (1813–1817)

5 JAMES MONROE
Democratic-Republican Party, 1817–1825

Born: Apr. 28, 1758, in Westmoreland County, Virginia

Married: Elizabeth Kortright (1768–1830); 1 son, 2 daughters

Died: July 4, 1831; buried in Richmond, Virginia

Vice President: Daniel D. Tompkins (1817–1825)

6 JOHN QUINCY ADAMS
Democratic-Republican Party, 1825–1829

Born: July 11, 1767, in Braintree (now Quincy), Massachusetts

Married: Louisa Catherine Johnson (1775–1852); 3 sons, 1 daughter

Died: Feb. 23, 1848; buried in Quincy, Massachusetts

Vice President: John C. Calhoun (1825–1829)

7 ANDREW JACKSON
Democratic Party, 1829–1837

Born: Mar. 15, 1767, in Waxhaw, South Carolina

Married: Rachel Donelson Robards (1767–1828); 1 son (adopted)

Died: June 8, 1845; buried in Nashville, Tennessee

Vice President: John C. Calhoun (1829–1833), Martin Van Buren (1833–1837)

8 MARTIN VAN BUREN
Democratic Party, 1837–1841

Born: Dec. 5, 1782, at Kinderhook, New York

Married: Hannah Hoes (1783–1819); 4 sons

Died: July 24, 1862; buried at Kinderhook, New York

Vice President: Richard M. Johnson (1837–1841)

9 WILLIAM HENRY HARRISON
Whig Party, 1841

Born: Feb. 9, 1773, at Berkeley, Charles City County, Virginia

Married: Anna Symmes (1775–1864); 6 sons, 4 daughters

Died: Apr. 4, 1841; buried in North Bend, Ohio

Vice President: John Tyler (1841)

10 JOHN TYLER
Whig Party, 1841–1845

Born: Mar. 29, 1790, in Greenway, Charles City County, Virginia

Married: Letitia Christian (1790–1842); 3 sons, 5 daughters. Julia Gardiner (1820–1889); 5 sons, 2 daughters

Died: Jan. 18, 1862; buried in Richmond, Virginia

Vice President: none

11 JAMES KNOX POLK
Democratic Party, 1845–1849

Born: Nov. 2, 1795, in Mecklenburg County, North Carolina

Married: Sarah Childress (1803–1891); no children

Died: June 15, 1849; buried in Nashville, Tennessee

Vice President: George M. Dallas (1845–1849)

12 ZACHARY TAYLOR
Whig Party, 1849–1850

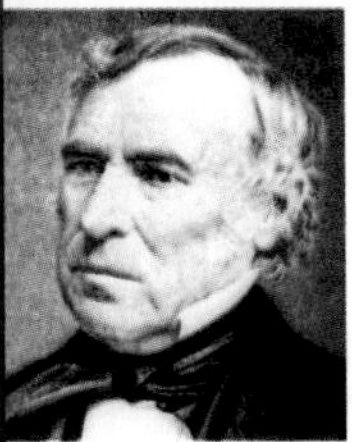

Born: Nov. 24, 1784, in Orange County, Virginia

Married: Margaret Smith (1788–1852); 1 son, 5 daughters

Died: July 9, 1850; buried in Louisville, Kentucky

Vice President: Millard Fillmore (1849–1850)

13 MILLARD FILLMORE
Whig Party, 1850–1853

Born: Jan. 7, 1800, in Cayuga County, New York

Married: Abigail Powers (1798–1853); 1 son, 1 daughter. Caroline Carmichael McIntosh (1813–1881); no children

Died: Mar. 8, 1874; buried in Buffalo, New York

Vice President: none

14 FRANKLIN PIERCE
Democratic Party, 1853–1857

Born: Nov. 23, 1804, in Hillsboro, New Hampshire

Married: Jane Means Appleton (1806–1863); 3 sons

Died: Oct. 8, 1869; buried in Concord, New Hampshire

Vice President: William R. King (1853–1857)

15 JAMES BUCHANAN
Democratic Party, 1857–1861

Born: Apr. 23, 1791, Cove Gap, near Mercersburg, Pennsylvania

Married: Never

Died: June 1, 1868, buried in Lancaster, Pennsylvania

Vice President: John C. Breckinridge (1857–1861)

16 ABRAHAM LINCOLN
Republican Party, 1861–1865

Born: Feb. 12, 1809, in Hardin County, Kentucky

Married: Mary Todd (1818–1882); 4 sons

Died: Apr. 15, 1865; buried in Springfield, Illinois

Vice President: Hannibal Hamlin (1861–1865), Andrew Johnson (1865)

17 ANDREW JOHNSON
Democratic Party, 1865–1869

Born: Dec. 29, 1808, in Raleigh, North Carolina

Married: Eliza McCardle (1810–1876); 3 sons, 2 daughters

Died: July 31, 1875; buried in Greeneville, Tennessee

Vice President: none

18 ULYSSES S. GRANT
Republican Party, 1869–1877

Born: Apr. 27, 1822, in Point Pleasant, Ohio

Married: Julia Dent (1826–1902); 3 sons, 1 daughter

Died: July 23, 1885; buried in New York City

Vice President: Schuyler Colfax (1869–1873), Henry Wilson (1873–1877)

19 RUTHERFORD B. HAYES
Republican Party, 1877–1881

Born: Oct. 4, 1822, in Delaware, Ohio

Married: Lucy Ware Webb (1831–1889); 7 sons, 1 daughter

Died: Jan. 17, 1893; buried in Fremont, Ohio

Vice President: William A. Wheeler (1877–1881)

20 JAMES A. GARFIELD
Republican Party, 1881

Born: Nov. 19, 1831, in Orange, Cuyahoga County, Ohio

Married: Lucretia Rudolph (1832–1918); 5 sons, 2 daughters

Died: Sept. 19, 1881; buried in Cleveland, Ohio

Vice President: Chester A. Arthur (1881)

21 CHESTER A. ARTHUR
Republican Party, 1881–1885

Born: Oct. 5, 1829, in Fairfield, Vermont

Married: Ellen Lewis Herndon (1837–1880); 2 sons, 1 daughter

Died: Nov. 18, 1886; buried in Albany, New York

Vice President: none

22 GROVER CLEVELAND
Democratic Party, 1885–1889

Born: Mar. 18, 1837, in Caldwell, New Jersey

Married: Frances Folsom (1864–1947); 2 sons, 3 daughters

Died: June 24, 1908; buried in Princeton, New Jersey

Vice President: Thomas A. Hendricks (1885–1889)

23 BENJAMIN HARRISON
Republican Party, 1889–1893

Born: Aug. 20, 1833, in North Bend, Ohio

Married: Caroline Lavinia Scott (1832–1892); 1 son, 1 daughter. Mary Scott Lord Dimmick (1858–1948); 1 daughter

Died: Mar. 13, 1901; buried in Indianapolis, Indiana

Vice President: Levi Morton (1889–1893)

24 GROVER CLEVELAND See 22, above
Democratic Party, 1893–1897

Vice President: Adlai E. Stevenson (1893–1897)

25 WILLIAM MCKINLEY
Republican Party, 1897–1901

Born: Jan. 29, 1843, in Niles, Ohio

Married: Ida Saxton (1847–1907); 2 daughters

Died: Sept. 14, 1901; buried in Canton, Ohio

Vice President: Garret A. Hobart (1897–1901), Theodore Roosevelt (1901)

26 THEODORE ROOSEVELT
Republican Party, 1901–1909

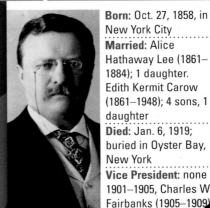

Born: Oct. 27, 1858, in New York City

Married: Alice Hathaway Lee (1861–1884); 1 daughter. Edith Kermit Carow (1861–1948); 4 sons, 1 daughter

Died: Jan. 6, 1919; buried in Oyster Bay, New York

Vice President: none 1901–1905, Charles W. Fairbanks (1905–1909)

27 WILLIAM HOWARD TAFT
Republican Party, 1909–1913

Born: Sept. 15, 1857, in Cincinnati, Ohio

Married: Helen Herron (1861–1943); 2 sons, 1 daughter

Died: Mar. 8, 1930; buried in Arlington National Cemetery, Virginia

Vice President: James S. Sherman (1909–1913)

28 WOODROW WILSON
Democratic Party, 1913–1921

Born: Dec. 28, 1856, in Staunton, Virginia

Married: Ellen Louise Axson (1860–1914); 3 daughters.
Edith Bolling Galt (1872–1961); no children

Died: Feb. 3, 1924; buried in Washington, D.C.

Vice President: Thomas R. Marshall (1913–1921)

29 WARREN G. HARDING
Republican Party, 1921–1923

Born: Nov. 2, 1865, near Corsica (now Blooming Grove), Ohio

Married: Florence Kling De Wolfe (1860–1924); no children

Died: Aug. 2, 1923; buried in Marion, Ohio

Vice President: Calvin Coolidge (1921–1923)

30 CALVIN COOLIDGE
Republican Party, 1923–1929

Born: July 4, 1872, in Plymouth, Vermont

Married: Grace Anna Goodhue (1879–1957); 2 sons

Died: Jan. 5, 1933; buried in Plymouth, Vermont

Vice President: none 1923–1925, Charles G. Dawes (1925–1929)

31 HERBERT C. HOOVER
Republican Party, 1929–1933

Born: Aug. 10, 1874, in West Branch, Iowa

Married: Lou Henry (1875–1944); 2 sons

Died: Oct. 20, 1964; buried in West Branch, Iowa

Vice President: Charles Curtis (1929–1933)

32 FRANKLIN DELANO ROOSEVELT
Democratic Party, 1933–1945

Born: Jan. 30, 1882, in Hyde Park, New York

Married: Anna Eleanor Roosevelt (1884–1962); 4 sons, 1 daughter

Died: Apr. 12, 1945; buried in Hyde Park, New York

Vice President: John N. Garner (1933–1941), Henry A. Wallace (1941–1945), Harry S. Truman (1945)

33 HARRY S. TRUMAN
Democratic Party, 1945–1953

Born: May 8, 1884, in Lamar, Missouri

Married: Elizabeth Virginia "Bess" Wallace (1885–1982); 1 daughter

Died: Dec. 26, 1972; buried in Independence, Missouri

Vice President: none 1945–1949, Alben W. Barkley (1949–1953)

34 DWIGHT D. EISENHOWER
Republican Party, 1953–1961

Born: Oct. 14, 1890, in Denison, Texas

Married: Mary "Mamie" Geneva Doud (1896–1979); 2 sons

Died: Mar. 28, 1969; buried in Abilene, Kansas

Vice President: Richard M. Nixon (1953–1961)

35 JOHN FITZGERALD KENNEDY
Democratic Party, 1961–1963

Born: May 29, 1917, in Brookline, Massachusetts

Married: Jacqueline Lee Bouvier (1929–1994); 2 sons, 1 daughter

Died: Nov. 22, 1963; buried in Arlington National Cemetery, Virginia

Vice President: Lyndon Baines Johnson (1961–1963)

36 LYNDON BAINES JOHNSON
Democratic Party, 1963–1969

Born: Aug. 27, 1908, near Stonewall, Texas

Married: Claudia "Lady Bird" Alta Taylor (1912–2007); 2 daughters

Died: Jan. 22, 1973; buried in Johnson City, Texas

Vice President: none 1963–1965, Hubert H. Humphrey (1965–1969)

37 RICHARD MILHOUS NIXON
Republican Party, 1969–1974

Born: Jan. 9, 1913, in Yorba Linda, California

Married: Thelma "Pat" Ryan (1912–1993); 2 daughters

Died: Apr. 22, 1994; buried in Yorba Linda, California

Vice President: Spiro T. Agnew (1969–1973), Gerald R. Ford (1973–1974)

38 GERALD R. FORD
Republican Party, 1974–1977

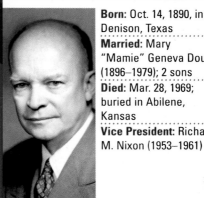

Born: July 14, 1913, in Omaha, Nebraska

Married: Elizabeth "Betty" Bloomer (1918–2011); 3 sons, 1 daughter

Died: Dec. 26, 2006; buried in Grand Rapids, Michigan

Vice President: Nelson A. Rockefeller (1974–1977)

39 JIMMY (JAMES EARL) CARTER
Democratic Party, 1977–1981

Born: Oct. 1, 1924, in Plains, Georgia

Married: Rosalynn Smith (b. 1927); 3 sons, 1 daughter

Vice President: Walter F. Mondale (1977–1981)

40 RONALD REAGAN
Republican Party, 1981–1989

Born: Feb. 6, 1911, in Tampico, Illinois

Married: Jane Wyman (1914–2007); 1 son, 1 daughter. Nancy Davis (b. 1923); 1 son, 1 daughter

Died: June 5, 2004; buried in Simi Valley, California

Vice President: George H. W. Bush (1981–1989)

41 GEORGE H. W. BUSH
Republican Party, 1989–1993

Born: June 12, 1924, in Milton, Massachusetts

Married: Barbara Pierce (b. 1925); 4 sons, 2 daughters

Vice President: Dan Quayle (1989–1993)

42 BILL (WILLIAM JEFFERSON) CLINTON
Democratic Party, 1993–2001

Born: Aug. 19, 1946, in Hope, Arkansas

Married: Hillary Rodham (b. 1947); 1 daughter

Vice President: Al Gore (1993–2001)

43 GEORGE W. BUSH
Republican Party, 2001–2009

Born: July 6, 1946, in New Haven, Connecticut

Married: Laura Welch (b. 1946); 2 daughters

Vice President: Dick Cheney (2001–2009)

44 BARACK OBAMA
Democratic Party, 2009–

Born: August 4, 1961, in Honolulu, Hawaii

Married: Michelle Robinson (b. 1964); 2 daughters

Vice President: Joe Biden (2009–)

DID YOU KNOW? In 2008, an estimated 1.8 million people crowded the Mall in Washington, D.C., for the inauguration of Barack Obama. But these swearing-in ceremonies used to be simpler affairs. The first president inaugurated in Washington, D.C., was Thomas Jefferson, in 1801. Wearing everyday clothes, he walked to the Capitol from the house where he had rented a room, took the oath of office, and then walked back to his boardinghouse, where he had lunch with other residents.

Meet the FIRST LADIES

For many years there was no title for the wife of the president. Wives of the early presidents were sometimes addressed as "Lady," "Mrs. President," "Mrs. Presidentress," or even "Queen." The term "First Lady" did not become common until after 1849. That year, President Zachary Taylor called James Madison's wife, Dolley, "First Lady" in a speech at her funeral. Here are a few of the best-known First Ladies of the United States.

← **MARTHA CUSTIS WASHINGTON**, wife of the first president, was a wealthy widow when she married George Washington. During the American Revolution, she helped manage Mount Vernon, their Virginia plantation, but also spent time with her husband at his military headquarters. When he became president, they moved to New York and then Philadelphia, the nation's first capitals.

ABIGAIL ADAMS, wife of John Adams, never went to school, but she learned to read at home. She was a close adviser to her husband. She is well-known for the many letters she wrote to him when they were separated. The Adamses became the first family to move into the White House.

MARY TODD LINCOLN, wife of Abraham Lincoln, was a well-educated Southerner who strongly opposed slavery. She suffered many tragedies in her lifetime. Her husband was assassinated, and three of her four children died young.

LUCY WEBB HAYES, wife of Rutherford B. Hayes, was the first First Lady to have graduated from college. A popular figure, she visited disabled soldiers and gave large sums of money to the poor. Because alcohol was banned at the White House for most of her time there, she got the nickname "Lemonade Lucy."

EDITH WILSON, wife of Woodrow Wilson, was one of the most powerful First Ladies in U.S. history. After her husband suffered a stroke in 1919, she played a key role, in his last 18 months in office, in deciding whom he would meet with and what papers he would see. According to some, she made decisions that normally would have been made by a president.

ELEANOR ROOSEVELT, wife of Franklin D. Roosevelt, supported the New Deal policies of her husband and was a strong advocate for civil rights. She had a lifelong career as a writer and champion of causes she believed in. After her husband's death in 1945, she served as a delegate to the United Nations.

JACQUELINE KENNEDY, wife of John F. Kennedy, met her husband while she was working as a photographer and reporter. As First Lady, she filled the White House with historic furnishings and artwork. Her elegant clothes and hairstyles were copied by millions of women.

NANCY REAGAN, wife of Ronald Reagan, met her husband when they both were Hollywood actors in the 1940s. As First Lady, she led a campaign to encourage young people to "just say no" if offered illegal drugs.

HILLARY RODHAM CLINTON, wife of Bill Clinton, met him when they were both in law school. She acted as Arkansas's First Lady when he was governor of that state. After her time as the nation's First Lady, she ran for office herself, winning election to the U.S. Senate. She unsuccessfully sought the presidency in 2008. After Barack Obama won the office, she served as his secretary of state.

WHITE HOUSE Pets

The White House has been home to many animals, beginning with John Adams's favorite horse, Cleopatra. Here are some other famous White House pets.

The Clinton family cat, Socks

- John Quincy Adams had an alligator that sometimes hung out in the East Room.
- The Lincolns had a variety of animals, including cats, dogs, goats, and a white rabbit.
- Theodore Roosevelt's family had a badger and a macaw, along with horses, dogs, cats, snakes, guinea pigs, and even bears.
- The Coolidge family kept a small zoo that included lion cubs, a bobcat, a pygmy hippo, and a raccoon that got walked on a leash.
- Franklin D. Roosevelt's Scottish terrier, Fala, was often seen with FDR at the White House and went with the president on many trips.
- Millie, a springer spaniel owned by Barbara and George H. W. Bush, was the make-believe writer of a book published by the First Lady.
- The Clintons had a cat named Socks and a chocolate Labrador retriever named Buddy.
- The Obama family has a Portuguese water dog, Bo.

Franklin D. Roosevelt's dog, Fala

American Indians

People may have arrived in the Americas more than 15,000 years ago, most likely from northeast Asia. Although the American Indian population decreased significantly through the 17th, 18th, and 19th centuries from disease and war, there are still hundreds of tribes, or nations, each with unique languages and traditions.

WHAT CAME FROM AMERICAN INDIANS

GAMES AND SPORTS

Many of today's games and sports came from practices and inventions of American Indians or other native peoples. The game of lacrosse began as an ancient Indian event called *baggataway*. Algonquian Indians in the northeastern U.S. used birchbark canoes for fishing and travel. The toboggan started out as an American Indian bark-and-skin runnerless sled to move heavy objects over snow or ice. In the far north, the Inuit wore snowshoes strung with caribou skin to walk on deep, soft snow. Many people today canoe, toboggan, or travel on snowshoes just for fun.

NAVAJO (DINE) WAR CODE

With almost 300,000 members, the Navajo make up the largest American Indian group in the U.S. The Dine (dee-NAY), as they call themselves, belong to clans in which members trace descent through the mother. Many Dine still speak a highly descriptive and unique language called Athapaskan. This language, which almost no non-Navajo knew, became the basis for a code used by U.S. forces in World War II. Navajo "code talkers" served in combat zones, sending and receiving top-secret messages in this code, which was never cracked. Local radio still broadcasts sports, including New Mexico State University's football games, in Athapaskan.

PLACE NAMES

The names of many places in the U.S. have origins in American Indian languages and people. For example, the city of Seattle, Washington, is named after a Suquamish chief. Alachua County in Florida takes its name from the Timucuan word for "sinkhole." In fact, the names of almost half the U.S. states have a link to American Indian culture (see pages 290-291).

TIMELINE **NORTH AMERICAN INDIANS**

For events before 1492, see page 279.

1492	Christopher Columbus made contact with Taino tribes on the island he named Hispaniola.
c. 1600	Five tribes—the Mohawk, Oneida, Onondaga, Cayuga, and Seneca—formed the Iroquois Confederacy in the Northeast.
1637	Settlers in Connecticut defeated Pequot Indians in the Pequot War.
1754–1763	Many American Indians fought as allies of either French or British troops in the French and Indian War.
1804–1806	Sacagawea served as an interpreter and guide for Lewis and Clark.
1827	Cherokee tribes in what is now Georgia formed the Cherokee Nation with a constitution and elected governing officials.
1830	Congress passed the Indian Removal Act, the first law that forced tribes to move so that U.S. citizens could settle certain areas of land.
1834	Congress created the Indian Territory for tribes removed from their lands. It covered present-day Oklahoma, Kansas, and Nebraska.
1835–1842	Seminoles battled U.S. troops in the Second Seminole War. They lost the conflict and their homeland in Florida.
1838–1839	The U.S. government forced Cherokees to move to Indian Territory. Thousands died during the so-called Trail of Tears.
1876	Sioux and Cheyenne Indians defeated troops led by U.S. colonel George Armstrong Custer in the Battle of the Little Bighorn.
1877	After the U.S. government tried to remove his people to Idaho, Chief Joseph led a Nez Percé retreat to Canada but surrendered before reaching the border.
1890	U.S. soldiers massacred more than 200 Sioux, including unarmed women and children, in the Battle of Wounded Knee, the last major conflict between U.S. troops and American Indians.
1912	Jim Thorpe, an American Indian, won the decathalon and the pentathalon in the 1912 Olympic Games.
1924	Congress granted all American Indians U.S. citizenship.
1929	Charles Curtis, a member of the Kaw Nation, became the first American of Indian ancestry elected vice president of the U.S.
1934	Congress passed the Indian Reorganization Act to increase tribal self-government.
1968	The American Indian Movement, a civil rights organization, was founded.
1985	Wilma Mankiller became the first female chief of the Cherokee Nation.
2004	The National Museum of the American Indian opened in Washington, D.C.
◄2012	The U.S. Mint released the 2012 Native American dollar coin, celebrating trade routes in the 17th century.

MAJOR CULTURAL AREAS OF NATIVE NORTH AMERICANS

Climate and geography influenced the culture of the people who lived in these regions. On the plains, for example, people depended on the great herds of buffalo for food. For the Aleut and Inuit in the far north, seals and whales were an important food source. There are more than 560 tribes officially recognized by the U.S. government today and more than 56 million acres of tribal lands. Below are some of the major cultural areas of North American Indians and other native peoples.

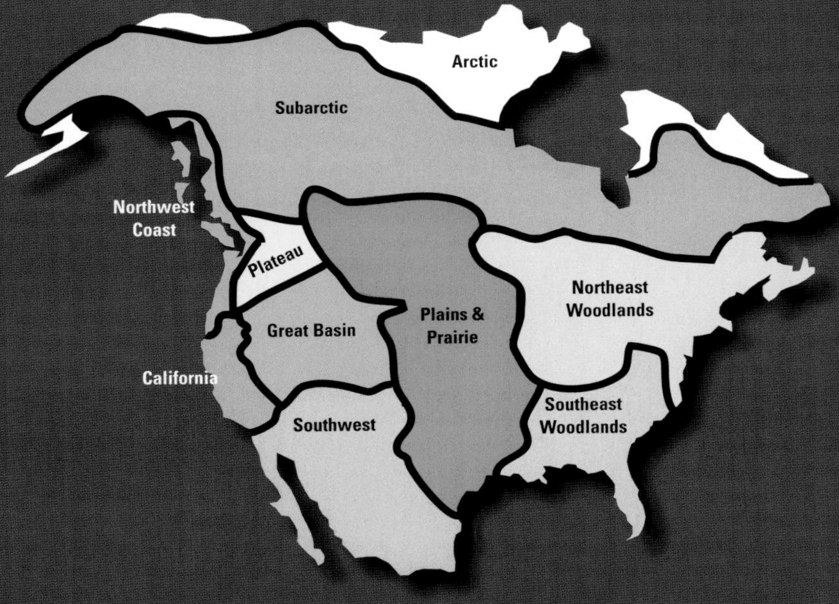

NORTHEAST WOODLANDS The Illinois, Iroquois (Mohawk, Onondaga, Cayuga, Oneida, Seneca, and Tuscarora), Lenape, Menominee, Micmac, Narragansett, Potawatomi, Shawnee

SOUTHEAST WOODLANDS The Cherokee, Chickasaw, Choctaw, Creek, Seminole

PLAINS & PRAIRIE The Arapaho, Blackfoot, Cheyenne, Comanche, Hidatsa, Kaw, Mandan, Sioux

SOUTHWEST The Apache, Navajo, Havasupai, Mojave, Pima, Pueblo (Hopi, Isleta, Laguna, Zuñi)

GREAT BASIN The Paiute, Shoshoni, Ute

CALIFORNIA The Klamath, Maidu, Miwok, Modoc, Patwin, Pomo, Wintun, Yurok

PLATEAU The Cayuse, Nez Percé, Okanagon, Salish, Spokan, Umatilla, Walla Walla, Yakima

NORTHWEST COAST The Chinook, Haida, Kwakiutl, Makah, Nootka, Salish, Tillamook, Tlingit, Tsimshian

SUBARCTIC The Beaver, Chipewyan, Chippewa, Cree, Ingalik, Kaska, Kutchin, Montagnais, Naskapi, Tanana

ARCTIC The Aleut, Inuit, and Yuit

Whaling Traditions of Alaska Natives

The native peoples of Alaska, called Alaska Natives, have hunted whales for several thousand years. These peoples include the Inuit, or Eskimos, and Aleuts. In the past, Eskimos hunted with harpoons from kayaks. Aleuts, traveling in wooden dugout boats, used spears poisoned with boiled wildflower roots.

In keeping with tradition and a respect for the natural world, Alaska Natives used as much of the kill as possible. A captured whale provided meat to eat and oil for fuel and light. The whalebones were valuable for building shelters and creating tools. It took members of the village many hours to butcher the catch. Everyone got a share of the meat and oil.

Today, the International Whaling Commission allows the native peoples of Alaska to hunt a limited number of whales to meet their cultural and survival needs. In 2012, Alaska Natives were permitted to catch no more than 75 bowhead whales to protect the population of this animal. Although they still use traditional, hand-built whaling boats, they sometimes fit boats with gasoline motors or other modern technology. Hunters use nets, harpoons with explosive contact, or rifles to kill the animals humanely.

AMERICAN INDIAN NUMBERS*

	American Indians	Total U.S. Population
Median age	**29 years**	**37.2 years**
Percentage of people 5 years and older who speak only English at home	**72%**	**79%**
Percentage of households owning their own home	**54%**	**65%**
Percentage of people without health insurance	**29.2%**	**15.5%**

***2010 U.S. Census Bureau estimates. Figures refer to the American Indian population who reported only one race.**

A Native Hawaiian Dance

The original Hawaiians came to the islands from Polynesia in about A.D. 400—traveling north through the Pacific Ocean for 2,000 miles or more. To honor their gods and chiefs, they performed the *hula*. Native Hawaiians dance with hip, arm, and finger movements, accompanied by rhythmic drumming and chants called *mele*. Legend says the goddess Hi'iaka first danced the hula to appease her sister, Pele, the goddess of volcanoes and fire. To today's native Hawaiians, the art form remains an important expression of their culture.

United States HISTORY

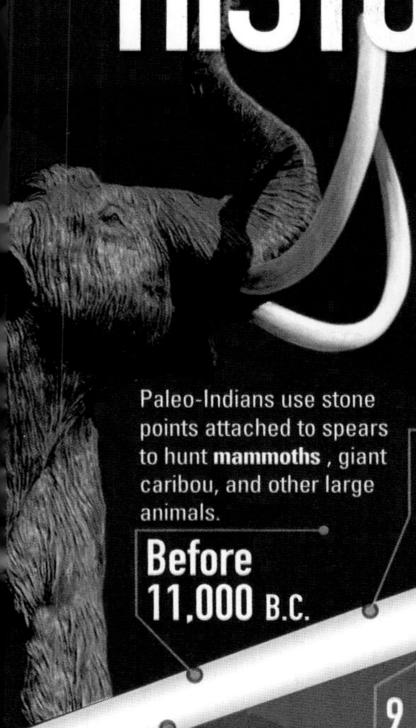

Before 13,000 B.C.

People called **Paleo-Indians** cross from Siberia to Alaska and begin to move into North America.

Before 11,000 B.C.

Paleo-Indians use stone points attached to spears to hunt **mammoths** , giant caribou, and other large animals.

11,000 B.C.

Mammoths and other large animals disappear, and Paleo-Indians begin to gather **plants** for food.

9,500 B.C.–1,000 B.C.

North American Indians begin using **stone** to grind food and to hunt bison and smaller animals.

1,000 B.C.–A.D. 1,000

Woodland Indians, who lived east of the Mississippi River, bury their dead under large **mounds** of earth (which can still be seen today).

After A.D. 500

The Ancestral Puebloans in the Southwestern United States live in homes on cliffs, called **cliff dwellings**. These people's pottery and dishes are known for their beautiful patterns.

After A.D. 700

Mississippian Indians in the Southeastern United States **develop farms** and continue to build burial mounds.

700–1492

Many **different Indian cultures** develop throughout North America. Several million American Indians probably live on the continent by 1492.

Colonial America AND THE AMERICAN REVOLUTION: 1492–1783

1492 Christopher **Columbus** sails across the Atlantic Ocean and reaches an island in the Bahamas in the Caribbean Sea.

1513 Juan **Ponce de León** explores the Florida coast.

1524 Giovanni da **Verrazano** explores the coast from Carolina north to Nova Scotia, enters New York harbor.

1540 Francisco Vásquez de **Coronado** explores the Southwest.

1565 St. Augustine, Florida, the **first permanent town** established by Europeans in the United States, is founded by the Spanish.

1607 **Jamestown,** Virginia, the first permanent English settlement in North America, is founded by Captain John Smith.

1609 Henry Hudson sails into **New York Harbor**, explores the Hudson River. Spaniards settle Santa Fe, New Mexico.

1619 The first African **slaves** are brought to Jamestown. (Slavery is made legal in 1650.)

1620 **Pilgrims** from England arrive at Plymouth, Massachusetts, on the *Mayflower*.

1626 Peter Minuit buys **Manhattan** island for the Dutch from Manahata Indians for goods worth $24. The Dutch settlement is named New Amsterdam.

1630 **Boston** is founded by Massachusetts colonists led by John Winthrop.

Benjamin Franklin (1706–1790)

was a great American leader, printer, scientist, and writer. In 1732, he began publishing a magazine called ***Poor Richard's Almanack***. Poor Richard was a make-believe person who gave advice about common sense and honesty. Many of Poor Richard's sayings are still known today. Among the most famous are "God helps them that help themselves" and "Early to bed, early to rise, makes a man healthy, wealthy, and wise."

1634 **Maryland** is founded as a Catholic colony, with religious freedom for all granted in 1649.

1664 The English seize **New Amsterdam** from the Dutch. The city is renamed New York.

1669 **French settlers** move into Mississippi and Louisiana.

1732 Benjamin Franklin begins publishing ***Poor Richard's Almanack***.

1754–1763 **French and Indian War** between Great Britain and France. The French lose their lands in Canada and the Midwest.

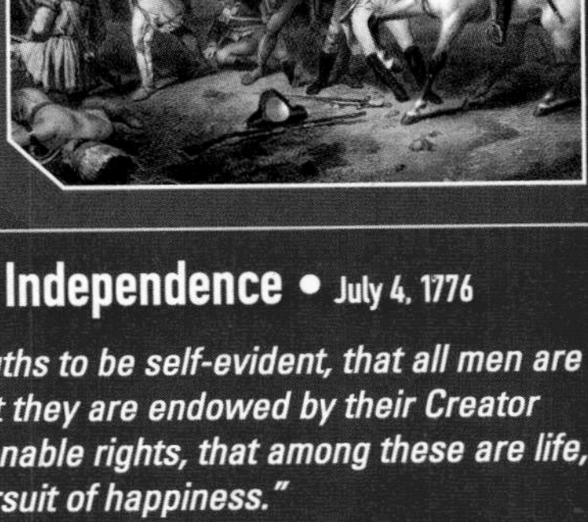

1764–1766 Britain places taxes on sugar that comes from its North American colonies. Britain also requires colonists to buy stamps to help pay for royal troops. Colonists protest, and the **Stamp Act** is repealed in 1766.

1770 **Boston Massacre:** Demonstrators against British taxes throw rocks at British troops. The troops open fire, killing 7.

1773 **Boston Tea Party:** British tea is thrown into the harbor to protest a tax on tea.

1775 Fighting at **Lexington and Concord**, Massachusetts, marks the beginning of the American Revolution.

1776 **The Declaration of Independence** is approved July 4 by the Continental Congress (made up of representatives from the American colonies).

1781 British General **Charles Cornwallis** surrenders to the Americans at Yorktown, Virginia, ending major fighting in the Revolutionary War. In a 1783 peace treaty, Great Britain officially recognizes American independence.

Declaration of Independence • July 4, 1776

"We hold these truths to be self-evident, that all men are created equal, that they are endowed by their Creator with certain unalienable rights, that among these are life, liberty, and the pursuit of happiness."

1784–1900

1784 The first successful daily **newspaper** in the U.S., the *Pennsylvania Packet & General Advertiser*, is published.

Who Attended the Convention?

The **Constitutional Convention** met in Philadelphia in the hot summer of 1787. Most of the great founders of America attended. Among those present were George Washington, James Madison, and John Adams. They met to form a new government that would be strong and, at the same time, protect the liberties that were fought for in the American Revolution. The Constitution they created is still the law of the United States.

1787 The **Constitutional Convention** meets to write a Constitution for the U.S.

1789 The new **Constitution** is approved by the states. George Washington is chosen as the first president.

1800 The federal government moves from Philadelphia to a new capital, **Washington, D.C.**

1803 The U.S. makes the **Louisiana Purchase** from France. The Purchase doubles the area of the U.S.

1804–1806 **Lewis and Clark**, with their guide Sacagawea, explore what is now the northwestern United States.

1812–1815 **War of 1812** with Great Britain: British forces burn the Capitol and White House. Francis Scott Key writes the words to "The Star-Spangled Banner."

1820 The **Missouri Compromise** bans slavery west of the Mississippi River and north of 36°30′ latitude, except in Missouri.

1823 The **Monroe Doctrine** warns European countries not to interfere in the Americas.

1825 The **Erie Canal** opens, linking New York City with the Great Lakes.

1831 ***The Liberator***, a newspaper opposing slavery, is published in Boston.

1836 Texans fighting for independence from Mexico are defeated at the **Alamo**.

1838

Cherokee Indians are forced to move from the Southeast U.S. to Oklahoma, along "The **Trail of Tears**." On the long march, thousands die because of disease and the cold weather.

Civil War Dead and Wounded

The **Civil War** resulted in the death or wounding of hundreds of thousands of people—perhaps more than three-quarters of a million. Little was known at the time about infections and the spread of diseases. As a result, many soldiers died from illnesses such as influenza and measles. Many also died from infections from battle wounds.

1844

The **first telegraph** line connects Washington, D.C., and Baltimore.

1846–1848

U.S. war with Mexico: Mexico is defeated, and the United States takes control of the Republic of Texas and of Mexican territories in the West.

1848

The discovery of **gold** in California leads to a "rush" of 80,000 people to the West in search of gold.

1852

Uncle Tom's Cabin, Harriet Beecher Stowe's novel about the suffering of slaves, is published.

1860

Abraham **Lincoln** is elected president.

1861

The **Civil War** begins when Confederate troops fire on Fort Sumter, South Carolina.

1863

President Lincoln issues the **Emancipation Proclamation**, freeing most slaves.

1865

The **Civil War** ends as the South surrenders. President Lincoln is assassinated.

1869

The **first railroad** connecting the East and West coasts is completed.

1890

Battle of Wounded Knee is fought in South Dakota—the last major battle between Indians and U.S. troops.

1898

Spanish-American War: The U.S. defeats Spain, gains control of the Philippines, Puerto Rico, and Guam.

UNITED STATES 1901–Present

World War I

In **World War I** the United States fought with Great Britain, France, and Russia (the Allies) against Germany and Austria-Hungary. The Allies won the war in 1918.

World War II

From 1941 to 1945 the United States, joining Britain, the Soviet Union, and other Allied powers, fought the Axis powers, led by Germany, Italy, and Japan, in the deadliest conflict in human history.

1903
The United States begins digging the **Panama Canal**. The canal opens in 1914, connecting the Atlantic and Pacific oceans.

1908
Henry Ford introduces the **Model T** car, priced at $850.

1916
Jeannette Rankin of Montana becomes the first woman elected to Congress.

1917–1918
The United States joins **World War I** on the side of the Allies against Germany.

1927
Charles A. **Lindbergh** becomes the first person to fly alone nonstop across the Atlantic Ocean.

1929
A stock market crash marks the beginning of the **Great Depression**.

1933
President Franklin D. Roosevelt's **New Deal** increases government help to people hurt by the Depression.

The Great Depression

The stock market crash of October 1929 led to a period of severe hardship for the American people—the **Great Depression**. As many as 25 percent of all workers could not find jobs. The Depression lasted until the early 1940s. The Depression also led to a great change in politics. In 1932, Franklin D. Roosevelt, a Democrat, was elected president. He served for 12 years, longer than any other president.

1941
Japan attacks **Pearl Harbor**, Hawaii. The United States enters World War II.

1945
Germany surrenders in May. The U.S. drops atomic bombs on **Hiroshima** and Nagasaki in August, leading to Japan's surrender and the end of **World War II**.

1947
Jackie Robinson becomes the **first black baseball player** in the major leagues when he joins the Brooklyn Dodgers.

1950–1953
U.S. armed forces fight in the **Korean War**.

1954
The U.S. Supreme Court **forbids racial segregration** in public schools.

1963
President John **Kennedy** is assassinated.

1964
Congress passes the **Civil Rights Act**, which outlaws discrimination in voting and jobs.

1965
The United States sends large numbers of troops to fight in the **Vietnam War**.

1968
Civil rights leader **Martin Luther King Jr.** is assassinated. Senator **Robert F. Kennedy** is assassinated.

1969
U.S. astronaut Neil Armstrong becomes the **first person** to walk **on the moon**.

1973
U.S. participation in the **Vietnam War ends**.

1974
President Richard **Nixon resigns** because of the **Watergate** scandal.

1979
U.S. **hostages** are taken **in Iran**, beginning a 444-day crisis that ends with their release in 1981.

1991
The Persian Gulf War: The U.S. and its allies force Iraq to withdraw its troops from Kuwait.

2001
Hijacked jets crash into the **World Trade Center**, the **Pentagon**, and a field in Pennsylvania, September 11, killing about 3,000 people.

2003
U.S.-led forces invade Iraq and remove dictator **Saddam Hussein**.

2008
Barack Obama defeats John McCain to become the first African American president.

2011
U.S. forces kill **Osama bin Laden**, mastermind of the September 11, 2001 terrorist attacks.

AFRICAN AMERICANS: A Time Line

From the era of slavery to the present, African Americans have struggled to obtain freedom and equal opportunity. The timeline below pinpoints many of the key events and personalities that helped shape this long struggle.

Colin Powell ▶

1619 — **First slaves** from Africa are brought to Virginia.

1831 — Nat Turner starts a **slave revolt** in Virginia that is unsuccessful.

1856-1857 — **Dred Scott**, a slave, sues to be freed because he had left slave territory, but the Supreme Court denies his claim.

1861-1865 — The North defeats the South in the brutal Civil War; the **13th Amendment** ends nearly 250 years of slavery. The Ku Klux Klan is founded.

1865-1877 — Southern blacks play leadership roles in government under **Reconstruction**; the 15th Amendment (1870) gives black men the right to vote.

1896 — Supreme Court rules in a case called *Plessy v. Ferguson* that racial segregation is legal when facilities are **"separate but equal."** Discrimination and violence against blacks increase.

1910 — W. E. B. Du Bois (1868–1963) founds National Association for the Advancement of Colored People (**NAACP**), fighting for equality for blacks.

1920s — African American culture (jazz music, dance, literature) flourishes during the **Harlem Renaissance**.

1954 — Supreme Court rules in a case called ***Brown v. Board of Education of Topeka*** that school segregation is unconstitutional.

1955-1965 — Black students, backed by federal troops, enter recently desegregated Central High School in **Little Rock**, Arkansas.

1957 — **Malcolm X** (1925–1965) emerges as key spokesperson for black nationalism.

1963 — **Rev. Dr. Martin Luther King, Jr.** (1929–1968) gives his "I Have a Dream" speech at a march that inspires more than 200,000 people in Washington, D.C.—and many others throughout the nation.

1964 — Sweeping **civil rights bill** banning racial discrimination is signed by President Lyndon Johnson.

1965 — Martin Luther King leads protest march in **Selma**, Alabama. Blacks riot in **Watts** section of Los Angeles.

1967 — Gary, Indiana, and Cleveland, Ohio, are first major U.S. cities to elect black mayors. **Thurgood Marshall** (1908–1993) becomes first African American on the U.S. Supreme Court.

2001 — **Colin Powell** becomes first African American secretary of state.

2005 — **Condoleezza Rice** becomes first African American woman secretary of state.

2008 — Barack Obama becomes the **first African American elected president** of the United States.

They Made HISTORY

People of many different backgrounds have played important roles in the history of the United States.

1818–1895 FREDERICK DOUGLASS escaped from slavery at age 20. In the decades before the Civil War (1861–1865), he had a major influence on the anti-slavery movement through his lectures and writings. He became an adviser to President Abraham Lincoln and encouraged him to issue the Emancipation Proclamation (1863), freeing slaves in Confederate-controlled territory in the South.

1840–1904 CHIEF JOSEPH was a leader of the Nez Percé Indians of the Pacific Northwest. When the U.S. government ordered the tribe to move to a small reservation, many refused. Pursued by the U.S. Army and severely outnumbered, Chief Joseph led several hundred Nez Percé on a 1,400-mile retreat toward Canada. Trapped just 40 miles from the border, he surrendered, promising, "I will fight no more forever."

1913–2005 ROSA PARKS refused to give up her bus seat to a white man one day in 1955. Spurred on by her brave action, blacks in Montgomery, Alabama, started a boycott of the bus system. It led to desegregation of the city's buses, a key event in the history of the civil rights movement.

1924– DANIEL INOUYE is the highest-ranking Asian American government official in U.S. history. He won the Medal of Honor for his bravery in combat during World War II, in which he lost an arm. He served in the U.S. House of Representatives and, since 1963, in the U.S. Senate. In 2010, he became president pro tempore of the Senate, making him third in the line of succession to the presidency.

1927–1993 CESAR CHAVEZ, a Mexican American who was raised in migrant worker camps, started the union known as the United Farm Workers of America in 1966. Along with UFW cofounder **DOLORES HUERTA** (born 1930), he organized boycotts that eventually made growers agree to better conditions for field workers.

1929–1968 REV. DR. MARTIN LUTHER KING JR. was the most influential leader of the civil rights movement from the mid-1950s to his assassination in 1968. A believer in peaceful protest, he received the Nobel Peace Prize in 1964. The federal government and all 50 states now have a holiday in his honor. His wife, **CORETTA SCOTT KING** (1927–2006), helped carry on his work.

1954– SONIA SOTOMAYOR, who grew up in a public housing project in New York City, went on to graduate from Princeton University and Yale Law School. Experienced as a prosecutor and a judge, she was named to the U.S. Supreme Court in 2009, becoming the court's first Hispanic justice.

1961– BARACK OBAMA is the son of an American mother and a Kenyan father. After serving in the Illinois Senate for eight years, he was elected to the U.S. Senate in 2004. From there he launched a successful campaign to become president of the U.S. Inaugurated in 2009, he worked to help resolve the nation's economic problems.

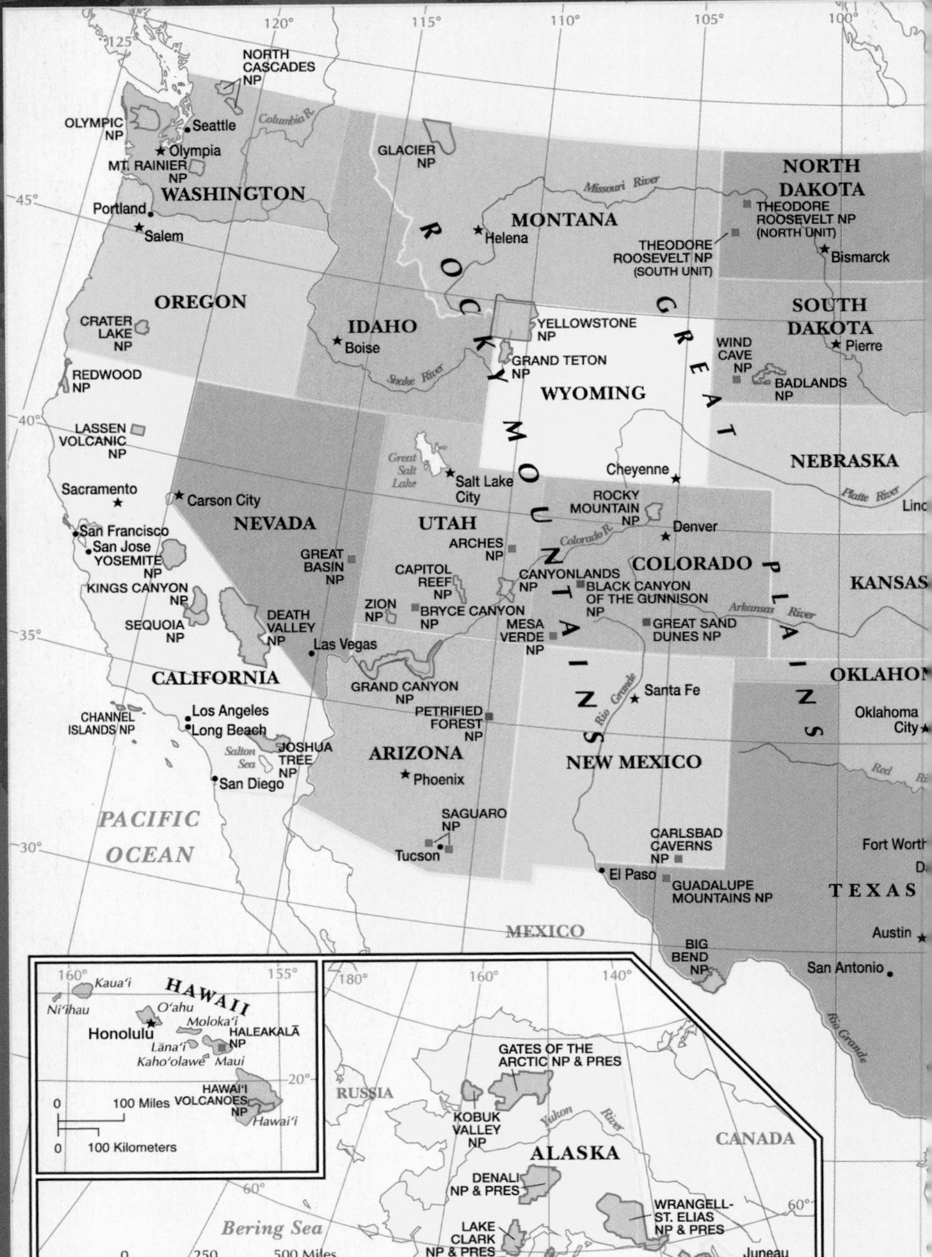
NORTH CASCADES NP
OLYMPIC NP
Seattle
Olympia
MT. RAINIER NP
WASHINGTON
Columbia R.
Portland
Salem
OREGON
CRATER LAKE NP
REDWOOD NP
LASSEN VOLCANIC NP
Sacramento
Carson City
San Francisco
San Jose
YOSEMITE NP
KINGS CANYON NP
SEQUOIA NP
DEATH VALLEY NP
NEVADA
CALIFORNIA
Las Vegas
CHANNEL ISLANDS NP
Los Angeles
Long Beach
Salton Sea
JOSHUA TREE NP
San Diego
PACIFIC OCEAN
GLACIER NP
MONTANA
Helena
Missouri River
IDAHO
Boise
Snake River
ROCKY MOUNTAINS
YELLOWSTONE NP
GRAND TETON NP
WYOMING
Great Salt Lake
Salt Lake City
UTAH
GREAT BASIN NP
ARCHES NP
CAPITOL REEF NP
CANYONLANDS NP
ZION NP
BRYCE CANYON NP
MESA VERDE NP
GRAND CANYON NP
PETRIFIED FOREST NP
ARIZONA
Phoenix
SAGUARO NP
Tucson
Cheyenne
ROCKY MOUNTAIN NP
Denver
Colorado R.
COLORADO
BLACK CANYON OF THE GUNNISON NP
GREAT SAND DUNES NP
Arkansas River
Rio Grande
Santa Fe
NEW MEXICO
CARLSBAD CAVERNS NP
El Paso
GUADALUPE MOUNTAINS NP
BIG BEND NP
MEXICO
NORTH DAKOTA
THEODORE ROOSEVELT NP (NORTH UNIT)
THEODORE ROOSEVELT NP (SOUTH UNIT)
Bismarck
SOUTH DAKOTA
Pierre
WIND CAVE NP
BADLANDS NP
GREAT PLAINS
NEBRASKA
Platte River
KANSAS
OKLAHOMA
Oklahoma City
Red River
Fort Worth
TEXAS
Austin
San Antonio
125° 120° 115° 110° 105° 100°
45° 40° 35° 30°
HAWAII
Kaua'i
Ni'ihau
O'ahu
Honolulu
Moloka'i
Lāna'i
HALEAKALĀ NP
Kaho'olawe
Maui
HAWAI'I VOLCANOES NP
Hawai'i
0 100 Miles
0 100 Kilometers
160° 155° 20°
180° 160° 140° 60°
RUSSIA
GATES OF THE ARCTIC NP & PRES
KOBUK VALLEY NP
Yukon River
ALASKA
CANADA
DENALI NP & PRES
WRANGELL-ST. ELIAS NP & PRES
Bering Sea
LAKE CLARK NP & PRES
KENAI FJORDS NP
Juneau
GLACIER BAY NP & PRES
KATMAI NP & PRES
0 250 500 Miles
0 250 500 750 Kilometers
ALEUTIAN ISLANDS
Gulf of Alaska

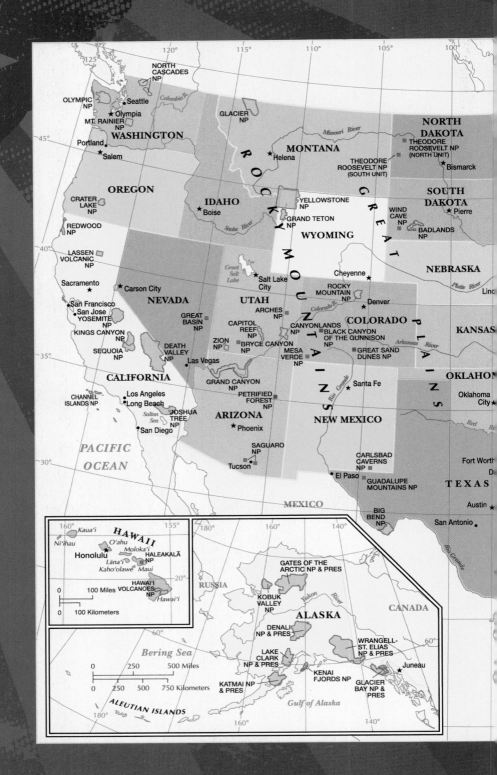

CANADA
Lake of the Woods
Lake Superior
Lake Huron
Lake Michigan
Lake Ontario
Lake Erie
ISLE ROYALE NP
MINNESOTA
St. Paul
WISCONSIN
Madison
Milwaukee
MICHIGAN
Lansing
Detroit
IOWA
Des Moines
Chicago
ILLINOIS
Springfield
St. Louis
INDIANA
Indianapolis
OHIO
Columbus
Cleveland
CUYAHOGA VALLEY NP
Kansas City
Jefferson City
MISSOURI
KENTUCKY
Frankfort
MAMMOTH CAVE NP
Ohio River
WEST VIRGINIA
Charleston
VIRGINIA
Richmond
SHENANDOAH NP
APPALACHIAN MTNS.
PENNSYLVANIA
Harrisburg
Philadelphia
NEW YORK
Albany
New York City
Trenton
N.J.
Baltimore
Annapolis
Washington, D.C.
MD.
Dover
DEL.
MAINE
Augusta
ACADIA NP
Montpelier
VT.
N.H.
Concord
MASS.
Boston
Hartford
CONN.
Providence
R.I.
NORTH CAROLINA
Raleigh
GREAT SMOKY MTNS. NP
TENNESSEE
Nashville
Tennessee River
ARKANSAS
Little Rock
HOT SPRINGS NP
Memphis
Mississippi River
SOUTH CAROLINA
Columbia
CONGAREE NP
GEORGIA
Atlanta
ALABAMA
Montgomery
MISSISSIPPI
Jackson
Tallahassee
Jacksonville
Baton Rouge
LOUISIANA
New Orleans
Houston
FLORIDA
Orlando
Tampa
St. Petersburg
Miami
BISCAYNE NP
EVERGLADES NP
DRY TORTUGAS NP
ATLANTIC OCEAN
Gulf of Mexico
THE BAHAMAS
CUBA
MEXICO
THE UNITED STATES
National Capital
State Capital
Other City
National Park
0 200 400 Miles
0 200 400 600 Kilometers

How the STATES

ALABAMA comes from the name of an Indian tribe, which may mean "gathering thick vegetation."

Glacier Bay, Alaska

ALASKA comes from *alakshak*, an Aleut word meaning "peninsula" or "land that is not an island."

ARIZONA comes from a Pima Indian word meaning "little spring place" or the Aztec word *arizuma*, meaning "silver-bearing."

ARKANSAS is a variation of Quapaw, the name of an Indian tribe. Quapaw means "south wind."

CALIFORNIA was probably named by Spanish explorers after an imaginary island in a Spanish story.

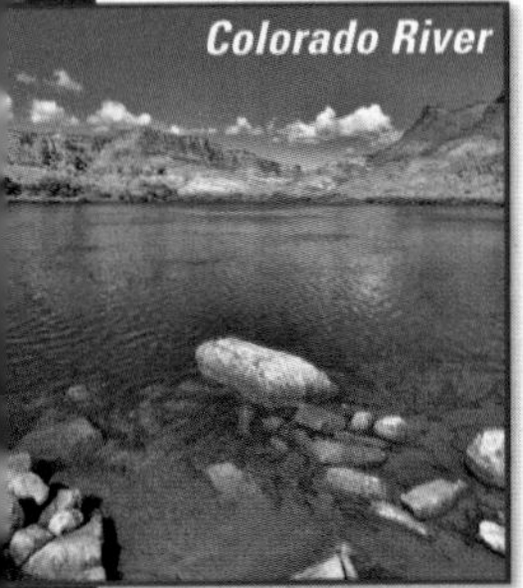
Colorado River

COLORADO comes from a Spanish word meaning "red." It was first given to the Colorado River because of its reddish color.

CONNECTICUT comes from an Algonquin Indian word meaning "long river place."

DELAWARE is named after Lord De La Warr, the English governor of Virginia in colonial times.

FLORIDA was named by the Spanish explorer Ponce de León, who landed there during Easter season, called *pascua florida* ("festival of flowers") in Spanish.

GEORGIA was named after King George II of England, who granted the right to create a colony there in 1732.

HAWAII probably comes from *Hawaiki,* or *Owhyhee,* the native Polynesian word for "homeland."

IDAHO's name may come from a Kiowa Apache name for the Comanche Indians.

ILLINOIS is the French version of *Illini,* an Algonquin Indian word meaning "men" or "warriors."

INDIANA means "land of the Indians."

IOWA comes from the name of an American Indian tribe that once lived in the region.

KANSAS comes from a Sioux Indian word that possibly meant "people of the south wind."

KENTUCKY comes from an American Indian word, possibly meaning "meadowland."

LOUISIANA, which was first settled by French explorers, was named after King Louis XIV of France.

MAINE means "the mainland." English explorers called it that to distinguish it from islands nearby.

MARYLAND was named after Queen Henrietta Maria, wife of King Charles I of England, who granted the right to establish an English colony there.

MASSACHUSETTS comes from an Indian word meaning "large hill place."

MICHIGAN comes from the Chippewa Indian words *mici gama*, meaning "great water" (referring to Lake Michigan).

MINNESOTA got its name from a Dakota Sioux Indian word meaning "cloudy water" or "sky-tinted water."

MISSISSIPPI is probably from Chippewa Indian words meaning "great river" or "gathering of all the waters," or from an Algonquin word, *messipi.*

MISSOURI comes from an Algonquin Indian term meaning "river of the big canoes."

MONTANA comes from a Latin or Spanish word meaning "mountainous."

GOT THEIR NAMES

NEBRASKA comes from an Omaha or Otos Indian word meaning "flat river" or "broad water," referring to the Platte River.

Sierra Nevada

NEVADA means "snow-clad" in Spanish. Spanish explorers gave the name to the Sierra Nevada mountains.

NEW HAMPSHIRE was named by an early settler after his home county of Hampshire, in England.

NEW JERSEY was named for the English Channel island of Jersey.

NEW MEXICO was given its name by 16th-century Spaniards in Mexico.

New York City

NEW YORK, first called New Netherland, was renamed for the Duke of York after the English took it from Dutch settlers.

NORTH CAROLINA, the northern part of the English colony of Carolana, was named for King Charles I.

NORTH DAKOTA comes from a Sioux Indian word meaning "friend" or "ally."

OHIO is the Iroquois Indian word for "good river."

OKLAHOMA comes from a Choctaw Indian word meaning "red man."

OREGON may have come from *Ouaricon-sint,* a name on an old French map that was once given to what is now called the Columbia River.

PENNSYLVANIA meaning "Penn's woods," was the name given to the colony founded by William Penn.

RHODE ISLAND may have come from the Dutch *Roode Eylandt* ("red island") or may have been named after the Greek island of Rhodes.

SOUTH CAROLINA, the southern part of the English colony of Carolana, was named for King Charles I.

SOUTH DAKOTA comes from a Sioux Indian word meaning "friend" or "ally."

TENNESSEE comes from *Tanasi,* the name of a Cherokee Indian village.

TEXAS comes from a word meaning "friends" or "allies," used by the Spanish to describe some of the Indians living there.

UTAH comes from the name given to the Ute Indians. The likely meaning is "people of the high land."

Green Mountains, Vermont

VERMONT comes from two French words, *vert* meaning "green" and *mont* meaning "mountain."

VIRGINIA was named in honor of Queen Elizabeth I of England, who was known as the Virgin Queen because she was never married.

WASHINGTON was named after George Washington. It is the only state named after a president.

WEST VIRGINIA got its name from the people of western Virginia, who formed their own government during the Civil War.

WISCONSIN comes from a Chippewa name that is believed to mean "grassy place."

WYOMING comes from Algonquin Indian words that may mean "at the big plains," "large prairie place," or "on the great plain."

Facts about the STATES

Area includes both land and water; it is given in square miles (sq mi) and square kilometers (sq km). Numbers in parentheses after Population, Area, and Entered Union show the state's rank compared with other states. State populations are for 2011. City populations are from the 2010 U.S. Census. The postal abbreviation for each state appears in a circle to the left of the state's population.

ALABAMA

Heart of Dixie, Camellia State

AL **POPULATION:** 4,802,740 (23rd)

AREA: 52,420 sq mi (30th) (135,768 sq km)

F Camellia
B Yellowhammer
T Southern longleaf pine
S "Alabama"

ENTERED UNION: December 14, 1819 (22nd)

LARGEST CITIES (WITH POP.): Birmingham, 212,237; Montgomery, 205,764; Mobile, 195,111; Huntsville, 180,105

★ Montgomery

P motor vehicles, metal products, chemicals, paper, food products, clothing, lumber, coal, oil, natural gas, chickens, livestock, peanuts, cotton

DID YOU KNOW? About 9,000 years ago Indians came to live in Russell Cave, in northern Alabama. They hunted, fished, and gathered nuts and other foods from plants. The cave is part of a national monument today.

ALASKA

The Last Frontier State

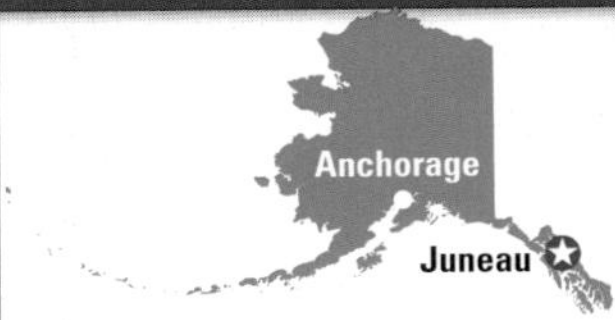

AK **POPULATION:** 722,718 (47th)

AREA: 665,384 sq mi (1st) (1,722,319 sq km)

F Forget-me-not
B Willow ptarmigan
T Sitka spruce
S "Alaska's Flag"

ENTERED UNION: January 3, 1959 (49th)

LARGEST CITIES (WITH POP.): Anchorage, 291,826; Fairbanks, 31,535; Juneau, 31,275

★ Juneau

P oil, natural gas, fish, food products, lumber and wood products, nursery and greenhouse products, hay, fur

DID YOU KNOW? Alaska was once owned by Russia. Many Americans thought it was a vast useless wasteland. They made fun of Secretary of State William Seward when he bought it from Russia in 1867, for about 2 cents an acre.

ARIZONA

Grand Canyon State

AZ **POPULATION:** 6,482,505 (16th)

AREA: 113,990 sq mi (6th) (296,234 sq km)

F Blossom of the Saguaro cactus
B Cactus wren
T Paloverde
S "Arizona"

ENTERED UNION: February 14, 1912 (48th)

LARGEST CITIES (WITH POP.): Phoenix, 1,445,632; Tucson, 520,116; Mesa, 439,041; Chandler, 236,123; Glendale, 226,721; Scottsdale, 217,385; Gilbert, 208,453

★ Phoenix

P electronic equipment, transportation and industrial equipment, aerospace products, copper and other minerals

DID YOU KNOW? At the Petrified Forest National Park, in northeast Arizona, you can see the remains of fallen trees that have turned into colorful rock over millions of years.

ARKANSAS

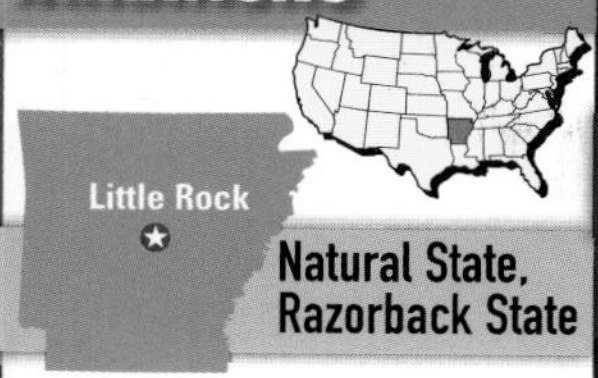

Natural State, Razorback State

AR **POPULATION:** 2,937,979 (32nd)

AREA: 53,179 sq mi (29th) (137,732 sq km)

- F Apple blossom
- B Mockingbird
- T Pine
- S "Arkansas"

ENTERED UNION: June 15, 1836 (25th)

LARGEST CITIES (WITH POP.): Little Rock, 193,524; Fort Smith, 86,209; Fayetteville, 73,580; Springdale, 69,797; Jonesboro, 67,263

★ Little Rock

P food products, transportation and industrial equipment, paper, metal products, lumber and wood products, chickens, soybeans, rice, cotton, natural gas

DID YOU KNOW? In 1906, a farmer named John Huddleston became rich and famous after discovering diamonds in the soil of his field near Murfreesboro. The site is now a state park—where visitors can look for diamonds.

CALIFORNIA

Golden State

CA **POPULATION:** 37,691,912 (1st)

AREA: 163,395 sq mi (3rd) (423,967 sq km)

- F Golden poppy
- B California valley quail
- T California redwood
- S "I Love You, California"

ENTERED UNION: September 9, 1850 (31st)

LARGEST CITIES (WITH POP.): Los Angeles, 3,792,621; San Diego, 1,307,402; San Jose, 945,942; San Francisco, 805,235; Fresno, 494,665; Sacramento, 466,488; Long Beach, 462,257; Oakland, 390,724; Bakersfield, 347,483; Anaheim, 336,265.

★ Sacramento

P electronic equipment, oil, transportation and industrial equipment, motion pictures, printed materials, wine, food products, milk, cattle, fruit, vegetables

DID YOU KNOW? San Francisco is said to be the second-hilliest city in the world, after La Paz, Bolivia. Some of the hills are very high and steep, with great views of the city and surrounding area.

COLORADO

Centennial State

CO **POPULATION:** 5,116,796 (22nd)

AREA: 104,094 sq mi (8th) (269,601 sq km)

- F Rocky Mountain columbine
- B Lark bunting
- T Colorado blue spruce
- S "Where the Columbines Grow"

ENTERED UNION: August 1, 1876 (38th)

LARGEST CITIES (WITH POP.): Denver, 600,158; Colorado Springs, 416,427; Aurora, 325,078; Fort Collins, 143,986; Lakewood, 142,980

★ Denver

P electronic equipment, instruments and industrial machinery, food products, metal products, oil, natural gas, coal, cattle

DID YOU KNOW? The small town of Dinosaur, CO, is located near Dinosaur National Monument. Street names in the town include Brontosaurus Boulevard, Tyrannosaurus Trail, Stegosaurus Freeway, and Triceratops Terrace.

Key: F Flower B Bird T Tree S Song ★ Capital P Important Products

CONNECTICUT

Constitution State, Nutmeg State

CT POPULATION: 3,580,709 (29th)

AREA: 5,543 sq mi (48th) (14,357 sq km)

F Mountain laurel
B American robin
T White oak
S "Yankee Doodle"

ENTERED UNION: January 9, 1788 (5th)

LARGEST CITIES (WITH POP.): Bridgeport, 144,229; New Haven, 129,779; Hartford, 124,775; Stamford, 122,643; Waterbury, 110,366; Norwalk, 85,603; Danbury, 80,893

★ Hartford

P aircraft parts, helicopters, metals and metal products, electronic equipment, medical instruments, chemicals, greenhouse and nursery products, dairy products, stone

DID YOU KNOW? Famous people who were born in Connecticut include the Revolutionary War hero Ethan Allen, the banker J. P. Morgan, the actresses Katharine Hepburn and Glenn Close, and the former president George W. Bush.

DELAWARE

First State, Diamond State

DE POPULATION: 907,135 (45th)

AREA: 2,489 sq mi (49th) (6,446 sq km)

F Peach blossom
B Blue hen chicken
T American holly
S "Our Delaware"

ENTERED UNION: December 7, 1787 (1st)

LARGEST CITIES (WITH POP.): Wilmington, 70,851; Dover, 36,047; Newark, 31,454

★ Dover

P chemicals, drugs, transportation equipment, food products, chickens

DID YOU KNOW? Pea Patch Island, in the Delaware River, got its name because people believed a ship carrying peas was wrecked there in the 1700s. Fort Delaware, on the island, was used to hold thousands of Confederate prisoners during the Civil War.

FLORIDA

Sunshine State

FL POPULATION: 19,057,542 (4th)

AREA: 65,758 sq mi (22nd) (170,312 sq km)

F Orange blossom
B Mockingbird
T Sabal palmetto palm
S "Old Folks at Home"

ENTERED UNION: March 3, 1845 (27th)

LARGEST CITIES (WITH POP.): Jacksonville, 821,764; Miami, 399,457; Tampa, 335,709; St. Petersburg, 244,769; Orlando, 238,300; Hialeah, 224,669; Tallahassee, 181,376; Ft. Lauderdale, 165,521; Port St. Lucie, 164,603

★ Tallahassee

P electronic and transportation equipment, instruments, printed materials, food products, nursery plants, oranges and other citrus fruits, vegetables, phosphates, fish

DID YOU KNOW? The city of St. Augustine, on the east coast of Florida, was founded by the Spanish explorer Pedro Menéndez de Avilés in 1565. It is the oldest European settlement in North America that has continued to be occupied up to today.

GEORGIA

Empire State of the South, Peach State

GA **POPULATION:** 9,815,210 (9th)

AREA: 59,425 sq mi (24th) (153,910 sq km)

- F Cherokee rose
- B Brown thrasher
- T Live oak
- S "Georgia on My Mind"

ENTERED UNION: January 2, 1788 (4th)

LARGEST CITIES (WITH POP.): Atlanta, 420,003; Augusta, 195,844; Columbus, 189,885; Savannah, 136,296; Athens, 115,452

★ Atlanta

P clothing and textiles, carpets, transportation equipment, food products, paper, chickens, eggs, cotton, peanuts, peaches, clay

DID YOU KNOW? At the Okefenokee National Wildlife Refuge in southern Georgia, visitors can explore forests, marshes, and prairies and see many kinds of animals, including alligators, sandhill cranes, and red-cockaded woodpeckers.

HAWAII

Aloha State

HI **POPULATION:** 1,374,810 (40th)

AREA: 10,932 sq mi (43rd) (28,314 sq km)

- F Yellow hibiscus
- B Hawaiian goose
- T Kukui
- S "Hawaii Ponoi"

ENTERED UNION: August 21, 1959 (50th)

LARGEST CITIES (WITH POP.): Honolulu, 337,256; East Honolulu, 49,914; Pearl 47,698; Hilo, 43,263; Kailua, 38,635; Waipahu, 38,216; Kaneohe, 34,597

★ Honolulu

P food products, pineapples, nursery and greenhouse products, sugar, concrete, printing and publishing, fish

DID YOU KNOW? Hawaii is the only state that is made up entirely of islands. There are about 130 of them, but most are tiny. People live on only a few large islands. Ka Lea, on the south side of the largest island (also named Hawaii), is the southernmost point in the United States.

IDAHO

Gem State

ID **POPULATION:** 1,584,985 (39th)

AREA: 83,569 sq mi (14th) (216,443 sq km)

- F Syringa
- B Mountain bluebird
- T White pine
- S "Here We Have Idaho"

ENTERED UNION: July 3, 1890 (43rd)

LARGEST CITIES (WITH POP.): Boise, 205,871; Nampa, 81,557; Meridian, 75,092; Idaho Falls, 56,813; Pocatello, 54,255

★ Boise

P electronic products, lumber and wood products, cattle, dairy products, food products, potatoes, sugar beets, hay, wheat

DID YOU KNOW? The average American eats about 140 pounds of potatoes a year, more than any other food except dairy products. Idaho grows about one-third of the U.S. fall potato crop, more than any other state.

Key: F Flower B Bird T Tree S Song ★ Capital P Important Products

ILLINOIS

Prairie State

IL **POPULATION:** 12,869,257 (5th)

AREA: 57,914 sq mi (25th) (149,995 sq km)

F Native violet
B Cardinal
T White oak
S "Illinois"

ENTERED UNION: December 3, 1818 (21st)

LARGEST CITIES (WITH POP.): Chicago, 2,695,598; Aurora, 197,899; Rockford, 152,871; Joliet, 147,433; Naperville, 141,853; Springfield, 116,250; Peoria, 115,007; Elgin, 108,188

★ Springfield

P industrial machinery, metals and metal products, coal, electronic equipment, food products, corn, soybeans, hogs

DID YOU KNOW? In the city of Lincoln, Illinois, there is a statue of a watermelon. It commemorates the day in 1853 when Abraham Lincoln came there. It was the first place that was ever named after him with his permission. He christened the new town with watermelon juice and gave watermelons to people in the crowd.

INDIANA

Hoosier State

IN **POPULATION:** 6,516,922 (15th)

AREA: 36,420 sq mi (38th) (94,326 sq km)

F Peony
B Cardinal
T Tulip poplar
S "On the Banks of the Wabash, Far Away"

ENTERED UNION: December 11, 1816 (19th)

LARGEST CITIES (WITH POP.): Indianapolis, 820,445; Fort Wayne, 253,691; Evansville, 117,429; South Bend, 101,168; Hammond, 80,830; Bloomington, 80,405; Gary, 80,294

★ Indianapolis

P motor vehicles and parts, electronic equipment, iron and steel, coal, metal products, drugs, corn, soybeans, hogs, coal

DID YOU KNOW? Two main routes of the Underground Railroad, a movement that helped free black slaves, went through Indiana. From 1827 to 1847, the Coffin family ran a stop, in Newport (now Fountain City). They helped more than 2,000 runaway slaves escape.

IOWA

Hawkeye State

IA **POPULATION:** 3,062,309 (30th)

AREA: 56,273 sq mi (26th) (145,746 sq km)

F Wild rose
B Eastern goldfinch
T Oak
S "The Song of Iowa"

ENTERED UNION: December 28, 1846 (29th)

LARGEST CITIES (WITH POP.): Des Moines, 203,433; Cedar Rapids, 126,326; Davenport, 99,685; Sioux City, 82,684

★ Des Moines

P corn, soybeans, hogs, cattle, food products, industrial machinery

DID YOU KNOW? Every year in July, thousand of cyclists, from all 50 states and even from a number of foreign countries, get together for RAGBRAI (the *Register's* Annual Great Bicycle Ride Across Iowa). This seven-day, 460-mile group bike ride is said to be the oldest, largest, and longest bicycle touring event in the world. It was started in 1973 by two reporters for the *Des Moines Register* newspaper.

KANSAS

Sunflower State

KS POPULATION: 2,871,238 (33rd)

AREA: 82,278 sq mi (15th) (213,100 sq km)

F Native sunflower
B Western meadowlark
T Cottonwood
S "Home on the Range"

ENTERED UNION: January 29, 1861 (34th)

LARGEST CITIES (WITH POP.): Wichita, 382,368; Overland Park, 173,372; Kansas City, 145,786; Topeka, 127,473; Olathe, 125,872

★ Topeka

P cattle, aircraft and other transportation equipment, industrial machinery, food products, wheat, corn, soybeans, hay, oil, natural gas

DID YOU KNOW? In October 2005, Steven Arnold discovered a 1,400-pound meteorite—a piece of rock from outer space—on farmland in Kansas. He found it by searching with a metal detector and then digging into the ground at a likely spot.

KENTUCKY

Bluegrass State

KY POPULATION: 4,369,356 (26th)

AREA: 40,408 sq mi (37th) (104,656 sq km)

F Goldenrod
B Cardinal
T Tulip poplar
S "My Old Kentucky Home"

ENTERED UNION: June 1, 1792 (15th)

LARGEST CITIES (WITH POP.): Louisville, 597,337; Lexington-Fayette, 295,803; Bowling Green, 58,067; Owensboro, 57,265

★ Frankfort

P coal, industrial machinery, electronic equipment, motor vehicles, chickens, horses, cattle, corn, tobacco.

DID YOU KNOW? A building in Kentucky, commonly known as Fort Knox, holds most of the gold owned by the federal government. The gold is kept in a vault behind a locked door that weighs more than 20 tons. No one person knows the whole combination needed to open it.

LOUISIANA

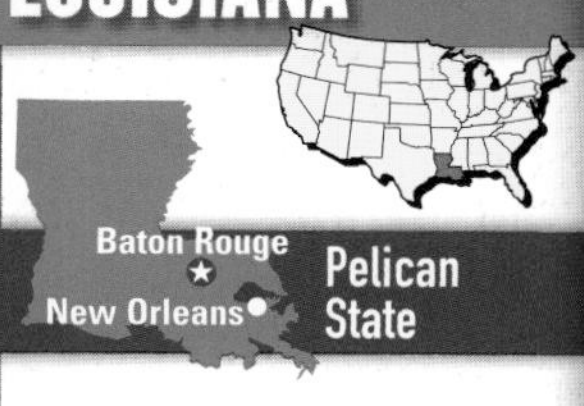

Pelican State

LA POPULATION: 4,574,836 (25th)

AREA: 52,378 sq mi (31st) (135,659 sq km)

F Magnolia
B Eastern brown pelican
T Cypress
S "Give Me Louisiana"

ENTERED UNION: April 30, 1812 (18th)

LARGEST CITIES (WITH POP.): New Orleans, 343,829; Baton Rouge, 229,493; Shreveport, 199,311; Metaire, 138,481; Lafayette, 120,623

★ Baton Rouge

P natural gas, oil, chemicals, transportation equipment, paper, food products, sugar, cotton, cattle, fish

DID YOU KNOW? In 1827, students returning to Louisiana from Paris put on costumes and danced in the streets of New Orleans on the last day before the Catholic religious season known as Lent. Special celebrations on that day, called "Fat Tuesday," or "Mardi Gras," had been common in parts of Europe for centuries. Since 1827, Mardi Gras in New Orleans has gotten bigger and bigger.

Key: F Flower B Bird T Tree S Song ★ Capital P Important Products

MAINE

Pine Tree State

POPULATION: 1,328,188 (41st)

AREA: 35,380 sq mi (39th) (91,633 sq km)

- **F** White pine cone and tassel
- **B** Chickadee
- **T** Eastern white pine
- **S** "State of Maine Song"

ENTERED UNION: March 15, 1820 (23rd)

LARGEST CITIES (WITH POP.): Portland, 66,194; Lewiston, 36,592; Bangor, 33,039

★ Augusta

P paper, ships and boats, plastics, wood and wood products, food products, potatoes, blueberries, milk, eggs, fish, shellfish

DID YOU KNOW? Maine is known for its rocky seacoasts, lobsters, and fishing villages—and for having the highest tides found anywhere in the United States. The easternmost point in the lower 48 U.S. states, along the Maine coast, is marked by a lighthouse.

MARYLAND

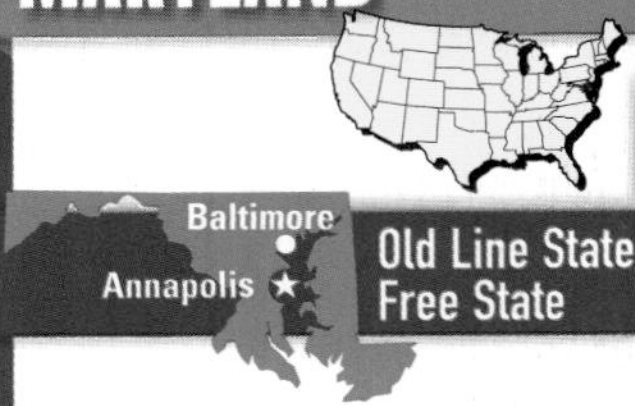

Old Line State, Free State

POPULATION: 5,828,289 (19th)

AREA: 12,406 sq mi (42nd) (32,131 sq km)

- **F** Black-eyed susan
- **B** Baltimore oriole
- **T** White oak
- **S** "Maryland, My Maryland"

ENTERED UNION: April 28, 1788 (7th)

LARGEST CITIES (WITH POP.): Baltimore, 620,961; Columbia, 99,615; Germantown, 86,395; Silver Spring, 71,452; Waldorf, 67,752; Glen Burnie, 67,639

★ Annapolis

P food products, electronic equipment, chemicals, instruments, drugs, chickens, soybeans, corn, stone

DID YOU KNOW? Maryland is the narrowest of the 50 states. In one part of the northwest, around the town of Hancock, the state is only about a mile wide (between Pennsylvania to the north and West Virginia to the south).

MASSACHUSETTS

Bay State, Old Colony

POPULATION: 6,587,536 (14th)

AREA: 10,554 sq mi (44th) (27,336 sq km)

- **F** Mayflower
- **B** Chickadee
- **T** American elm
- **S** "All Hail to Massachusetts"

ENTERED UNION: February 6, 1788 (6th)

LARGEST CITIES (WITH POP.): Boston, 617,594; Worcester, 181,045; Springfield, 153,060; Lowell, 106,519; Cambridge, 105,162

★ Boston

P electronic equipment, instruments, chemicals, drugs, metal products, fish, flowers, shrubs, cranberries

DID YOU KNOW? The first shots of the American Revolution were fired on the village green in Lexington on April 19, 1775. Massachusetts residents remember the events of that day with a state holiday, called Patriots' Day. It is celebrated each year on the third Monday in April. The Boston Marathon is held on that day.

MICHIGAN

Great Lakes State, Wolverine State

MI **POPULATION:** 9,876,187 (8th)

AREA: 96,714 sq mi (11th) (250,487 sq km)

- F Apple blossom
- B Robin
- T White pine
- S "Michigan, My Michigan"

ENTERED UNION: January 26, 1837 (26th)

LARGEST CITIES (WITH POP.): Detroit, 713,777; Grand Rapids, 188,040; Warren, 134,056; Sterling Heights, 129,699; Ann Arbor, 113,934; Lansing, 109,565; Flint, 102,434

★ Lansing

P automobiles, chemicals, industrial machinery, metal products, furniture, plastic products, iron ore, food products, milk, corn, blueberries

DID YOU KNOW? Known for her patriotism and love of adventure, Sarah Emma Edmonds enlisted in a Michigan army regiment in 1861 disguised as a man. She spent most of the Civil War as a battlefield nurse and a Union spy, but she eventually deserted to keep her secret from being discovered. She later wrote a book about her exploits.

MINNESOTA

North Star State, Gopher State

MN **POPULATION:** 5,344,861 (21st)

AREA: 86,936 sq mi (12th) (225,163 sq km)

- F Pink and white lady slipper
- B Common loon
- T Red pine
- S "Hail! Minnesota"

ENTERED UNION: May 11, 1858 (32nd)

LARGEST CITIES (WITH POP.): Minneapolis, 382,578; St. Paul, 285,068; Rochester, 106,769; Duluth, 86,265; Bloomington, 82,893

★ St. Paul

P food products, electronic products, petroleum and asphalt, scientific and medical instruments, iron ore, paper, milk, turkeys, hogs, cattle, corn, soybeans

DID YOU KNOW? The city of St. Paul grew from a tiny settlement first known as Pig's Eye Landing. It got its new name from a log cabin chapel built there by a Catholic missionary priest.

MISSISSIPPI

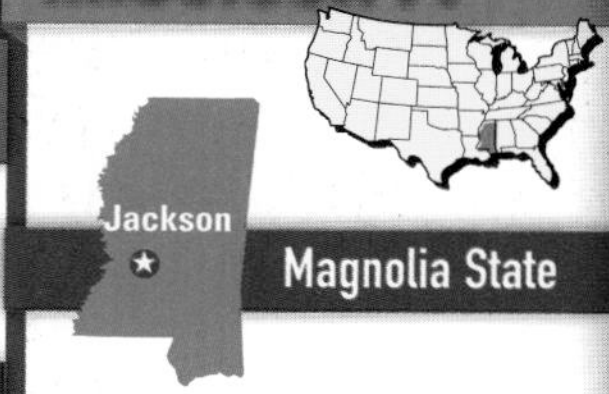

Magnolia State

MS **POPULATION:** 2,978,512 (31st)

AREA: 48,432 sq mi (32nd) (125,438 sq km)

- F Magnolia
- B Mockingbird
- T Magnolia
- S "Go, Mississippi!"

ENTERED UNION: December 10, 1817 (20th)

LARGEST CITIES (WITH POP.): Jackson, 173,514; Gulfport, 67,793; Hattiesburg, 48,982; Biloxi, 45,989

★ Jackson

P transportation equipment, chemicals, furniture, electrical machinery, lumber and wood products, cotton, soybeans, rice, chickens, cattle

DID YOU KNOW? The Natchez Trail Parkway is a scenic road that runs 444 miles from Natchez, on the Mississippi River, to Nashville, Tennessee. It closely follows the route of a famous "trace," or forest trail, used in past centuries by American Indians.

Key: F Flower B Bird T Tree S Song ★ Capital P Important Products

MISSOURI

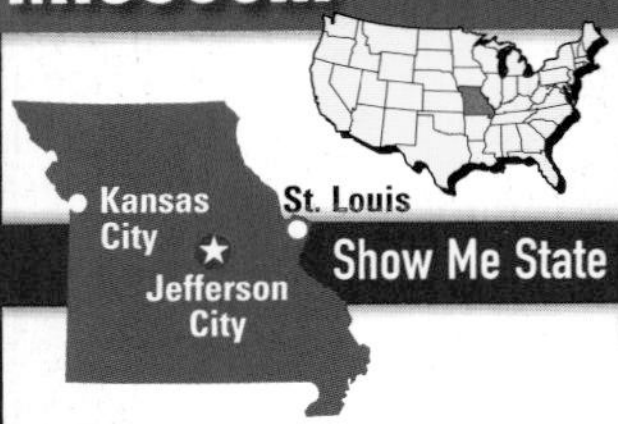

Kansas City ★ St. Louis

Jefferson City

Show Me State

MO POPULATION:
6,010,688 (18th)

AREA: 69,707 sq mi (21st)
(180,540 sq km)

F Hawthorn
B Bluebird
T Dogwood
S "Missouri Waltz"

ENTERED UNION:
August 10, 1821 (24th)

LARGEST CITIES (WITH POP.): Kansas City, 459,787; St. Louis, 319,294; Springfield, 159,498; Independence, 116,830; Columbia, 108,500

★ Jefferson City

P motor vehicles, aerospace equipment, chemicals, electrical and electronic equipment, food products, cattle, hogs, milk, soybeans, corn, hay, lead

DID YOU KNOW? The stainless steel Gateway Arch (630 feet high), in St. Louis, is the state's most famous landmark. The state's most famous citizen is probably President Harry S. Truman. He was born and lived most of his life in Missouri.

MONTANA

Helena ★

Treasure State

MT POPULATION:
998,199 (44th)

AREA: 147,040 sq mi (4th)
(380,831 sq km)

F Bitterroot
B Western meadowlark
T Ponderosa pine
S "Montana"

ENTERED UNION:
November 8, 1889 (41st)

LARGEST CITIES (WITH POP.): Billings, 104,170; Missoula, 66,788; Great Falls, 58,505; Bozeman, 37,280

★ Helena

P cattle, copper, gold, coal, petroleum products, food products, wheat, barley, wood and paper products

DID YOU KNOW? The Little Bighorn National Monument, in southeastern Montana, commemorates "Custer's last stand." U.S. Army cavalry troops, under Lt. Col. George Armstrong Custer, were outnumbered and crushed by Sioux and Northern Cheyenne Indians, in a famous 1876 battle on that site.

NEBRASKA

Omaha ●
Lincoln ★

Cornhusker State

NE POPULATION:
1,842,641 (38th)

AREA: 77,348 sq mi (16th)
(200,330 sq km)

F Goldenrod
B Western meadowlark
T Cottonwood
S "Beautiful Nebraska"

ENTERED UNION:
March 1, 1867 (37th)

LARGEST CITIES (WITH POP.): Omaha, 408,958; Lincoln, 258,379; Bellevue, 50,137; Grand Island, 48,520

★ Lincoln

P cattle, hogs, milk, corn, soybeans, hay, sorghum, food products, chemicals, industrial machinery

DID YOU KNOW? The actor Marlon Brando, the Lakota Indian chief Red Cloud, the African-American activist Malcolm X, former Vice President Dick Cheney, and former President Gerald Ford were all born in Nebraska. So was the billionaire businessman Warren Buffett, known as the "Oracle of Omaha."

NEVADA

Sagebrush State, Battle Born State, Silver State

NV **POPULATION:** 2,723,322 (35th)

AREA: 110,572 sq mi (7th) (286,380 sq km)

- F Sagebrush
- B Mountain bluebird
- T Single-leaf piñon, bristlecone pine
- S "Home Means Nevada"

ENTERED UNION: October 31, 1864 (36th)

LARGEST CITIES (WITH POP.): Las Vegas, 583,756; Henderson, 257,729; North Las Vegas, 216,961; Reno, 225,221; Paradise, 223,107

★ Carson City

P gold, silver, cattle, hay, food products, plastics, cement, chemicals

DID YOU KNOW? The state's population grew by 35% between 2000 and 2010, according to the 2010 U.S. Census, making Nevada the fastest-growing U.S. state. North Las Vegas grew by 88% during those years. It was the second-fastest-growing big city in the United States.

NEW HAMPSHIRE

Granite State

NH **POPULATION:** 1,318,194 (42nd)

AREA: 9,349 sq mi (46th) (24,214 sq km)

- F Purple lilac
- B Purple finch
- T White birch
- S "Old New Hampshire"

ENTERED UNION: June 21, 1788 (9th)

LARGEST CITIES (WITH POP.): Manchester, 109,565; Nashua, 86,494; Concord, 42,695

★ Concord

P electric and electronic equipment, machinery, metal products, plastic products, greenhouse and dairy products, apples, maple syrup and maple sugar

DID YOU KNOW? Mount Washington, in New Hampshire, is the highest mountain in the northeastern United States. Visitors can ride to the top on a cog railway. But it's windy up there! A weather observatory on the mountain once reported a wind speed of 231 miles an hour.

NEW JERSEY

Garden State

NJ **POPULATION:** 8,821,155 (11th)

AREA: 8,723 sq mi (47th) (22,591 sq km)

- F Purple violet
- B Eastern goldfinch
- T Red oak
- S none

ENTERED UNION: December 18, 1787 (3rd)

LARGEST CITIES (WITH POP.): Newark, 277,140; Jersey City, 247,597; Paterson, 146,199; Elizabeth, 124,969; Edison, 99,967; Woodbridge, 99,585

★ Trenton

P chemicals, drugs and medical equipment, electronic equipment, petroleum products, nursery and greenhouse products, food products, tomatoes, blueberries, peaches

DID YOU KNOW? New Jersey has parks, meadows, farms, and beaches, but it also has several big cities. On the whole, New Jersey is the most crowded U.S. state, with an average of around 1,200 people per square mile.

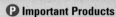

Key: F Flower B Bird T Tree S Song ★ Capital P Important Products

NEW MEXICO

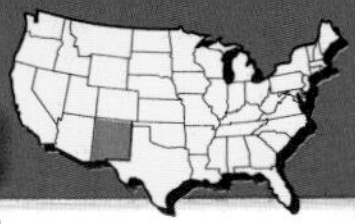

Land of Enchantment

NM **POPULATION:** 2,082,224 (36th)

AREA: 121,590 sq mi (5th) (314,917 sq km)

F Yucca
B Roadrunner
T Piñon
S "O, Fair New Mexico"

ENTERED UNION: January 6, 1912 (47th)

LARGEST CITIES (WITH POP.): Albuquerque, 545,852; Las Cruces, 97,618; Rio Rancho, 87,521; Santa Fe, 67,947

★ Santa Fe

P electronic equipment, medical equipment, aircraft, natural gas, oil, copper, potash, uranium, cattle, hay, onions, chilies

DID YOU KNOW? Every summer, hundreds of thousands of bats come to stay and give birth to their young at the Bat Cave in Carlsbad Caverns National Park. When weather permits, adult bats fly out at night in huge swarms to search for insects, their main food source. During the day, bat colonies rest, hanging from the ceiling of the dark cave.

NEW YORK

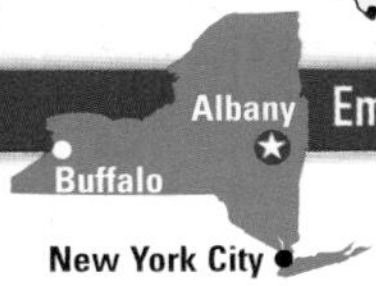

Empire State

NY **POPULATION:** 19,465,197 (3rd)

AREA: 54,555 sq mi (27th) (141,297 sq km)

F Rose
B Bluebird
T Sugar maple
S "I Love New York"

ENTERED UNION: July 26, 1788 (11th)

LARGEST CITIES (WITH POP.): New York, 8,175,133; Buffalo, 261,310; Rochester, 210,565; Yonkers, 195,976; Syracuse, 145,170

★ Albany

P chemicals, drugs, automobile and aircraft parts, electronic equipment, machinery, metal products, books and magazines, milk, cattle, hay, nursery and greenhouse products apples, salt, stone

DID YOU KNOW? In January 1892, Annie Moore, an Irish teenager, became the first of some 12 million immigrants to enter the United States through Ellis Island in New York Harbor. A bronze statue at the museum there honors her memory.

NORTH CAROLINA

Tar Heel State, Old North State

NC **POPULATION:** 9,656,401 (10th)

AREA: 53,819 sq mi (28th) (139,391 sq km)

F Dogwood
B Cardinal
T Pine
S "The Old North State"

ENTERED UNION: November 21, 1789 (12th)

LARGEST CITIES (WITH POP.): Charlotte, 731,424; Raleigh, 403,892; Greensboro, 269,666; Winston-Salem, 229,617; Durham, 228,330; Fayetteville, 200,564

★ Raleigh

P tobacco and tobacco products, chemicals, drugs, electronic equipment, clothing and textiles, furniture, chickens, hogs, nursery and greenhouse products, sweet potatoes, cotton, soybeans, peanuts

DID YOU KNOW? In 1587, a group of 112 English colonists arrived on Roanoke Island off the coast of North Carolina. Their leader, John White, sailed back to England to get more supplies. When he returned in 1590, after many delays, the people were all gone. No one knows what happened to them.

NORTH DAKOTA

Peace Garden State

POPULATION: 683,932 (48th)

AREA: 70,698 sq mi (19th) (183,108 sq km)

F Wild prairie rose
B Western meadowlark
T American elm
S "North Dakota Hymn"

ENTERED UNION: November 2, 1889 (39th)

LARGEST CITIES (WITH POP.): Fargo, 105,549; Bismarck, 61,272; Grand Forks, 52,838; Minot, 40,888

★ Bismarck

P wheat, soybeans, barley, hay, sunflowers, sugar beets, cattle, oil, food products, farm equipment, transportation equipment, metal products

DID YOU KNOW? In the 1880s, well before he became president, Theodore Roosevelt went to the "badlands" of North Dakota to hunt bison (buffalo). He ended up owning 2 ranches in this dry, rocky, windswept region. You can see these sites today if you visit Theodore Roosevelt National Park in North Dakota.

OHIO

Buckeye State

POPULATION: 11,544,951 (7th)

AREA: 44,826 sq mi (34th) (116,098 sq km)

F Scarlet carnation
B Cardinal
T Buckeye
S "Beautiful Ohio"

ENTERED UNION: March 1, 1803 (17th)

LARGEST CITIES (WITH POP.): Columbus, 787,033; Cleveland, 396,815; Cincinnati, 296,943; Toledo, 287,288; Akron, 199,110; Dayton, 141,527

★ Columbus

P metals and metal products, motor vehicles, chemicals, machinery, rubber and plastic products, electronic equipment, food products, corn, soybeans, livestock, milk

DID YOU KNOW? Wilbur and Orville Wright, the famous brothers who made the world's first plane flight, grew up mostly in Dayton, OH. They became interested in aviation when their father gave them a toy helicopter powered by a rubber band.

OKLAHOMA

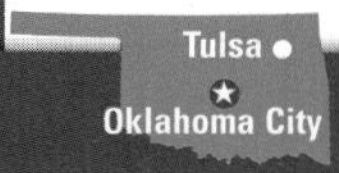

Sooner State

POPULATION: 3,791,508 (28th)

AREA: 69,899 sq mi (20th) (181,037 sq km)

F Mistletoe
B Scissor-tailed flycatcher
T Redbud
S "Oklahoma!"

ENTERED UNION: November 16, 1907 (46th)

LARGEST CITIES (WITH POP.): Oklahoma City, 579,999; Tulsa, 391,906; Norman, 110,925; Broken Arrow, 98,850; Lawton, 96,867

★ Oklahoma City

P natural gas, oil, machinery, transportation equipment, metal products, food products, cattle, hogs, wheat, hay

DID YOU KNOW? At the popular National Cowboy and Western Heritage Museum in Oklahoma City you can visit a replica of an old Western town and see exhibits about cowboy life and the history of the working cowboy.

Key: F Flower B Bird T Tree S Song ★ Capital P Important Products

OREGON

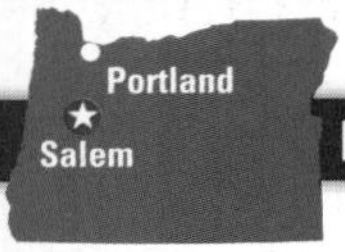

Beaver State

OR **POPULATION:** 3,871,859 (27th)

AREA: 98,379 sq mi (9th) (254,799 sq km)

F Oregon grape
B Western meadowlark
T Douglas fir
S "Oregon, My Oregon"

ENTERED UNION: February 14, 1859 (33rd)

LARGEST CITIES (WITH POP.): Portland, 583,776; Eugene, 156,185; Salem, 154,637; Gresham, 105,594; Hillsboro, 91,611; Beaverton, 89,803

★ Salem

P electronic products and semiconductors, lumber and wood products, cattle, dairy products, hay, fruits and vegetables

DID YOU KNOW? Crater Lake, in southern Oregon, is almost 2,000 feet deep. It is the deepest lake in the United States and the seventh-deepest lake in the world. The lake occupies the crater of a huge volcano that erupted thousands of years ago.

PENNSYLVANIA

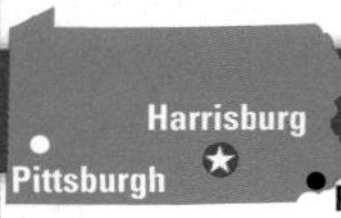

Keystone State

PA **POPULATION:** 12,742,886 (6th)

AREA: 46,054 sq mi (33rd) (119,280 sq km)

F Mountain laurel
B Ruffed grouse
T Hemlock
S "Pennsylvania"

ENTERED UNION: December 12, 1787 (2nd)

LARGEST CITIES (WITH POP.): Philadelphia, 1,526,006; Pittsburgh, 305,704; Allentown, 118,032; Erie, 101,786; Reading, 88,082; Upper Darby, 82,795; Scranton, 76,089

★ Harrisburg

P food products, iron and steel, coal, petroleum products, metal products, drugs, machinery, transportation equipment, stone and glass products, nursery plants, mushrooms

DID YOU KNOW? Philadelphia was the capital of Pennsylvania for many years in the 1600s and 1700s and capital of the U.S. from 1790 to 1800. Independence Hall is perhaps the city's most famous building. The Declaration of Independence was approved there in 1776, and the U.S. Constitution was written there in 1787.

RHODE ISLAND

Little Rhody, Ocean State

RI **POPULATION:** 1,051,302 (43rd)

AREA: 1,545 sq mi (50th) (4,001 sq km)

F Violet
B Rhode Island red
T Red maple
S "Rhode Island"

ENTERED UNION: May 29, 1790 (13th)

LARGEST CITIES (WITH POP.): Providence, 178,042; Warwick, 82,672; Cranston, 80,387; Pawtucket, 71,148

★ Providence

P metal products, plastics, chemicals, costume jewelry, electronic equipment, nursery and greenhouse products, corn, fish

DID YOU KNOW? Newport is known for its huge mansions, many built during the "Gilded Age" of the late 19th century. Years before then, the city was a major whaling port. Still earlier, Newport was known as a haven for pirates.

SOUTH CAROLINA

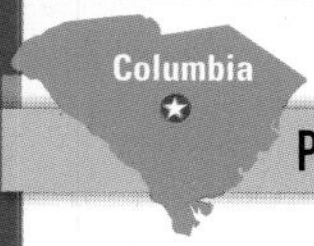

Palmetto State

SC POPULATION: 4,679,230 (24th)

AREA: 32,020 sq mi (40th) (82,933 sq km)

F Yellow jessamine
B Carolina wren
T Palmetto
S "Carolina"

ENTERED UNION: May 23, 1788 (8th)

LARGEST CITIES (WITH POP.): Columbia, 129,272; Charleston, 120,083; North Charleston, 97,471; Mount Pleasant, 67,843; Rock Hill, 66,154

★ Columbia

P chemicals, motor vehicles, plastics, machinery, metal products, chickens, nursery and greenhouse products, tobacco, cement

DID YOU KNOW? More Revolutionary War battles were fought in South Carolina than in any other state. The famous South Carolina soldier Francis Marion was known as the "Swamp Fox" because he was so successful at leading surprise attacks on British troops and then slipping back into the swamps.

SOUTH DAKOTA

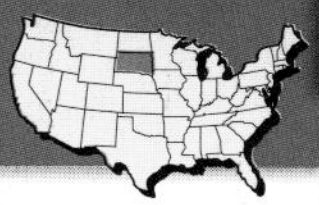

Mt. Rushmore State, Coyote State

SD POPULATION: 824,082 (46th)

AREA: 77,116 sq mi (17th) (199,729 sq km)

F Pasqueflower
B Chinese ring-necked pheasant
T Black Hills spruce
S "Hail, South Dakota"

ENTERED UNION: November 2, 1889 (40th)

LARGEST CITIES (WITH POP.): Sioux Falls, 153,888; Rapid City, 67,956; Aberdeen, 26,091

★ Pierre

P food products, chemicals, machinery, electrical and electronic equipment, corn, soybeans, oats

DID YOU KNOW? The four presidents whose faces are carved on South Dakota's famous Mount Rushmore are George Washington, Thomas Jefferson, Abraham Lincoln, and Theodore Roosevelt. Each head is 50 to 70 feet high.

TENNESSEE

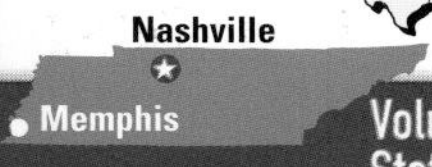

Volunteer State

TN POPULATION: 6,403,353 (17th)

AREA: 42,144 sq mi (36th) (109,153 sq km)

F Iris, Passionflower
B Mockingbird
T Tulip poplar
S "My Homeland, Tennessee," "When It's Iris Time in Tennessee," "My Tennessee," "Tennessee Waltz," "Rocky Top"

ENTERED UNION: June 1, 1796 (16th)

LARGEST CITIES (WITH POP.): Memphis, 646,899; Nashville-Davidson, 601,222; Knoxville, 178,874; Chattanooga, 167,674; Clarksville, 132,929; Murfreesboro, 108,755

★ Nashville

P motor vehicles, chemicals, machinery, metal products, electronic equipment, rubber and plastic products, food products, cattle, chickens, soybeans, nursery products, tobacco

DID YOU KNOW? Every year more than 600,000 people come to Graceland, Elvis Presley's former home in Memphis. This mansion is said to be the most frequently visited home in the United States, except for the White House.

Key: F Flower B Bird T Tree S Song ★ Capital P Important Products

TEXAS

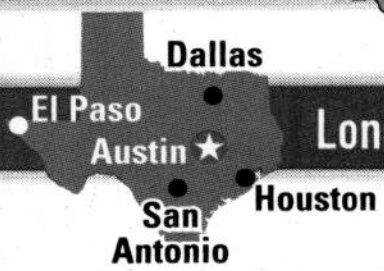

Lone Star State

TX **POPULATION:** 25,674,681 (2nd)

AREA: 268,596 sq mi (2nd) (695,661 sq km)

F Bluebonnet
B Mockingbird
T Pecan
S "Texas, Our Texas"

ENTERED UNION: December 29, 1845 (28th)

LARGEST CITIES (WITH POP.): Houston, 2,099,451; San Antonio, 1,327,407; Dallas, 1,197,816; Austin, 790,390; Fort Worth, 741,206; El Paso, 649,121; Arlington, 365,438; Corpus Christi, 305,215; Plano, 259,841; Laredo, 236,091

★ Austin

P oil, natural gas, coal, cattle, chemicals and resins, aerospace products, machinery, electrical and electronic equipment, cotton, corn, wheat, dairy products, nursery and greenhouse products, fish

DID YOU KNOW? In 1836, during Texas's war for independence, several thousand troops under the Mexican commander Santa Anna captured the Alamo in San Antonio after a long siege. Some 200 men tried to defend the fortress. Nearly all of them were killed, either in fierce hand-to-hand fighting or by execution.

UTAH

Beehive State

UT **POPULATION:** 2,817,222 (34th)

AREA: 84,897 sq mi (13th) (219,882 sq km)

F Sego lily
B Seagull
T Blue spruce
S "Utah, This Is the Place"

ENTERED UNION: January 4, 1896 (45th)

LARGEST CITIES (WITH POP.): Salt Lake City, 186,440; West Valley City, 129,480; Provo, 112,488; West Jordan, 103,712; Orem, 88,328; Sandy, 87,461; Ogden, 82,825

★ Salt Lake City

P food products, petroleum products, transportation equipment, medical instruments, electronic equipment, metal products, sporting goods, copper, cattle, hogs, dairy products, hay, wheat

DID YOU KNOW? The Great Salt Lake, in northwest Utah, is the biggest lake in the U.S. outside of the Great Lakes. It is also the world's saltiest lake except for the Dead Sea. It holds 6 billion tons of dissolved salts, mostly common table salt.

VERMONT

Green Mountain State

VT **POPULATION:** 626,431 (49th)

AREA: 9,616 sq mi (45th) (24,906 sq km)

F Red clover
B Hermit thrush
T Sugar maple
S "These Green Mountains"

ENTERED UNION: March 4, 1791 (14th)

LARGEST CITIES (WITH POP.): Burlington, 42,417; South Burlington, 17,904; Rutland, 16,495

★ Montpelier

P computers and electronic equipment, machinery, furniture, books, dairy products, cattle, apples, maple syrup

DID YOU KNOW? More than 3,000 black bears are believed to be living in the woods of Vermont. Black bears are shy and are seldom seen by people. They are the smallest of the three bear species found in North America, but they are still pretty big. An adult male usually weighs around 300 to 400 pounds.

VIRGINIA

Old Dominion

VA **POPULATION:** 8,096,604 (12th)

AREA: 42,775 sq mi (35th) (110,787 sq km)

F Dogwood
B Cardinal
T Dogwood
S none

ENTERED UNION: June 25, 1788 (10th)

LARGEST CITIES (WITH POP.): Virginia Beach, 437,994; Norfolk, 242,803; Chesapeake, 222,209; Arlington, 207,627; Richmond, 204,214; Newport News, 180,719

★ Richmond

P food products, transportation equipment, chemicals, machinery, electronic equipment, coal, chickens, cattle, hogs, dairy products, tobacco, hay, wood products, furniture

DID YOU KNOW? The world's biggest candy company is based in McLean, Virginia. Mars Incorporated makes Snickers, M&Ms, Milky Way, Twix, Mars bars, and many other candies, along with various other products such as Uncle Ben's rice and Pedigree dog food.

WASHINGTON

Evergreen State

WA **POPULATION:** 6,830,038 (13th)

AREA: 71,298 sq mi (18th) (184,661 sq km)

F Western rhododendron
B Willow goldfinch
T Western hemlock
S "Washington, My Home"

ENTERED UNION: November 11, 1889 (42nd)

LARGEST CITIES (WITH POP.): Seattle, 608,660; Spokane, 208,916; Tacoma, 198,397; Vancouver, 161,791; Bellevue, 122,363; Everett, 103,019

★ Olympia

P aircraft, electronic products and computer software, lumber and wood products, machinery, metal products, food products, wheat, apples, potatoes, fish

DID YOU KNOW? The Seattle suburb of Redmond is the home of the computer software giant Microsoft, founded in the 1970s by Seattle native Bill Gates. Seattle also helped give birth to Starbucks coffee and Amazon.com.

WEST VIRGINIA

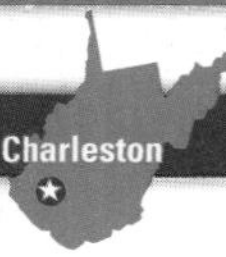

Mountain State

WV **POPULATION:** 1,855,364 (37th)

AREA: 24,230 sq mi (41st) (62,756 sq km)

F Big rhododendron
B Cardinal
T Sugar maple
S "The West Virginia Hills"; "This Is My West Virginia"; "West Virginia, My Home Sweet Home"

ENTERED UNION: June 20, 1863 (35th)

LARGEST CITIES (WITH POP.): Charleston, 51,400; Huntington, 49,138; Parkersburg, 31,492; Morgantown, 29,660; Wheeling, 28,486

★ Charleston

P chemicals, automobile parts, metal products, coal, aluminum, chickens, cattle, eggs, hay, apples, peaches, tobacco

DID YOU KNOW? When Virginia seceded from the Union in 1861 and joined the Confederacy, people in the northwestern counties got together and agreed to split off from the rest of Virginia. "West Virginia" was admitted to the Union in June 1863. It became the 35th state.

Key: F Flower B Bird T Tree S Song ★ Capital P Important Products

WISCONSIN

Badger State

POPULATION: 5,711,767 (20th)

AREA: 65,496 sq mi (23rd) (169,635 sq km)

- **F** Wood violet
- **B** Robin
- **T** Sugar maple
- **S** "On, Wisconsin!"

ENTERED UNION: May 29, 1848 (30th)

LARGEST CITIES (WITH POP.): Milwaukee, 594,833; Madison, 253,335; Green Bay, 104,057; Kenosha, 99,218; Racine, 78,860

★ Madison

P food products, milk, butter, cheese, machinery, transportation equipment, lumber and wood products, electrical and electronic products, plastics, cattle, corn, hay, vegetables

DID YOU KNOW? Architect Frank Lloyd Wright, artist Georgia O'Keeffe, *Little House on the Prairie* author Laura Ingalls Wilder, and Supreme Court Chief Justice William H. Rehnquist were all born in Wisconsin.

WYOMING

Cowboy State

POPULATION: 568,158 (50th)

AREA: 97,813 sq mi (10th) (253,334 sq km)

- **F** Indian paintbrush
- **B** Western meadowlark
- **T** Plains cottonwood
- **S** "Wyoming"

ENTERED UNION: July 10, 1890 (44th)

LARGEST CITIES (WITH POP.): Cheyenne, 59,466; Casper, 55,316; Laramie, 30,816; Gillette, 29,087

★ Cheyenne

P oil, natural gas, coal, petroleum and coal products, chemicals, cattle, hay, wheat, sugar beets

DID YOU KNOW? Buford, Wyoming, which has been called the "smallest town in America," was sold at auction in April 2012 to a man who came all the way from Vietnam to bid on it. He paid $900,000 for the tiny town, which had only one resident. It covers about 10 acres and includes an old schoolhouse, a gas station and convenience store, and a three-bedroom home.

COMMONWEALTH OF PUERTO RICO

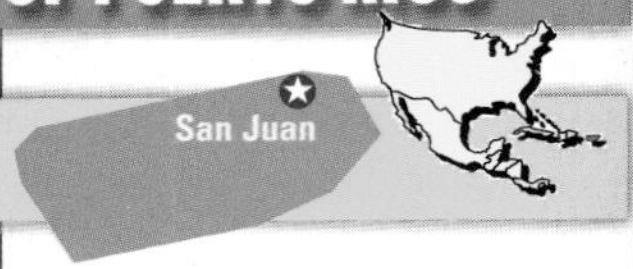

HISTORY: Christopher Columbus landed in Puerto Rico in 1493. Puerto Rico was a Spanish colony for centuries, then was ceded (given) to the United States in 1898 after the Spanish-American War. In 1952, still associated with the United States, Puerto Rico became a commonwealth with its own constitution.

POPULATION: 3,706,690

AREA: 5,325 sq mi (13,791 sq km)

- **F** Maga
- **B** Reinita
- **T** Ceiba

NATIONAL ANTHEM: "La Borinqueña"

LARGEST CITIES (WITH POP.): San Juan, 381,931; Bayamon, 185,996; Carolina, 157,832; Ponce, 132,502; Caguas, 82,243

★ San Juan

P drugs, medical equipment, electronic equipment, clothing and textiles, dairy products, chickens, cattle, coffee, fruit

DID YOU KNOW? The coqui, a tiny tree frog about 1 inch long, is found only in Puerto Rico. It has become a symbol of the island.

Key: **F** Flower **B** Bird **T** Tree **S** Song **★** Capital **P** Important Products

WASHINGTON, D.C.

The Capital of the United States

DC **POPULATION (2011):** 617,996 **AREA:** 68 sq mi (177 sq km)

FLOWER: American beauty rose **BIRD:** Wood thrush

FOR MORE INFORMATION, SEE: ***www.dc.gov* • *www.washington.org***

HISTORY: The District of Columbia, or Washington, D.C., became the capital of the United States in 1800, when the federal government moved there from Philadelphia. The city, named after George Washington, was designed and built to be the capital. Many of its major sights are on the **Mall**, a grassy open area that runs from the Capitol to the Potomac River.

CAPITOL, which houses the U.S. Congress, is at the east end of the Mall on Capitol Hill. Its dome can be seen from far away.

FRANKLIN DELANO ROOSEVELT MEMORIAL includes statues of Franklin D. and Eleanor Roosevelt, in a park-like setting near the Potomac River.

JEFFERSON MEMORIAL, a circular marble building located near the Potomac River, is partly based on a design by Thomas Jefferson for the University of Virginia.

LIBRARY OF CONGRESS, research library for Congress and the largest library in the world, is across the street from the Capitol.

◄ **LINCOLN MEMORIAL**, at the west end of the Mall, features a large, seated statue of Abraham Lincoln. His Gettysburg Address is carved on a nearby wall.

NATIONAL ARCHIVES, on Constitution Avenue, holds the Declaration of Independence, Constitution, and Bill of Rights.

NATIONAL WORLD WAR II MEMORIAL, located near the Lincoln Memorial, honors the 16 million Americans who served in that war.

SMITHSONIAN ► INSTITUTION has 19 museums, including the National Air and Space Museum and the Museum of Natural History.

U.S. HOLOCAUST MEMORIAL MUSEUM presents the history of the Nazis' murder of more than six million Jews and millions of other people from 1933 to 1945.

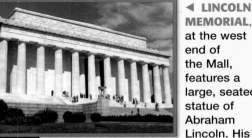

VIETNAM VETERANS MEMORIAL ► includes a wall with the names of those killed or missing in action during the conflict.

WASHINGTON MONUMENT is a white marble pillar, or obelisk, standing on the Mall and rising to more than 555 feet.

WHITE HOUSE, at 1600 Pennsylvania Avenue, has been the home of every U.S. president except George Washington.

VOLUNTEERING

→What does Plant Patrol do? PAGE 311

Environmental threats, poverty, natural disasters . . . sometimes the problems of the world seem so large that it's hard to imagine how we can help. But just one person really can make a difference. And people who help others also help themselves! Studies have shown that kids who volunteer perform better in school, are happier, and feel more positive about themselves. Does this win-win situation have you ready to take action? Here's how to get started.

RESEARCH Pick an area that interests you, and research different ways you can help. The web site ***www.dosomething.org*** features a great search tool to get you started. First pick a cause—such as the environment, animal welfare, or disaster relief. Then decide whom you want to work with (alone? with your family? with friends?), where you want to help, and how much time you have to volunteer. The search generates a list of action guides that fit your needs.

ASK AROUND There's a good chance that different groups in your community already have projects under way—and would welcome another helping hand. Many people volunteer through their **religious community**. Churches, synagogues, and mosques often organize ways to help the needy. Many **schools** also offer opportunities for their students to volunteer. Schools may sponsor plant sales to raise money for a worthy cause or ask students to visit elderly people in a nursing home. Girl Scout councils, county 4-H organizations, American Red Cross chapters, and other **community groups** participate in volunteering projects such as cleaning up a local park or organizing a car wash to raise money for a cause.

MAKE A CHOICE Do you want to provide direct services or raise money for your cause? For example, you can read to patients in a children's hospital or hold a bake sale and buy an acre of rain forest with the money you raise.

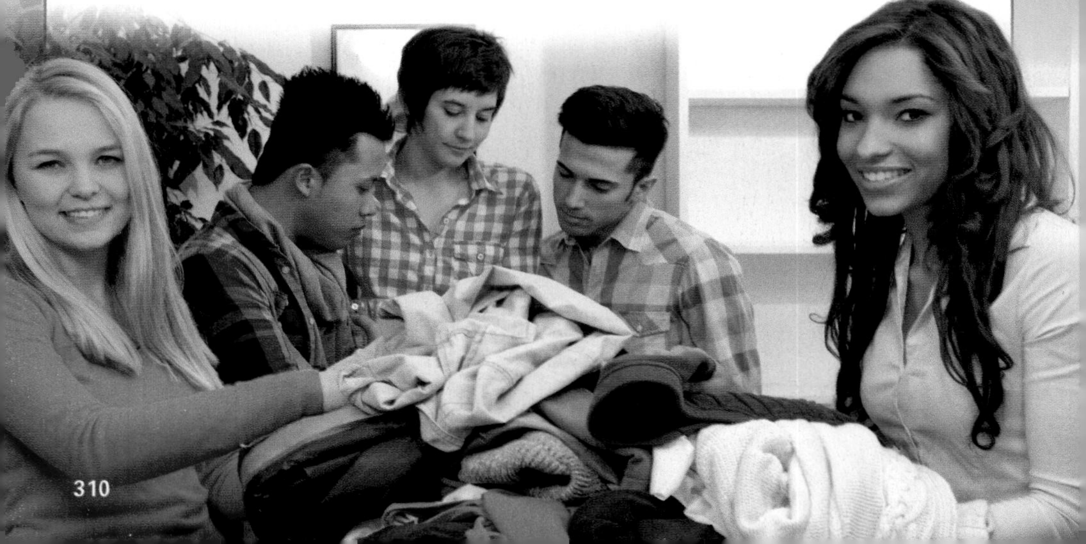

Volunteering **All-Stars**

Ashlee's Toy Closet

When Ashlee Smith, 13, of Sparks, Nevada, was five years old, her family lost everything in a house fire—including her favorite stuffed animal. A few years later, when her firefighter father was battling wildfires in neighboring California, he sent her pictures of the destroyed houses. "I knew right away how the kids were feeling, and I knew I had to help," says Ashlee. She posted flyers, asked for donations, and collected and sent a truck full of toys. "You do not have to be an adult to make a difference, and you never know until you try," Ashlee explains. Since then, her Ashlee's Toy Closet organization has distributed more than 175,000 toys to children in need.

Inspiring to Lead

"Bullying, racist comments, sexist comments, and overall prejudicial actions run rampant in schools," says Iko'tsimiskimaki ("Ekoo") Beck, 16, of Missoula, Montana, who is part American Indian. "I know how it feels. I am, and often have been, the target of those prejudicial comments." After winning a $10,000 grant in 2010, Ekoo set up a program to prevent bullying and reduce prejudice among students through training workshops and after-school clubs. Participants learn about the effects of bullying and racist behaviors and about ways to end them. Ekoo's program, called Inspire to Lead, includes peer-led workshops, and so far, more than 800 students have taken part in Missoula.

A Group Called Plant Patrol

Five years ago, Eric Babb, now 16, went for a hike near his home in Highland, Utah, and noticed many weeds along the trail. He did some research and discovered that they were nonnative (not originally from the region) and invasive (spread easily and quickly). The plants were also poisonous to local wildlife. Eric organized a group called Plant Patrol to identify, remove, and dispose of the invasive plants. Since then, he has educated dozens of 4-H groups, school classes, and scout troops totaling more than 2,000 people. "[The invasive plant] tends to skyrocket and, in turn, crowd out the native species," Eric explains. "I feel I have just begun to mobilize and educate my community about this serious environmental problem."

DID YOU KNOW?

The Prudential Spirit of Community Awards honor young people for outstanding volunteer community service. Find out more at *spirit.prudential.com*

WEATHER

→ Which state holds the hottest temperature record? PAGE 313

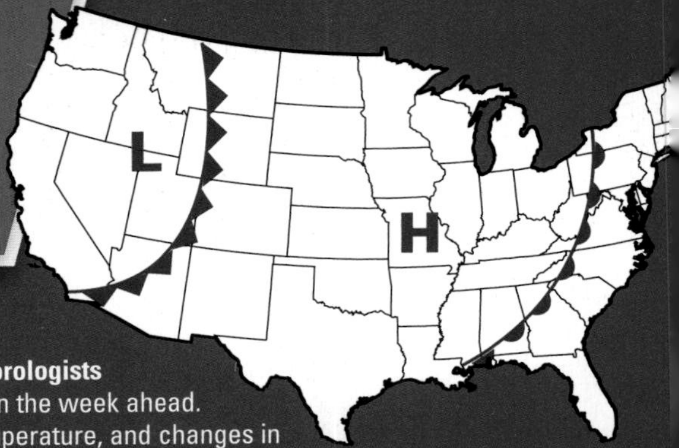

Weather Forecasting

Rain or shine? Weather scientists called **meteorologists** help forecast the weather for tomorrow or even the week ahead. They are able to do this by studying winds, temperature, and changes in the atmosphere. For example, an area of high pressure usually means dry, calm weather, while an area of low pressure often brings rain, clouds, and wind.

A **front** is a sharp change in air temperature. Storms usually come before a cold front. As a cold front passes through an area, the temperature drops. Light rain might bring a warm front. As a warm front moves in, the air gets warmer.

Around the world, meteorologists use the same set of symbols to show weather conditions (see the table below and the map above). These common symbols let them share weather data.

Selected Weather Symbols		
Sky Cover	**Fronts**	**Weather**
◯ Clear	▲▲ Cold front	▪ Rain ═ Fog
◔ Scattered	●●● Warm front	✳ Snow ∞ Haze
● Overcast	⌄⌄ Stationary front	⋉ Thunderstorm
Wind: ◎ Calm	── 1-2 knots (1-2 mph)	──⌐ 3-7 knots (3-8 mph)
L Low Pressure Center	**H** High Pressure Center	

WILD WEATHER FACTS

- A lightning bolt can be as hot as 55,000 degrees Fahrenheit. That's about five times hotter than the surface of the sun!

- In 2012, the United States had its hottest March on record. Average temperatures in most of the country were 8.6 degrees Fahrenheit above normal for the month.

- Barrow Island, off the coast of Australia, marks the spot of the fastest wind gust ever recorded in the world. The gust, measured at 253 miles per hour, occurred during a cyclone in 1996.

DID YOU KNOW?

It was a White Halloween for tens of millions of Americans in 2011. Just two days before Halloween, a rare October snowstorm struck the northeastern United States. It caused many power outages and school closings. In some places, trick-or-treating and other Halloween celebrations were canceled or postponed.

RECORD TEMPERATURES BY STATE (Through May 2012)

Coldest Temperature

Hottest Temperature

STATE	Lowest °F	Lowest Latest date	Highest °F	Highest Latest date
Alabama	–27	Jan. 30, 1966	112	Sept. 5, 1925
Alaska	–80	Jan. 23, 1971	100	June 27, 1915
Arizona	–40	Jan. 7, 1971	128	July 5, 2007
Arkansas	–29	Feb. 13, 1905	120	Aug. 10, 1936
California	–45	Jan. 20, 1937	134	July 10, 1913
Colorado	–61	Feb. 1, 1985	118	July 11, 1888
Connecticut	–32	Jan. 22, 1961	106	July 15, 1995
Delaware	–17	Jan. 17, 1893	110	July 21, 1930
Florida	–2	Feb. 13, 1899	109	June 29, 1931
Georgia	–17	Jan. 27, 1940	112	Aug. 20, 1983
Hawaii	12	May 17, 1979	100	Apr. 27, 1931
Idaho	–60	Jan. 18, 1943	118	July 28, 1934
Illinois	–36	Jan. 5, 1999	117	July 14, 1954
Indiana	–36	Jan. 19, 1994	116	July 14, 1936
Iowa	–47	Feb. 3, 1996	118	July 20, 1934
Kansas	–40	Feb. 13, 1905	121	July 24, 1936
Kentucky	–37	Jan. 19, 1994	114	July 28, 1930
Louisiana	–16	Feb. 13, 1899	114	Aug. 10, 1936
Maine	–50	Jan. 16, 2009	105	July 10, 1911
Maryland	–40	Jan. 13, 1912	109	July 10, 1936
Massachusetts	–35	Jan. 12, 1981	107	Aug. 2, 1975
Michigan	–51	Feb. 9, 1934	112	July 13, 1936
Minnesota	–60	Feb. 2, 1996	114	July 6, 1936
Mississippi	–19	Jan. 30, 1966	115	July 29, 1930
Missouri	–40	Feb. 13, 1905	118	July 14, 1954
Montana	–70	Jan. 20, 1954	117	July 5, 1937
Nebraska	–47	Dec. 22, 1989	118	July 24, 1936
Nevada	–50	Jan. 8, 1937	125	June 29, 1994
New Hampshire	–47	Jan. 29, 1934	106	July 4, 1911
New Jersey	–34	Jan. 5, 1904	110	July 10, 1936
New Mexico	–50	Feb. 1, 1951	122	June 27, 1994
New York	–52	Feb. 18, 1979	108	July 22, 1926
North Carolina	–34	Jan. 21, 1985	110	Aug. 21, 1983
North Dakota	–60	Feb. 15, 1936	121	July 6, 1936
Ohio	–39	Feb. 10, 1899	113	July 21, 1934
Oklahoma	–31	Feb. 10, 2011	120	June 27, 1994
Oregon	–54	Feb. 10, 1933	119	Aug. 10, 1898
Pennsylvania	–42	Jan. 5, 1904	111	July 10, 1936
Rhode Island	–25	Feb. 5, 1996	104	Aug. 2, 1975
South Carolina	–19	Jan. 21, 1985	111	June 28, 1954
South Dakota	–58	Feb. 17, 1936	120	July 15, 2006
Tennessee	–32	Dec. 30, 1917	113	Aug. 9, 1930
Texas	–23	Feb. 8, 1933	120	June 28, 1994
Utah	–69	Feb. 1, 1985	117	July 5, 1985
Vermont	–50	Dec. 30, 1933	105	July 4, 1911
Virginia	–30	Jan. 22, 1985	110	July 15, 1954
Washington	–48	Dec. 30, 1968	118	Aug. 5, 1961
West Virginia	–37	Dec. 30, 1917	112	July 10, 1936
Wisconsin	–55	Feb. 4, 1996	114	July 13, 1936
Wyoming	–66	Feb. 9, 1933	115	Aug. 8, 1983

Source: National Climatic Data Center

Record temperatures may have occurred on earlier dates. Dates listed here are for most recent occurrence of a record temperature.

WEIGHTS & MEASURES

→What does a fathom measure? PAGE 316

Metrology isn't the study of weather. (That's meteorology.) It is the science of measurement. Almost everything you use (or eat or drink) is measured—either when it is made or when it's sold. Materials for buildings and parts for machines must be measured carefully so they will fit together. Clothes have sizes so you'll know what to buy. Recipes help you measure the ingredients so your cookies bake properly.

ANCIENT MEASURE

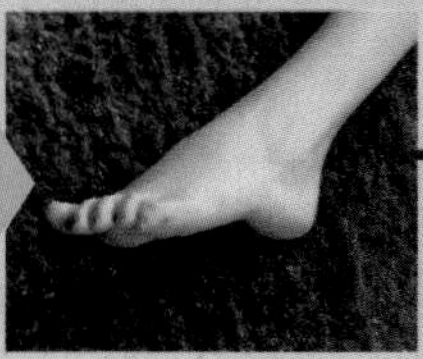

1 foot = length of a person's foot

1 yard = from nose to fingertip

1 acre = land a pair of oxen could plow in a day

MODERN MEASURE

1 foot	1 yard	1 acre
12 inches	**3 feet or 36 inches**	**4,840 square yards**

EARLIEST MEASUREMENTS

The human body was the first "ruler." An "inch" was the width of a thumb; a "hand" was five fingers wide; a "foot" was—you guessed it—the length of a foot! A "cubit" ran from the elbow to the tip of the middle finger (about 20 inches), and a "yard" was roughly the length of a whole arm.

Later, measurements came from daily activities, like plowing a field. A "furlong" was the distance a pair of oxen could plow before stopping to rest (now we say it is about 220 yards). The trouble with these units is that they vary from person to person, place to place, and ox to ox.

MEASUREMENTS WE USE TODAY

The official system in the U.S. is the customary system (sometimes called the imperial or English system). Scientists and most other countries use the International System of Units (SI, or the metric system). The Weights and Measures Division of the U.S. National Institute of Standards and Technology (NIST) makes sure that a gallon of milk is the same in every state. When the NIST was founded in 1901, the U.S. had as many as eight different "standard" gallons, and there were four different legal measures of a "foot" in Brooklyn, New York, alone.

TAKING TEMPERATURES

There are two main systems for measuring temperature. One is **Fahrenheit** (abbreviated F). The other is **Celsius** (abbreviated C). Another word for Celsius is Centigrade.

Zero degrees (0°) Celsius is equal to 32 degrees (32°) Fahrenheit.

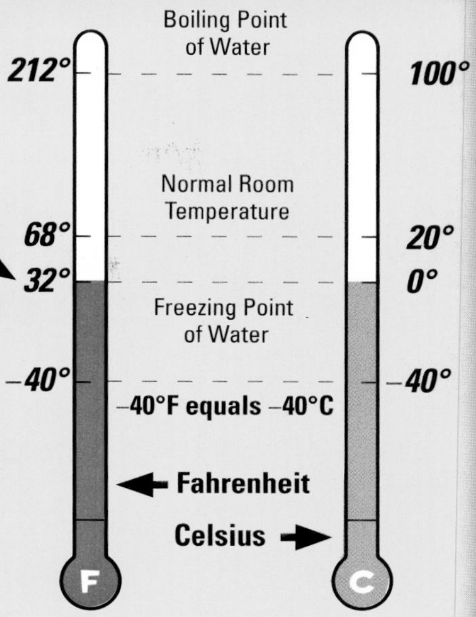

To convert from Celsius to Fahrenheit:

Multiply by 1.8 and add 32.
(°F = 1.8 × °C + 32)

Example: 20°C × 1.8 = 36; 36 + 32 = 68°F

To convert from Fahrenheit to Celsius:

Subtract 32 and divide by 1.8.

Example: 68°F – 32 = 36; 36 ÷ 1.8 = 20°C

HOTTEST and COLDEST Places in the World

Hottest Temperature → AFRICA

Coldest Temperature → ANTARCTICA (Vostok)

Continent	Highest Temperature	Lowest Temperature
AFRICA	El Azizia, Libya, 136°F (58°C)	Ifrane, Morocco, –11°F (–24°C)
ANTARCTICA	Vanda Station, 59°F (15°C)	Vostok, –129°F (–89°C)
ASIA	Tirat Tsvi, Israel, 129°F (54°C)	Verkhoyansk, Russia, and Oimekon, Russia, –90°F (–68°C)
AUSTRALIA	Cloncurry, Queensland, 128°F (53°C)	Charlotte Pass, New South Wales, –9°F (–23°C)
EUROPE	Seville, Spain, 122°F (50°C)	Ust'Shchugor, Russia, –67°F (–55°C)
NORTH AMERICA	Death Valley, California, U.S., 134°F (57°C)	Snag, Yukon, Canada, –81°F (–63°C)
SOUTH AMERICA	Rivadavia, Argentina, 120°F (49°C)	Sarmiento, Argentina, –27°F (–33°C)

DID YOU KNOW? The summer of 2011 brought record-setting heat to the U.S. Oklahoma averaged 88.9°F (31.6°C) in July. That was the hottest monthly temperature for any U.S. state ever.

LENGTH

The basic unit of **length** in the U.S. system is the **inch**. Length, width, and thickness all use the inch or larger related units.

1 foot (ft) = 12 inches (in)
1 yard (yd) = 3 feet = 36 inches
1 rod (rd) = 5½ yards
1 furlong (fur) = 40 rods = 220 yards = 660 feet
1 mile (mi) (also called statute mile) = 8 furlongs = 1,760 yards = 5,280 feet
1 nautical mile = 6,076 feet = 1.15 statute miles
1 league = 3 miles

CAPACITY

Units of **capacity** measure how much of something will fit into a container. **Liquid measure** is used to measure liquids such as water or gasoline. **Dry measure** is used with large amounts of solid materials such as grain or fruit. Although both liquid and dry measures use the terms "pint" and "quart," they mean different amounts and should not be confused.

Dry Measure

1 quart (qt) = 2 pints (pt)
1 peck (pk) = 8 quarts
1 bushel (bu) = 4 pecks

Liquid Measure

1 gill = 4 fluid ounces (fl oz)
1 pint (pt) = 4 gills = 16 ounces (oz)
1 quart (qt) = 2 pints = 32 ounces
1 gallon (gal) = 4 quarts = 128 ounces

For measuring most U.S. liquids,
1 barrel (bbl) = 31½ gallons

For measuring oil, 1 barrel = 42 gallons

Cooking Measurements

The measurements in cooking are based on the **fluid ounce**.
1 teaspoon (tsp) = ⅙ fluid ounce (fl oz)
1 tablespoon (tbsp) = 3 teaspoons = ½ fluid ounce
1 cup = 16 tablespoons = 8 fluid ounces
1 pint = 2 cups
1 quart (qt) = 2 pints (pt)
1 gallon (gal) = 4 quarts

AREA

Area measures a section of a two-dimensional surface like a floor or a piece of paper. Most area measurements are given in **square units**. Land is measured in **acres**.

1 square foot (sq ft) = 144 square inches (sq in)
1 square yard (sq yd) = 9 square feet = 1,296 square inches
1 square rod (sq rd) = 30¼ square yards
1 acre = 160 square rods = 4,840 square yards = 43,560 square feet
1 square mile (sq mi) = 640 acres

VOLUME

The amount of space taken up by a three-dimensional object (or the amount of space available within an object) is measured in **volume**. Volume is usually expressed in **cubic units**.

1 cubic foot (cu ft) = 12 inches x 12 inches x 12 inches = 1,728 cubic inches (cu in)
1 cubic yard (cu yd) = 27 cubic feet

DEPTH

Some measurements of length measure ocean depth and distance.

1 fathom = 6 feet (ft)
1 cable = 120 fathoms = 720 feet

WEIGHT

Although 1 cubic foot of popcorn and 1 cubic foot of rock take up the same amount of space, lifting them isn't the same. We measure heaviness as **weight**. Most objects are measured in **avoirdupois weight** (pronounced a-ver-de-POIZ):

1 dram (dr) = 27.344 grains (gr)
1 ounce (oz) = 16 drams = 437.5 grains
1 pound (lb) = 16 ounces
1 hundredweight (cwt) = 100 pounds
1 (short) ton = 2,000 pounds

THE METRIC SYSTEM

The metric system was created in France in 1795. Standardized in 1960, the International System of Units is now used in most countries and in scientific works. The system is based on 10, like the decimal counting system. The basic unit for length is the **meter**. The **liter** is a basic unit of volume or capacity, and the **gram** is a basic unit of mass. Related units are made by adding a prefix to the basic unit. The prefixes and their meanings are:

milli- = $\frac{1}{1,000}$

centi- = $\frac{1}{100}$

deci- = $\frac{1}{10}$

deka- = 10

hecto- = 100

kilo- = 1,000

For Example

millimeter (mm) = $\frac{1}{1,000}$ of a meter

kilometer (km) = 1,000 meters

milligram (mg) = $\frac{1}{1,000}$ of a gram

kilogram (kg) = 1,000 grams

To get a rough idea of measurements in the metric system, it helps to know that a **liter** is a little more than a quart. A **meter** is a little more than a yard. A **kilogram** is a little more than 2 pounds. And a **kilometer** is just over half a mile.

HOMEWORK TIP

Converting Measurements

If you have:	Multiply by:	To get:
inches	*2.54*	centimeters
inches	*0.0254*	meters
feet	*30.48*	centimeters
feet	*0.3048*	meters
yards	*0.9144*	meters
miles	*1.6093*	kilometers
square inches	*6.4516*	square centimeters
square feet	*0.0929*	square meters
square yards	*0.8361*	square meters
acres	*0.4047*	hectares
cubic inches	*16.3871*	cubic centimeters
cubic feet	*0.0283*	cubic meters
cubic yards	*0.7646*	cubic meters
quarts (liquid)	*0.9464*	liters
ounces	*28.3495*	grams
pounds	*0.4536*	kilograms

If you have:	Multiply by:	To get:
centimeters	*0.3937*	inches
centimeters	*0.0328*	feet
meters	*39.3701*	inches
meters	*3.2808*	feet
meters	*1.0936*	yards
kilometers	*0.621*	miles
square centimeters	*0.155*	square inches
square meters	*10.7639*	square feet
square meters	*1.196*	square yards
hectares	*2.471*	acres
cubic centimeters	*0.061*	cubic inches
cubic meters	*35.3147*	cubic feet
cubic meters	*1.308*	cubic yards
liters	*1.0567*	quarts (liquid)
grams	*0.0353*	ounces
kilograms	*2.2046*	pounds

→Why was Timbuktu important in the 1300s? PAGE 320

▼ *Sumerian temple*

◀ *hieroglyphics*

THE ANCIENT MIDDLE EAST

4000–3000 B.C. The world's first cities are built by the Sumerian peoples in Mesopotamia, now southern Iraq. Sumerians develop a kind of writing called **cuneiform**. Egyptians develop a kind of writing called **hieroglyphics**.

2700 B.C. Egyptians begin building the great pyramids in the desert.

1792 B.C. Some of the first written laws are created in Babylonia. They are called the **Code of Hammurabi**.

1200 B.C. Hebrew people settle in Canaan in Palestine after escaping from slavery in Egypt. They are led by the prophet Moses.

1000 B.C. King David unites the Hebrews.

ANCIENT PALESTINE Palestine is invaded by many different peoples after 1000 B.C., including the Babylonians, Egyptians, Persians, and Romans.

336 B.C. Alexander the Great, King of Macedonia, builds an empire from Egypt to India. ▼

ISLAM: A RELIGION GROWS IN THE MIDDLE EAST A.D. 610–632 Around 610, the prophet Muhammad starts to proclaim and teach Islam. This religion spreads from Arabia to all the neighboring regions in the Middle East and North Africa. Its followers are called Muslims.

The Koran

THE KORAN
The holy book of Islam is the Koran. It was related by Muhammad beginning in 611.

THE SPREAD OF ISLAM
The Arab armies that move across North Africa bring great change:

- The people who live there are converted to Islam.
- The Arabic language replaces many local languages as an official language. North Africa is still an Arabic-speaking region today, and Islam is the major faith.

63 B.C. Romans conquer Palestine and make it part of their empire.

Around 4 B.C. Jesus Christ, the founder of the Christian religion, is born in Bethlehem. He is crucified about A.D. 29.

A.D. 632 Muhammad dies. By now, Islam is accepted in Arabia as a religion.

641 Arab Muslims conquer the Persians.

Late 600s Islam begins to spread to the west into Africa and Spain.

THE MIDDLE EAST

THE UMAYYAD AND ABBASID DYNASTIES The Umayyads (661–750) and the Abbasids (750–1256) are the first two Muslim-led dynasties. Both empires include northern Africa and the Middle East.

711–732 Umayyads invade Europe but are defeated by Frankish leader Charles Martel in France. This defeat halts the spread of Islam into Western Europe.

1071 Muslim Turks conquer Jerusalem.

1095–1291 Europeans try to take back Jerusalem and other parts of the Middle East for Christians during the Crusades.

1300–1900s The Ottoman Turks, who are Muslims, create a huge empire, covering the Middle East, North Africa, and part of Eastern Europe. European countries take over portions of it beginning in the 1800s.

1914–1918 In World War I, the British officer known as Lawrence of Arabia▶ leads an Arab revolt against Turkish rule. After the war, most of the Middle East falls under British or French control.

1921 Two new Arab kingdoms are created: Transjordan and Iraq.

1922 Egypt becomes independent from Great Britain.

1945 After World War II, many Jews who survived the Holocaust migrate to Palestine.

1948 The state of Israel is created.

THE ARAB-ISRAELI WARS Arab countries near Israel (Egypt, Iraq, Jordan, Lebanon, and Syria) attack the new country in 1948 but fail to destroy it. Israel and its neighbors fight wars again in 1956, 1967, and 1973. Israel wins each war. In the 1967 war, Israel captures the Sinai Peninsula and Gaza from Egypt, the Golan Heights from Syria, and the West Bank from Jordan.

Anwar al-Sadat, Jimmy Carter, and Menachem Begin

1979 Egypt and Israel sign a peace treaty. Israel returns the Sinai to Egypt.▲

THE MIDDLE EAST AND OIL Many countries rely on oil imports from the region, which has more than half the world's crude oil reserves.

1991 The U.S. and its allies go to war with Iraq after Iraq invades Kuwait. Iraq is defeated and forced out of Kuwait.

2003–2011 The U.S. and its allies invade Iraq in 2003 and remove the regime of dictator Saddam Hussein. The U.S. declares the war officially over in December 2011.

2011 In what became known as the "Arab spring," demonstrations against repressive governments break out in the region, including in Syria, Lebanon, Egypt, Bahrain, and Yemen. Leaders in Egypt and Yemen are overthrown.

2012 Many countries oppose Iran's reported attempts to develop a nuclear weapon.

ANCIENT AFRICA

Sahara Desert

ANCIENT AFRICA In ancient times, northern Africa was dominated by the Egyptians, Greeks, and Romans. Ancient Africans south of the Sahara Desert did not have written languages. What we learn about them comes from weapons, tools, and other items from their civilization.

2000 B.C. The Nubian Kingdom of Kush, rich with gold, ivory, and jewels, arises south of Egypt. It is a major center of art, learning, and trade until around A.D. 350.

1000 B.C. Bantu-speaking people around Cameroon begin an 1,800-year expansion into much of eastern and southern Africa.

500 B.C. Carthage, an empire centered in Tunisia, becomes rich and powerful through trading. Its ports span the African coast of the Mediterranean. Rome defeats Carthage and

◀ Hannibal, its most famous leader, during the second Punic War, from 218 to 201 B.C.

• The Nok in Nigeria are the earliest users of iron for tools and weapons south of the Sahara Desert. They are also known for their terracotta sculptures.

• The Christian Kingdom of Aksum in northern Ethiopia becomes a wealthy trading center on the Red Sea.

By A.D. 700 Ghana, the first known empire south of the Sahara Desert, takes power through trade around the upper Senegal and Niger Rivers. Its Mande people control the trade in gold from nearby mines to Arabs in the north.

By 900 Arab Muslim merchants bring Islam to the Bantu speakers along the east coast of Africa, creating the Swahili language and culture. Traders in Kenya and Tanzania export ivory, slaves, perfumes, and gold to Asia.

1054–1145 Islamic Berbers unite into the Almoravid Kingdom centered at Marrakech, Morocco. They spread into Ghana and southern Spain.

1230–1400s A Mande prince named Sundiata (the "Lion King") forms the Mali Kingdom where Ghana once stood. Timbuktu becomes its main city.

TIMBUKTU Located on the trade routes between North Africa and West Africa, Timbuktu was one of the wealthiest cities in Africa in the 1300s, as well as a center for scholarship. Gold, ivory, cloth, salt, and slaves were all traded in Timbuktu.

1250–1400s Great Zimbabwe becomes the largest settlement (12,000–20,000 Bantu-speaking people) in southern Africa.

1464–1591 As Mali loses power, Songhai rises to become the third and final great empire of western Africa.

1481 Portugal sets up the first permanent European trading post south of the Sahara Desert at Elmina, Ghana. Slaves, in addition to gold and ivory, are soon exported.

1483–1665 Kongo, the most powerful kingdom on central Africa's west coast, provides thousands of slaves each year for Portugal. Portugal's colony Angola overtakes the Kongo in 1665.

AFRICA

1650–1810 Slave trading peaks across the "Slave Coast" from eastern Ghana to western Nigeria as African states sell tens of thousands of captured foes each year to European traders.

THE AFRICAN SLAVE TRADE
African slaves are taken to the Caribbean to harvest sugar on European plantations and then taken to South America and the United States. The ships from Africa are overcrowded and diseased. About 20% of the slaves die during the long journey.

1652 The Dutch East India Company sets up a supply camp in southern Africa at the Cape of Good Hope (later Cape Town). Dutch settlers and French Protestants (Huguenots) establish Cape Colony. Their descendants are known as the Boers or Afrikaners.

1803 Denmark is the first European country to ban slave trading. Britain follows in 1807, the U.S. in 1808. Most European nations ban the trade by 1820, but illegal trading continues for decades.

1814 Britain purchases the Dutch South African colony at Cape Town. British colonists arrive after 1820.

1835–1843 The "Great Trek" (march) of the Boers away from British Cape Town takes place.

1884–1885 European nations meet in Berlin and agree to divide control of Africa. The "Scramble for Africa" lasts until World War I.

1899–1902 Great Britain and the Boers fight in South Africa in the Boer War. The Boers accept British rule but are allowed a role in government.

1948 The white Afrikaner-dominated South African government creates the policy of apartheid ("apartness"), the total separation of races. Blacks are banned from many public places.

1957 Ghana gains independence from Britain, becoming the first territory in Africa below the Sahara to regain freedom from European rule. Over the next 20 years, the rest of Africa gains independence.

1990–1994 South Africa abolishes apartheid. In 1994, Nelson Mandela becomes South Africa's first black president.

1994 Members of Rwanda's Hutu majority launch a genocide against the country's Tutsi minority, killing about 800,000 people.

1998–2004 Fighting in the Democratic Republic of the Congo involves 9 nations. About 4 million die, mostly from starvation and disease.

2006 Ellen Johnson-Sirleaf becomes president of Liberia and Africa's first elected female leader.

2011 South Sudan becomes Africa's newest independent nation, on July 9. Protesters in Tunisia overthrow that country's longtime dictator. In Libya, rebels helped by Western governments overthrow dictator Muammar al-Qaddafi. Johnson-Sirleaf and another Liberian leader share the Nobel Peace Prize.

Libyans celebrate Qaddafi's downfall

ANCIENT ASIA

The Great Wall

3500 B.C. People settle in the Indus River Valley of India and Pakistan and the Yellow River Valley of China.

Around 1523 B.C. Shang peoples in China build walled towns and use a kind of writing based on pictures. This writing develops into the writing Chinese people use today.

Around 1050 B.C. Zhou peoples in China overthrow the Shang and control large territories.

563 B.C. Siddhartha Gautama is born in India. He becomes known as the Buddha—the "Enlightened One"—and is the founder of the Buddhist religion (Buddhism). ▶

551 B.C. The Chinese philosopher Confucius is born. His teachings—especially rules about how people should treat each other—spread throughout China and are still followed. ▼

320–232 B.C.
- Northern India is united under the emperor Chandragupta Maurya.
- Asoka, emperor of India, sends Buddhist missionaries throughout southern Asia to spread the Buddhist religion.

221 B.C. The Chinese begin building the Great Wall. Its main section is more than 2,000 miles long and is meant to keep invading peoples out.

202 B.C. The Han people of China win control of all of China.

A.D. 320 The Gupta Empire controls northern India. The Guptas, who are Hindus, drive the Buddhist religion out of India. They are well known for their many advances in mathematics and medicine.

618 The Tang dynasty begins in China. The Tang dynasty is well known for music, poetry, and painting. They export silk and porcelains as far away as Africa.

THE SILK ROAD Around 100 B.C., only the Chinese know how to make silk. To get this light, comfortable material, Europeans send fortunes in glass, gold, jade, and other items to China. The exchanges between Europeans and Chinese create one of the greatest trading routes in history—the Silk Road. Chinese inventions such as paper and gunpowder are also spread via the Silk Road. Europeans find out how to make silk around A.D. 500, but trade continues until about 1400.

960 The Northern Sung dynasty in China makes advances in banking and paper money. China's population of 50 million doubles over 200 years, thanks to improved ways of farming that lead to greater food production.

ASIA

◀ **1000** The Samurai, a warrior people, become powerful in Japan. They live by a code of honor known as *Bushido*.

1180 The Khmer Empire in Cambodia becomes widely known for its beautiful temples.

1206 The Mongol leader Genghis Khan creates an empire that stretches from China to India, Russia, and Eastern Europe.

1264 Kublai Khan, grandson of Genghis Khan, rules China as emperor from his new capital at Beijing.

1368 The Ming dynasty comes to power in China and drives out the Mongols.

1526 The Mughal Empire in India begins under Babur. The Mughals are Muslims who invade and conquer India.

1644 The Ming dynasty in China is overthrown by the Manchu peoples.

1839 The Opium War takes place in China between the Chinese and the British. The British and other Western powers want to control trade in Asia. The Chinese want the British to stop selling opium to the Chinese. Britain wins the war in 1842.

1858 The French begin to take control of Indochina (Southeast Asia).

1868 In Japan, Emperor Meiji comes to power. Western ideas begin to influence the Japanese.

THE JAPANESE IN ASIA In the 1930s, Japan begins to invade some of its neighbors. In 1941, the United States and Japan go to war after Japan attacks the U.S. Navy base at Pearl Harbor, Hawaii.

1945 Japan is defeated in World War II after the U.S. drops atomic bombs on the Japanese cities of Hiroshima and Nagasaki.

1947 India and Pakistan become independent from Great Britain.

1949 China comes under the rule of the Communists led by Mao Zedong, ▶ who abolishes private property and businesses.

1950–1953 THE KOREAN WAR Communist North Korea invades South Korea. The U.S. and allies fight the invasion. China sides with North Korea. The fighting ends in a truce in 1953.

1954–1975 THE VIETNAM WAR The French are defeated in Indochina in 1954 by Vietnamese nationalists. The U.S. sends troops in 1965 to help South Vietnam fight against the Communists in the North. The U.S. withdraws in 1973. In 1975, South Vietnam is taken over by North Vietnam.

1989 Chinese students protest for democracy, but the protests are crushed by the army in Beijing's Tiananmen Square.

1997 Britain returns Hong Kong to China.

2004 A powerful earthquake in the Indian Ocean in December sets off huge waves (tsunamis) that kill more than 225,000 people in Indonesia, Sri Lanka, and other countries.

THE U.S. IN AFGHANISTAN U.S.-led military action overthrows the Taliban regime in Afghanistan in 2001 and seeks to root out terrorists there. In 2009 and 2010, the United States sends additional troops to fight the Taliban, which had regained strength. The U.S. announces plans to remove most troops by 2014.

2011 A massive earthquake and tsunami in March cause widespread destruction and thousands of deaths in northeastern Japan. In North Korea, longtime dictator Kim Jong Il dies and is replaced by his son, Kim Jong Un.

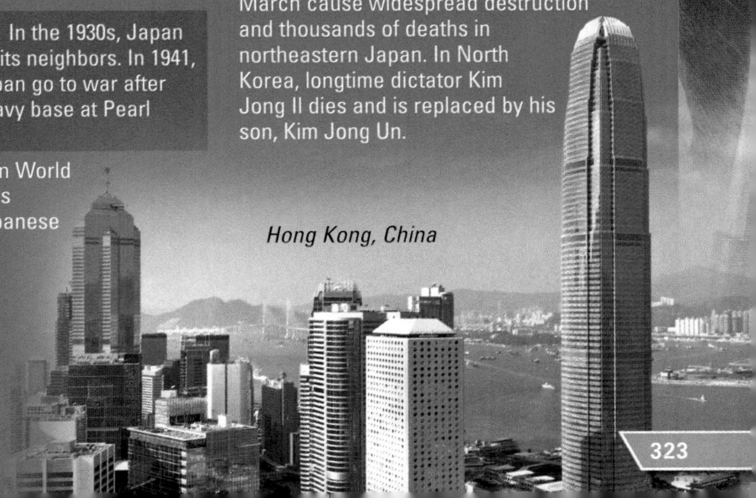

Hong Kong, China

ANCIENT EUROPE

Stonehenge, England

4000 B.C. People in Europe start building monuments out of large stones called megaliths, such as Stonehenge in England.

2500 B.C.–1200 B.C.

The Minoans and the Mycenaeans

- People on the island of Crete (Minoans) in the Mediterranean Sea build great palaces and become sailors and traders.
- People from Mycenae invade Crete and destroy the power of the Minoans.

THE TROJAN WAR The Trojan War is a conflict between invading Greeks and the people of Troas (Troy) in southwestern Turkey around 1200 B.C. Although little is known today about the real war, according to legend, a group of Greek soldiers hides inside a huge wooden horse. The horse is pulled into the city of Troy. Then the soldiers jump out and conquer Troy. ▼

900–600 B.C. Celtic peoples in Northern Europe settle on farms and in villages and learn to mine for iron ore.

600 B.C. Etruscan peoples take over most of Italy. They build many cities and become traders.

SOME ACHIEVEMENTS OF THE GREEKS

The early Greeks are responsible for:

- the first governments elected by the people.
- great poets such as Homer, who composed the *Iliad* and the *Odyssey*,
- great thinkers such as Socrates, Plato, and Aristotle,
- great architecture, including the Parthenon ▶ on the Acropolis in Athens.

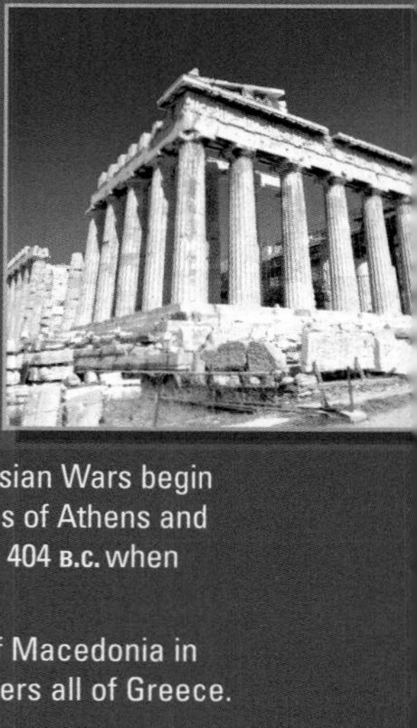

431 B.C. The Peloponnesian Wars begin between the Greek cities of Athens and Sparta. The wars end in 404 B.C. when Sparta wins.

338 B.C. King Philip II of Macedonia in northern Greece conquers all of Greece.

336 B.C. Philip's son Alexander the Great becomes king. He creates an empire from the Mediterranean Sea to India. For the next 300 years, Greek culture dominates this area.

264 B.C.–A.D. 476 **THE ROMAN EMPIRE**

The city of Rome in Italy begins to expand and capture surrounding lands. The Romans gradually build a great empire and control all of the Mediterranean region. At its height, the Roman Empire includes Western Europe, Greece, Egypt, and much of the Middle East. It lasts until A.D. 476.

ROMAN ACHIEVEMENTS

- Roman law; many of our laws are based on Roman law.
- Great roads to connect their huge empire; the Appian Way, south of Rome, is a Roman road that is still in use today.
- Aqueducts to bring water to large cities.
- Great sculpture; Roman statues can still be seen in Europe.
- Great architecture; the Colosseum, which still stands in Rome today, is an example.
- Great writers, such as the poet Virgil, who wrote the *Aeneid*.

49 B.C. A civil war breaks out that destroys Rome's republican form of government.

45 B.C. Julius Caesar becomes the sole ruler of Rome but is murdered one year later by rivals. ▶

27 B.C. Octavian becomes the first emperor of Rome. He takes the name Augustus.

THE CHRISTIAN FAITH Christians believe that Jesus Christ is the Son of God. The history and beliefs of Christianity are found in the New Testament of the Bible. Christianity spreads slowly throughout the Roman Empire. The Romans try to stop the new religion, and they persecute Christians. Over time, however, more and more Romans become Christian.

THE BYZANTINE EMPIRE, centered in modern-day Turkey, is the eastern half of the old Roman Empire. Byzantine rulers extend their power into western Europe. Constantinople (now Istanbul, Turkey) becomes the capital of the Byzantine Empire in A.D. 330.

A.D. 313 The Roman Emperor Constantine gives full rights to Christians. He eventually becomes a Christian himself.

410 The Visigoths and other barbarian tribes from northern Europe invade the Roman Empire and begin to take over its lands.

476 The last Roman emperor, Romulus Augustus, is overthrown.

768 Charlemagne ▶ becomes king of the Franks in northern Europe. He rules a kingdom that includes most of France, Germany, and northern Italy.

800 Feudalism becomes important in Europe. Feudalism means that poor farmers are allowed to farm a lord's land in return for certain services to the lord.

896 Magyar peoples found Hungary.

800s–900s Viking warriors and traders from Scandinavia begin to move into the British Isles, France, and parts of the Mediterranean.

989 The Russian state of Kiev becomes Christian.

Colosseum, Rome

EUROPE

Venice, Italy

1066 William of Normandy, a Frenchman, successfully invades England and makes himself king. He is known as William the Conqueror.

1096–1291 THE CRUSADES Christian leaders send a series of armies to try to capture Jerusalem from the Muslims. The Christians do not succeed, but trade increases between the Middle East and Europe.

King John

1215 The Magna Carta is agreed to by King John of England and the nobility. The king agrees that he does not have absolute power and has to obey the laws of the land. The document is an important step toward democracy.

1290 The Ottoman Empire begins. It is controlled by Turkish Muslims who conquer lands in the eastern Mediterranean and the Middle East.

1337 The Hundred Years' War begins in Europe between France and England. The war lasts until 1453 when France wins.

1348 The bubonic plague (Black Death) begins in Europe. As much as one-third of the whole population of Europe dies from this disease.

1453 The Ottoman Turks capture the city of Constantinople and rename it Istanbul.

1517 THE REFORMATION The Protestant Reformation splits European Christians apart. It starts when German priest Martin Luther breaks away from the Roman Catholic pope.

1534 King Henry VIII of England breaks away from the Roman Catholic church. He names himself head of the English (Anglican) Church. ▶

1558 The reign of King Henry's daughter Elizabeth I begins in England.

1588 The Spanish Armada (fleet of warships) is defeated by the English Navy as Spain tries to invade England.

1600s The Ottoman Turks expand their empire through most of eastern and central Europe.

1618 Much of Europe is destroyed in the Thirty Years' War, which ends in 1648.

1642 The English Civil War begins. King Charles I fights against the forces of the Parliament. The king is defeated and is executed in 1649. His son, Charles II, returns as king in 1660.

1762 Catherine the Great becomes Empress of Russia. She extends the Russian Empire.

1789 THE FRENCH REVOLUTION The French Revolution begins. It brings a temporary end to royal rule in France. During the revolution, dictators take control, and many people die on the guillotine. King Louis XVI and Queen Marie Antoinette are executed in 1793.

1799 Napoleon Bonaparte, an army officer, becomes dictator of France. Under his rule, France conquers most of Europe by 1812.

1815 Napoleon's forces are defeated by the British and German armies at Waterloo (in Belgium). Napoleon is exiled to a remote island and dies there in 1821.

1848 Revolutions break out in countries of Europe. People force their rulers to make more democratic changes.

1914–1918 **WORLD WAR I IN EUROPE** At the start of World War I in Europe, Germany, Austria-Hungary, and the Ottoman Empire oppose Britain, France, Russia—later joined by the U.S. (the Allies). The Allies win in 1918.

1917 Tsar Nicholas II ▶ is overthrown in the Russian Revolution. The Bolsheviks (Communists) under Vladimir Lenin take control. Millions are starved, sent to labor camps, or executed under Joseph Stalin (1929–1953).

▲*Italian leader Benito Mussolini and Adolf Hitler*

THE RISE OF HITLER
Adolf Hitler becomes dictator of Germany in 1933. He joins forces with rulers in Italy and Japan to form the Axis powers. In World War II (1939–1945), the Axis powers are defeated by the Allies— Great Britain, the Soviet Union, the U.S., and others. During his rule, Hitler's Nazis kill millions of Jews and other people in the Holocaust.

1990s Communist governments in Eastern Europe are replaced by democratic ones. Divided Germany is reunited, and the Soviet Union breaks up. The European Union (EU) forms.

2009–2012 Europe goes into a major economic recession, and unemployment surges. Some countries' economies later begin to improve, but others remain weak.

2012 In Great Britain, London hosts the Summer Olympics.

All About AUSTRALIA

Aborigines (native peoples) have lived there for more than 60,000 years. In the 17th century, Portuguese, Dutch, and Spanish expeditions explored Australian coasts. In the 1770s, Capt. James Cook of Britain made three voyages to the continent, cementing Britain's claims of ownership. On May 13, 1787, Capt. Arthur Phillip brought 11 ships from Britain, carrying convicts and guards. Although the first communities were prison colonies, other immigrants settled around the continent over the 19th century. Wool and mining were major industries. Australia was established as a commonwealth of Great Britain on January 1, 1901. Today, it is a country of 22 million people. It is famous for both its modern cities and the spectacular beauty of its rugged interior.

Uluru-Kata Tjuta National Park, Australia

THE AMERICAS

Pyramid at Teotihuacán

10,000–8000 B.C. People in North and South America gather plants for food and hunt animals using stone-pointed spears.

Around 3000 B.C. People in Central America begin farming, growing corn and beans for food.

1500 B.C. Mayan people in Central America begin to live in small villages.

500 B.C. People in North America begin to hunt buffalo to use for meat and for clothing.

100 B.C. The city of Teotihuacán is founded in Mexico. It becomes the center of a huge empire extending from central Mexico to Guatemala. Teotihuacán contains many large pyramids and temples.

A.D. 150 Mayan people in Guatemala build many centers for religious ceremonies. They create a calendar and learn mathematics and astronomy.

900 Toltec warriors in Mexico begin to invade lands of Mayan people. Mayans leave their old cities and move to the Yucatan Peninsula of Mexico.

1000 Native Americans in the southwestern United States begin to live in settlements called pueblos. They learn to farm.

1325 Mexican Indians known as Aztecs create the huge city of Tenochtitlán and rule a large empire in Mexico. They are warriors who practice human sacrifice.

1492 Christopher Columbus sails from Europe across the Atlantic Ocean and lands in the Bahamas, in the Caribbean Sea. This marks the first step toward the founding of European settlements in the Americas.

1500 Portuguese explorers reach Brazil and claim it for Portugal.

Christopher Columbus ▶

1519 Spanish conqueror Hernán Cortés ▼ travels into the Aztec Empire in search of gold. The Aztecs are defeated in 1521, and Spain takes control of Mexico.

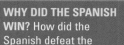

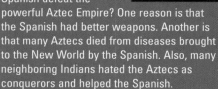

WHY DID THE SPANISH WIN? How did the Spanish defeat the powerful Aztec Empire? One reason is that the Spanish had better weapons. Another is that many Aztecs died from diseases brought to the New World by the Spanish. Also, many neighboring Indians hated the Aztecs as conquerors and helped the Spanish.

1534 Jacques Cartier of France explores Canada.

1583 The first English colony in Canada is set up in Newfoundland.

1607 English colonists led by Captain John Smith settle in Jamestown, Virginia. Virginia becomes the oldest of the thirteen colonies that will form the United States.

1619 First African slaves arrive in English-controlled America.

1682 The French explorer René-Robert Cavelier, sieur de La Salle, sails down the Mississippi River. The area is named Louisiana after the French King Louis XIV.

EUROPEAN COLONIES By 1700, most of the Americas are under European control.

Spain: Florida, southwestern United States, Mexico, Central America, western South America

Portugal: eastern South America

France: central United States, parts of Canada

England: eastern U.S., parts of Canada

Holland: West Indies, eastern South America

1756–1763 France loses its lands in eastern North America to Britain in the French and Indian War.

1775–1783 AMERICAN REVOLUTION The American Revolution begins in 1775 when the first shot is fired in Lexington, Massachusetts. The thirteen British colonies that become the United States officially gain independence in 1783.

SIMÓN BOLÍVAR: LIBERATOR OF SOUTH AMERICA

In 1810, Simón Bolívar begins a revolt against Spain. As a result of his leadership, nine South American countries gain their independence by the 1820s.

Becoming Independent

Most countries of Latin America gained independence from Spain.

COUNTRY	YEAR OF INDEPENDENCE
Argentina	1816
Bolivia	1825
Brazil	1822[1]
Chile	1818
Colombia	1819
Ecuador	1822
Guyana	1966[2]
Mexico	1821
Paraguay	1811
Peru	1824
Suriname	1975[3]
Uruguay	1825
Venezuela	1821

(1) From Portugal. (2) From Britain. (3) From the Netherlands.

1846–1848 MEXICAN-AMERICAN WAR In 1846, Mexico and the United States go to war. Mexico loses most of the Southwest and California to the U.S.

1867 Canadian provinces are united as the Dominion of Canada.

1898 SPANISH-AMERICAN WAR Spain and the U.S. fight a brief war in 1898. Spain loses its colonies Cuba, Puerto Rico, and the Philippines.

1911 A revolution in Mexico that began in 1910 overthrows Porfirio Díaz. ▼

1959 Fidel Castro becomes president of Cuba, which becomes a Communist country allied with the Soviet Union.

1962 U.S. President John F. Kennedy forces the Soviet Union to withdraw missiles it had installed in Cuba.

1994 The North American Free Trade Agreement (NAFTA) increases trade between the U.S., Canada, and Mexico.

2001 On September 11, Muslim terrorists crash planes into U.S. targets, killing about 3,000 people. The U.S. launches a "war on terrorism."

2009 Barack Obama becomes the first African American president of the U.S.

2010 More than 220,000 people are killed in a devastating earthquake in Haiti.

2011 U.S. Navy Seals enter a compound in Pakistan and kill Osama bin Laden, who was behind the September 11, 2001, terrorist attack on the U.S.

THEN & NOW 2013

10 YEARS AGO—2003

THEN: An invasion of Iraq, led by the U.S. and Britain, topples Saddam Hussein's government in three weeks.

NOW: After withdrawing troops from Iraq in 2011, the U.S. government plans to reduce the size of its embassy, which is currently the world's largest.

THEN: The space shuttle *Columbia* explodes shortly after takeoff, killing all seven crew members.

NOW: After 135 space shuttle missions, NASA retires the 30-year-old program and sends the space shuttles to museums around the U.S.

50 YEARS AGO—1963

THEN: Civil rights leader Martin Luther King Jr. helps organize the March on Washington, where he gives his famous "I Have a Dream" speech (right) about the goal of equal treatment and opportunity.

NOW: The Martin Luther King Jr. National Memorial in Washington, D.C., opened in 2011, draws thousands of visitors each year. The 4-acre memorial is part of the National Mall.

THEN: John F. Kennedy, the 35th U.S. president, is shot and killed in Dallas, Texas.

NOW: Founded in 1936 and later named for the slain president, Harvard's Kennedy School of Government (located in Cambridge, Massachusetts) has more than 1,000 full-time students.

100 YEARS AGO—1913

THEN: Henry Ford develops his moving assembly line (right), which produces the popular Model T car. More than 15 million of the so-called Tin Lizzies are sold before their production ends in 1927.

NOW: With about 70 plants and more than 160,000 workers, the Ford Motor Company manufactures or distributes cars on six continents.

THEN: The 16th and 17th amendments to the U.S. Constitution are ratified. The 16th allows the U.S. government to collect income tax, and the 17th requires the popular election of U.S. senators.

NOW: The Constitution has a total of 27 amendments, including those guaranteeing women the right to vote and lowering the voting age to 18.

500 YEARS AGO—1513

Explorer Juan Ponce de León sails from Puerto Rico in search of gold and a "fountain of youth." He lands near today's Saint Augustine and claims what is now Florida for Spain. Every year, the Spain-Florida Foundation presents the Juan Ponce de León Award to someone who has promoted understanding of the Hispanic community in the United States.

THEN & NOW 2014

10 YEARS AGO—2004

THEN: An underwater earthquake in the Indian Ocean causes a tsunami that kills more than 225,000 people in Southeast Asia.

NOW: Tsunami warning centers have been established in Indonesia, Australia, and New Zealand. Centers in the Caribbean and Mediterranean seas are planned.

THEN: George W. Bush, 43rd U.S. president, wins a second term, defeating U.S. senator John Kerry of Massachusetts in the national presidential election.

NOW: Completion of the George W. Bush Presidential Center, on the Southern Methodist University (SMU) campus in Dallas, Texas, is planned for 2013.

50 YEARS AGO—1964

THEN: The Summer Olympics, held in Tokyo, Japan, are Asia's first Olympic Games.

NOW: Sochi, Russia, is set to host the 2014 Winter Olympics. They will be the first Russian-hosted Winter Games.

THEN: After "I Want to Hold Your Hand" hits number one on the U.S. charts, the British rock group The Beatles performs live for the first time on American TV on the popular variety program *The Ed Sullivan Show.*

NOW: The Beatles remain the best-selling band ever, with more than 1 billion recordings sold.

100 YEARS AGO—1914

THEN: World War I begins—an international conflict between the Central Powers (mainly Germany, Austria-Hungary, and Turkey) and the Allied Powers (mainly France, Britain, Russia, Italy, Japan, and as of 1917, the U.S.).

NOW: Growing out of efforts begun in the 1950s by European countries to work together for growth and peace, the European Union (EU) is an economic and political confederation of more than two dozen nations.

THEN: The Panama Canal, one of the world's greatest engineering projects, opens officially, connecting the Pacific and Atlantic oceans.

NOW: An expansion of the Panama Canal doubling its shipping capacity is scheduled for completion in 2014.

WOMEN IN HISTORY

69–30 B.C. CLEOPATRA

Queen of Egypt who used her association with Roman leaders Julius Caesar and Mark Antony to increase her power. After her father's death, Cleopatra and her brother Ptolemy jointly ruled. By custom, they were forced to marry each other. After Caesar defeated her enemies, she lived for a time with Caesar in Rome, but she later went back to Egypt, where she met and married Antony.

1533–1603 QUEEN ELIZABETH I

One of the greatest rulers of England. She was the daughter of King Henry VIII and his second wife, Anne Boleyn. Elizabeth ruled for 45 years, until her death. She built England into a world power, especially after her navy's victory in 1588 over the Spanish Armada, an invasion fleet sent by Spain's king, Philip II. Elizabeth never married. She used the possibility of marriage to increase her political power.

1717–1780 MARIA THERESA

Empress of Austria-Hungary for 40 years who ruled over much of Eastern Europe as well as other areas. When she came to the throne, many regions refused to accept a woman as ruler, which led to a nine-year war. As empress, Maria Theresa was a strong leader who put in place many educational reforms and encouraged the growth of commerce and industry. Among her 16 children was Marie-Antoinette, who as queen of France was guillotined during the French Revolution.

1775–1817 JANE AUSTEN

English author whose works remain as popular today as when they were written 200 years ago. Her six novels focus on the daily lives of families in small, rural villages and gently mock social conventions. Austen began writing stories as a young child. As an adult, she traveled very little and disliked large cities. Four of her books, including her most famous, *Pride and Prejudice*, were published in her lifetime (without her name on them, since it was not acceptable for a woman to be an author). All her books have been made into movies, some many times.

1797–1883 SOJOURNER TRUTH

American abolitionist and activist (born Isabella Baumfree). She was raised as a slave on an estate in New York state. She escaped in 1826. In 1843, she became a traveling preacher and took the name Sojourner Truth. She traveled widely, speaking out against slavery and for women's rights.

1821–1910 ELIZABETH BLACKWELL

First woman to receive a degree from a medical school in the U.S. At first she couldn't find a medical school that would accept her, but finally she did—and she graduated first in her class. She later trained nurses and founded the New York Infirmary for Women and Children. She also started a medical school for women.

1907–1964 RACHEL CARSON

American scientist and author. She is often credited with launching the modern environmental movement with the publication of her book *Silent Spring* (1962), about the dangers of pesticides. (The book brought her much criticism from the chemical industry.) Carson worked for many years as a scientist with the U.S. Fish and Wildlife Service.

1917–1984 INDIRA GANDHI

India's powerful prime minister from 1966 to 1977 and again from 1980 to 1984. The daughter of Jawaharlal Nehru, the first prime minister of India after independence, she helped India modernize and grow into a world power. She negotiated a peace with rival Pakistan, reduced the food shortages that had long been a problem for India, and developed a nuclear weapon. However, she also took on unpopular dictatorial powers and was defeated for reelection in 1977. She returned to power in 1980, but four years later, she was assassinated.

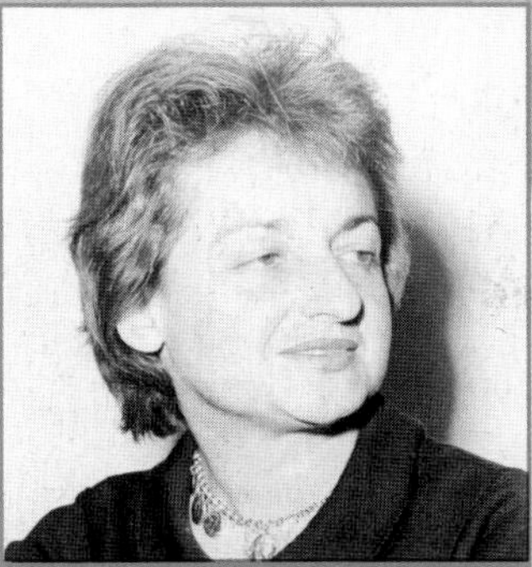

1921–2006 BETTY FRIEDAN

American leader of the women's movement that began in the 1960s. A graduate of Smith College and a psychologist, Friedan gave up her career after having children to stay home with them. Bored and frustrated, she surveyed other Smith graduates. Her study developed into *The Feminine Mystique* (1963), which urged women to pursue careers. She cofounded the National Organization for Women and remained an activist all her life, working for equal rights for women and an end to discrimination against women.

1929–1945 ANNE FRANK

German-born Jewish girl. Her diary of her family's two years in hiding in an Amsterdam office building during the German occupation of the Netherlands in World War II became a worldwide classic in literature. The Gestapo arrested the occupants of her hiding place after acting on a tip. Frank died in the Bergen-Belsen concentration camp in 1945. Her diary was published in the U.S. as *Anne Frank: The Diary of a Young Girl.*

1943– BILLIE JEAN KING

American tennis player who became a symbol for women's equality. King won 12 Grand Slam singles titles. But her most famous victory may have been in the 1973 "Battle of the Sexes" match, when she beat male player Bobby Riggs. King helped start the first women's pro tennis tour in 1970. In 1971, she became the first woman athlete to win more than $100,000 in one season.

1945– AUNG SAN SUU KYI

Burmese political activist and winner of the Nobel Peace Prize (1991). Suu Kyi's father is considered the founder of modern Burma, now called Myanmar. Suu Kyi opposed the country's military government and became a leader of the pro-democracy movement. She spent many years under house arrest in Myanmar but, as the country democratized, was released in 2010. She was elected to Parliament in 2012 and became the leader of the opposition.

ANSWERS

Animals Word Scramble p. 31

Florida panther
cheetah
colossal squid
kangaroo
giant panda
Bactrian camel

Celebrity Crossword Puzzle p. 43

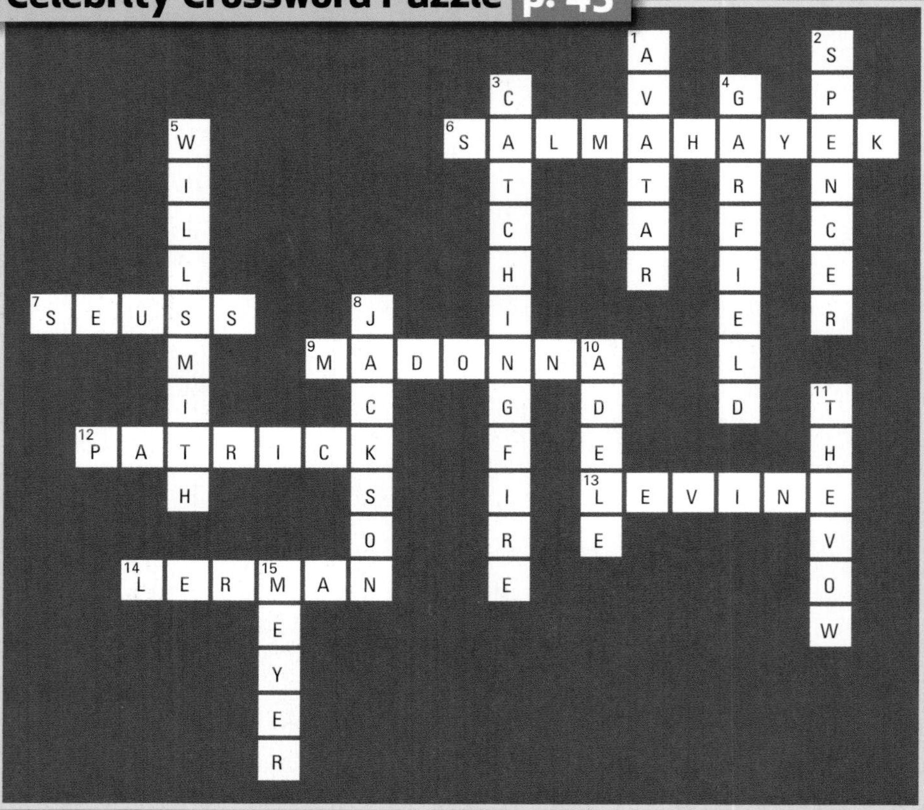

Building Quiz p. 54

Alhambra	Palace in Spain
The Crooked House	Most-photographed building in Poland
Borobudur Temple	Biggest tourist attraction in Indonesia
Burj Khalifa	Tallest building in the world

Movies & TV Word Search p. 131

X	Y	C	H	E	M	W	G	J	V	D	O	I	R	R
E	A	X	A	T	D	G	L	I	U	M	D	I	Q	R
I	Q	R	V	T	J	A	C	D	U	G	I	P	N	F
S	J	B	O	U	C	T	Q	M	R	H	K	S	T	B
S	C	U	G	L	O	H	M	N	V	H	D	O	W	T
E	B	J	C	R	E	U	I	E	T	G	R	S	X	O
J	A	D	I	C	N	H	Z	N	C	Z	V	G	R	T
H	D	O	W	K	Q	P	T	E	G	T	B	H	R	A
Y	U	G	Y	L	I	M	A	F	T	F	S	P	C	L
S	Y	G	E	T	L	R	B	S	T	K	I	X	D	R
A	M	E	R	I	C	A	N	I	D	O	L	R	T	E
P	L	X	W	X	M	N	I	P	K	E	N	T	E	C
G	D	S	Y	N	S	I	C	K	K	S	X	I	S	A
M	Q	L	C	U	W	O	K	E	A	K	B	V	D	L
R	W	H	V	P	H	Q	F	S	P	B	B	V	K	L

Roman Numerals p. 179

Super Bowl XLVI was the 46th Super Bowl.
2012 = MMXII
Super Bowl XXI (21) was played in 1987.

Homework Tip: Decimals to Fractions p. 180

0.5 = 1/2   0.6 = 6/10   0.75 = 3 /4

Cross-Number Puzzle p. 181

[1] 2	[2] 1			[3] 9		[4] 1		[5] 1	[6] 2
	1			9		[7] 6	[8] 4		3
		[9] 1	[10] 4	7			6		5
[11] 1	[12] 2		0		[13] 9		[14] 8	6	7
	0			[15] 8	9		9		1
[16] 9	0			0			[17] 1	2	1
	0				[18] 1		0		1
		[19] 1	[20] 8		[21] 7	[22] 5		[23] 3	3
	[24] 3		[25] 5	[26] 5		2			1
[27] 1	0	0		[28] 2	3	4	5	6	7

Sports Star Challenge p. 239

A	V	E	N	U	S	H	A	U	N
H	E	I	S	M	A	N	R	V	Q
T	R	M	M	Y	J	J	O	H	N
W	L	K	J	O	H	L	S	C	E
K	A	M	U	K	O	A	B	E	L
C	N	A	I	S	M	I	T	H	S
U	D	W	Z	K	S	A	N	T	O
L	E	V	O	N	N	F	R	E	N
X	R	E	N	I	R	G	X	J	D

Match It! p. 239

1. (e)	2. (d)	3. (a)	4. (b)
5. (g)	6. (h)	7. (f)	8. (c)

INDEX

Note: Words in **boldface** refer to key content sections. Page numbers in **boldface** refer to maps.

D

E

J

K

L

PHOTO CREDITS

FRONT COVER: AP Images: Paul Jasienski (Manning). **Newscom:** Everett Collection (Bieber); Lionsgate/Album (*The Hunger Games*). **BACK COVER: Newscom:** DLM Press, PacificCoastNews (Stewart); Mike Gray/LFI/Photoshot (Drake); Pacific Rim Photo Press (Perry). **INTERIOR: 2K Sports:** 90 (*Major League Baseball 2K12*). **Alamy:** © Ashley Cooper, 73 (wind farm); © North Wind Picture Archives, 67 (Portugal). **AP Images:** 263 (Taft & Kennedy), 330 (King), 331 (Beatles); Ben Liebenberg, 18 (Manning); Bettmann/Corbis, 121 (Vietnam), 204 (Mayer), 226 (Naismith), 247 (helicopter), 263 (Reagan), 333 (Gandhi); Cal Sports Media, 228 (Summit), 235 (Marta); David Drapkin, 179 (Manning); David Goldman, 227 (Augustus), 265 (Romney); Evan Agostini, 88 (Lauren); Frank Augstein, 234 (women's soccer); Frank Micelotta/PictureGroup, 17 (Swift); Gerald Herbert, 226 (Hall of Fame inductees); Harry Harris, 333 (King); Jason Redmond, 88 (Stewart); Jeff Chiu, 19 (Cain); Jim Mone, 35 (Oldenburg); John Donegan, 236 (Djokovic); Julie Jacobson, 18 (Tebow), 19 (Griner); Kelly Kline, 21 (Griffin); Kerstin Joensson, 219 (Youth Olympics); Keystone/ Georgios Kefalas, 217 (badminton); Korean Central News Agency via Korea News Service, 7 (Kim Jong Un); Marcy Nighswander, 274 (Socks); Matt Sayles, 132 (Minaj); Michael Dwyer, 4, 134 (step dancing); Mike McCarn, 4, 230 (Newton); Nati Harnik, 124 (Buffett); Nigel Kinrade, 222 (Bayne & Stewart); North Wind Picture Archives, 279 (longhouse); Peter Byrne/PA Wire URN:11371307, 25 (Chester Zoo); Phil Sears, 262 (Biden); Picture Group, 132 (Phillips); Pier Paolo Cito, File, 7 (*Costa Concordia*); Pontus Lundahl, 20 (Vonn); PRNewsFoto/Nickelodeon, Robert Voets, 129 (Cruikshank); Rex Features, 3, 112 (glasses), 3, 12, 130 (*The Hunger Games*), 9 (Romney), 14 (*The Dark Knight Rises*), 15 (*The Vow*), 128 (Madonna), 262 (Obama); Scott Kirkland, 124 (Parker); Seth Wenig, 187 (Korean Americans); Stew Milne, 235 (Wondolowski); The News & Observer, Shawn Rocco, 9 (Obama); Tim Wright, 278 (hula). **Bridgeman Art Library International:** © Czartoryski Museum, Cracow, Poland, 35 (da Vinci); Metropolitan Museum of Art, New York, USA/Giraudon, 35 (Vermeer); The Stapleton Collection, 137 (Pandora). **Timothy Bryk:** 314 (1 yard). **Jimmy Carter Library and Museum:** 319 (Peace treaty). **Courtesy of Cedar Point:** 5, 249 (rollercoaster). **Central Intelligence Agency (CIA):** 172 (Slovakia), 174 (Swiss Alps). **J. Delanoy:** 239 (Stanley Cup). **Courtesy of Meredith Evans:** 3, 89. **Everett Collection:** Adam Rose/© Fox, 131 (*Glee*); © Copyright Fox 2000 Pictures, 129 (*Percy Jackson and the Olympians:The Lightning Thief*); © Sony Pictures, 14 (*The Pirates! Band of Misfits*); © Universal Pictures, 130 (*Dr. Suess' The Lorax*); Zade Rosenthal/© Walt Disney Studio Motion Pictures, 13 (*The Avengers*). **© The Exploratorium, www.exploratorium.edu:** 250 (Exploratorium). **Reprinted by permission of Farrar, Straus and Giroux, LLC:** 44 (Jacket design from DEAD END IN NORVELT by Jack Gantos. Jacket art copyright © 2011 by Greg Call). **J. Patrick Fischer:** 31 (tiger). **Flashlightmuseum.com:** 112 (Flash-Matic). **Getty Images:** Adam Pretty, 232 (Douglas); Adam Taylor/ABC, 134 (*Dancing With the Stars*); AFP, 321 (Libya); Al Bello, 231 (Luck); Al Diaz/Miami Herald/MCT, 226 (James); Alex Livesey – FIFA, 234 (Wambach); Alvis Upitis, 135 (orchestra); Archive Photos, 41 (Austen), 64 (Rathbone), 280 (Minuit), 281 (French & Indian War), 319 (Lawrence); Ben Hider, 50 (One World Trade Center); Bill Wallace/NY Daily News Archive, 69 (Long Island Express hurricane); Bob Levey, 225 (Rodriguez); The Bridgeman Art Library, 332 (Elizabeth I); Bryn Lennon, 218 (Olympic stadium); Bulent Kilic/AFP, 6 (Syria); Cavan Images, 3, 49 (young man); Chip Somodevilla, 250 (Saturn V),

261 (Supreme Court); Chris Trotman, 223 (Franchitti); Clive Brunskill, 237 (Bryan brothers); CQ-Roll Call Group, 91 (Smithsonian); Dan MacMedan/WireImage, 39 (Adele); Daniel Boczarski/Caesars Entertainment, 16 (Levine); Dave M. Benett, 4, 130 (Twilight actors); David Drapkin, 231 (Martin); David McNew, 8 (Martin), 78 (recycled bag); DEA/P. MANUSARDI/ VENERANDA BIBLIOTECA AMBROSIANA/De Agostini, 87 (ruff); Dennis Hallinan/Archive Photos, 91 (*Pac-Man*); Emmanuel Dunand/AFP, 34 (Degas); Eric McCandless/© ABC, 11 (*Pretty Little Liars*); Feng Li, 221 (fencing); FilmMagic, 45 (Meyer); Focus on Sport, 217 (John); Fred Vuich/Sports Illustrated, 20 (NASCAR); Frederick Breedon, 233 (Rinne); Gandee Vasan, 49 (girl); Gedeon Picaso/AFP, 215 (meterorite); Hulton Archive, 274 (Fala), 284 (WWI), 330 (Model T); Hulton Royals Collection, 325 (Charlemagne); James Devaney/WireImage, 86 (Diaz); Jamie Squire, 230 (Cruz & Woodsen); Jason Alden/Bloomberg, 3, 90 (*Angry Birds*); Jeff Kravitz/ FilmMagic, 189 (Gomez); Jeff Swenson, 264 (voters); Jemal Countess, 39 (Sendak); Jerry Cooke/Sports Illustrated, 220 (Rudolph); John W. McDonough/Sports Illustrated, 228 (Davis); Justin Lubin/NBC/NBCU Photo Ban, 11 (*The Voice*); Justin Sullivan, 124 (Zuckerberg); Ken Charnock, 39 (Angelou); Kevin Winter, 16 (Adele), 189 (Muppets), ACMA2012, 133 (Underwood); Kevork Djansezian, 91 (Sony PS Vita); Luciana Whitaker/LatinContent, 278 (Eskimo); Mark Davis/WireImage, 133 (Bieber); Michael Ochs Archives, 40 (Charles); Mike Ehrmann, 232 (McIlroy); Monty Brinton/CBS, 10 (*The Big Bang Theory*); New Zealand Ministry of Fisheries, 22 (squid); Odd Andersen/AFP, 188 (2012 Nobel laureates); Peter Adams, 195 (Hindu Holi); Peter Dazeley, 109 (picnic); Peter "Hopper" Stones/© ABC, 10 (*Modern Family*); Peter Kramer/NBC/ NBC NewsWire, 17 (One Direction); Popperfoto, 285 (Nixon), 326 (Henry VIII); Richard Bord, 238 (White); Richard Mackson/Sports Illustrated, 229 (McCarron); Romeo Gacad/AFP, 60 (Eid Al-Fitr); Ron Vesely/MLB Photos, 224 (Freese); Ronald Martinez, 21 (James); Scott Olson, 8 (tornado); Sean Gallup, 193 (synagogue); Stan Honda/AFP, 3, 64 (forensics); Stock Montage, 204 (Jenner); Superstock, 282 (Erie Canal); Taylor Hill, 38 (Patrick); Ted Aljibe/AFP, 3, 66 (earthquake); Tim Laman/National Geographic, 22 (bowerbird); Tim Rue/Bloomberg, 76 (hydrogen car); Time & Life Pictures, 263 (Wilson), 287 (Chavez); for TOMS, 88 (Mycoskie); Vladimir Rys, 221 (Special Olympics). **Glow Images:** Hill Street Studios, 108 (class). **Groundwood Books:** 47 (cover: *Sita's Ramayana*, by Samhita Arni). **HarperCollins Children's Books:** 44 (covers: *Heart and Soul: The Story of America and African Americans,* by Kadir Nelson, *Inside Out & Back Again*, by Thanhha Lai), 46 (cover: *Down the Rabbit Hole: An Echo Falls Mystery*, by Peter Abrahams), 47 (cover: *Justin Bieber: First Step 2 Forever: My Story*, by Justin Bieber). **Houghton Mifflin Harcourt Children's Book Group:** 48 (Lowry). **Infobase Learning:** 47 (cover: *The World Almanac for Kids 2013*). **International Astronomical Union:** Martin Kornmesser, 206 (sun & planets). **Joe Johnson:** 239 (NBA trophy). **Kansas City Public Library:** Mike Sinclair, 52 (Community Bookshelf). **John F. Kennedy Library:** 274 (Kennedy). **Courtesy of Richard King:** 205. **Library of Congress:** LC-DIG-jpd-02548, 36 (Japanese landscape); LC-DIG-ppmsca-19301, 38 (Lincoln); LC-USZ61-452, 41 (Alcott); LC-USZC4-10986, 71 (Lusitania); LC-USZ62-101298, 87 (corset); LC-DIG-pga-02616, 94 (Cartier); LC-USZC4-7503, 95 (Henson); LC-USZC4-2737, 120 (American Revolution); LC-USZC4-6893,120 (War of 1812); LC-B8184-10086, 120 (Civil War); LC-USZC4-2678, 120 (Spanish-American War); LC-USZC4-3859, 121 (World War I); LC-D4-22602, 245 (steamboat); LC-USZ62-43058, 245 (balloon); LC-USZ62-47579, 245 (streetcar); LC-DIG-highsm-11904, 246 (cable car); LC-USZ62-6166A, 246 (Wright plane); LC-USZ62-21222, 246 (Model T); 266-272 (U.S. Presidents, Washington-Clinton), LC-USZC2-3273, 273 (Washington); LC-USZ62-56782, 273 (Adams); LC-USZ62-15325, 273 (Lincoln); LC-USZ62-25792, 273 (Hayes); LC-G432-0932, 273 (Wilson); LC-DIG-pga-02388, 280 (Columbus); LC-DIG-highsm-13647, 280 (Ponce de Leon); LC-H8-CT-C01-063-E, 281 (Declaration of Independence); LC-USZC2-3796; 282 (War of 1812); LC-DIG-pga-02502, 283 (Emancipation Proclamation); LC-DIG-stereo-1s00612, 283 (train); LC-DIG-hec-18526, 284 (Rankin); LC-USZ61-2088, 287 (Chief Joseph); LC-USZ62-109426, 287 (Parks); LC-DIG-ppmsca-15836, 321 (slave trade); LC-USZC4-8655, 323 (samurai); LC-DIG-hec-04921, 327 (Tsar Nicholas); LC-DIG-pga-00710,328 (Columbus); LC-USZ62-47764, 328 (Cortes); LC-USZ62-100275, 329 (Diaz); LC-USZ62-119343, 332 (Truth); LC-USZ62-115884, 333 (Friedan). **Courtesy of Morgan McCann:** 65. **Courtesy of the Musical Instrument Museum:** 251 (family). **National Aeronautics and Space Administration (NASA):** 40 (Armstrong), 95 (Ride), 112 (Goddard), 207 (Sun), 285 (man on the Moon); Johnson Space

Center, 247 (shuttle); Johns Hopkins University Applied Physics Laboratory/Southwest Research Institute, 212 (New Horizons); JPL, 4, 212 (Mariner 2), 211 (moon); JPL/GSFC/Ames, 207 (Saturn rings); JPL-Caltech, 214 (Curiosity); Ken Shiflett, 214 (*Endeavour*); Robert Markowitz, 9 (*Discovery*); Space Telescope Science Institute, 215 (galaxy). **National Archives:** 256 (Constitution), 275 (code talkers); Army Signal Corps Collection, 121 (D-Day); Collection of Foreign Records Seized, 327 (Mussolini and Hitler). **Courtesy of National Fluid Milk Processor Promotion Board:** 191 (Chojnacky & Hsiao). **Newscom:** Ahmad Elatab-SaleemElatab/Splash News, 88 (Jay-Z); akg-images, 48 (monk); Alexander Pöschel Image Broker, 87 (wig); D Huang/AFP/Getty Images, 197 (fossil); HO/AFP/Getty Images, 113 (Honda); Mark Thiessen/AFP/Getty Images, 6 (Cameron); Michael Holahan/ZUMA Press, 3, 58 (St. Patrick's Day); Picture History, 283 (Trail of Tears); PIXAR ANIMATION STUDIOS/WALT DISNEY PICTURES/Album, 13 (*Brave*); Ralph, PacificCoastNews, 86 (Usher); Zhang Qi Authorized/ZUMA Press, 139 (health worker); ZUMA Press, 52 (Crooked House), 124 (Helú), 238 (Pastrana). **Courtesy of Vivian Ng:** 33. **NOAA:** 70 (tornado). **Nuclear Regulatory Commission:** 74 (nuclear power plant). **Penguin Young Readers Group:** 46 (cover: *Al Capone Does My Shirts*, by Jennifer Choldenko). **Photofest:** Columbia Pictures, 12 (*Men in Black III*), 15 (*The Amazing Spider Man*). **Ronald Reagan Presidential Library:** 274 (Reagan). **Courtesy of Chris Robley:** 243. **Franklin D. Roosevelt Library:** 273 (Roosevelt). **Russell Knightly Media:** 203 (mimivirus). **Courtesy of Dan Sabia:** 77. **Scholastic Inc.:** 45 (Collins), 46 (covers: *The Hunger Games,* by Suzanne Collins; *13 Gifts* by Wendy Mass, jacket photograph copyright © 2011 by Michael Frost, published by Scholastic Inc./Scholastic Press). **David Shankbone:** 51 (Chrysler Building). **Courtesy of ShurTech Brands, LLC:** 191 (Duct tape prom). **Courtesy of Ericka Smith:** 311 (Smith). **Spaceport America Conceptual Images URS/Foster + Partners:** 214 (Spaceport). **Thinkstock:** iStockphoto, 87 (hippie), 244 (3-mast ship); Photos.com, 281 (Franklin). **© Edward A. Thomas:** 318 (hieroglyphics). **Taka Kira/TokyoFashion.com:** 86 (platform sneakers). **TurboPhoto:** 194 (church). **U.S. Department of Agriculture:** 101 (food plate). U.S. Air Force: Airman 1st Class Laura Goodgame, 122 (Afghanistan). **U.S. Army:** 240 (ENIAC), Spc. April Stewart/Released, 318 (ziggurat). **U.S. Department of Defense:** Erin A. Kirk-Cuomo, 122 (Iraq). **U.S. Mint:** 126 (5 National Park quarters), 276 (Indian coin). **U.S. Navy:** Aviation Ordnanceman 2nd Class Charles Reeves/Released, 59 (Memorial Day); Photographer's Mate 2nd Class Jim Watson, 285 (9/11). **U.S. Department of State:** 274 (Clinton), 286 (Powell). **U.S. Treasury:** 123 (front & back $1 bill). **University of Oklahoma Libraries:** Courtesy History of Science Collections, 203 (van Leeuwenhoek). **Visuals Unlimited, Inc.:** Wim van Egmond, 203 (amoebas). **Courtesy of Heidi Wallace:** 311 (Beck). **WalterDeanMyers.net:** 45 (Myers). **The White House:** 272 (George W. Bush, Obama); Lawrence Jackson, 258 (Congress). **Works Progress Administration:** Federal Art Project: 35 (Blossom Restaurant).

THE WORLD ALMANAC® FOR KIDS 2013

#1 for Facts and Fun

Amazing facts fill every page of *The World Almanac for Kids*. Here are just a few...

Where can you find a building that looks as if it had melted in the sun? see page 52

What is the world's most popular theme park? see page 248

Who was the first person to locate the wreck of the *Titanic*? see page 95

Which was the first war in which airplanes played a major role? see page 121

What is the world's smallest bird? see page 26

Who was the first president to throw out the first pitch on baseball's opening day? see page 263

When is National Cookie Day? see page 63